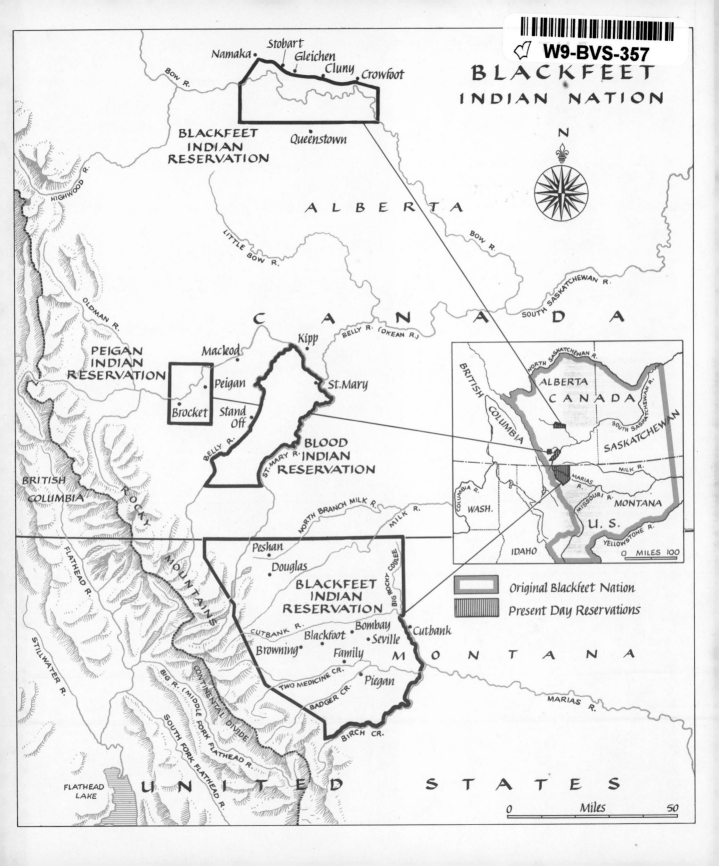

BLACKFEET
INDIAN NATION

Namaka
Stobart
Gleichen
Cluny
Crowfoot

BLACKFEET
INDIAN
RESERVATION

Queenstown

BOW R.

N

HIGHWOOD R.

A L B E R T A

LITTLE BOW R.

BOW R.

SOUTH SASKATCHEWAN R.

OLDMAN R.

C A N A D A

PEIGAN
INDIAN
RESERVATION

Macleod

Kipp

BELLY R. (OKEAN R.)

Peigan

St.Mary

Brocket

Stand
Off

BELLY R.

ST. MARY R.

BLOOD
INDIAN
RESERVATION

BRITISH
COLUMBIA

ROCKY

NORTH BRANCH MILK R.

MILK R.

MOUNTAINS

Peshan

Douglas

BLACKFEET
INDIAN
RESERVATION

BIG ROCKY COULEE

FLATHEAD R.

CUTBANK R.

Blackfoot

Bombay

Cutbank

Browning

Seville

M O N T A N A

STILLWATER R.

Family

CONTINENTAL DIVIDE

TWO MEDICINE CR.

Piegan

BIG R. (MIDDLE FORK FLATHEAD R.)

BADGER CR.

MARIAS R.

SOUTH FORK FLATHEAD R.

BIRCH CR.

FLATHEAD
LAKE

U N I T E D   S T A T E S

BRITISH
COLUMBIA

NORTH SASKATCHEWAN R.

ALBERTA

CANADA

SASKATCHEWAN

COLUMBIA R.

WASH.

MILK R.

MARIAS
R.

MISSOURI R.

MONTANA

IDAHO

U.S.

YELLOWSTONE R.

0   MILES   100

Original Blackfeet Nation

Present Day Reservations

0   Miles   50

THE BLOOD PEOPLE

THIS BOOK IS THE EIGHTH IN HARPER & ROW'S NATIVE AMERICAN PUBLISHING PROGRAM. ALL PROFITS FROM THIS PROGRAM ARE USED TO SUPPORT PROJECTS DESIGNED TO AID THE NATIVE AMERICAN PEOPLE.

OTHER BOOKS IN THE PROGRAM

Seven Arrows, by Hyemeyohsts Storm
Ascending Red Cedar Moon, by Duane Niatum
Winter in the Blood, by James Welch
Indians' Summer, by Nas'Naga
Carriers of the Dream Wheel, edited by Duane Niatum
Riding the Earthboy 40, by James Welch
Going for the Rain, by Simon Ortiz

THE BLOOD PEOPLE

A Division of the Blackfoot Confederacy

AN ILLUSTRATED INTERPRETATION OF THE OLD WAYS

Adolf Hungry Wolf

HARPER & ROW, PUBLISHERS
New York   Hagerstown   San Francisco   London

Library of Congress Cataloging in Publication Data

Hungry Wolf, Adolf.
The Blood People.
1. Kainah Indians. I. Title.
E99.K15H86   1977   970'.004'97   76–8706
ISBN 0–06–450600–2

FIRST EDITION

Designed by Christine Aulicino

Contents

Preface

As a child I lived far from the lands of the Blackfoot People. Yet my dreams often took me among these People. As I grew older I went to schools, studied American history, and became a schoolteacher. I wanted to relate to this land and its People, both past and present. So I finally traveled to the lands of the Blackfoot People to see if there was any truth to my childhood dreams. I met an old Blackfoot man who told me there was.

This old man was 116 years old when he finally passed away, a few years after I met him. He was the last Blackfoot warrior and buffalo hunter. I met him in time to receive his introduction to the Old People and their Old Ways.

From this first old man I was guided north into Canada to the land of the Bloods—a tribe of the Blackfoot Confederacy. These People became the relatives that I saw in my childhood dreams. They are the People of my children's mother. I am proud to be raising my children according to the ways of their ancestors.

Blackfoot ways of living in harmony with nature are traditionally passed on by Teachers who have, themselves, been initiated into those ways. Anyone may apply to such Teachers. The guidance varies according to the wisdom of each Teacher, as well as the sacrifices and devotions made by each student. My family is fully devoted to this way of life. Our Teachers have passed much wisdom on to us, for us to live and grow with. Also for us to share. The ancient wisdoms are still with us only because they have been shared all along.

The actual writings in this book were mostly put down in 1972. Our Teachers were among the last wise ones of Blackfoot traditions. They felt that the ancient wisdoms should continue on, even though the young generations showed little interest in the required disciplines. The Old Ones accepted the arrival of this modern world, and they agreed that the time was right for making a permanent record, like this book, so that the future generations might yet benefit from the spiritual ways of their ancestors.

Two of our wisest Teachers were also relatives of our family. We traveled with them. We camped with them. We ate and prayed with them. We made incense and sang with them, many mornings and evenings, before going to sleep. The idea for this book originated with them, and grew because of their continuous faith and encouragement. Without the love and understanding of Willie Scraping White (Wolf Old Man) and Willie Eagle Plume (Prairie Owl Man) this book would not be.

THE BLOOD PEOPLE

Our Sun Dance Encampment of 1972, as seen from the Belly Buttes, looking west.

Introduction to the Sun Dance Encampment

Setting Up Camp

It was the middle of summer, the time when Sun is closest to us and to our Mother Earth. It was a good time to gather with friends and relatives. The long, hot days were perfect for relaxing by a tipi and visiting with others. On printed calendars the year was 1972.

Within that summer camp one of our People's ancient Medicine Pipe Bundles could be seen hanging over the doorway of a yellow-painted tipi that had figures of otters drawn all around it. This was the tipi of my own family—and within it, our household.

To most of my friends I am Hungry Wolf, though our Old People call me Natosina, or Sun Chief. The first name was given to me long ago as a reflection of some of my personal characteristics. The second name was given me by my "uncle" when I became a Medicine Pipe Man. Natosina had been the name he had inherited from his father. All who carried this name were Medicine Pipe Men and lived to old age.

My wife is SikskiAki, or "Black-Faced Woman." The name was inherited from an old relative and has nothing to do with her appearance.

We hope in this book to share with you some of the Spirit of the Old Ways, the Spirit that is a part of our family's life. You will learn about many things that have come to us as Teachings, Teachings from our Old People. Some we have learned directly from them; some have come through the records of the Old People who are still living with us; and some we have from those in the past who offered their stories to be written down. You will see that this book is a guide to the life-style of my family. If you are inspired while reading these pages, that will be good. The Spirit of our Old People and their Ways is good and Powerful, and those of us who have the Spirit are happy to share it with you.

An eagle soared silently overhead. Perhaps he knew that our camp was holy and that no one would disturb his passing. From up in the sky, he may have noticed that our camp was set up in a circle just like the path of his flight, just like the roundness of Earth, and just like the roundness of the universe. He may have noticed that the camp circle was made up of tipis that were also round. With his sharp eyesight he could have looked through the smokeholes at the tops of our tipis,

Top left: Teachers and follower constructing a sweat lodge.

Bottom left: 1972 family portrait in our backyard. The sweat lodge was specially built for one ceremony with the Old Man, Mokakin, and Atsitsina.

Top right: Teachers Wolf Old Man and Mokakin carrying on with the Old Ways, as they enter the sweat lodge in a sacred manner.

and seen that our fireplaces in the centers of our tipis were surrounded by circles of stones, and that around the fireplaces our People were seated in circles. As each of these circles had no beginning and no end, so we were reminded that the Great Spirit of the Universe has no beginning and no end.

We were gathered together in the circle encampment to sing and pray and dance in many ceremonies. The ceremonies were to remind us of all the Spirits that gave us the Powers to live during the seasons since our last sacred gathering. Our songs were of the birds and animals, of the People and mountains, of the trees and flowers, of

the sky and Sun. Especially of Sun! Sun is our constant reminder of the endless Power of the Universe. Sun is our father. The warm love that he sends to our Mother, Earth, brings life and makes everything grow. It is the same warm love that Sun provided for Earth in the times of our grandfathers and their grandfathers. Our prayers to Sun give us the same Holy Power he gave them in long-ago times. It is that endless Holy Power of the Universe that we refer to as *Natojewa*. It is our godhead and our Great Spirit.

To the Blood People the Belly Buttes are Natojewa; they are our Holy Land. Every year thousands of tourists speed through this land on their way to Waterton and Banff National Parks or to the famous Calgary Stampede in Canada. Yet there are areas far enough away from the speeding traffic for the Belly Buttes to remain the isolated center of the Holy Spirit among the Blood People.

The Power of the Buttes is felt by all who go near them, even when there is no encampment in progress. One winter a desperate family searched an old Sun Dance campsite for firewood, which is scarce out on the prairie. This family discovered they were using the fallen log of the sacred Center Pole for fuel when they were awakened during a cold night by an unseen Power singing the holy Center Pole songs in a loud voice. Another time, an enterprising rancher from our reserve began to fence in the Buttes so that his cattle could graze there. But he was discouraged from building his fence when strange sensations overtook him; older relatives reminded him that Holy Spirits must not be disturbed without some sacrifice.

□

In 1972 the Sun Dance Encampment was located near the edge of the flat that overlooks the tree- and brush-lined Belly River bottoms. As the flat rises up from the river, the Belly Buttes rise up from the flat, farther to the east. It is in those Buttes that many men have gone to find their visions and Spirit helpers. Bears lived there not long ago. Today, eagles sometimes build their nests there, and mountain lions cross tracks with porcupines and coyotes. In some of the many caves and crevices are now the final resting places of those Old People who passed away after laws were made forbidding the traditional practice of placing bodies near to the Spirit World on top of scaffolds or in branches of trees.

It was still morning when we arrived at the campground with our outfit. Our spiritual grandparents, Mokakin and Ponah, pointed out a vacant spot next to their tipi where they thought we should camp. Mokakin, who was attending his

seventy-second Sun Dance Encampment, reminded us that he had taken on a new name to celebrate reaching the status of Old Man. From now on he would be known by his late uncle's name, PitachPikis, or Eagle Ribs. For most of his life he had been Mokakin, or Pemmican, although his many friends in towns and on other reservations usually called him by his recorded name, Pat Weaselhead.

We hung our sacred Bundle from its wooden tripod at the rear of the space selected for our tipi, in keeping with the traditions taught to us. SikskiAki's dad was along to help us set up properly. It was not long before we had the four main poles for our tipi tied correctly and raised into place. Other poles were leaned against the crotch formed by the tops of these four. With a strong pole we lifted up the tipi's canvas cover and fastened it down. Then we adjusted the poles, tied up our inner lining, spread out our floor mats and bedding, and moved in the rest of our supplies of food, water, and clothing. In other parts of the camp circle, tipis and tents were being set up at the same time.

Ours was the second Yellow-Otter Tipi set up in the camp. Mokakin's and Ponah's, next door, was of the same painted design. Their design had been transferred to them many years before by a man from the North Blackfoot division of our People. Their canvas cover was so old that the otters painted on the south side (male otters, by tradition) had lost all their black paint and were now only white outlines against the faded yellow background. Sun shines on the land of the Bloods from the south, as He travels from east to west; the north side of the old tipi was not nearly so faded. Mokakin remarked, "Those otters on the south side look like a bunch of white-haired old men! That's the last Sun Dance for this tipi. Next year we use a new one, one with a different design. Ponah is gonna make it up this winter and I am going to paint it myself."

I asked which design it would have and he

said, "The half-red, half-yellow design. We got it long time ago, too."

It was a familiar story. We had just finished making our own new tipi. Our old one, with another design, had been too frail to stand for the three weeks of the encampment, exposed to winds, rains, and Sun on the unprotected Belly Buttes. SikskiAki sewed the new cover, and we both painted it with the red, yellow, and black of the otter design. This particular design had belonged to SikskiAki's grandfather, Joe Beebe. It had been given to him as a present by his first wife's brother. That brother was Old Weaselhead, Mokakin's stepfather. Joe Beebe had given him his favorite racehorse, with split ears, in return. The tipi was later transferred to a North Blackfoot man, and Joe Beebe bought it back when he married SikskiAki's grandmother. The canvas cover they used fell victim to old age, but the rights to use the design were saved from a similar fate when it was transferred to us by Grandma.

After our tipi was set up, we were invited by Harry Shade to have lunch at his lodge. It was a new white tipi that had been made by SikskiAki's mother just before the encampment. Harry Shade, or IshtapatauMachkan ("Running in the Back"), had planned to paint the lodge with the snake design, so that his old grandfather, Wolf Old Man, could transfer the rights to him during the Sun Dance. The rights were transferred as planned, but the tipi painting had to wait until later, since the family was preparing for the ceremony in which Mrs. Shade would become a member of the women's society known as the Motokiks.

Wolf Old Man was the leading holy man left among our People, having spent most of his ninety-four years giving spiritual leadership and physical doctoring. By the Powers of our Old Ways he remained active and well, and by these same Powers, I was brought to him to become, in his opinion, the one who would carry on his Spirit through the Teachings he gave to me and my family. Some of these Teachings are too sacred for me to pass on in writing, but many others can be shared. Wolf Old Man, or the Old Man, was one of four holy men whose Teachings most influenced my interpretation of our Old Ways.

□

Our first chance to relax in the new camp came just before dark. Everything inside the lodge was in order, and our young son Wolf Child was securely tucked into his bed. The long, hot day and the fresh air gave his mind a cushion that immediately carried him into the world of sleep. A few small sticks of burning cottonwood crackled inside the stone circle of our fireplace and gave a cheery warmth to the cooling evening air. SikskiAki took one of the burning sticks and held the glowing end to the bowl of my long-stemmed pipe while I puffed until its contents were lit. The sacred herb glowed brightly within the shiny stone bowl that I had recently made with old Uncle Atsitsina's guidance. I offered the mouthpiece of the pipe to the Spirits of our sacred Bundle, then to Sun and Earth.

For some time we sat in silence and puffed on the polished mouthpiece, watching little clouds of smoke whirl upward around us, and toward the smokehole of our tipi. The sacred tobacco comes from our Mother Earth in the form of leaves and it goes to our Father, Sun, in the form of smoke. We watched it diffuse into the air. It seemed to disappear. Yet we knew that it was only changing into a shape invisible to our eyes, just like the Spirits that dwell all around us.

At the rear of our tipi, facing east through the doorway, is our altar. An altar is a small area of earth cleared of pebbles and grasses, a place where we burn incense. The shape of an altar is determined by the traditions of each household's sacred Bundles. Ours requires an altar in the shape of a rectangle.

After we finished our smoke, SikskiAki took the incense tongs—a forked serviceberry branch—from their place next to the altar. Between the burnt, pointed ends, she picked up a small glowing coal from the fire. Carefully, she carried the coal and placed it in the middle of the altar. From a little buckskin pouch she took a pinch of the sweet pine needles that are the sacred incense for our Bundle. Lifting them up high to symbolize the Holy Power of the Universe, she then slowly lowered the needles and let them fall onto the glowing coal. As the pine needles made contact with the coal, a spiral of smoke rose upward, its sweet fragrance filling our lodge with goodness and holiness.

Earlier, before Sun went down over the mountains, SikskiAki had brought in our ancient Medicine Pipe Bundle. The Bundle, which hung from a tripod, was covered with a fringed shawl. As the smoke rose up under the shawl and caressed the Bundle, we breathed deeply of the sweet smell and bathed ourselves, rubbing the smoke between the palms of our hands and then brushing our hands downward from the tops of our heads to the ends of our toes. Our Old People taught us this way of symbolically removing the evil from our minds and bodies with the Power of the Good represented by the sacred incense smoke. I prayed:

HiYo sacred smoke! HiYo Good Spirits of the Universe! Hear me! Let us take your Holy Power into our minds and into our bodies, so that your Holy Power will help us to be good. HiYo holy Pipe and all of you Good Spirits who are with our holy Pipe! Give us your strength and Power, as you have given it to the many good People in the past who had you with them while they followed their holy Ways. Inspire us to think of your Holy Power all of the time, you Good Spirits, so that we may learn to be holy, ourselves, so that we may be able to inspire others with your Holy Power and with these holy Ways. Be the center of our family, so that we may, someday, teach others those songs and ceremonies. . . . Help us to do what is right, you Good Spirits, with our holy Pipe. . . . Give us your strength and guidance so that we may give it to any others who wish to have it. . . . HiYo, hear my prayers! . . . Okohe, you Holy Powers of the Universe! Hear me! HiYo Natosi, our Father, Sun above! Let us see you for as long as we live so that we may always be reminded of the Holy Power that exists all around us in the universe. . . . Make our paths bright with your light so that we may see our way clearly, so that we may be able to follow our paths easily and safely and that we may find all the goodness that lies along the way. HiYo Ksaxkom, our Earth Mother! Let us always live close to you and treat you with respect. Give us strength beneath our feet as we walk along our paths, and give us good foundations for our homes. Let us raise children near you and help us to feed them well. Let us grow good crops. Let us find success with our hunting. . . . Let our sacred Tobacco grow well. Let us always have this small part of you in the midst of our home, so that we may always make incense upon you and so that we will always be reminded of your sacred body beneath us. Let us think of good things when we burn that sacred incense on you every morning and every night. HiYo all of you birds and animals! you trees and flowers! you rivers and mountains! you thunder and rains! Let us live a life in harmony with all of you in nature. . . . Teach us to have respect for all of you, and for all that we meet, you Good Spirits. Teach us to think good thoughts about everyone and to overcome those who may have bad thoughts about us. HiYo all of you good Medicines who are with us! Teach us your good Medicine so that all our Spirits may come together to be good Medicine. . . . HiYo HiYo! . . . Hear me you Good Spirits! . . . HiYo—HiYo!"

□

Outside it was dusk. We could hear a few kids still playing. Their voices seemed distant, even though only a thin layer of canvas separated us from their vast outdoor playground. Here and there a dog barked, and from the nearby brush we could hear the whinny of a horse. A mother called for her children to come home and get ready for bed. Then we heard the voice of old Mokakin. He called out for all to hear:

"All of you children who are still playing around the camp, all of you young people, hear me! This is a holy camp, and the older people wish to pray now. They will be praying that all of you will live good lives and reach old age. You must help them by going to your homes and keeping quiet for the rest of the night. Tomorrow will be another day for playing and visiting with your friends. Mothers and fathers, see that your children are at home now, so that they will disturb no one in the camp."

Mokakin slowly walked around the camp circle while he talked. He was headed for the west side of the camp, toward Sun. He stayed close to the tipis, so that everyone could clearly hear his words. He was the main camp crier, often called upon to make announcements for others.

Slowly Mokakin made his way back to our side of the circle. He was wearing his very old Hudson's Bay point blanket, the kind with one black stripe instead of several colored ones. The blanket was wrapped around his body, over his left shoulder and under his right arm, allowing it to hang free. This arm he waved in the air, making gestures to support his words. He came to the door of our lodge and coughed lightly, letting us know that he was about to enter. From the reflection of the fire on our tipi's walls he knew that we were still up. He did not know that we had been watching him through the small opening. Quickly, we rushed back to our seats and waited for his entrance. One of the many rules of respect shown to Medicine Pipe Bundles is that the Keepers must never call out to anyone from within the tipi where the Bundle is kept. Peace and quiet should be maintained around such a tipi at all times. If someone calls from outside and does not come in, we must step outside to speak with him. Mokakin, himself a former Medicine Pipe Owner, was well aware of this rule.

"Oki, OmachKinna," I said to him, as he came through the doorway. I used a standard greeting of respect to an older man.

"Oki, Natosina ki SikskiAki," said Mokakin in return. He glanced around our tipi and said, "It's all fixed up now," giving an approving nod, then shaking his head to the side with pleasure. We felt happy and proud that our traditional Ways gladdened the old man's thoughts.

"Do you have time to sit and have a smoke and some tea?" I asked hesitantly. I knew that Mokakin was already serving as advisor, as grandfather, to the soon-to-be Horns. I wasn't sure how long he had for a visit with us.

No sooner had I asked the question than we heard Ponah's strong voice call out, "PitachPikis!" And for insurance she followed with, "Mokakin!" Knowing that there would be no excuse for not hearing his wife call at least one of his names, he apologetically mumbled something and hurried out. One of the future members of the Horns was probably waiting to be advised on some ceremonial matter. We knew that Mokakin would spend as much time at our place as he could, and we looked forward to his later visits.

Behind Mokakin's and Ponah's tipi was the tipi of their son, Charlie Weaselhead. His parents had given him the new white tipi to honor his joining the Horns Society. His joining meant a lot to them. They had been members in the past.

While sitting quietly in our tipi, we suddenly became aware of a gathering of voices, soon followed by a few beats on a large bass drum. The camp was about to be entertained by "tobacco singers," a group of friends who sit before the door of a lodge and sing until the lodge owner offers them a pipe to smoke. If the owner has no pipe, he may offer cigarettes or food.

After a few brief high-pitched solos to warm up voices, the leader of the group sang the first line of his song. His loud falsetto voice echoed across the camp. The others with him joined in on the second line, which was a repeat of the first. The silence inside our tipi was overcome by the chorus of voices singing: "Ja, He-Ja, He-Ja, He-Ja, He-Le-Le, He-Le-Le, He-Yoooo . . ."

For some time we sat without moving, the chant creating vivid scenes in our minds. Our tipi seemed like a loudspeaker, the sound coming down through our smokehole as though sent by the stars.

We decided to go out into the cool night air to be closer to the thrill and spirit of the drumming and singing. The vast expanse of countless stars lit up the night through a clear sky. Like the light in a distant ceiling, Moon was full and round. The brightness reflecting on the tipis made them look like lanterns, the unpainted white ones glowing especially brightly. A short distance away we could see the sacred Buttes, silhouetted against the bright sky like a dark, jagged wall. Looking west toward the Rocky Mountains we could see that even though night was fully upon us, Sun still added a touch of his light to the horizon. Just above the jutting mountain peaks stretched a thin ribbon of deep orange, lingering stubbornly from Sunset.

The singers began their song quietly and with an easy tempo. The sounds of the song are not words with meanings but syllables that create a feeling. The drumbeat was slow and steady; the voices sang softly but distinctly. The five singers were sitting on chairs they carried with them. About twenty of us, wearing blankets over our clothes, stood in a loose circle around the singers, watching their faces and the movements of their drumsticks.

We were listening to the music of our ancestors, standing on soil where they once stood. We were watching the singers by the same heavenly lights that had lit up the nights for them, too. Their Spirits are always in the air. With each breath we took in some of our Old People's Spirits.

Most of us gathered around the drum were young people. Some wore cowboy hats, bell-bottomed trousers, and mod boots. But we were joined together by Spirits that transcended these external things.

The tempo of the song began to quicken. After it had been repeated several times, we caught on to the tune and joined the singing, tapping our feet and rocking in time to the rapid drumbeats. The group's enthusiasm continued to grow. At the end of each round the leader quickly repeated the opening line, before anyone could attempt a concluding note and interrupt the Spirit that was flowing with the music. Our whole world was centered there, before that tipi. We barely recognized our own voices within the thrilling harmony and Spirit of our one voice.

The leader finally struck four extra-hard drumbeats, signifying his intention to end the song after that round. Everyone was physically exhausted from such intense involvement. When the last note died away, a moment of absolute silence reigned in the camp. Suddenly, someone from within the tipi called out, in an intentional understatement, *"Okinn?"*—Is that all? The tense air disappeared and we all broke out in laughter. Then someone from inside passed out a pack of cigarettes, which the singers shared with each other.

□

We were awakened quite early the next morning. Someone outside loudly called something we were too sleepy to understand. We stood up in the chilly morning air. The tipi was bathed in the stark, bright light of Sun's early rays. There are only a few hours of total darkness during these midsummer nights this far north on the plains.

While I combed and braided my hair, Sikski-Aki lit a small fire of cottonwood twigs so that we could have a coal for our morning smudge of incense. With the forked stick, she picked up a piece of one of the twigs and placed it in the center of our altar. She sprinkled a few sweet pine needles on the coal, but sparingly, for the trees that give us this holy incense are usually found only in remote and scattered mountain places. A little spiral of smoke again marked the place where the hot coal and the dry pine needles met. The pungent odor brought the Good Spirits to us through our sense of smell. With our hands held in the smoke we again took the Spirit, brought it to us, and accepted it into our minds and bodies by rubbing ourselves from head to toe. We prayed:

HiYo Good Spirits who are here with us! You who make up everything that is Good and holy! Let us take your Holy Power and use it well. Let us be thankful for being aware of the goodness of your presence. . . . Let us think of your goodness as we go through this day, so that this day will be good for us. HiYo Natosi, our sacred Sun above! Help us to see the goodness along our paths. Let us be thankful for being able to see you again this day. Let us feel your warmth in our bodies, Natosi, and let us reflect your warmth in our food and in our homes, so that our families may be healthy. HiYo Earth, our holy Mother! Let us feel your strength beneath our feet as we walk upon you this day. Let us be strong and safe as long as we remain close to your body . . . all of you Good Spirits! Let us go through this day with respect and holy thoughts, and let us learn from our mistakes and trials, so that we may end this day with happiness. HiYo! Hear me!

□

After we finished praying, SikskiAki took our sacred Bundle outside and fastened it over our doorway. In the Old Days, the Bundle would have been hung from its tripod and placed at the rear of our tipi, even though horses would sometimes knock over such tripods. Nowadays, few people hang their sacred Bundles on tripods, not for fear of horses, but for fear of mischievous children who are not taught an understanding and respect for our holy Ways.

Dipping water out of our tin cream cans to wash the sleep from our faces, we thought of the Old Days, when our People were forced to use cleaned-out buffalo paunches to store water. Such containers were usually tied to tipi poles or hung from smaller tripods. They were hard to handle and keep clean. Water from them had an odd taste. It is no wonder that our Old People treasured metal buckets and kettles brought to this country by the early traders.

I stepped outside and walked over to the rim of the coulee that ran past our side of the camp. Most everyone in camp made at least one trip to this coulee each day. Across the coulee, I could see horses tied to bushes, where their owners had left them to graze. Some of these horses were later to be given as payment in transfer ceremonies during the encampment. Most of the bushes were covered with ripe berries, and all day long women and children would go back and forth to fill their berry containers.

Although it was still early in the morning, Sun was already over the top of the Belly Buttes, on his way across the sky. It seemed as though only the Old People were awake so early in the morning. Some were just sitting, waiting to wake up fully in the fresh morning air. Others were quietly standing, facing Sun, praying in quiet voices. One old lady was walking along with the help of a cane, her eyes almost shut. I could hear her prayer plainly as she called out the names of her children and grandchildren and asked Sun to pity them and keep them safe on this day.

Soon the smoke from many morning fires rose above the tipis and tents, sharply contrasted against the cool air. The fires made with cotton-wood burned quietly and calmly; but loud crack-ling and popping could be heard from those fires made with pine, which was gathered from lumberyard scrap piles. Pine is not a popular firewood in tipis, especially if it is not thoroughly dry. It usually produces more smoke than the smoke-holes can let out, and this makes for very tearful scenes! The smoke also carries little cinders throughout the tipi, burning holes in blankets and clothes. Pine is just no good in a tipi, although tent-dwellers have no trouble with it in their iron cooking stoves. Cottonwood is the favorite firewood, usually found in river bottoms. It is also the proper wood on which to burn incense. Unlike pine, cottonwood coals will continue to glow for a long time after being taken from a fire. This is helpful during ceremonies. Cottonwood coals are often placed on altars before prayers are begun. Later, incense is placed on a coal when the one who is praying wishes to make the sacred smoke.

As I returned to our tipi I heard the deep voice of an old man beginning a song inside his lodge. Perhaps this man's Medicine, which came to him during some dream or vision, called for daily singing, although most Medicine Bundles don't require this. He was probably singing a song his Spirit helpers taught him many years ago. No one in the camp would ask him about it or dare to sing it.

Our breakfast consisted of rose hips tea, fried bread, and oatmeal. The tea was made from the red buds of roses, which we had gathered after the first frost the previous fall. The fried bread was made from white-flour dough, shaped into large patties and quick-fried in a skillet of hot grease. The oatmeal was made from the same kind of rolled oats that our Old People of the long-ago obtained from traders. Ours was a typical camp breakfast, but many of the Old People still prefer the traditional breakfast food—a piece of boiled or fried meat, washed down with water.

Black coffee or tea is often drunk instead of plain water, though most everyone knows that water is healthier.

Two more criers made their way around the camp circle. One announced the name of the person whose tipi would be the meeting place for the future Horns. The other crier called out the names of two members, inviting one to visit the other. Even though PitachPikis was recognized as the camp's main crier, anyone could announce something the others should know. Generally, certain recognized Old Men were asked to make the announcements. For this favor they were given a present of tobacco, food, or money.

It was about midday when SikskiAki lit our fire again to put a kettle of soup over it. Earlier, we had invited our friend Albert Wolf Child to come over for lunch and a visit. Albert is the grandson of the man whose common name, Wolf Child, is now a last name for his descendants. When our People first settled on the reserve, government officials arbitrarily assigned family names based on the common name of the head of the family. Unfortunately, the man who interpreted all these names was not fully familiar with the complicated Blackfoot language. He was a Negro named Dave Mills, who was married to a Blood woman. His descendants are now active members of the tribe. Dave Mills was well liked by the Old People, even though he did not adopt their traditions. They gave him the name Young Scabby Bull.

WOLF OLD MAN VISITS

While SikskiAki went next door to invite Pitach-Pikis to join us, Albert Wolf Child arrived. He hesitated until I pointed to the seat at my left. Just as he sat down, the door curtain opened wide. It was our grandfather, Wolf Old Man, thrusting his two canes through the opening and carefully lifting his legs over the canvas that formed the base of the doorway. His brother, his

11

companion, Mike Yellow Bull, held him steady from behind until he was safely inside. Slowly, he walked around the fireplace toward me.

"T'kcha?"—Who is that?—the Old Man called out, as he pointed to Albert with one of his canes. In our tipi, he always sits at the place of honor, immediately to my left, where Albert was sitting.

"Makwi Poka," Albert replied. The Old Man was momentarily confused, since our little boy, also named Makwi Poka, usually sits at my right. Then he recognized the voice and said, "Oh, my old son-in-law," his tone implying that he should have known who it was. He was referring to Albert's first marriage to his daughter, Victoria.

Albert got up and we helped the Old Man sit down in the honored place. At ninety-four, his vigorous outdoor life had helped him grow old in good health. Although his eyes were nearly worn out and his knees were weak, he was one of the few Old People who could sit through our all-night ceremonies and still be alert and joking when Sun came up in the morning.

The Old Man was the last holy man to follow the Old Ways of our People. He had spent his lifetime giving spiritual guidance to our People, doctoring them when their health failed, and leading their ceremonies when they came together to pray.

He had been born in the year 1877. His father's name was also Wolf Old Man, and his mother was the younger of Wolf Old Man's two wives. Not long after our Old Man's birth, Wolf Old Man died. Our Old Man's mother then mar-

Students of the Calgary Industrial School in 1897. The Old Man, then seventeen years old, is second from right in the back row. To his left is his instructor, Charles Pippy. Most of the boys in the picture are from the North Blackfoot, North Piegan, and Sarsi reserves. In the center are Rev. and Mrs. Hogbin. Next to Mrs. Hogbin is Charlie Goodrider. Second from the right in front row is Percy Creighton. (Glenbow Archives)

ried a young warrior named Scraping White, who already had one wife and three children. When Scraping White's oldest daughter saw her new little brother she told her mother, "I like my new brother—I want his name to be Napi." So he was called Napi, "Old Man." Many years later he took the name of his original father, Wolf Old Man. On the tribe records his name is Willie Scraping White, and it was by this name that he was called during the three years that he attended the Calgary Industrial School in the 1890s.

"No, I didn't get much schooling at that place," he once told us, "because the instructors thought that a fellow my size would be more use to them out in the fields than in the classroom. I'm glad," he said with a smile, "because I liked the outdoors much better than the insides of buildings." The Old Man speaks only very broken English and he never did learn to read or write. But he did become the school's star football player. He used to tuck his long braids up under his helmet. "When I came back to the reserve the kids wanted me to teach them how to play, and the girls sure admired me when I passed the ball a long ways," he said with a combined look of pride and embarrassment. He was usually too modest to tell of his personal accomplishments. Unfortunately, several accidents while playing football and ice hockey weakened his knees. "Better to have weak knees than a weak mind," he sometimes said to console himself. After three years in the school's fields he finally decided to ask how much longer he would have to stay. "I never knew that I was allowed to ask the principal such a question," he said, "so I felt pretty foolish when he told me that I was free to go whenever I wanted. I packed up pretty fast and left." He was also one of the first students at St. Paul's Anglican School, on the Blood Reserve, though he did not stay long.

The Old Man learned much about our Old Ways from his stepfather, Scraping White, who was Owner of many sacred Medicines and knew how to lead Medicine ceremonies. He also received many Teachings from his stepfather's friends and from his own neighbors, respected leaders like Sun Chief, Big Wolf, and Packs His Tail. The Old Man was one of the last of our People to know the Spirit of these ancient Teachings. For that reason he was happy to have me as "grandson" and student. It pleased him to know that many of those Teachings are now written down for people who are yet unborn. "I sometimes wonder," he told me, "why our Old People never learned to read and write their own languages, so that they could have passed on all their wonderful knowledge of the old-time world."

Wolf Old Man was noted among our People for his knowledge of herbs and his methods of doctoring. He was the last of our old-time doctors. However, it was his spiritual leadership of which he was most proud. He enjoyed telling about a recent incident that occurred while he was returning home from a holy ceremony held on the reservation of our Piegan division, in nearby Browning, Montana. It was Sunday evening, a time when some members of our reserve return home with U.S. spirits tucked under their car seats or stored in their stomachs. In Canada, liquor is not sold on Sundays. The car in which the Old Man was riding was filled with others who had gone to the ceremony. When they reached the Canadian customs office, the men in charge prepared to make their usual inspection. But when the chief inspector looked inside and saw the Old Man, he called out to his assistant, "It's alright, we don't have to check this one—he's the Indian Bishop!"

Some time before us, the Old Man had been Keeper of our Medicine Pipe Bundle for ten years. Most of the Teachings he passed on to us concern this Bundle. Although he was the oldest leader of Medicine Pipe ceremonies among our People, he never learned all the fifty-six songs that were sung during these ceremonies in the Old Days; his own Teacher, old Heavy Head, very slow and thorough, had passed away before finishing his instructing. By that time the Old Man felt he was too old to begin studying under another Teacher, and decided to make the best of what he had already learned.

Other Teachings the Old Man gave to us include the Ways of our Sun Dance and our Nighttime ceremonies, as well as our traditional legends and some of the many true stories about the adventures of various people of the past.

For many years, the Old Man's chief function during our Sun Dances was that of Weather Dancer. He was given the rights and Teachings for this sacred duty by the former Weather Dancer, Crow Spreads His Wings, who was his brother. He gave the position up to the present Weather Dancer, Mark Old Shoes, who was informed through a dream that he would grow old if he accepted this duty. When I sought to fulfill a personal vow to take over the duties of a Weather Dancer, it was necessary for me to consider Old Shoe's conditional assurance of his old age. I did not wish to break the spiritual strength of this dream nor cause him any sudden anxiety about the span of his life. So I recently became

Wolf Old Man as head Weather Dancer during the Medicine Lodge ceremonies. He is holding an eagle-wing fan and sprigs of Creeping Juniper, the Sun Dance incense. He is blowing on an eagle bone whistle to keep time to his dancing and the drumming and singing. (Glenbow Archives)

14

Weather Dancer among the South Piegan division of our People. Weather Dancers from various divisions often join together for Sun Dances.

Another of the Old Man's spiritual duties was to serve as advisor to the Horns Society. Among our People he was considered to have the greatest knowledge of the society's songs and ceremonies, having held seven different memberships in the society, including that of leader. The recent transfer was the tenth for which he had served as advisor. In his younger days, the Old Man also belonged to the now-extinct Brave Dogs and Pigeons societies.

As always, it was an honor to have the Old Man visit our home. His presence inspired us with the knowledge that it was still possible to find spiritual satisfaction with many of our Old Ways in this modern age. The strength of his old age let us find Power in his Teachings. With each visit he gave us more of his Good Spirits.

We sat in silence for a few moments after the Old Man settled next to me. It is not proper to ply a guest with many questions as soon as he arrives; nor does a guest usually begin a lengthy conversation until he has learned what mood is current in the lodge he has just entered. During that period of silence, SikskiAki came in, followed by Mokakin. As an old *Ninamskan*, or Pipe Man, he was given the second place of honor in the tipi, to the left of the Old Man.

Mokakin is learning to carry out two of the Old Man's duties. During his past memberships with the Horns he became acquainted with many of that society's functions, and is now looked upon as an advisor by the new members. In addition, Mokakin is a successful doctor of several minor physical ailments. He was given, in dreams this Power and shown the plants to use while he was sleeping near some old open-air burials in a secluded part of the reserve. His dreams came unexpectedly, while sleeping alone during a wintertime trapping expedition.

While SikskiAki served lunch to our three guests, the two Horns advisors discussed business. Albert Wolf Child took part in the conversation, since he is a former member of the Horns and is sometimes called on for advice. During this time I filled my smoking pipe and in my mind rehearsed the songs for our sacred Bundle. It is a tradition for a Medicine Pipe Owner to invite one or more former Owners for a meal and to offer them a smoke. They, in turn, will pray for the present Owner and his family, and will sing some of the Bundle's songs. Before the coming of tape recorders, this was the only way such songs could be learned. Many songs were lost between the years when the People stopped camping by each other and when songs could finally be recorded. Even now, few people will take the time to listen to these songs as often as it takes to learn them.

I asked the Old Man to sing one song, meaning one set of seven songs. Many of our holy songs are sung in sets of seven, although no one seems to remember why. I could have asked the Old Man to sing more than one set, but I realized he had plenty of singing to do in his affairs with the Horns.

SikskiAki placed a hot coal in the center of our altar, while I took a pinch of sweet pine needles and held them with the thumb and first finger of my right hand. The Old Man took that hand in his and held it high above the smoldering coal. He said a prayer of thanks to the Holy Powers that brought us together. Then he prayed for good thoughts and long life for all of us and asked our holy Pipe to inspire my family to live a straight life. He thanked the Pipe's Powers for being with him for so many years and with us now. Then he began to sing: "The Above . . . it is holy . . . the earth . . . it is holy!"

He lowered my hand during the singing, letting the sweet pine fall on the hot coal, making the incense. While chanting, we all reached out our hands toward the sacred smoke and rubbed it on our arms and over our bodies from our heads down. Each song consisted mostly of chanting and a few sacred words, all repeated four times. I handed my filled pipe to the Old Man during the final song. The sacred words were, "My smoking . . . it is holy!"

Before the pipe was lit the Old Man prayed again. He pointed the mouthpiece of the stem upward and asked all that is holy to come with the smoke into our minds and bodies. He asked that my family and I have long life and good health for taking proper care of our holy Bundle. Then he told SikskiAki to take a brand from the fire and hold it inside the shiny black bowl to light the sacred tobacco. The pipe lit well, which was a good sign, and burnt for a long time. Everyone took a turn, smoking contentedly. When the smoking was finished, the ashes were carefully knocked out at the edge of the fireplace.

Wolf Child and Mokakin had things to do at their own lodges, so they got up and left. Suddenly it seemed very still in our lodge. We just sat quietly. SikskiAki and I let the Old Man's Spirit overpower us in silence. His eyes were closed. He was no doubt thinking of the many Powerful things that dwelled in his mind. We sat without moving, waiting for him to speak. Even though he requires two canes to walk and needs help getting up and down from the floor, I felt very weak next to him.

The Old Man did not care for gaudy "Indian" garb, unlike some of the "Medicine Men" of today. Yet his appearance was very striking. His face was freshly painted with sacred red earth. It was streaked up on his forehead into the pompadourlike forelock of his white hair. His hair had thinned so that he could only form two small braids, which he fixed himself. When he was younger he wore his long hair with a third braid hanging down his back in our traditional warrior style. The ends of his braids were always wrapped with red cloth, another tradition of our People. He used to wear shell earrings until a few years ago, when one of them got hooked on something and tore the ear's small hole into a slit. Enough of

his own teeth remained to allow him to chew his favorite food—meat. He would have been content with a diet of meat and bread, and lots of water that he claimed helped stimulate digestion. Though he liked fruits and desserts, he was not overly fond of vegetables. Like most of our Old People of the long-ago, he did not eat fish, because they belong to the Underwater Spirits. Around his neck was his customary black scarf; his feet were covered with moccasins. He was wearing his special dress moccasins with a blue-and-white geometric design beaded on them. One of his canes was plain, while the other was carved and vividly decorated with paint.

When he finally spoke, he asked if we knew the story of how things were in the beginning of the world. Of course we had read several versions of the traditional creation myth told among our People, but we didn't know his version and were anxious to hear it. He lapsed into silence, sorting out the story in his mind. We sat quietly so that he would not get the feeling we were impatient.

Although the heat of the afternoon was becoming very noticeable, the brightness of the outdoors was greatly subdued by the yellow coating of paint and the black silhouettes of the eight otters that circled the outside of our lodge.

The Old Man's voice began in a commanding tone:

HOW THE EARTH WAS MADE AND PEOPLE ORIGINATED

Oki, the first ones here were a man named Sun, a woman named Earth Woman, and a Dog. These were the first three that inhabited Earth. So that makes four. The man did all the hunting. He always cut open whatever he got and then went home. The woman was given just a limited time to go and get what he cut open. The man put a thong in his mouth, soaked it, and then put it down. The woman had to bring the food home before the thong dried. They lived in abundance.

One day Earth Woman told her husband, Sun, "There are only two of us, and Dog is useless, I wish we could have somebody else to live with us." He told her, "No, there will only be the two of us." It started at that point that women will always beat men in an argument, because the man finally said, "Oki, let it be your way."

Time passed and the woman had a baby boy. Sun told her, "Please give him a name." The woman said no. She said, "If it was a girl I would name her, but since it is a boy you give him a name." He told her, "You are right, I will give him a name. His name will be Napi."

Time went on, and the woman said, "I think it is lonely for our son. He is alone. It is better that there be two of them." Sun said no. But the woman won again. And again it was a boy. Sun named him Creator.

Now, whenever the man went out hunting, the woman also went out. Since they were mysterious people, she always knew when it was time for her husband to come back and she always went back into her tipi before he returned.

More time went on, and one day while the woman was gone to bring in the food, one of the boys told Sun, "Father, as soon as you are gone hunting Mother goes out."

"Hiya," replied Sun, "She has somebody else. I am just now discovering that." He sharpened his knife and he went off to hunt. When he came back he gave his wife the wrong direction to the food, and then he followed her. Soon he came

War Tipi in the Blood Sun Dance Camp of 1891. This is one of two traditional War Tipis among the Bloods. It is recognized by its circle of fringe, under which are the picture-writings of various men's exploits. (R. N. Wilson)

17

to a place where it was very slippery. This slippery place was made by the great big Snake. "That is the one that she meets," he thought. So he kicked at the door of Snake's den.

As Snake came creeping out, Sun cut off its head and its short feet. He told Snake, "For your punishment you will no longer have feet to walk on. You will always be creeping around on your stomach, just like you did with my wife."

When Sun got home he told his boys, "Your mother is Powerful and she will kill us when she learns what I have done." He advised them to run away and told them, "Take this sod and these thorns and this mountain rock and this water moss. When she comes close behind you, drop one of these things in her path and run.

Just then Earth Woman stuck her head in through the tipi and said, "Yes, I will kill you all." Sun pulled his knife and cut off her head. They all ran outside and fled. It is said that Sun ran toward the east.

On and on they ran, as fast as they could. When the boys looked back they said, "Our mother is catching up to us!" She was chasing them with her head in her hands. When she got close behind them, they dropped the sod and a deep coulee was created. She had a hard time to climb that.

They went on running across the prairie and soon their mother was behind them again. One of the boys said to the other, "She is near behind!" So they dropped the thorns, and a great big thick growth of thorn bushes formed this way and that way. She had a hard time to pick her way through, almost losing her head.

But she got through and again was almost up to the boys when they dropped the mountain rock, and big mountains formed between them and their mother. By the time she climbed over, the boys had fled a long distance ahead.

Nevertheless, she soon was upon them. The boys threw down the last thing they carried, the water moss. A huge body of water formed be-

tween them and the place where they last saw their mother. They could no longer see the opposite shore and it is said that this was the beginning of the big waters, which are called the oceans.

After the boys had roamed in their new land for some time, Napi told his brother, "It is lonely here. It was better where we were born."

"Well," said Creator, "you may go back over there, but I will stay and see what is to be done."

Napi replied, "Oki, I will go my way."

Creator told Napi, "Close your eyes; I will tell you when to open them." When Napi was told to open his eyes he looked around and saw that he was back on the land where he was born.

Oki, I will tell you what I know about the meaning of this story. This took place long, long ago. Napi stayed on this side of the big water and used his mysterious Powers to make the People and shape the land over here. His brother, Creator, stayed on the other side and made the People and the land over there. That is why we are all related. Earth Woman forgave her children and said that she would always be the mother of her descendants. She and her husband now live far apart, but he still uses his Power to provide her with food, which she gives to her children. Dog tried to follow his master, but got lost and ended up on the Moon. That is why dogs and wolves always howl up at Moon. The descendants of that dog are all the animals. They are also related to us, but they did not learn the Ways of people because that dog was too busy chasing its master while those things were being taught. So that is what I know about the story that our Old People have handed down from very long ago.

□

SikskiAki and I didn't ask the Old Man about the contrast between this story and the many sacred stories about Sun and Earth and their children. We knew the custom among our People to see all things in life in many ways—good, bad, and humorous. Many of these stories are not meant to be taken literally but to illustrate that everything in life can be seen in different ways. A common example of this attitude is the joking and fun-making that sometimes erupts spontaneously when a serious participant makes an error in the middle of a sacred ceremony. Human nature is often allowed to take precedence over serious ritual. If human nature causes people to laugh, then they should be allowed to laugh. Laughter, too, is a holy Way among people who live in harmony with nature.

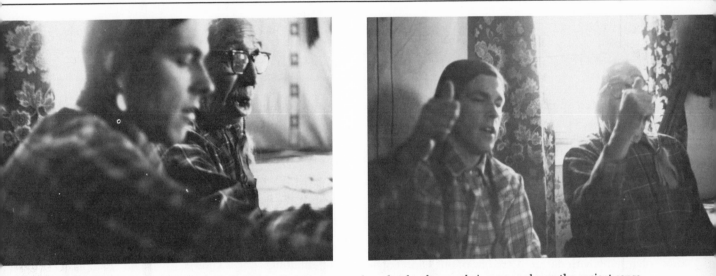

The highlight of each visit from the Old Man was when we sat down by the altar, made incense, and sang the ancient songs for the Medicine Pipe ceremony. Thus has the knowledge passed from Teacher to Teacher, through countless generations.

19

Stories of Our
Sun Dance Ceremonies

The greatest spiritual celebration of our People is commonly called the Sun Dance. A lifetime of Teachings and a massive book could not cover all the variations that were a part of the many Sun Dance celebrations of the past. Like most everything else among our People, the Ways of the Sun Dance continually change in response to dreams, visions, and living conditions. The most dramatic changes, of course, came with the end of the Old Days of hunting the buffalo and living in harmony with nature. Very few of our Old People still know even the basic Ways of the celebration. Although we meet annually to form the circle camp we call the Sun Dance Encampment, it has been several years since even an abbreviated version of the ceremony itself has been held. If our People should ever call for another spiritual celebration, it would best be done in a New Way, using what remains known of the Old Ways only for inspiration.

The closing ceremony of Sun Dance celebrations is the building of the sacred Medicine Lodge. The entire Sun Dance celebration is also known as the Medicine Lodge ceremony or Okan. Some of the past Okans are recounted here to show what they meant to our Old People, and hopefully to inspire our young to again seek spiritual communion with nature through sacred tribal festivals.

THE BLOOD OKAN
IN THE YEAR 1892

One of the most thorough records of a Sun Dance Encampment was made by Robert N. Wilson during the summer of 1892. For many years, beginning in the 1890s, Wilson operated a store in the log building once known as David Lambert's Trading Post. The old building stood, until a few years ago, on a bluff near Stand Off, overlooking the Waterton River (called the Kootenay River by our Old People) and Highway No. 2.

Wilson traded foodstuffs, hardware, guns, and blankets for furs, beadwork, relics, and, of course, money. He was a representative of the Hudson's Bay Company and carried their popular point blankets. Most Blood men in those days wore blanket coats made from these point blankets. Wilson was also a representative for the Chicago Field Museum, where he sold most of the craftwork and relic items he obtained in trade from our People.

Wilson was well liked by our Old People. They called him Inuskaisto, or "Long-Faced

David Lambert's Trading Post, at Stand Off, in 1886, not long before it was taken over by Robert Wilson. (Russel Photo)

Robert N. Wilson and his favorite horse. (Mrs. Frank Red Crow collection)

Crow." He spoke the Blackfoot language and took an interest in the Old Ways. With notebook and camera he recorded some of those Ways from those who still knew their traditional meanings. He wrote down the Blood versions of many old tales told among the tribe. These were given to him by the master storyteller, old Eagle Ribs. He also wrote accounts of Medicine Pipe, Beaver Bundle, and Nighttime ceremonies as they were led by such holy men as Moon and Running Wolf. He used both paper and camera to record the last Medicine Lodge self-torture ceremony, at which men who had promised to torture themselves physically, in exchange for spiritual help during some earlier time of need, fulfilled their vows. Many of the customs and rituals Wilson recorded still are alive in the Old Ways we observe today.

Copies of Wilson's unpublished papers and photographs are in the collections of the Glenbow Foundation Archives in Calgary, Alberta. The foundation's historical director, Hugh Dempsey, was most helpful in my efforts to record all these

Old Ways; his staff also gave time, locating and duplicating photographs and papers. It is good to know that some museums and ethnologists care more for our People's Ways than just to collect their belongings.

□

In 1892, people were already living in log cabins instead of tipis. They could not roam beyond the limits of the reserve, and cows had replaced buffalo as the source of meat. Nevertheless, most of the Blood People still taught their young and lived according to the Teachings of the Old Ways. They continued to be proud to be of the Blood tribe, and worked hard to learn the songs and ceremonies that had inspired their parents and grandparents.

An example of how closely the People still followed the Old Ways occurred during the winter before the Okan. Seven women felt called upon to vow to make the personal sacrifice of "putting up the Medicine Lodge." Among our People, the person who represents the tribe in the holy place of the Medicine Lodge ceremony is a woman, a virtuous woman who has lived a straight life and knows the Good Spirits. The holy woman's spiritual responsibilities are many and her physical sufferings are strong. That's why it was unusual to have as many as seven making the sacred vows in one year.

Only a woman who has lived a pure life will approach the Holy Powers and offer to exchange her physical suffering for the spiritual good of her People. The vow is usually made in a time of extreme need, such as a severe illness in her family or a male relative gone on the warpath. (The last battle between enemy war parties was fought five years before the 1892 Okan. However, many Blood men were still following the traditional practice of proving their bravery and finding adventure by raiding for horses or material trophies in places distant from the reserve. This continued well into the present century.)

After a woman has vowed to make the sacrifice of putting up the Medicine Lodge, she goes to an old man, usually a respected member of her family, and walks with him outdoors. He calls out for Sun and all the Holy Powers to hear that this woman is seeking protection for her family and herself, so that she might fulfill her vow for the good of all the People. The vow is usually made during wintertime, giving her half the year to prepare for the holy ceremony—the erection of the holy temple in the center of the Sun Dance camp.

Early in the summer of 1892, the People of the Blood tribe began to gather on the large flat that lies north of Stand Off and to the east below the Belly Buttes. Nearby was a large grove of cottonwoods where firewood was gathered. Next to the camp flowed fresh mountain water in the Belly River.

As the Blood tribe forms a division of the Blackfoot Confederacy, so do several lesser bands form divisions within the Bloods. In the Old Days, these lesser bands often camped apart from each other, depending on their preferences of hunting and camping sites. The bands camped together only during the Medicine Lodge ceremony. But in 1892, although the people still lived with their own bands, they were not separated by such great distances as before. Each band had a traditional place where its members put up their tipis and tents. Their place was left unoccupied whether the members of the band arrived late or not at all.

The Bloods were made up of ten or twelve bands at any one time. The number of bands varied because people were free to leave a band if they disagreed with its chief or if they preferred to follow the chief of another band. Some of the larger bands had more than one chief.

Let me tell you the names of some of the bands that existed around the turn of the century and the names of some band chiefs. The Lone Fighters were led jointly by One Spot and Heavy Shield, and later solely by Running Wolf. The Fish Eaters were led by Crop-Eared Wolf, and later by Many White Horses. This was the band of Blood's tribal head chief, Red Crow, and his family. The Bite-Throats were led by Low Horn. The Followers of Buffalo were led by Bull Horn; the Black Elks, by Bull Shield; the Many Children, by Young Pine; the Skinny People, by Running Antelope; and the Many Tumors, by Strangling Wolf.

Many of the People still used travois to haul their belongings to the 1892 camp. Others came in wagons, while a few in their slim-wheeled buggies challenged the rocks and holes lining the pathways to camp. The travois consisted of two tipi poles tied together near the end attached to the horse, with the untied ends spread apart to drag on the ground behind the horse. Padding was placed where the poles crossed, for they rested on the horse's shoulders. Crosspieces, tied to the poles near where they dragged, provided a frame on which the family could tie their belongings. Small items were rolled between tipi covers and fur robes, while larger bags were either tied to

A travois at a Blood camp along the Belly River in 1887. The woman's tipi cover is packed on her travois, and her lodge poles are fastened to the top of the cover. (Boorne & May)

the outside of the main bundle or slung over the horse's back. Sacred Bundles were carried only on a special horse and travois. Usually no one but the Bundle's Owner could ride such a horse. Nor was that horse used to carry meat. This was to keep the Spirit of the animal pure and clean for its holy duties.

The seven vowing Okan women and their families were among the first to arrive at the camp circle. They pitched their tipis closer to the center of the circle than the others. Cottonwood boughs were piled up outside against the base of their tipis. In this way, people would know that these tipis were sitting holy and should not be disturbed. The green leaves hiding the bottoms of the tipis of these holy women served as spiritual guards for those who were within. Children were

taught not to play nearby, lest they disturb the holy thoughts inside.

Dried tongue is the meal of communion during the Medicine Lodge ceremony. One hundred tongues must be dried and prepared beforehand in the spring so that everyone in the camp can share in this communion. The tongues, symbols of the natural foods of the buffalo as well as the main foods of our People, represent the Spirits of buffalo.

Traditionally, buffalo tongues were brought to the vowing holy woman by generous hunters. With the help of her family, she dried and stored them in preparation for the holy ceremony. But by 1892, beef had replaced buffalo in the diets of our People, so beef tongues were used instead. (The last buffalo killed by our People—around the year

1884—was a lone bull who was found in one of the prairie coulees.)

When the camp circle was filled with enough people to represent the Spirit of the tribe, the Okan women gave word to move the camp. After a short ride, the camp was set up again. Three times the camp was moved this way. On the fourth day, the final move was made to a site where the Medicine Lodge was to be built. In 1892 the seven holy women and their parties used four tipis for their preparatory ceremonies. One of these tipis belonged to the family of Big Wolf, whose wife was one of the vowing women.

The men who took part in the preparations for the Medicine Lodge ceremony were purified by sweat baths several times, beginning on the day before the final move to the Medicine Lodge site. The sweat houses were built by the members of four different men's societies. Each society built one sweat house whose frames were constructed of one hundred long, straight willows. The members of each society went out into the woods to collect the willows. When they returned, they rode together as a group, holding the branches in their hands and singing an ancient song, in imitation of a victorious war party returning home with trophies. All the People came out of their tipis to witness the event.

The four sweat lodges were built a short distance outside the camp circle, near the holy women's tipis. Older men supervised the construction of the lodges. Half the willows were stuck into the ground on the south side of the lodge. These were painted with red earth, representing the Power of the warm summers. The rest of them were placed on the north side and were covered with black paint, representing the Power of the winters. Wider spaces were left on the east and west sides, for entering and leaving, breaking the otherwise complete willow circle. Opposing willows were bent toward the center and intertwined with each other, forming a basketlike frame. Over this frame, fur robes,

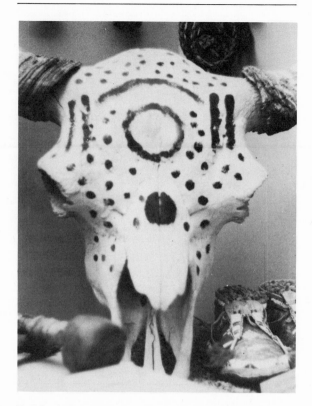

Buffalo skull painted for the Medicine Lodge ceremony, on display at the Glenbow Museum. Symbols represented include: Sun in the center; pairs of Sun Dogs on each side; crescent Moon above; Morning Star below; and hail stones, or Thunder, all around.

blankets, and quilts were draped in such a way that the inside became absolutely dark and fairly airtight. A buffalo skull, representing the Power and Spirit of the traditional food source, was painted with ceremonial colors and laid on top of each lodge facing the east.

As the sweat lodges neared completion, fires were started to heat the rocks—one hundred rocks for the fires in each lodge. One hundred is a sacred number during the Medicine Lodge ceremony because it is many, like the People of the tribe.

Each holy woman had a spiritual mother, a former holy woman, who gave her a sacred Bundle and the knowledge and rights to use it for the ceremony. Their husbands were instructed by spiritual fathers, who were in turn the husbands of former holy women. While the husbands engaged in the sweat baths, the holy women sat outside the lodge and prayed. The purifying sweat baths marked the beginning of the holy fast. During this fast, the holy women and their husbands concentrated completely on their efforts to inspire their People. The only thing they consumed was a shell full of water each morning and evening. Only the participants of the Medicine Lodge ceremony were allowed near their tipis, and they spoke not at all or in whispers.

The fourth and final move was made early in the morning. While the camp's lodges were being set up, the holy leaders marked out the site for the Medicine Lodge in the center of the camp circle, and dug the holes for the posts. While the women arranged their households, the children gathered firewood. The men went down to the river bottom, where they ceremoniously cut one upright post and one rafter log for the frame of the Medicine Lodge, then returned to the camp with the Spirit of a successful victory and again sang the ancient song. Some men fired their guns into the air. The excitement spread around the camp and strengthened the Spirits of everyone.

The construction of the Medicine Lodge began with the placement of twelve upright cottonwood logs. These posts stood in a circle about thirty-five feet in diameter; in the center was the large hole into which would go the Center Pole. The posts, long enough to extend about nine feet above the ground, forked at the top end. Eleven smaller logs, each about twelve feet long, were laid so that their ends rested in the forks of adjacent uprights, thus forming a circle. The remainder of the Holy Lodge was constructed the following day, the most important day of the ceremony.

Wilson observed in his notes:

That morning as I neared the camp I saw that most of the lodges had sacrifices or offerings of some garment or blanket elevated upon an extra lodge-pole leaning against the lodge; these were tied to cross sticks. . . . At each of the four lodges occupied by the O-Kon people an extension rite was, in the forenoon, begun.

Wilson did not often explain the spiritual meanings of the details of ceremonies he recorded. For instance, the customary purpose of an offering is to give every family an opportunity to participate in building the sacred lodge. A gift of fabric, fastened to a small frame, is presented to the holy people, who are acting in behalf of the Spirits, just before the main construction of the lodge takes place. The frame is made by tying two scraped willow sticks in the shape of a cross, representing the Four Holy Directions of the Universe. Bunches of sage tied to the cross represent the gifts obtained from our Mother Earth. The cloth is added to share our material wealth with the Holy Powers. Each family hangs its offering above its tipi early in the morning so that the Spirits of Sun and the Universe can see where it came from. The family members, observing their offering in this way, derive spiritual pride for their part in the proceedings.

On the day the Center Pole is raised, the holy women end their fasting and praying, and the former holy women (or woman) transfer their sacred Bundles to the new holy women. In 1892, the seven transfers were conducted simultaneously in the four main tipis.

The holy woman's sacred Bundle is called the Natoas. It is kept in a cylindrical rawhide case decorated with painted designs and long fringes. On the outside of the rawhide case the sacred digging stick is fastened, the same kind of stick our women used to dig edible roots like camas. During the transfer ceremony, a set of dried moose hooves is tied to the stick. The hooves and stick symbolize our Old People's main foods—meat and roots. They also represent two of the spiritual helpers who are said to have contributed their Powers to the original Natoas. The meanings of these items were revealed in a dream to a Beaver Bundle man who kept the original Natoas.

The holy woman's sacred headdress is the most important item in the rawhide case. Like our other tribal Medicines of ancient origin, this one is made up of things symbolic of the natural world. The base of the headdress is a rawhide band of buffalo skin, shaped like a lizard. Plumes and feathers of eagles and other birds are fastened to it so that they stand up. Skins of weasels are attached so that they hang down, and an ancient arrowhead hangs from one side. A tiny image-doll stuffed with sacred tobacco seeds is attached to the rawhide band to represent mystical Spirits known as the Little People. Back when our Old People still grew sacred tobacco, the Little People would mysteriously come and give it their Power to be sacred.

Wilson made these observations during the transfer ceremonies of these sacred headdresses:

Simultaneously, the initiation rite was performed in '92 in all four of the lodges. I witnessed that in which three women were initiated at once in Running Wolf's lodge. The front had been enclosed and poles of the lodge had been spread far apart and a second lodge pitched in front, so

Mrs. Rides-at-the-Door is the last Blood Holy Woman. She is seen wearing her Natoas headdress as she entered the last Blood Medicine Lodge ten years ago.

that when their canvas was joined a double lodge was formed. At back end of the lodge proper, sitting in a row, were the old and new O-Kon women and the master of ceremonies [Wilson means the holy women and the priest]; also the husbands of the women about to be initiated. In middle of lodge a hole had been dug 2½ by 3 feet square and 4 inches deep; the sod taken from it was piled around three sides and covered with pine boughs [actually, boughs of creeping juniper —a species commonly found in our country; it grows close to the earth and is the sacred incense for Medicine Lodge ceremonies]. Bottom of hole was covered with white clay in which had been drawn, an inch deep, this design [showing the main symbols of the Universe]; the bottom of all the marks was painted black by sprinkling in them black paint, the edges yellow. A cottonwood tree was planted in ground to the left of hole. Tree 7 or 8 feet high. Upon the tree were hanging the head dresses to be disposed of.

The hole Wilson describes was the incense alter, representing our Mother Earth. The designs indicated Moon, in the shape of a crescent; Sun; Morning Star; and Sun Dogs. The black paint was for Night Sky, the yellow paint for the Powers represented. The small cottonwood tree stood as a symbol of the Old People's main source of firewood, without which they would have perished. In the midst of these spiritual symbols, the sacred headdresses were hung. In addition, the leader of the sacred ceremonies regularly made incense on the altar, for its sweet smell symbolized the presence of the Holy Spirits.

Wilson continues:

Seven men rattled and sang, and the three old O-Kon women took each a root digger, and leaning upon them, dance upon their knees, rattling against the stick each a bundle of buffalo toes [moose hooves], and at end of the song tied the toes to the stick securely and in next songs they, still keeping time, danced pointing the sticks towards the clay [symbolically giving them the Power of the sacred incense]. Sticks were then put down and the candidates were robed in new clothes; an elk skin tanned on both sides is the proper robe for O-Kon to wear. Part of the lodge was screened off [by blankets held up by some of the other participants], behind which . . . the re-dressing of the woman was done. At this stage, relatives of one of the O-Kon women [such as Red Crow's wife] brought in piles of dry goods etc., and deposited them on the ground, after which they were all gathered up by children of the old woman who was installing her, and taken away home.

There was more singing and rattling, during which the holy women kept time to the rhythm. The new holy women were painted by the old ones with sacred red earth.

Then the three older women [took] the head-bands from the tree and [danced] them towards the clay [for] 2 or 3 songs. Next they placed head-bands upon their own head, and [danced] on their knees towards the tree, which all 3 butted with their heads and grunted as they did so several times. [They were imitating the elk cow, who gave her Powers with the original Natoas after knocking down a cottonwood tree to prove her strength to her husband and to the dreamer.] Head-bands were then taken off and held by each woman in front of the younger one whom she was installing; and after dancing it there in front of her awhile and passing it 4 times around the younger's head, put it on and tied it in place.

Singing without rattles, three old men [husbands of the three retiring holy women] painted the three O-Kon men black from head to foot, with a yellow streak across the face and a yellow ring around each wrist. [The yellow paint again represented the Above Powers, especially Sun.]

Renewing the rattling as they sang and after many flourishes, a crow's tail was tied to the back lock of each black man's hair, and a scalp tied around his neck, which was first passed 4 times around his head and handed to him and taken again by the priest to tie. In the meantime, the women's faces had been painted, and the root diggers stuck in their belts behind, the rattles dangling therefrom.

The O-Kon necklaces were next produced and with usual flourishes and songs were tied about each man's neck and wrists. This concluded that part of it.

These necklaces, *O-Koch-Kindt*, are still worn by the man and woman during Medicine-Lodge ceremonies. They consist of a thong with four blue beads strung on each side, representing the clear sky. A white dentalium shell is strung between the beads to represent the purity and holiness of the Spirit World. A thin braid of hair hangs down from the center of the necklace to represent the Power of the People. The holy woman may make extra necklaces to transfer to anyone requesting such a spiritual Medicine, as the wearer is believed to possess the spiritual power of the holy ceremony. Our last holy woman, old Mrs. Rides-at-the-Door, transferred a holy necklace to SikskiAki when we attended the recent Okan among the Southern Piegans.

When the 1892 ceremonial transfer and painting were done, and the women were dressed in their holy headdresses and elk robes, they were ready to go outside and perform the main ceremonial functions. From within the tipi in which Wilson was an observer, came a procession led by No Chief, who was the priest. Behind him came the three black-painted husbands, wearing black blankets over their heads. And behind them came the holy women, each one following the woman whose Natoas she had just taken over. From the other holy tipis came similar processions.

Wilson's narrative continues:

Very slowly they walked to the south side of the half-built medicine lodge, stopping at intervals to pray, but not loudly. They circled the medicine-lodge once, taking the course of the Sun, and then sat down in a shelter which had been constructed for them to the West of the medicine lodge.

This shelter was made up of travoix poles and canvas. Those using it sat facing the sacred edifice. The shelter was about 60 feet long, and sitting in a row, extending from one end to the other [were] seven parties of people, each composed of the woman who had sold her O-Kon [Wilson should have said Natoas; he uses the word O-Kon in various ways, although it actually describes only the Medicine Lodge ceremony itself], her husband, the new O-Kon, and her husband. . . . In front of these people and about 20 feet from them was a row of 7 parfleche bags, 4 placed on each side of a central space through which those going and coming passed. [The bags belonged to the holy women and contained the dried sacred tongues.] In front again of this entrance space was deposited a green beef hide wrapped in a black blanket; the use of the hide will appear later on.

While the holy people prepared to receive those who wished their blessings, the Horns Society mounted horses and rode to the cottonwood grove to obtain the sacred Center Pole. The party rode off as if headed for war and approached the chosen tree as they would a powerful enemy. After brave deeds were recounted and prayers for success were made, the tree was cut down amidst shooting and shouting. While the Horns were preparing to haul the sacred tree back to camp, Wilson made these observations:

People in camp now began taking down the offerings before mentioned from the tops of their lodges, and soon a woman came to the O-Kon, leading a child and bearing her offering. She went to one of the old O-Kon [priests] and reluctantly [she was probably shy before the holy man] knelt in front of the man and handed him a filled pipe which she had brought, and deposited the offering at his feet. The vendor took the pipe and pointed the stem to the Sun and prayed in favor of the suppliant, who knelt through the prayer with bowed head. At the end of the prayer the latter passed her hands to head of the prayer-maker and down his shoulders and arms to the hands, taking the pipe from him and laying it aside. The old man's wife then painted a black ring around the face of both mother and child and her husband. The old man took up the offering and made a pass with it down each side of the woman's body; the latter turned about without rising and the offering was leaned against her back at which she arose and departed. Four members of the Society, "Crazy Dogs," were sitting near at hand, their duty being to light the pipe. One of these now came and took the late suppliant's pipe from [the] old man who handed it to him, went out to the front of the enclosure, past the before-mentioned hide, to a little fire built there for the purpose, and lit the pipe. Puffing it on the way to keep it from going out, he returned it to the old man who first took a few whiffs himself, then handed it to the black man of his set who smoked and handed it around.

When the pipe was emptied, it was passed out to someone of the owner's family waiting for it. That is a close description of the mode of giving the offerings, which were brought by all sorts of people, young and middle aged. Some were boys, some were girls, bringing children with them, and others alone. All were dressed in their best clothing. Some boys wore their fathers' war bonnets. Many sacred pipes were brought, the young men "attendants" were called upon, but the pipe bearer himself took the pipe to the fire, after he was painted, the old man going with him to pray as he lit it for the other. The bearer of the pipe now presented the mouthpiece to each man and woman in the row of O-Kons and then to everyone sitting outside. Great rows of people were sitting in a half circle on either side of the shelter. Each person to whom the pipe was presented took 4 draws only. These sacred pipes were always passed a long time after they had ceased to emit smoke. They seemed to go out before many people had smoked.

As is the case with our People now, anyone in camp could make an offering, a symbolic gift to the Holy Spirits—to Sun, Moon, sky, stars, birds, animals. The offering would be brought to the holy people by a family member. At this stage of the Medicine Lodge ceremony, these holy people were thought to be in strong communication with the Spirits. Each person bringing an offering selected one of the holy people waiting in the Sun shelter for this purpose. The chosen holy person would then pray to the Spirits on behalf of the offerer. Later, all the offerings would be brought to the Medicine Lodge and tied, permanently, to the lodge's Center Pole.

Families keeping the tribe's sacred Medicine Pipes and Beaver Bundles had the opportunity for an unusual and powerful spiritual experience during the Medicine Lodge ceremony. Only at this time were these sacred Pipes fitted with bowls for smoking; at no other time were they smoked. The Owners of the sacred Pipes gathered their families inside their lodges. Usually, past Owners were present, especially if the current Owner did not know the Bundle's songs very well. There are songs to sing while opening the Bundle and many more songs to sing afterwards, when the People pray and dance with its contents.

After incense was made, the leader of the opening painted the Owner's family with Medicine Pipe symbols on their faces and wrists. The sacred Pipestem was taken from its cloth wrapping and carefully laid on top of the Bundle. At this point the sacred Bowl was removed from the Bundle and filled with ceremonial tobacco. With

29

a prayer for success and good thoughts, the Bowl was fitted to the Stem. The Owner took hold of the Pipe—one hand on the Stem and one on the Bowl. It would have been a bad sign if the Stem became separated from the Bowl during the rest of the ceremony.

With the guidance of some old man, the Owner took his sacred Pipe outside. He was followed by his family, all wearing blankets or shawls, as a sign of modesty during holy occasions. The old man would call out, "Make way, People, here comes the bearer of a sacred Pipestem. Give him your respect." Quickly, the People would move aside, leaving a clear path for the bearer to walk, straight to the holy people's shelter.

As Wilson stated, the sacred Pipe would first be offered to one of the priests. A helper from the Crazy Dogs Society would hold a glowing stick into the Bowl while the priest puffed on the mouthpiece. The Owner, holding Stem and Bowl in his hands, would offer the Pipe among the people, who placed their lips against the mouthpiece to smoke it. They would not hold the Pipe, not being purified with the sacred incense, and not trained in handling it. Some people would brush their hands reverently over the sacred Stem and then down their bodies, taking its ancient Holy Spirit within themselves. For many, this was the only chance to be in the presence of one of the tribe's sacred Pipes and to give their prayers directly to the Holy Spirits within it.

Wilson noted on his watch that not quite two hours had passed since the Horns Society left camp to go after the Center Pole:

Offerings were still being brought when, at 4:30, appeared in sight those with the centre pole. They came in a great procession, scores of

Medicine Pipe Owner offering smokes from his sacred Pipe to those gathered outside the Medicine Lodge of 1907. (Van Wangen)

mounted men and women accompanying them. All had wreaths of green leaves upon their heads and were singing the same song referred to before. The pole, a large cottonwood tree, was brought on a wagon followed by many travoix loaded with boughs. The procession came around the back of the shelter and stopped at front of the medicine lodge, where they unloaded the pole, as related.

The Center Pole was unloaded from its wagon inside the unfinished Medicine Lodge. Its butt end rested on the ground near the hole it was to go in; its forked end was propped up in the air so that it could be lifted easily later. But before that, the ceremony known as "cutting the hide" had to be performed. The green, or raw, beef hide mentioned earlier was cut round and round into a long, narrow strip. This strip was in turn cut into lengths for tying together the poles of the Medicine Lodge. Since these strips were to hold up the Temple of the Holy Spirits, a strong man was needed to ensure that the hide was properly cut. In the long-ago days, the hide-cutter was a man known to have performed at least four brave deeds. Recently, an old man who had committed such deeds came forward and recounted them while holding up the hand of the hide-cutter. After this, a former hide-cutter painted his successor and prayed for him.

Roached Mane, who had been hide-cutter at the Okan previous to 1892, sat before the uncut hide, waiting for someone to come forward and accept the duty from him. Members of the Horns Society approached him and began singing and dancing, while "one of their members, Old Bull Horn, counted 4 coups." The coups represented brave deeds such as touching an enemy, stealing a horse or weapon, or taking a scalp.

Raising the Center Pole in 1892. The Pole has just dropped into its hole. In another moment the rafters will be pushed up into the crotch and tied in place on the surrounded framework. (R. N. Wilson)

At last "Gambler" came forward and began to take off his clothes. Calf Shirt [who had the Power of Rattlesnakes] painted him red all over and dressed him in new . . . garments. Gambler's relatives now brought in piles of goods and put them on the ground as presents to Roached Mane, [who] produced a knife, which was painted red, and placed it in Gambler's hand.

During the year previous to the Okan, a number of women had vowed to "feed Sun" some of the sacred tongue. These women wanted the inspirational power obtained by taking part in the Medicine Lodge ceremony, but were not able to take on the responsibility of holy women. At this stage these women came forward, accompanied by the person for whose benefit they first made the vow—usually a child or some other relative.

A number of virtuous women in the tribe had during the year vowed to distribute the sacred tongues, which duty can only be done by such women. These now came forward and opened up the sacks and each took out a number of pieces. Each walked out to where she could see the Sun, and pinching off a little piece of the dried meat, held it up and prayed aloud. At the conclusion of her prayer each put the little pieces of meat into the ground at her feet, giving it to her mother the Earth Person [as] a duty.

While the virtuous women held up pieces of sacred tongue, they usually called out something like this: "As I have lived a pure and honest life, I feed you this piece of sacred tongue, our Sun, and ask you to keep my family safe and healthy." After finishing their prayers,

These women, assisted by some men, then distributed to the assembled populaces all of the sacred tongue meat. Nearly all of the recipients prayed where they sat and put a little into the earth as before.

Lazy Going Man's 2 children were brought in and painted, then both were mounted upon a horse. Their father stood up and presented a rifle to the outgoing "hide cutters" party by laying it upon the ground. His wife and others also made various presents of lodge furniture and wearing apparel.

Lazy Going Man was a close friend of Gambler, the new hide-cutter. By contributing presents to the past hide-cutter, he was helping Gambler assume his new duties. At the same time, he obtained the right to help his friend with the sacred hide-cutting. Having his children painted was to give them the inspiration to look for success in later life.

The hide was then uncovered and spread out; Gambler stood up before it and made a speech. He, Strangled Wolf and Lazy Going Man each counted 4 coups . . . holding the knife in hand as he did so. . . . Gambler, assisted by others, cut up the hide. Beginning at the tail, he cut around the edge and continued cutting until the whole hide was made into a single, long thong about an inch in width, the tail being one extremity. To the tip of the tail was tied an eagle tail feather. The offerings were now all brought from where they had been piled behind the A-Kax [Medicine Lodge] and were tied to the ends of all the rafters. Many of the offerings were also tied to the [top] end of the centre pole, as it lay, and others were wrapped and tied about the middle. . . . The tail end of the raw hide was now pulled along and made fast to the top end of the centre pole, in such a manner that the ox-tail [beef hide] would hang near the ground when this pole became erect. The raw hide was then all cut into lengths sufficient to tie the smaller poles together . . . and several men went to work tying them.

The tail left hanging down from the Center Pole represents the tail that hung from the bottom of the rawhide rope Morning Star made for his wife—in the very long ago—so that she could come back down to her home on Earth and bring the Medicine Lodge ceremony to the People.

A strange sight next appeared. Four processions of young men approached from the lodges, one from each of the cardinal points. Each procession was made up of pairs of young men, walking, each pair behind the other. Each man held aloft a lodge pole, which was strongly connected at the top to the pole of his companion. So in all 4 of the processions, the poles of every pair of young men were tied together, a foot and a half or two feet apart. They approached a few yards at a time until, when within 50 or 60 yards of the Sun-Lodge, they changed their formation from column to line. This resulted in the ends of their 4 lines uniting so that they, as a whole, formed a large circle, the centre of which was the half erected medicine lodge. The completion of the lodge by raising the heavy timbers in place [with their lodge poles] was the errand of all these young men.

We are here in the midst of a symbolic battle. The young men with their lodge poles represent the warriors of the tribe, the tribe's defenders, carrying their weapons. The warriors are about to converge upon the Center Pole, representing the enemy, and overpower it by raising it up. This is symbolic of the People's power to triumph in battle. The holy people wait by the Center Pole to lend their spiritual power to the victory. The husbands wear the black paint worn by a victorious war party.

Completing the Medicine Lodge follows:

The A-Kax [holy party] now left their positions and entered the circle; the black men each carried the scalps tied to a short stick, climbed upon the resting centre pole and, all bending their heads close to the top and covering their heads with their blankets, prayed silently. At the end of this prayer, they jumped down and the circle of young men closed in amid deafening yells and attacked the centre pole with their poles. Each pair worked together. Placing the connecting cord against the pole, most of them pushing from the under side, they soon had it upright in its hole, being assisted at first by some other men who put their shoulders to it. Next they attacked the rafters which were lifted up. The butt end of one of them was placed upon the centre of each stringer and all the small ends bearing offerings were resting in the fork of the centre pole. The butts were tied in place with raw hide, the whole being completed in a very short time to the satisfaction of the Indians, who consider the completion of the lodge a cause for joy.

The vows of the holy women were completed once the Center Pole was up. Having made their sacrifice to help build the Medicine Lodge, they returned to their tipis and removed their sacred outfits. Their husbands entered a sweat lodge where the husbands of the former holy women ceremonially wiped the black paint from their "sons" with handfuls of sage. The sacred objects used by the men were passed outside during the sweat bathing. After all the holy people had returned to their own lodges, the former Owners of the Natoas Bundles showed the new Owners how to pack up the sacred articles, and gave them final instructions for everyday care. By this time it was probably dark, since the Center Pole is usually raised as Sun sets. Relatives of the holy people brought food, since the period of fasting was over.

On the following day most of the young people and many adults were busy in the forenoon bringing the cottonwood boughs, with which to cover the sides of the sacred lodge. For 4 or 5 hours previous to 1 o'clock, mounted processions continually were arriving in camp, singing, shooting and shouting. The women formed a considerable proportion of these, many having travoix attached to their horses, loaded with *boughs. At 1 p.m. the Lodge was quite completed and quietness reigned in the camp, broken only by the occasional shouting of some chief calling guests to a feast, or a caller assembling the members of some fraternity.*

With the completion of the Holy Lodge, the participants returned to their own lodges to await the next ceremony which was, in effect, the start of the second half of the Okan. The first four days had led up to the construction of it; the last three or four days were taken up with ceremonies within it.

The next part of the Okan began when two men came out of their lodges wearing sacred dress and carrying fans of eagle wings and boughs of creeping juniper. Four old men came behind them with hand drums, singing a sacred song. The two men, known as the Weather Dancers, danced forward to the rhythm of the song, at the same time blowing on whistles of eagle bone, which stuck from their mouths.

The Weather Dancers are the priests for the activities that take place inside the Medicine Lodge. The People placed their spiritual faith in these men, who were considered to have Power to attract good weather to the encampment. It was up to the Weather Dancers to decide how many more days the Okan ceremonies would continue, and they would remain within the Medicine Lodge throughout that time to fast, pray, and dance. It is as a result of their duties that the Okan is often referred to as a Sun Dance.

The only clothing the Weather Dancers usually wore were moccasins and breechcloths. They painted their bodies with designs shown to them in dreams or given by some previous dancer. Around their heads and wrists they wore wreaths of creeping juniper boughs, and eagle bone whistles hung from thongs around their necks. On their backs they sometimes wore white robes, pinned together in front of their necks. They tried to concentrate their thoughts on the Holy Power that Sun passes on to all the creatures on Earth.

On their way to the Medicine Lodge, the Weather Dancers made four stops. At each stop they intensified their holy thoughts and danced more vigorously, while the drumming and singing continued behind them. The People stood quietly before their tipis, watching the brightly colored dancers make their way around the north side of the Medicine Lodge and then enter through the large opening on the east side of the cottonwood boughs.

The Weather Dancers entered this sacred booth and sat down, facing the Center Pole and the entrance of the Holy Lodge at the east. The holy people followed and sat down on their robes at the northwest side. The drummers sat on logs at the southwest side and were soon joined by several old men who knew the ceremonial songs. People approached the Holy Lodge to see inside, so that the entrance was blocked. Others found places around the outside where they could look through.

According to our Old Man, who was a young boy at the 1892 Okan, the head Weather Dancer was Ki-soum, or Sun, still remembered as one of our finest holy men. Wilson often refers to this man by the name Moon. The other was a former Weather Dancer who had vowed to help Ki-soum. Among the small bundle of things Ki-soum had brought into the Weather Dancers' booth was a black-bowled pipe. He filled the pipe with sacred tobacco and handed it to the drummer nearest the booth. The drummer raised the stem, prayed for the spiritual success of the People, lit the pipe, and passed it among the other drummers to smoke. It was then passed into the booth, where the Weather Dancers smoked quietly.

When the pipe was smoked out, Ki-soum signaled the drummers, who began to drum and sing a Weather Dancers song. The Weather Dancers placed their bone whistles between their lips and stood up. Raising their heads so they

Outside the 1892 Medicine Lodge, while ceremonies take place inside. (R. N. Wilson)

Inside the 1892 Medicine Lodge. In the foreground is the pit where the sticks representing war adventures were burned. Behind the pit is the sacred Center Pole, with offerings tied to it. The man standing is believed to be the Weather Dancer, Ki-soum. The others are his drummers. (R. N. Wilson)

could see the top of the sacred Pole, they blew on their whistles with short blasts while they bounced up and down with the drum beats.

Before them was the center of the Earth, marked by the sacred Center Pole. From Earth it reached to the heavens above, symbolically connecting the two into one Universe. The bright colors of the many offerings fluttered at the top of the Center Pole, marking the place where Sky and Earth met. The fork joint represented that all the directions in the Universe are joined together by the Great Spirit to make One. The prayers of the Above Spirits were represented by Wind, which could be heard all around; the prayers of the Earth Spirits were represented by the rustling of the green leaves on the cottonwood boughs.

"Cheep—cheep—cheep—cheep," sounded the eagle bone whistles as the Weather Dancers rocked on the balls of their feet, accompanied by the rhythm of the drumming and chanting. If a cloud threatened to hide Sun's light, the intensity of the dancing and music increased until the cloud passed out of sight.

I believe in this Power of Universal Harmony, for I experienced it myself during the Piegan Medicine Lodge celebration of 1972. The former Weather Dancer, an old man named Makes Summer, taught me the way to use spiritual power passed on from the long-ago. As dark rain clouds threatened overhead, the singing and dancing became more and more intense. The clouds finally separated and Sun shined brightly until the ceremony was over; not until then did it begin to rain. No one remembers a Medicine Lodge ceremony that was ever disturbed by rain.

Wilson brought his notebook and joined the crowd around the Holy Lodge:

35

Late in the afternoon those members of the Pigeon Society [who were able to relate personal exploits of bravery] formed a line, standing. Two of them rode a single horse; the others were all dismounted. They began to sing and approached the A-Kax and entered, then took a position in two rows; the riders rode their horses once completely around the enclosure, passing at the back between the banner [Weather Dancers' booth] and centre pole. Four Tom-toms [hand drums] and the same number of rattles were obtained for music. While the Pigeons danced and sang, relatives brought in piles of goods which were deposited at the feet of the dancer related to the giver. These presents were all gathered up by an old man and distributed to other people. Eagle Ribs [the uncle of our Mokakin] was taken by the arm and led out to the centre and left standing there. Pails of food were now brought in; generally a row of 4 or more pails were strung upon a stick and carried in by two squaws, each taking an end of the stick. Squaws [a foreign word to us, even though Wilson uses it often; a man calls his wife Aki, "woman," or Nitokeman, "my wife"] always put down the pails, and either left the enclosure or joined the crowd of women at the south and near the entrance. The food was distributed to all the people who had seated themselves inside, with bowls in front of them. Next pipes were filled, presented to an old man, blessed and smoked. They then danced three times without changing their positions in rows. Bob Tailed Chief [then a young member of the Pigeon Society—he later became one of our holy leaders] went and placed a stick at the feet of an old man, which meant that he had given him a horse, at which the old man stood up and made a long blessing over the liberal young man, whose wife came forward and shared it with him. A 4th dance was indulged in at close of which they danced out. Time was 8:10.

The Pigeon Society was composed of young men who had few exploits to their record, and so they were the first to perform in the Medicine Lodge. This was an opportunity for the societies to inspire the People, as well as themselves, with their ceremonies and comradeship. And it was an honor for members to donate food to the gathered People, who were given good thoughts through the gesture.

After the presentation, the People were asked to return to their lodges and spend the night quietly. There was to be no noise, especially near the Medicine Lodge. The Weather Dancers were fasting and meditating on the Holy Powers created by the sacred encampment.

THE SELF-TORTURE CEREMONIES

Another group to participate in the Medicine Lodge ceremony came to fulfill their own vows. These were men who had made vows of physical sacrifice in exchange for spiritual help from Sun. Such vows were usually made during dangerous situations, perhaps on the hunt or warpath, when death seemed imminent. A vowing man might call out to Sun, "Help me, O holy Sun, my Father, and let me see you again with happiness. Give me your strength so that I may survive this danger, and I will give myself to you. I will help my People to remember your Holy Power by performing the physical torture dance during the next Holy Lodge ceremony of our People." Fulfilling such vows was truly a Sun Dance, and inspiring to those who watched.

WILSON'S OBSERVATIONS: 1892

The last time self-torture vows were fulfilled during a Blood Medicine Lodge ceremony was in 1892. The days of warpaths were already past. Although our young men still went on regular horse raids then, there was seldom any fighting, even when the raiders were caught. Government agents knew that the self-torture ceremony inspired a spirit of adventure, which they opposed. Follow-

Goes to War suspended from the Center Pole during his self-torture. The man standing near him is his advisor, who underwent this ordeal at some earlier time. (R. N. Wilson)

A vow of self-torture being fulfilled during an earlier Medicine Lodge Ceremony in 1887. A shield is suspended from the dancer's back by thongs. (W. H. Boorne)

ing the 1892 Okan, the agents sent word to the People that participants in self-torture would henceforth be jailed. They aroused outside backing for their move by calling the ceremonies "heathen rituals." The missionaries hoped that this ban would lead to an end of the Medicine Lodge ceremony itself. However, Medicine Lodges continued to be built. Self-torture vows were carried out in places that were not so public.

In writing and with his camera, Wilson recorded the details of the last ceremonies to fulfill self-torture vows:

Next day nothing occurred until afternoon, when some members of two Societies, "Crazys" [Wilson's own name for the Crazy Dogs, who were not actually crazy in any way] and "Black Soldiers," came out of their rows. At this, Sitting Bull's son entered in the paint garb of the "self-torture" as follows: no clothing except breach cloth and a blanket wrapped about him. A wreath of wild sage about the head, a ring of same about each arm and ankle. Painted with white dirt from head to foot. He sat down upon his blanket and presently some one placed a pillow and quilt on the ground upon which he laid down. A man assisted by others put a skewer in each breast and a 3rd [behind] one shoulder. When he arose to his feet a shield was fastened to the skewer in the back and the ropes from top of centre pole, to the others [on his breasts]. He walked up and embraced the centre pole and silently prayed. Then [he] went back until the ropes tightened and, reaching around behind, grasped the shield, tore it from his flesh with a jerk and cast it upon the ground. Giving a yell, he next caught hold of one of the ropes in each hand and gave them a couple of good jerks which pulled the skin out from his breast several inches each jerk. Then he threw back his full weight upon the ropes, having first inserted a whistle in his mouth, the string of it depending from around the neck. The drums started up and the boy danced in time to their

beating; he danced in a curve about the north side of the centre pole, blowing the whistle also in time and looking up at the top of the lodge, throwing more and more of his weight upon the ropes [until] his body was almost at right angles to the ropes, tied far above him. As his weight seemed insufficient to break loose the skin through which the skewers were, a man sitting near quickly got up, threw his arms around the young fellow's body, pulled backwards and tore him loose. He lay upon the ground while one of the attendants [not a priest or a doctor] cut away the torn end[s] of skin which were handed to him. He then arose to his feet and buried the said piece of skin in the loose dirt at foot of sacred pole, took off all the sage ornaments and hung them upon the offerings of the sacred pole, and went home. A young man named A-suc [Goes to War] was also put through the torture and I succeeded in getting a pretty fair photo of him, an instantaneous one taken as he was on the jump in his dance. When these young men are having the incisions made in their breasts, they often whisper to the operator stating how they wish the cuts to be, deep so that there will be difficulty in getting loose, or shallow cuts that will be easily broken. Those who do the cutting make it a rule to do the reverse to what they are requested, thus they reward the stout-hearted who say "cut deep" and punish the cowards. The Ats-Knax Society [Itski-naiks, or Horns] furnished the music for this day. They sat at the back of the enclosure upon the South side of the banner; the other, or North Side of the banner was occupied by the women who "made the lodge" and others.

Calf Tail and Goes to War were the first two dancers to fulfill their vows to suffer before the People, as just described. They had promised to "give themselves to Sun." Thus, the long rawhide ropes were attached to their breasts so that as the flesh opened, the blood nearest their hearts would flow upon the ropes. From there the Spirit

Powers took it up to the top of the Center Pole, where the ropes were fastened, and then up to Sun, who was looking down on the ceremony.

The remainder of that day was taken up with ceremonies that helped the People learn some of the history of their tribe. Men came forward who had personal exploits, mainly war adventures, to their record, and proceeded to tell their stories, giving a demonstration of the main scenes. Wilson for some reason calls these men dancers.

The dancers, one at a time, now related their heroic deeds in a theatrical manner, during which they would go through all sorts of antics in imitations of the original event. Some built little lodges on the ground and alongside were placed two or three little boys, who represented so many picketed horses, and led them away or else made a bold dash and captured them that way. In other cases, the boaster would enlist the services of some of the other dancers and would divide them into two parties, one representing the enemy, the other his own. The squad, acting as the enemy, would stoop low behind an imaginary shelter and watch the others approach the horses to be stolen. When the horse-thieves were almost upon their prey, the others would suddenly jump in sight and fire off their guns in the air, then a sham battle would ensue during the cause of which one or more of the participators would fall as dead, and undergo the operation of scalping, and in some cases have both hands cut off, showing how the killed had been used in the fight long ago. Each man who entered the O-Kon as a member of a dancing party related his deeds of valor during which his relatives brought in goods and presented them to the sacred gathering. The people present took more than a usual interest in certain of these rehearsals which were those of events in tribal history dear to the memory of all. This pride was, of course, more noticeable during the narratives of the older men. A comical feature of these performances appeared in their manner of showing mounted men as distinct from those who had fought on foot. The former would thrust a stick between his legs with the end trailing on the ground and ride it about the arena exactly like we used to in our boyhood. This absurd pantomime was performed numbers of times by middle-aged Indians who in their ordinary life were most circumspect in matters of behaviour. Several hours were spent thus, until the last warrior had related his glorious deeds. Much ammunition was shot off and all kinds of trophies were captured from bogus enemies. Each here began his story by mounting a horse and riding it around the inside of the sacred lodge, singing his war song and shouting. He would then dismount, hand the horse to someone outside, and enter upon the details of his past.

Thus ended the second day of activities inside of the Medicine Lodge. The Crazy Dogs and the Black Soldiers, both leading societies of brave warriors, have always had a great many exploits to relate during the Medicine Lodge ceremonies. Two more societies were to tell and perform their stories during the next several days. Meanwhile, the camp was silent again.

On the next day, Sunday, no one entered the structure until late, 4 or 5 o'clock in the evening [the Weather Dancers were inside, of course]; [then entered] the principal heroes in the society called "Crow Carriers." Their performances were much like the former, and one used a wagon to illustrate how he had killed some Cree he found travelling in a cart. This exploit could not be acted inside the O-Kon, so he and those who assisted him went outside to the front or East and performed the first part of the tragedy, which ended after a retreat inside the sacred lodge. In this case the boaster took by main force a gun from the hands of a living foe and afterwards slew him with a knife. A man, Sum-a-ke, appeared in the torture paint and, after sitting on the ground for a few minutes, was punctured as usual and fastened to the ropes. I also took his photo but the Sun was so low that the picture did not turn out as well as the one the day before.

The next day of the ceremonies turned out, unexpectedly, to be the last day. Two unrelated incidents caused camp to break: an undisclosed dispute among the Horns and an unidentified charge of adultery.

Monday. It was expected that the "Horned Ones" would enter today but a dispute arose among [them], one of their members taking down his lodge, which formed half of the fraternal abode, and moving from camp. The night before, a man accused one of the religious women of the tribe of adultery [this was a separate affair from the Horns dispute]. He claimed he had seen her at dusk indulging in immoral conduct with a certain young man, the son of a prominent chief. This caused a great commotion in camp, which coupled with the trouble in the Horned Society, had the effect of breaking up the camp, all dispersing to the different villages up and down the river.

It may be added that the criminal affair mentioned, which was for a long time the one interesting topic of tribal talk, had a somewhat impressive ending. Sentiment was divided in regard to the guilt or innocence of the woman, who declared that her accuser was blasting her character because she had repelled improper advances of his own. She had hitherto bourne a good reputation; in fact she had filled positions in religious rites that only those who solemnly swore to their virtue can occupy. The people therefore were loath to misjudge the woman. The old men said, "Time will tell who speaks the truth; death inside of a year is the penalty which all women pay who make false vows; the young man commits an equally serious crime who accuses a good woman falsely, therefore the liar in this case must die before the end of a year. It is not a long time to wait [and see] which of them will it be." Strange to relate, the woman died in childbirth in January following above incident.

The disagreements that brought the Okan of 1892 to an end did not affect most of the People. They went back home with the Good Spirits that had presided over the holy ceremonies. Disagree-

Robert Wilson standing by the Center Pole of the 1892 Medicine Lodge. The offerings at the top of the lodge remain, but those around the bottom of the Center Pole are missing. None of our People would have dared to remove such offerings, as they are the spiritual property of Sun. Wilson's adopted brother, Mean Bandolier, stands on the right. (R. N. Wilson)

40

ments among the People were becoming more common by that time, anyway, as their life in harmony with the Old Ways was being disturbed by outside interferences, both physical and spiritual.

SCRAPING WHITE'S AND HEAVY HEAD'S ACCOUNT: 1889

I once asked the Old Man if he had seen the self-torture dancing during the 1892 Okan, among the Bloods. He told me, "I was at that Okan with my parents, I remember . . . but I was too young to understand what was really going on. Some families had favorite children (Minipokaiks) who were taken along to holy ceremonies and had things explained to them. I wasn't one of those. Most of the kids were expected to play with their friends and not come near enough to disturb holy places until they were old enough to take part in things. I spent most of my time with my partners, riding across the prairie on my horse and looking for childhood adventure." Then, sensing that I had hoped for a more exciting answer, he added, "But my stepfather, Scraping White, later told me about the self-torture dancing. He helped to make the incisions and gave the dancers encouragement. Three summers before that last time of self-torture he had made and fulfilled a vow of his own."

I learned that old Scraping White was one of three men who fulfilled his self-torture vows during the Okan in 1889. Besides Scraping White, who was then twenty-three years old, there was Tough Bread (also known as Flint and Heavy Forehead) and old Heavy Head, who was then twenty. Heavy Head later became the Old Man's advisor and teacher. In 1947, an anthropologist named John Ewers recorded old Scraping White's story about his experience. Scraping White was then eighty-one years old—a fact that disproves the common theory that men who took part in the self-torture did not live long afterward. This theory might have been true in the long-ago days,

when men were sometimes left suspended from the Center Pole for several days and nights, going without food or water. Scraping White was only suspended for a short time, and was not required to fast at all. Here is his story.

Three of us tortured ourselves in the Sun Dance that year—Tough Bread, Heavy Head, and I. I was the oldest of the three.

I was on a war party to take horses from the Assiniboine [a neighboring tribe] when I made my vow to be tortured. Shortly before Sun went down, when we were in sight of the enemy camp, I turned to Sun and said, "I want good luck. Now I go to the enemy. I want to capture a good horse and go home safely. I'll be tortured this coming Sun Dance." As soon as it was dark I went into the enemy camp and took two fast horses out of their corral without any of them knowing it. I had good luck and reached home safely.

Then I told my relatives of the vow I had made. Yellow Horn, an older relative, who had been through the torture before, told me, "Put up a sweat lodge for me and I shall look after you." I made the sweat lodge the very next day.

Not long after that the Sun Dance was held. The torture took place the day after the Center Pole was raised for the Medicine Lodge. I was the first one to be tortured. The torture began about noon. Old Yellow Horn cut my breasts with an iron arrowhead and inserted a skewer through the cuts at each breast. These skewers were of serviceberry wood, flattened on both sides, thinned toward the ends but not sharpened, and about this long (showing two inches with his fingers). Then sinew was wrapped around the ends of the skewers and they were tied, each skewer to a 4-strand plaited rawhide rope. The two ropes were fastened at their far ends to the Center Pole at its forks.

I stood up and Yellow Horn told me, "Now you walk up, put your arms around the Center Pole and pray. Tell Sun, now your vow is being fulfilled." I did just as he told me. Then I stepped back. Yellow Horn pulled hard on the rawhide ropes attached to the skewers. Then I danced. I didn't dance long before my flesh gave way and the skewers pulled out. Yellow Horn came to me and cut the skin that had broken. He trimmed it off even. Then he gave me the pieces of skin he had cut away and told me to take them and stick them in the ground at the base of the Center Pole, saying, "Now, Sun, I have completed my vow."

The Old Man said that he often saw on his father's chest the scars where he had been pierced, but that old Scraping White suffered no other permanent injuries from the experience. He said that his father had asked for deep cuts and had been fortunate in actually having the mildest torture of the three. He remembers his Old People telling that Heavy Head suffered more than anyone they had ever seen. Here is how Heavy Head told his story to the same anthropologist:

There were only two of us, Buffalo Teeth, my partner, and I. We went to war together to take horses. At Medicine Hat we found a small camp of Cree half-breeds. It was night when we saw their camp. It was moonlight. I looked up at Moon and prayed, "I shall be tortured at the Sun Dance if I have good luck and get home safely." Then I stole up to the camp and got one bay that was tied in front of a lodge without any of the enemy waking or seeing me. Buffalo Teeth took a roan. We started back to the Blood camp, traveled three days and three nights with no food other than a black rabbit. We got awfully weak and hungry.

When I reached home I told my story to my father, Water Bull. The old man got up and sang his honoring song. Then he told me, "My son, you have done something worth doing. You have made a vow that you will be tortured at the Sun Dance. You must do it this coming Sun Dance."

A few days later, I went out to the east point of Belly Butte to fast. While I fasted I dreamed that a sacred person came to me and gave me a drum and certain herbs to use for doctoring. Then I returned home.

A short time after that the bands began to come together for the Sun Dance Encampment. I prepared myself to go to an old man named Little Bear, a relative of mine [SikskiAki's great-grandfather], who had been through the torture himself, years before. I filled my pipe and took it to him. I gave him the pipe and a buckskin horse, and said, "Here is a horse for you. Keep this pipe too. I want you to look after me in the torture." When I gave him the pipe he put it down and went over to the next lodge. There were two old men there, Green Grass Bull and Red Bead. These men were not related to me, but they were both older than Little Bear, and both had been through the torture. Little Bear asked them to come to his lodge, to take my pipe and pray for me. After they prayed, they told me not to take any food or water the day I was to be tortured.

The day before the torture I ate or drank nothing. Next day I ate or drank nothing until after the torture. However, the three old men gave me some sagebrush to chew.

I was the last of the three Bloods to undergo the torture that day. Scraping White, who was the oldest, was first. Then Tough Bread, then I. I was the youngest. Inside the Medicine Lodge, on the west side of the Center Pole and north of the Weather Dancer's arbor, a shelter was built of sticks like a sweat lodge, covered with willow leaves. I went there before noon of the day of the torture. I was laid on my back with my head pointed north. I was barefoot, and wore only a breechcloth made from a small red trade shawl purchased from the Hudson's Bay Company. There was a little bowl of white paint and another of black paint nearby. The three old men painted four black dots, one below the other, under each of my eyes. This was called "tear paint." If I cried the tears would run down there. Then they painted a double row of six black dots. The rest of my body was painted white, also my face. They took some of the broad-leafed sagebrush from the ground inside the sweat lodge and bound it together, placed a wreath of it around my head, and bands of it around each wrist and ankle.

I was taken from the sweat lodge and laid upon a blanket on the ground at the north side of the Center Pole with my head to the north, my feet toward the Center Pole. Other people were told to keep back away from me. Then an old man named Low Horn was brought forward. He counted four of his coups. The three old men, Little Bear, Red Bead, and Green Grass Bull, held me—one at each arm, and one at my head. Red Bead took a sharp iron arrowhead in his hand, and asked me, "How do you want me to cut them? Thick or thin?" I said, "Thin." I learned later that this question was always asked of the man undergoing the torture before his breasts were pierced, and the one doing the cutting always did just the opposite of the young man's request. So when I said "thin," Red Bead knew to make his incisions deep. Red Bead gave four of his own war coups. He made no prayer. Then he pierced my breasts with the sharp arrowhead and inserted a serviceberry stick through each breast. The sticks were not sharp but flattened at the ends. The other two men held my arms as he cut and inserted the sticks. Blood flowed down my chest and legs over the white paint. Then Red Bead pressed the sticks against my body with his hands. They turned me around to face Sun and pierced my back. To the skewers on my back they hung an imitation shield, not so heavy as a war shield. The shield had feathers on it, but I don't remember how it was painted. It belonged to a man named Peninsula.

The ropes were brought out from the Center Pole and tied to the skewers in my breasts—right side first, then left side. Red Bead then grabbed the ropes and jerked them hard twice. Then he told me, "Now you go to the Center Pole and pray that your vow will come true." I walked up there. I knew I was supposed to pretend to cry. But oh! I really cried. It hurt so much. Coming back from the Center Pole I was shouting. Then, before I started to dance, I jerked the shield off my back.

I leaned back and began dancing, facing the Center Pole. It felt just like the Center Pole was pulling me toward it. I began to dance from the

Heavy Head, around 1940, carrying his Crazy Dogs Society Rattle, and wearing one of the last weasel-tail shirts to have been made and transferred among the Bloods.

43

west toward the doorway of the Sun Lodge and back. Then, when the skewers did not break loose, the old men realized that the incisions had been made too deep. Red Bead came up and cut the outside of the incisions again so they would break loose. As I started dancing again the left side gave way and I had to continue dancing with only my right side holding. An old man named Strangling Wolf jumped up from the crowd and came toward me shouting. He called out four coups he had counted and jumped on me. The last rope gave way and I fell to the ground.

The three old men came to me and cut off the rough pieces of flesh hanging from my breasts. They told me to take this flesh that had been trimmed off, and the sagebrush from my head, wrists, and ankles, and place them at the base of the Center Pole. I did as they told me.

Then I took my robe and walked out of the Medicine Lodge alone. I went to a lonely place and fasted for a night. I wanted to dream. But I couldn't sleep because of the pain. At sunrise I prayed to Sun.

Some time after that I saw a man approaching on horseback. He said, "I'm going to take you home right away." He took me up behind him on his horse and rode me slowly back to camp. My breasts were swollen and hurt. The rider's name was Red Crane. He told me of a mix-up that took place at the Sun Dance over horses stolen from the Gros Ventres.

When I got to my lodge, my mother gave me something to eat. She and my father told me what had happened at the Sun Dance gathering—a mix-up between the Mounted Police and Indians. I had to stay in the lodge several days. My breasts were so swollen that I could hardly move. Indian doctors used herb medicines to take away the swelling and to cure my wounds.

Heavy Head and Scraping White both passed away a few years after their stories were recorded. They were the last of our People who had undergone the self-torture ceremony. With some variations in the details, their stories are still told whenever our Old People get together to talk about the past. The mentioned mix-up with the Mounted Police will be more fully described later in a story about old Calf Robe, who was the object of the mix-up.

THE 1908 OKAN, SPONSORED BY HEAVY SHIELD

We are fortunate to have Wilson's written account of the 1892 Okan. Without it, many of the details of the ceremony would have been lost to us. Nevertheless, many details were not recorded and are lost because he did not understand all that went on around him. He was given no Teachings about Medicine Lodge ceremonies. Among the Old People who were given such Teachings is George First Rider, the son of a priest and doctor. Here is his story of another, later Sun Dance, as he told it recently.

My grandmother, Catching Amongst, was going to sponsor a Holy Lodge in the year 1908, but she didn't. Something happened in the family of the people that were going to transfer the Natoas Bundle to her. [Probably a death; a mourning family cannot take part in holy ceremonies.]

If there is no one to sponsor a Holy Lodge, then the Horns Society will look for someone.

The Horns Society took one of the tongues [from the cows that were butchered on ration day], and the ceremonial leader painted it black. The Horns Society sang, "The black paint I take. . . . It is holy."

The seven high-ranking members went out in a procession bearing the painted tongue. They all wore holy moccasins, breechcloths, and robes. The procession led to the east entrance of the camp circle. They walked slowly. When they got to the south side, they stopped and prayed. They stopped and prayed several times as they pro-

ceeded around the camp circle, each time waiting for someone to approach them. This is what they prayed: "Help, O Sun, may someone take this tongue. O Sun, bless the tongue yourself so that someone may build a holy lodge for you."

The elderly Horns members sang a song of praise for each band in the camp circle—the Fish Eaters band, the Many Children band, and also for the women who sponsor Holy Lodges. . . .

Still, there was no one to sponsor a Holy Lodge. The men continued carrying the tongue around the camp circle. They stopped a little way from the east entrance of the camp circle. They were worried. This was their last stop, the camps of the Lone Fighters band. For this band they sang, "My children, when they were long gone, I was still happy."

The members prayed again and were about to go back to their lodge when a woman came out of her tipi. As she walked toward them, Chief Calf came out and sang a song of praise for the woman. The woman was the wife of Iron Necklace [better known as Heavy Shield]. Her name was Many Kill. She walked straight up until she stood in front of the leader who carried the tongue. She held out her robe in bowl-like fashion. The tongue carried around the camp was held with sage grass and a braid of sweetgrass. It was not carried in a dish.

Many Kill did not say a word; the leader did not say a word. He just gave her the tongue. As he did, the rest said, "Aye," and made a downward brushing motion at the woman, showing their acceptance of her holy effort. She stood facing northeast. She turned to her right and went home. The leader was the woman's father. He sang, "Many Kill Woman—when she started to walk I was very happy."

The People all sang praise. The Horns Society members returned to their lodge. They walked around it from the south side to the north side, in the direction that Sun travels, and then they went inside. Some of them came out and called out invitations: "All you Horns Society members are all invited." The Horns said [to themselves], "Oki, it's us that took the tongue around the camps and we are the ones that will make the payments—Many Kill will just sponsor the Holy Lodge—us, we will make the payments."

The virtuous women, past holy women, were individually invited. They assembled immediately. Many Kill said, "You Horns Society members will get me a father." Getting a father meant that they would look for someone to transfer a Natoas Bundle to her. She would need dry goods and horses as payments for the transferral. In the future, when Many Kill transferred her Natoas Bundle, she would pay back anyone who had helped with these payments.

The women who were to work on the tongues all went to the holy woman's tipi. The Horns Society members gathered the tongues, wrapped them in a blanket, and the leader took them to Heavy Shield's tipi. In the tipi, sitting at the back in the place of honor was Wolf Shirt, a respected holy man. The leader told Wolf Shirt, "Come to the Horns Society tipi." When Wolf Shirt went to the Horns, they said, "You will get a father for Many Kill. Who shall we ask?"

Wolf Shirt went out from the Horns Society tipi to tell the one who was going to give up her Natoas. She did not refuse. She said, "I am glad to transfer my Natoas to Many Kill." Wolf Shirt first returned to the Horns and told them, "It is agreed. She will transfer her Natoas to Many Kill." Then he went back to Heavy Shield's tipi and told Many Kill, "I got you a father." With that settled, Heavy Shield moved his camp to the other side of the camp circle.

I have heard a lot of Old People say the holy woman's tipi is never pitched on the north side of the camp circle, always on the south side. But if the woman who is going to sponsor the Holy Lodge is from the north side, she will have to move her tipi to the south side.

Heavy Shield's friends took down his tipi. Just

45

the tipi and bedding were moved—back rests are not used in the tipis of holy women. The tipi has to have beds all around the inside because the holy men and the holy women gather there and they take care of the tongues. A holy woman's travois, all painted, is also moved.

Many Kill covered her head when she took the tongue, and she would not uncover her head from then on. She would not see anybody, and nobody would see her face. Many Kill was a pious woman from the time she took the tongue. Many Kill's bed was made and then she was taken to her tipi by the former holy women. She walked very slowly across to her tipi. She could not look around. If she were going to cough she would cover her mouth with her hand so that the People would not hear her coughing. That is how hard it was to sponsor a Holy Lodge.

So, Many Kill was taken from the north side across to her tipi. The virtuous women walked with her. She sat on her bed. She did not braid her hair. She did not have on wristlets; she wore no necklace and no earrings. She had brought herself into loneliness and she had no material things to distract her.

The tongues had not been prepared beforehand, since no Holy Lodge had been planned. Now they had to be prepared in a hurry. They were sliced very thin while a fire was built in the fireplace. It was a small fire, just big enough to heat the tongues. Tripods were set over the fire where the tongues were hung to dry.

Many Kill was a pious woman from the time she took the tongue. She is a tall woman. She is not fat, just stout. Heavy Shield is tall, thin, and left-handed. He suffered with his wife.

By the next morning the Horns Society preparations were finished. One of the Horns members was sent to tell the holy woman that the Medicine Lodge ceremony could begin.

The messenger didn't have to wear holy moccasins. He wore his ordinary moccasins, a breechcloth, and a robe. He ran to the Holy Lodge tipi.

Before he entered he coughed; the people inside all sat in order. The messenger went inside. He put his robe on the right-hand side of the door and he went around the tipi making downward brushing motions on the People, except for the holy woman and her helpers. He passed in front of her and continued to make downward brushing motions on the men. When he got back to his robe he picked it up, secured it around his waist, and sat down. He sat on one of his feet.

The messenger told them, "I came over to notify you that the Horns Society has finished the preparations." Neither the holy woman nor her husband spoke a word. The priest spoke, saying to everyone in the tipi, "Everything is prepared." And then, someone in the Holy Lodge who counted the tongue slices told the messenger there were not enough. The messenger immediately returned and told this to the Horns. Some Horns members went out of camp to get more beef tongues. They brought these tongues to the holy woman's tipi, where they were cut and sliced and set to dry.

At the Horns tipi, they selected their best singers from amongst the members. The singers formed themselves into two rows, the men in one row, the women in the other. They paraded to the east side of the camp circle. Then, starting at the east entrance they paraded by all the camps within the camp circle. At each camp they stopped and sang. After singing their song, one of the men called out: "Woo-Ka-Hai! For you People all to know: after tomorrow a sweat lodge will be constructed. Nobody is to leave the camps, so that we will all help with the construction of the Holy Lodge. We all will work on it after tomorrow."

The reason why the Horns set this date to build the lodge was so that there would be time for the newly cut tongues to dry. The tongues were to be used in two days' time.

The next morning everything was arranged, and the following morning the sweat lodge was built. The young Horns got their saddle ponies and rode down to the river. They gathered one hundred rocks. The rocks were smaller than a folded fist. White flint rocks and sand rocks were not taken. They picked all ordinary rocks. About noon the riders were heard returning, singing plainly. There were no women among the riders. The riders paraded around the inside of the camp circle. They all dismounted at the Holy Lodge tipi and their horses were led away.

The sweat lodge was constructed. There are one hundred willows to a holy sweat lodge. The entrance is on the east side and the exit is on the west side, just like the daily path of Sun. The fifty willows on the south side were colored with real paint [red earth] and the other fifty willows were colored with black paint. The real paint represents the day; the black paint represents the night. The buffalo hides used to cover the sweat lodge were also colored, the hides on the south side with real paint, the hides on the north side with black paint. In recent years the willows and the canvases are not colored anymore.

In legends of the long-ago, only one rock was used in the sweat lodge. Lately, one hundred rocks were used. In this sweat lodge the rocks were not heated red hot. It was a sweat lodge just to reinforce the spiritual powers.

The buffalo skull, which is offered to Sun, was laid on a small pile of dirt that had been scooped out from a hole inside the sweat lodge. It is different with the Crow Indians, who put their buffalo skulls by the Center Pole. Buffalo skulls are no longer left out as offerings. They are put away for use in the next Sun Dance.

The night after the sweat lodge ceremonies, the Horns Society members were painted and the next morning they cut down the Center Pole. There were four singers, each with hand drums, which were invented by that time. The Center Pole was cut down, and as it was hauled to the center of the camp circle, the Horns Society members rode on it. A woman member was ap-

pointed to follow behind. The singers beat their drums as the procession moved along.

Many Kill was sitting out in the shade by her tipi. The People brought to her their offerings and pipes. After they unloaded the Center Pole, the Horns Society members brought forward to Many Kill their payments for the Natoas transferral. They carried dry goods in their arms and each led a horse to the transferral.

The People tied tipi poles together, approximately a foot down from the top. Every separate band came forward, singing a song with no words. The People all jumped into the Holy Lodge. Heavy Shield sat on the Center Pole. He had on a black robe and his face was painted black. He was blowing on his whistle. As the Center Pole started to raise, he jumped down, leaving his robe on the Center Pole. That is the custom.

The Center Pole was raised. Some blew their whistles while others shot their guns into the air. Everybody helped set the Pole upright and the seven rafter poles in place. Two orderlies wearing crow-feather headpieces brought in the hide to tie the rafter poles and cross beams. The People got their horses again and rode down to the river to cut young trees to cover the sides of the circular structure of the Holy Lodge. Some riders attached stirrup-cover decorations. Some wore fur chaps, even though it was a hot day. Some men had on facial war paintings. The People sang a song with no words.

The riders were shooting and shouting. They came back through the east entrance, paraded once around the inside of the camp circle, and then they galloped to the Holy Lodge. Some were bucked off on the way—the horses shy at the trees dragged by the riders. They raced to the Holy Lodge as a reenactment of the time when the Plains Indians rode into enemy camps at full speed.

The trees were set up against the cross beams of the Holy Lodge. Then the riders went home and turned loose their horses.

At this point, Many Kill, the sponsor of the Holy Lodge, came out from her tipi and sat in its shade. The Horns Society sat on the east side, the Braves Society on the southeast side, and the Pigeon Society on the southwest side. The drumming of the various societies sounded at intervals. The Holy Lodge was completed.

I, First Rider, have told this story. I am a Blood Indian.

Back to Our Own Encampment

The Old Man ended his visit with us before supper. Because he did not like to travel after dark, he always insisted on being brought home before Sun sets. When darkness came he liked to sit at the edge of his iron-frame bed and sing songs of the Old Ways—they were holy songs, of which he knew many. The first time I had met him, that was what he had been doing in his little white one-room frame house. I had gone to him in search of inspiration and guidance, which he had given me. Here is how we began our deep spiritual relationship:

ON FIRST MEETING
OUR OLD MAN

As SikskiAki and I drove over the dirt road toward the Old Man's house, we could see a light burning through a window. Behind the house we could see the silhouettes of sweat lodge frames—reminders of holy experiences from his past.

We knocked, and a voice from within bid us enter. A blast of warm air rushed past us as we came in from the cold. Immediately, I felt the presence of holy Powers; a feeling of weakness overcame my original intentions. I began to wonder how I would explain my presence in the silence waiting for us. We left our overshoes in the entryway and stepped inside.

The room was lit by a bare light bulb. There was a strong contrast to everything I saw. While I tried not to look at anything in particular, my eyes were attracted at once to many pleasant scenes. Sacred Bags and Bundles hung up on the rear wall. Photographs were mounted inside old frames. In the middle of the room stood a vintage upright heater. Its stovepipe went up to the ceiling and then, along the ceiling far back through a hole in the wall, to the chimney. A box of coal sat next to the heater. The heater and stovepipe radiated considerable warmth in the little house. On the floor, between the heater and the Bundles on the rear wall, was a wooden box filled with earth. It was the Old Man's altar, on which he made incense. Sacred stones were inside the box and braids of sweetgrass lay on the floor next to it. Heavy winter coats and an assortment of cowboy hats and slouch caps hung from nails and hooks by the doorway. A worn dresser was pressed against the far wall. The clutter of things on the

48

Wolf Old Man, as he sat for his portrait in January, 1958. (Marsden Photo, from Glenbow Archives)

dresser top was doubled by their reflection in the dresser mirror. Three iron-frame beds took up most of the floor space. An old man sat on each of the beds. All three old men looked silently at us. I felt as though we had disturbed a harmonious scene, which now awaited us to announce why we came.

The Old Man was on the bed at the rear. He squinted, trying to see who was at the doorway. His many wrinkles and powerful features were all the more pronounced because his face was painted with sacred red earth. The paint went up into the forelock of his white hair. The forelock covered where his hair was parted into two braids, which fell over his ears. Pieces of red flannel cloth were tied at the ends of his braids. He wore a long-sleeved flannel shirt, gray trousers, and an old pair of buckskin moccasins. The toe of each moccasin was decorated with a yellow beaded flower and green leaves.

When the Old Man learned we had come to see him, he reached out his hand and we shook it in greeting. The size and strength of his younger years was still in the clasp of his hand. My lips were dry and my knees were trembling, but I decided to shake the hands of the other two men in the room. I walked first to the one across from the Old Man, realizing too late that I had stepped between the stove and the Bundles on the wall, thus disturbing their sacred path. The two men shook my hand. As one of them pointed out my error, the feeling within the room became even more Powerful. I had not been sure what to say first to the Old Man. But, in apologizing for my mistake, I explained the purpose of my visit—to learn from him how to live in harmony with the Spirit of the Old Ways. I told him that it would be best for me to end our first visit right then, and that I wished to come back at another time. He replied, "If your desire to learn is strong enough then I will look forward to your next visit."

Once outside, this Powerful experience caused an uncontrollable shaking in my body. In the darkness, I saw the laughing face of Apeso Machkan, my first spiritual master, who had passed away a couple of years earlier at the age of 116. He was telling me that I must learn something from what I had just experienced. Up to then I had been spending a great deal of time studying details of the Old Ways, but not how to apply those Ways.

In the time I knew the Old Man, he brought me far along the path of living a holy life. He showed me his footprints along the Old Way and inspired me to step into them wherever I could find them. Time passed too quickly for him to teach me all he knew—much of it passed on with him. Some of his knowledge concerned doctoring, about which he told me little. Some of his knowledge concerned songs and ceremonies to which I have never been properly initiated; and without proper initiation, those songs and ceremonies would be of no use to anyone. Even he had never been properly initiated for some of the songs and ceremonies he knew, so he did not speak about them to anyone. He told me that many of the Old Ways could no longer be put to use in this Changed World. His concern was only with saving those Ways that might help to inspire the People yet unborn to live with holiness.

Most important was the spiritual relationship the Old Man and I shared. The greatest Power he had was not so much in what he learned through initiation, or through information passed on to him from others, but in his ability to observe, absorb, and spiritually intuit many wordless things. The most Powerful exchanges that took place between us were often accompanied by complete silence. His Old People had given him their Spirits in the same manner. Theirs continued to grow with him as he got older, and that is how he wished for his Spirit to go on, as well. So the most Powerful legacy he has left is one essentially spiritual, one that lives with me each day of my life.

LEGENDS OF NAPI

Our second evening of the encampment at the Belly Buttes was beginning. We were in a mood to hear some old-time stories, so we decided to visit Mokakin and see if we could inspire him to tell us some. It is a tradition among our People that myths and legends should be told only at nighttime. It is said that early blindness comes to those who disobey this custom.

Stories of war and adventure have always been popular among our People, especially the men. Women and children, too, have their favorites. But the most well liked of all are the stories of our legendary Napi, or Old Man, whose mythical experiences are exciting and occasionally gruesome. Some of the most popular of them are obscene.

The word *Napi* is used in a number of ways in the Blackfoot language. It can mean "friend," if the *a* is pronounced "ah" and the *i* is drawn out properly. A common greeting among acquaintances, for instance, is, *"Oki, Napih."* It may also be used to greet an old man, if the word is pronounced with a longer "ah" and a very short *i*. This generally refers to a very old man. A man just old would be more commonly called *Omach-Kinna*, which means something like "big-aged man." Napi is pronounced with a short *i* when it is used to refer to the Old Man of legend. Finally, many of our People refer to our holy Sun as Napi, or Old Man, in their prayers. Because of this and the stories about Napi creating our part of the world, many observers have written that our People thought of Napi as God and prayed to him. Long, long ago, it is likely that our People believed that in the Sun was the spirit of an Old Man, to whom they gave thanks for the beginning of Earth. But the Napi of our myths and legends is a humorous prankster and troublemaker. He is not the Napi referred to in our prayers.

So we went to call on Mokakin next door. He was resting and Ponah was nearby visiting her sister, Mrs. Red Crow. He asked SikskiAki to pour some tea for us all from the kettle by the fire.

To start the conversation Mokakin said, *"Ah, Tsanitappi?"* He meant, "Yes, well, how are things going?" *"EkSokahpi,"* we replied, "Very good." I asked him if he could tell us any Napi stories. He told us, "Oh, I know lots of them. My grandmother taught them to me. My uncle, Eagle Ribs, he used to be real good at them—everybody knows him for that. That white man—we call him Long-Nosed Crow [Wilson]—he used to write them down when my uncle went to his store to tell him some. . . . Oh, I wish I could read good—I would have kept those stories and I could tell them to you just like my uncle did."

He didn't know that I had copies of those stories in a trunk at our tipi next door. I got them from the Glenbow Archives in Calgary. They had hired Philip H. Godsell in 1958 to edit Wilson's papers and combine them into a typewritten volume. When I told Mokakin about this he was anxious to have me read them.

I went to our tipi for the papers with Eagle Ribs's stories. As I read them to Mokakin he made a number of additions and variations. Our traditional stories always vary according to the person telling them. So, as I read each story to Mokakin, he made remarks here and there, in effect telling me his version of the same story. Therefore, I will now pass on to you the stories of old Eagle Ribs, as recorded by Wilson and, in a way, edited by the present Eagle Ribs (Mokakin).

☐

NAPI TEACHES THE PEOPLE TO USE BUFFALO

It used to be that buffalo ate People. Napi found the People hiding in the mountains, where the buffalo could not find them. He told the People: "This is not right. You were meant to hunt the

51

buffalo, not to be eaten by them." So he taught the People how to make bows and arrows of wood and how to chip arrowheads from flint. When all the People were armed in this way he led them out on the prairie near a herd of buffalo. He then changed himself into a calf and told the buffalo about the People nearby. The buffalo used to drive the people into a pound where they could butcher them easily. Two rows of large stones like a **V** led into this pound. Two of the buffalo would rise up from behind the stone piles, where they were hiding, and the People would become frightened and run farther into the **V** until they were trapped inside the pound. But this time, when the buffalo came after the People to butcher them, they shot their bows and arrows and killed most of the herd. Only two bulls and a few cows got away. From these few were descended all the buffalo that have since lived. One of the cows that survived was outside the pound before the shooting, applying sacred paint to her face. When the shooting began she took the piece of fat, which she was mixing with the paint, and stuck it between her toes. She also grabbed a piece of human meat—left from the last hunt—tucked it under her arm, and fled. Ever since then, buffalo have had fat between their toes and "human" meat under their "arms."

After the slaughter, Napi showed the People how to make use of the buffalo. He taught them how to remove the large skins and how to cut up the meat. He told them that all of the meat must be eaten and that they must not waste anything for which they could find a use. He taught the women how to stretch the hides on the ground with wooden pegs, and cut the hides with a flint knife. He showed them how to make a hide scraper from an elk's horn edged with flint. He taught them to soak the hide before scraping, and how to work it by first using mashed brains and later by pulling it back and forth through a loop of three-strand sinews taken from the buffalo's back. After they had tanned a number of

hides, he showed them how to make a lodge to live in, how to cut the poles, how to set them up, and how to make the beds and other furnishings. He showed the men how to hunt and use pounds, just as the buffalo had done before.

NAPI GIVES THE PEOPLE DEATH
Some time after this, Napi was standing with a woman by a river. He picked up a buffalo chip and threw it into the water. "As this chip rises to the surface and floats," he told the woman, "so will the People rise and return to life four days after death." The woman picked up a stone and threw it into the water. "As this stone sinks and stays gone," she told Napi, "so should People remain gone once they are dead." Napi agreed. Not long after this one of the woman's children took sick and died. She came to Napi, crying, and said, "Let us have death be as you said, so that my child will come back in four days." "No," said Napi, "you have decided for yourself. As the stone sinks, so will your child stay gone." Since that time the People have always gone and not returned when they died.

NAPI BRINGS MEN AND WOMEN TOGETHER
Some time after Napi saved the People from the buffalo, they separated into two groups—men and women. Napi spent his time with the women, with whom he always enjoyed himself. He showed the women how to build a Piskan, or buffalo pound, at the base of a cliff, so that they could drive herds of buffalo down into it and butcher them for meat and hides. [In the Rocky Mountain foothills, west of Claresholm, Alberta, you can still visit the Women's Buffalo Jump, which is supposed to be the one Napi helped to prepare.] Napi showed the women how to find and eat strawberries, raspberries, and other wild berries. He also showed them how to dry service-

berries and how to mix them with meat to make pemmican. He taught them how to crush chokecherries between two stones. He showed them how to make a digging stick to gather wild roots like camas and turnips. He told them that they could eat serviceberries from the bush in the fall, and wild tomatoes (rose hips) from the bush in winter. He taught them how to make wooden bowls from the large knots often seen in the trunks of pine trees.

After a long time, Napi decided to pay a visit to the men. He found them camped by themselves and in miserable condition. They made tipis by throwing raw buffalo hides over poles. They wore raw furs for clothing. They made moccasins by peeling the hide from the bottoms of buffalo ankles, like socks, and then pulling them over their own feet and ankles. They tied knots on the toe ends to close them up. They did not know how to furnish their tipis, how to cook, or how to do any other household work. They could only hunt.

After his stay with the men, Napi looked so miserable that the women did not recognize him when he returned. They asked him where he had been and when it was heard that he had come from a camp of men, the chief of the women called him to her lodge. She told him that she was greatly pleased to hear where he came from and that she would like him to return to that camp and invite all the men to come and visit. Napi immediately set out to present the invitation.

The women decided that each of them would choose one of the men for a husband. When the men arrived outside their camp, the chief of the women desired to honor them, so she dressed herself in raw furs and torn clothing and wiped her body with dirt. Then she led her women out to meet the men. She instructed her women not to choose Napi, for she wished to have him for her own. When she saw Napi among the men she walked over and took his hand and planned to lead him to her tipi. Napi quickly jerked his hand away and shrunk back, shouting, "Go away, you filthy woman, I wouldn't have you for my wife." The chief of the women was angered and returned alone to her lodge. She quickly cleaned herself and put on her fine buckskin outfit. She braided her hair and incensed her body in the smoke of sweetgrass. When Napi saw this well-dressed woman walking toward the gathering he thought, "My, what a fine-looking woman. I would like to have her for my wife." She walked right up to him and he thought that she was going to choose him. However, she walked on by and chose the man standing next to him. As she left with her new husband she reminded the other women that they were not to choose Napi. Thus, Napi was left alone while all the others became husbands and wives. For many centuries a large pine tree stood at the Women's Buffalo Jump. People said that it was the ghost of Napi mourning because he had no wife.

NAPI AND THE NIGHT HAWKS

South of Calgary, there is a place the Old People call Where Napi Slept. The shape of Napi's bed can still be plainly seen. Napi and Kit Fox were taking a trip through this area. They came to the top of a high hill, where Napi told his partner, "Let us slide down this hill to save ourselves the trouble of walking." As they reached the bottom, a huge slide of loose rocks came down after them. But they ran just in time. The Old People call this place Napi's Slide. As the two hiked over the hot prairie, Napi decided that his robe was getting too heavy. They passed by a lone boulder, and Napi laid his robe over it, saying, "Here, my friend the stone, take this robe to keep you warm." When they had not walked very much farther, they noticed dark clouds coming up. Napi feared that a thunderstorm was approaching. He told Kit Fox to go back and ask the stone to lend him his robe. Kit Fox went back, but soon returned. The stone had told him, "Napi gave me his robe, so I don't intend to give it to anyone else."

Napi sent Kit Fox back for two more unsuccessful tries. Then he went himself and took the robe by force, and they continued on their way north. Napi thought a great deal about his bad treatment of the stone and he worried that something might result. Periodically, he sent Kit Fox up to some ridge to look back and see if the stone was still in the same place. Three times Kit Fox returned and said yes. But the fourth time he came back running and shouting, "The stone is coming after us! The stone is coming after us!" By that time the stone was already rapidly closing the distance between them. Napi and Kit Fox ran as fast as they could, but the stone was still catching up to them. While running, they passed two large buffalo bulls. Napi called out to them, "Help, my friends, stop this boulder or it will kill us!" The bulls stepped into the stone's path, but the stone just rolled them flat on the ground and continued on. Next they passed two very large bears. Again Napi shouted for help. The bears stepped into the stone's path and were rolled over just as quickly as the buffalo. Then Kit Fox noticed a large hole ahead, so he dived into it, expecting to be safe. But the stone rolled over the hole and closed it up, forcing Kit Fox to raise all his descendants under the ground. Now Napi was running for his life all alone.

Above him Napi saw two night hawks flying. He called out to them for help. They considered what they could do and this is what they decided. They dived down and picked up large pebbles from the ground, then dropped the pebbles on the rolling boulder from high in the air. Each time they did this, a piece chipped off the boulder and that made its progress slow down. Before long, the boulder was only a small rolling stone. One more well-aimed shot broke it in two, so that it could roll no more.

Napi traveled on northward with good spirits.

On his way he came across a nest of young night hawks. "Where are your parents?" he asked them. "They are getting food for us," was the reply. Now he knew that these were the children of the two night hawks that had just saved his life. His ornery mood returned to him and he shouted at the young birds, "Your parents have just annoyed me greatly. They had no business spoiling my fun out on the prairie. No one asked them to break that stone apart." And with that he took the young birds and put his fingers in each one's mouth and stretched them wide. Then he took a stone and pounded their long beaks until they were quite crooked, and he said, "This is how your kind will look from now on." And that is why night hawks have large mouths and crooked beaks.

When the old night hawks returned and discovered what had happened to their children, they immediately flew off after Napi. Napi saw them coming and tried to run from them, but they caught up to him and began throwing stones at his robe. The night hawks told Napi, "You will not be bothered by your robe anymore after we are through with you." Each time they threw a stone, a piece broke off Napi's robe, until the last piece was knocked from his hand. As Napi ran, he turned his head to see if the night hawks were still coming after him. At that moment the birds each threw their last stone, which hit him directly in the mouth, knocking out all his teeth. The night hawks then returned to their nest, satisfied that they had revenged Napi's evil treatment. At Rocky Creek, near Calgary, you can still see the pieces of the big stone, lying in a row as they broke off.

☐

Ponah returned to her tipi while we were listening to Mokakin's last story of the night. Between stories, she had mentioned that her "old man" had often told Napi stories at home when she was still a child. She remembered sitting around the wood stove during winter blizzards, fascinated by Napi's escapades. With a shy smile she added, "Now I know some of those stories that my dad never told me." She was referring to the ribald Napi adventures that were left out of the series when children were around. Wilson recorded his own versions of these naughty Napi stories that I later discovered had been "censored" when I heard the original, adult versions from our Old People.

Ponah told us that her dad's name was Iron, but that he was also called Center Speaker. He died not many years ago at the age of ninety-six. His father was the famous Ki-soum, or "Sun"— the same man Wilson called Moon. Ki-soum was a holy man, a doctor, and a minor chief as head of the Fish Eaters band. The confusion over his name can be explained this way: Although the common word for Sun in Blackfoot is *Natosi*, an older, seldom-used word is *Ki-soum*; and the word for Moon is *Gho-Ghomae-Ki-Soum*, or "Night Sun."

Iron is famous among our People for having been Keeper of more sacred Medicines than anyone else. Bundles of all kinds were transferred to him, and he, in turn, transferred them to others. I asked Ponah which of the sacred Bundles he was best at leading ceremonies for. She said, "Oh no, my dad didn't lead any ceremonies. He was too stingy. He always said, 'My prayers help me. I want to keep them for myself. I don't want to give them away.' That's why he never led ceremonies for other people." Iron's attitude about his prayers was somewhat unusual. He was long known for this philosophy. When his father, Ki-soum, died in 1898, Iron was the likely successor as chief of the Fish Eaters. However, the People of that band chose Eagle Bear instead. Eagle Bear was the husband of Otter Woman, Iron's sister.

One of Iron's brothers took his father's name, Ki-soum. He was a Weather Dancer during Medicine Lodge ceremonies. Another brother of Iron, Wolf Shirt, was famous for having great Power with our Medicine Pipes. Many Old

Iron and his last wife, Istsimpski, or "Hateful Face." She was the former wife of Ghost Chest and the mother of Charlie Goodrider. The photo was taken in 1939, a time when the ancient symbols on his beaded rifle were coincidentally used as swastikas by Nazi Germany. (Esther Goldfrank)

People still remember seeing him dance with the sacred Pipestems. He would take the long, decorated Stem and toss it up on his head, where it would stay while he performed the sacred dance of Medicine Pipe ceremonies. Most people who dance with a sacred Stem hold it very tightly with both hands, for it is a sign of impending misfor-

55

tune if it should fall to the ground. Wolf Shirt proved his Power by never letting a Stem fall from his head. Mokakin and Ponah have seen him dance this way with all the Medicine Pipes still left among our People.

Ponah told us that her father, as a young man, was happily married to two sisters from the North Piegan divison. After one of the sisters died, Iron began investigating a young Blood woman for his next wife. The surviving sister became jealous and left him. So he married the Blood woman. She was the mother of Ponah and her sister, Mrs. Red Crow. After his third wife died he married the widow of Ghost Chest. She was an older woman, called Istsimpski, or "Hateful Face." Her son was Charlie Goodrider, who was quite a romantic character.

Ponah asked Mokakin to tell us about her father's horse raids. He related the time Iron was with One Spot and Head Walking when they raided the Crees. One Spot captured a Cree Medicine Pipe, against Iron's insistence, while Head Walking shot a Cree. Iron rode up to the Cree, dismounted, stabbed the man dead, and took his scalp.

As we talked, we began to hear singing faintly coming through the rising and falling of the wind outside. Slowly, the singing grew louder.

It was a serenade song. The voices came closer, passing by our part of the camp circle. The singers, four young men riding on three horses (two of the singers doubling up on one horse), ended one song with short, jovial shouts, and began another.

This was a treat to hear, as most young people today don't know the old serenade songs from the past. Long ago, several groups of serenade singers would go around the camp circle every night, in the days when camp circles had a circumference of a mile or more. Young people would tie strings of sleigh bells to their horses to add background music to their singing. Groups of young men usually sang together, sometimes doubling up on one horse. Married couples often rode the same way. Single men would ride alone, singing love songs with code words so that their sweethearts, bound by tradition to stay inside at night, would know the songs were for them.

The young men singing on this night continued until morning. Blankets drawn over their heads protected them against the wind. In between songs they talked and laughed quietly. During the night I woke up, and heard them still singing, talking, laughing, and their horses' hooves thudding.

56

Another Day in Camp

The following day we had a number of visitors—friends and relatives from the reserve. They thought it great that we should still be carrying on the tradition of coming together for the annual Sun Dance Camp in a holy place like the Belly Buttes. Many acted like tourists, having no conception of the spiritual meaning of the gathering. Several had to be asked to leave their children outside our tipi, for their running and noisy playing might have disturbed the Spirits of our Bundle, and insulted the tradition surrounding it. Some, however, including a few who don't follow the Old Ways, had a great deal of respect for the holiness in our lodge.

GRANDMA ANADAAKI

One of the visitors who knew how to respect our traditions had spent most of her eighty-four years as a very progressive ranch wife on the reserve. She was SikskiAki's grandmother, AnadaAki, or "Pretty Woman." Between her name on the tribe rolls—Hilda Beebe—and her light complexion and gray-blue eyes, she would have been readily accepted by those who hesitate to make friends with our People.

Grandma's father was a German named Joseph Trollinger. He came here in the early days of the reserve and married Lucy, whose common name was First to Kill. Sweetgrass was one of her brothers. Joe and Lucy Trollinger moved north to Mosquito Creek, along the trail from Fort MacLeod to Calgary, where they operated a halfway house, providing room and board. Joe became well known among the travelers of this area, who nicknamed him "Rutabaga Joe" because of his fondness for that vegetable. Our Old People named him Last to Get Angry, because he often said, "You got angry first, now I'm going to get angry." Grandma AnadaAki was the youngest of his five children with Lucy, but he never saw her. When Lucy was still carrying her, she learned of Joe's plan to take their eldest daughter, who was deaf and dumb, to Germany to have doctors operate on her. Afraid to have her child taken so far away, Lucy left Joe and returned to the reserve with all her children. She married Heavy Head shortly before Grandma was born. (This was about a year before he fulfilled his self-torture vow at the 1889 Okan.) The children were all given Heavy Head's name for their own last names. The memory of Trollinger lived on with two of Lucy's sons, both named Joseph.

Grandma married Joe Beebe, son of a white man also named Joe Beebe. Joe Beebe Senior was born in New York, but his Mormon parents soon moved by covered wagon to Utah. When he was about fifteen, Joe ran away from home and ended up at Fort Benton, the main trading post for the Piegans in Montana. He worked as a teamster on bull trains (wagon trains pulled by bulls) over the old Whoop-Up Trail between Fort Benton and Edmonton, Alberta. During these trips, he got to know the family of a Piegan named Red Tail Feathers and his two Blood wives, Mountain Lion Woman and Woman's Word. Among the children of this family was Bird Rattler and Awok-Aki, or "Smart Woman," who became Joe Beebe's wife. Their only child was Grandma's Joe Beebe. When the boy was born, AwokAki was not able to pass her afterbirth. Joe Beebe wanted to get the white doctor, but the wives of Red Tail Feathers had no faith in him and insisted on doctoring AwokAki themselves. She passed away after six days.

Old Joe Beebe married again, but continued to provide for his two mothers-in-law. Mountain Lion Woman raised little Joe for the first seven years of his life. After AwokAki's death, this old lady took him to women who had babies so that he could nurse from them. If they weren't available, she made broths for him, letting him suck on her own dry breasts for contentment. His continued sucking finally caused milk to come from her breasts, so that she was able to nurse her grandson for some time. The old lady delighted in showing off whenever visitors were around that she could nurse the baby.

When young Joe Beebe was about seven, his father placed him in the Dunbow Boarding School, where he stayed for most of the next twelve years. Many other boys from this reserve were sent to Dunbow. At the age of nineteen he returned to the reserve to work as interpreter and scout for the Mounted Police. Although his speech and appearance led many to think of him as a white man, he soon let his hair grow long enough to braid and began to take part in the frequent powwows. He became an excellent Grass Dancer, earning the right to dance with the Forked Stick during the Dog Feast, a ceremony our People had adopted from the Assiniboines.

Joe Beebe joined his father in British Columbia for a while and then moved on to live among the Colville and Yakima People in Washington. We call these People the Fish Indians, due to their favorite food. He didn't last very long there. Irate mothers chased him away for supplying liquor to their young daughters, among other things.

He wandered back to the Blood Reserve, married young Hilda, and settled down as a progressive rancher. Though a small man, he worked hard until a crippling disease disabled him. To carry on the farm, Grandma began to take on all his work in addition to her own chores. She learned to herd the horses, hitch the teams, gather the wheat, and pitch the hay. She did almost everything except drive the farm implements after the horses were hooked up to them; Joe was too proud to give that up. Grandma used to bring the team near the house and then help her crippled husband up on mower or plow or rake, so that he could do the driving himself.

They had two children. SikskiAki's mother, Ruth, is also known as Pretty Crow Woman or MastuitsoAki. Howard now has his uncle's name, Bird Rattler. Howard carries on his father's progressive farming, in addition to his duties on the Chief's Council.

In his final years, Joe Beebe took an interest in recording some of the Old Ways of our People. His grammar shows that his thoughts were influenced by the modern outside world as well as by the Old People still living around him. Let us hear him tell this ancient legend as he wrote it down in his notebook.

MANY SWANS RECOVERS HIS ARROW

This occurred before the fur traders came west to the Rockies, and while the different tribes of Indians were hostile to one another.

One of the members of the [Blood Sun Dance] encampment of long ago was an Indian named Many Swans. He was not a chief, he was a

Joe Beebe on his democrat while in Cardston in 1939. Behind him is John Red Crane, the man who sold the Long-Time Pipe. Joe Beebe, an invalid by this time, had hired John as driver. The old lady is John Red Crane's mother. (Esther Goldfrank)

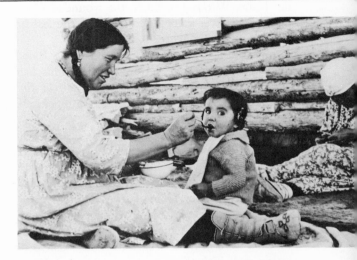

Grandma AnadaAki in 1939. She is feeding SikskiAki's brother, Gilbert, or Black Eyes. The old lady was Grandma's stepmother, one of old Heavy Head's wives. (Esther Goldfrank)

very fearless warrior. Considering what there was to be had at that time, this Indian was fairly well off. He had a big buffalo skin teepee, two wives, a marriageable daughter, and a fair sized bunch of horses, among which were some fast buffalo runners. In the way of weapons he had a quiver of bow and arrows, and a two-edged flint dagger, which answered the purpose of a butcher knife as well.

These Indians were constantly on the lookout for their horses, as prowling enemy Indians were always around. At night they staked their mares or leaders, turning them loose in the mornings and driving them to untrodden grass, within a watching distance of the camps. The Indian's wealth was in his band of horses in those days.

One morning, just at dawn, Many Swans woke up his Queen to go with him to attend his horses. He left the other woman still sleeping. He slung his bow and arrow on his back, and put his dagger in his belt. On no occasion must these things be left behind in such chores.

Turning loose their staked horses, the two started them up towards the summit of the Butte to cleaner feed. Arriving on the top, the woman came running on tiptoes towards her husband, making the sleeping motion sign. She told him that there were a couple of people fast asleep in a buffalo wallow, just on top of the Butte.

Pulling out his bow and arrow ready for action, Many Swans advanced on the sleepers. His first thought was that they must be from the home camps, perhaps lullaby singers who, having sung all night, went off some place to sleep so as to avoid the morning noise of the herald cryers.

It was all in an instant that the two were on their feet and were retreating from Many Swans. The Blood, recognizing them to be from the Crow tribe by the cut of their forelocks and their attire, at once knew that they were enemies from far away Big Horn River, in Montana. He let fly his arrow which struck the leader who dropped all in a heap. He drew another arrow and let it fly to the other, striking him just below the left shoul-

59

der blade. Without a flinch, the wounded Crow disappeared over a knoll and that was the last he saw of him, he thought.

After the Crow Indian had died, the Blood marked a line around the outer edge of his hair with his flint knife, and being an expert at this business, he popped off his scalp by a quick jerk on the braids.

After relieving the corpse of its charms and worthwhile apparel, Many Swans went back to where the two slept, and there he found two quivers of bows and arrows, two pairs of moccasins, and two robes. Going back down to the Big Circle encampment, Many Swans loudly announced his killing and scalping. The camps of warriors were only too eager to hold a dance of victory in which the raw scalp was the centre of attraction. The whole mob of them rushed to the summit of the Butte to witness the scene of the killing. Many Swans cut another notch on his bow.

Now believe it or not, the Crow Indian that Many Swans had wounded survived ten days and nights of intense pain, suffering and hard hoofings from the Belly River Buttes in Alberta, Canada, to his Big Horn River camp in Montana. Still in his shoulder was the arrow which he could not reach with either hand to extract. He was just a skeleton when he got home.

After his people had pulled out the arrow and he was given first aid, he was made to take a little broth and a much needed rest. He then told the tale of the arrow. He said the encounter he had was with a big Band of the Blackfoot Nation at Many Junctions, where the city of Lethbridge is now in Alberta, Canada.

He said being against great odds, he was compelled to fight a pit-fight, and that it was not until his brother was killed that he quit fighting and made his escape, and that it was in retreating that he got hit.

His people had deep sympathy for him and thought him a very brave man to have survived the ordeal. From a mere skeleton, the Crow In-

dian was revived on herbal medicine to a well man again, just as fit as he was. And in competition his deed had no equal.

Four winters passed, when, at another big encampment at the Belly Buttes in Alberta, Many Swans daughter got married. Now there is a custom among these Indians, which still exists, whereby in-laws are restricted from meeting and talking to one another; but this restriction can be bought by enemy property.

One evening as Many Swans took to the entrance of his daughter's teepee a wooden bowl of pemmican, his curiosity overpowered him, and through the tiny opening of the lodge's entrance he peeped and feasted his eyes on the handsome features of his son-in-law.

After his daughter had taken the bowl of food, the father went back to his own lodge, and confessed his guilt to his Queen, who gave him a thorough tongue-lashing and [asked] him if he did not know that he needed enemy property to pay his son-in-law to look in his face.

"Ah Okee" (all right then), said Many Swans to his Queen, "if it needs enemy property, enemy property he will get. We shall move our camp tonight and start for the Big Horn River to the Crow Nation."

The next morning just his circle camp stones were to be seen of his outfit. It was a puzzle to all, why he did not leave a word to any one; they saw that he went south, but that was all.

On the way, Many Swans killed Buffalo. The meat filled many parflesh bags of dried meat and pemmican. The trip took the Blood Indians eight days.

Arriving in [the Crow] camp in broad daylight, the enemy did not suspect foul play from Many Swans. Many Swans picked out a big painted teepee, and set his own up beside it. On sighting the new lodge by the painted one, the Crow Indians came over from all sides of the encampment to ascertain who the newcomer was, and the origin of his expedition.

The owner of the big painted teepee was

Chief Wolf Tail, Head Chieftain of all the Crow Nation. Wolf Tail, standing outside his teepee, called a loud invitation for Many Swans and his family.

During the conversation, Many Swans explained his mission to the Chief, who accepted everything and welcomed him to his tribe, also promising him Crow property when he was ready to go home. This old custom of restricting sons-in-law from meeting willfully his parents-in-law might seem very silly to some readers, but the old Indians are even now very serious in regards to it, although it is dying off among the younger generation, very sorry to say. However, considering the lashing of tongues of some mothers-in-law, we think this is a very good custom.

Many Swans, having fast buffalo runners, became very useful to the Crow Tribe in the way of getting Buffalo meat and was naturally welcomed by all. Now there is a custom among all Indians, that groups of men near the same age form Societies; these Societies meet and compete with their brave deeds.

The members of the groups whose deeds were not equalled by the opposing group would be the winners, and they would paint black on the faces of their rivals. It was great fun, and it was encouragement to the younger warriors to become real brave.

One evening, while Chief Wolf Tail was smoking with his friend Many Swans, he told him that there was to be a competition of deeds the next day, and that he belonged to one of the parties. Would he, the Blood, join his Society since he was the same age? "Ah, I will my friend," said the Blood, who spoke good Crow.

The next sun came with loud chantings of war songs, tom toms, and incantations from the opposing parties. Young men went about their chores with the staked horses. Smoke poured from the teepee tops while the morning meal was being cooked. Some did their cooking outside on tripods. After all this was over, the preparation for the competition began. The warriors began to come to the centre from all sides of the camp in full war paint and feathers. Some right nude but for breach cloths.

Then they began to take their places in the two rows marked out; the rows ran from west and east. The junior group with Running Rabbit their leader, were on the left from the west, the seniors with Chief Wolf Tail and Many Swans on the right.

After all were seated on their crossed legs, old men not interested in the contest got up and sang songs of praise in which they called out names from each party. The ones named would get up to relate their deed. Some merely related what they did, and gave proof such as scars of old wounds or scalps and weapons they got from the enemy. Others acted their doings as in sham fighting, with all the reality of a battle for life and death. It was looking gloomy and bad for the juniors when at last Running Rabbit got up. He was naked but for his breach cloth and feathers. An arrow tied to his left shoulder, and a big red blotch mark under his left shoulder blade, over an ugly old scar, he went towards the centre of the space; everybody kept mum. After chanting his warsong, he walked back and forth looking very brave and serious. He took the arrow off his shoulder, and holding it high up he said, speaking very loudly:

"You are all aware of the story of my arrow, you saw what condition I was in, when I came amongst you. And you yourselves my seniors extracted the arrow from my shoulder."

Holding the arrow high up. "But so that your friend, the Blood, will know, I will tell it again. It was at Many Rivers Junction that I fought in a pit fight against the whole Blackfeet Nation, and had not my brother got killed and my arrows run out, I'd be fighting yet, but I got hit and had to run." Then, sticking the arrow in the ground, he said, "Here it is, beat my deed if you can, and tell your friend, Many Swans, the Blood Indian who is amongst you now, to come forward and tell us what he has done. I see that he has his paint on."

The warwhoops and yells of applause from the juniors were deafening. After the noise had died down, Wolf Tail gave his friend a look, which he understood. He started to get up, but Wolf Tail motioned him down. Getting up, the Chief perambulated the lines, singing and chanting songs of praise for his friend, calling his name several times, then he went back to his place.

With that encouragement, the Blood Indian got up, dressed in the attire as he was four years ago back home. Singing his war song, and his woman walking closely behind, he went down between the lines and back, then strode near the arrow that Running Rabbit had stuck in the ground. Although the whole camp was standing around the contestants there was hardly a word to be heard.

"My juniors and my friends," he said, "I will not speak many words. I have one deed to relate, and it is this. What Running Rabbit has just related is my doing. That arrow there is mine, and I will vouch for this by having you compare that arrow with mine. The all powerful is looking and listening to me, this was my doing single handed."

At this, one of the juniors came forward and one of the Seniors. They took the arrows for examination, they saw that all the arrows were feathered with the same bird, a white feather with a black tip, and all headed with red flint, the same in length. They were identical in every respect.

The senior took all the arrows, holding them in front of him. He walked up his line with them for examination. Then over to the opposing line. Then giving them to Many Swans, said, "My friend, here is where you claim your arrow." Many Swans, taking them, bowed his head. This was his thanks.

Then turning to Running Rabbit, Many Swans said, "Now for your slur about my paint. You are well named, Running Rabbit. If you had

not run like your namesake, that time on the top of Belly Buttes, and I let loose another arrow at you, you would not be here today. There was no pit fight, no crowd. I've got your bow and arrows, your robe, your moccasins, and your brother's scalp. That is why I am painted."

The roar of warwhoops and yells from the whole camp was earsplitting. Then the seniors, as one, rushed forward to the juniors, blackening their faces. The contest broke up. It is not unusual in these contests for a defeated party to take their blackening good-naturedly. But in this case Running Rabbit was so insulted by the enemy Indian that he was uncontrollable with rage. He was indelibly branded as a false talker.

The losers withdrew to their teepees to wash their faces. Running Rabbit was without his famous relic, the arrow. The seniors, who were the winners, with Many Swans and Wolf Tail in the lead, marched around the inner circle of the camps with great triumph, beating their tomtoms, and singing their song of victory.

The Crow Indians had great admiration for their new member. But Running Rabbit swore revenge. Running Rabbit was very jealous. One night, after all the lights were out, he gave the Chief an unexpected visit.

"I'll listen," said Wolf Tail, "What do you want?"

"I want to buy your enemy friend from you, so as to kill him," said Running Rabbit. "I will give you four of my best horses and four mules. Give me the privilege of killing the Blood Indian in the next teepee."

"You don't ask for much," said the Chief. "What do you think he is, an elk or buffalo? You are sore because you had your face blackened. Well, it was coming to you for false talking. Go on out of here or I'll call my friend over."

Running Rabbit went out. The next day, thinking the matter over, he thought he would try the Chief's weakness, which was his passion for women. Running Rabbit had a grown-up daughter. The next night he went to the Chief's teepee again.

"Ah, what is it this time," said Wolf Tail.

"I mean what I speak this time," said the younger man. "I will double the animals and I will give you my daughter in wedlock. Let me kill the Blood Indian." It was brief and to the point. The Chief was silent for a long time and then said, "All right then, but leave my name out of this, and do your deed far out of the camps. Sometime when he is out running buffalo, for instance," said the Chief.

Wolf Tail's wives, who seemed to be fast asleep, heard everything and were very mad. These women were not going to have a younger woman with them. They were very jealous. The next day, after Many Swans had gone out for Buffalo meat, the Chief's wives went over to visit his wives.

These women told everything they had overheard, and that the Blood women were not likely to see their husband alive again. However, that evening Many Swans did come back and very much alive. The women, rushing out of their teepee, greeted their husband as if he really did come back from his Happy Hunting grounds on the Sand Hills. Many Swans, after recovering from the shock, demanded the reason for their unusual greeting. The women told what they had learned from Wolf Tail's wives. Hearing this, the Blood thought it was time to leave for home. It was now summer, and his People would be gathered on the sacred west slope of the Belly Buttes, and he owed the All Powerful many rites.

Garbed and painted in his war regalia, his bow and arrows slung on his back, Many Swans went around the inner circle of the camps, singing his war song and telling the Crow Indians that they were not enough in this camp to kill him and that he was going back into his lodge, and for them to come and try their luck, and see what would come out of it. The members of the Society he had joined learned that he was not in the

right temper, gathered together, and went over to his teepee. Many Swans went out to meet them. Seeing that they were unarmed and acting friendly, he went back into his teepee and invited them to come in.

After having been seated, one of them, talking very mildly, demanded the reason of their brother's loudtalking around the camps. Many Swans explained to them how he was being sold or betrayed by the Head Chief Wolf Tail to Running Rabbit, and that he had made up his mind to go back to his own tribe. The Crows, seeing that their brother member had no intention of staying with them any longer, told him,

"It is not our wish that you should leave this way. We owe you too much for what you have done for us, and we want to show you a little appreciation. Wait today anyway, we will hold a dance in which we'll give you things to go home with. Those staked horses and mules that the Chief got from Running Rabbit will be yours and we will dethrone him." Many Swans accepted their kind pleading.

The big give-away dance was held, and when it was over, Many Swans was richer by twenty head of horses and two pack loads of buckskin paraphernalia.

The next day Many Swans left the Crow's encampment after a sad farewell to his friends. Four of them went with him as far as Roaring River, which is now named Great Falls by the paleface. . . .

Many Swans made his last camping stop just across Spruce Pit Fall River, now named the St. Mary's River. From here Many Swans scouted ahead and sure enough the whole tribe was on the sacred slopes of the Buttes. He waited till darkness came, then he packed his stuff up for the last time.

Arriving in the dead of night, he put up his teepee in the gap of the circle of camps which was his place, near his son-in-law's. Next morning, early risers seeing his lodge announced his arrival, and relatives and friends rushed over to greet him.

After tenderly kissing his daughter, Many Swans told her that all the enemy property he brought was for her husband and that he may come over for a greeting. Thus was bought with enemy property this restriction which prevented these parents from seeing and meeting their son-in-law. The next day a big dance of victory was held in the Bougher Lodge over the arrow that Many Swans had recovered.

BIRD RATTLER

Joe Beebe's uncle, Bird Rattler, lived among the Crows for several years during his youth. Bird Rattler was born in 1859 to Red Bird Tail, a Piegan, and Woman's Word, a Blood. His grandfather was also named Bird Rattler. His mother's parents were The Tongue Eater and Fine Success Woman.

When Bird Rattler was just a boy, he left home and ended up at a camp of Crow People, who live today in southeast Montana. They were then still at war with our People, though their Old Ways were much like ours. When he arrived among the Crows, Bird Rattler went up to an old man standing outside his lodge by some horses. He asked the man, in sign language, if he could take care of the horses in exchange for a place to sleep. It was a custom in the old days for poor or orphaned boys to live with a successful family and help care for their horses and property.

At first the Crows suspected Bird Rattler to be a spy for a war party, but when no enemy showed up he became an accepted member of the camp. The old man asked him if he could hunt buffalo. Bird Rattler put his fists to the sides of his head and wiggled his thumbs, explaining he could only hunt the young ones. Boys began training to hunt buffalo by going after the less dangerous young ones. The old man gave Bird Rattler one of his choice buffalo runners for the hunt. To

prove his worth, the boy killed five good-sized bulls.

During Bird Rattler's stay among the Crows, he learned to speak their language and to know the People. When still a young man, he left them to return to his mother's People. His companions among the Bloods included Calf Robe and Weasel Tail, both of whom had also lived among the Crows. More than once they used their knowledge to raid the Crows for horses.

For many years a pictographic history of Bird Rattler's adventures was on display in one of the chalets in Glacier National Park. Among the exploits illustrated was the time he stole the Crows' best horse, as well as a headdress, shield, and other goods. Also illustrated was his theft from the Cheyennes; he took off with horses, travois, and some women—a complete household on the move.

Bird Rattler's stealing of the fine Crow horse went like this: With his brother and several companions, he crept up toward a small Crow camp. It was late afternoon, so they kept hidden in nearby brush looking over the camp until dusk. It was well after dark when they entered the Crow camp. Bird Rattler walked around the rear of the tipis, gathering a few of the prizes hung on the tripods there—a Powerful war shield, a spear, and bow and arrows. Such things were among the noblest items one could collect on the war trail. Without these weapons the enemy could inflict no injury in the event of a fight.

Bird Rattler then led the party to the horse corral, which was concealed in the nearby forest. He cut the rawhide straps holding up the poles of the corral and selected three fine horses from the herd. He took for himself an attractive-looking bay whose hind legs were all white, the whiteness coming up to and just over the rump. Quietly, they led the horses from the corral, then mounted them and rode safely home.

Bird Rattler kept his prize horse, Apistokinii, for many years. He trained it to race and it be-

64

Bird Rattler. (Glacier Studio)

came a famous winner. He warned anyone who came near the horse that no Medicine must ever be used on it, nor must it ever be ridden double. One weekend Bird Rattler let his brother Running Rattling take Apistokinii to a nearby race. Many good horses were participating, and Running Rattling became worried about the strong competition. So he asked a Medicine Man known for his successful Powers with horses to give some of his Power to Apistokinii. The Medicine Man did, and Apistokinii won the race. That evening Running Rattling rode the horse back home in the company of a friend. When the friend's horse stepped on a sharp stone and went lame, Running Rattling invited him to ride double. Not long after, they came to a narrow ravine. Running Rattling urged Apistokinii forward to jump over it. Burdened with two riders, Apistokinii did not complete the leap fully. His hind legs slipped back down the embankment, breaking both hips. Apistokinii sat, unable to rise. Running Rattling walked home the rest of the way greatly worried.

He went to bed and said nothing until the next morning. Bird Rattler was quite saddened when he was told what happened. He took his rifle and shot Apistokinii, then covered him with his finest Hudson's Bay blanket. It was not until much later that he discovered his brother had disobeyed his orders.

Bird Rattler's last raid did not end as well as his others. On returning to camp with newly stolen Crow horses, he and his partners, Weasel Tail and Black Looking, were arrested by Mounted Police. They were put in ball and chains in the guardhouse at Fort MacLeod. Managing to escape, they fled south to their relatives among the South Piegans of Montana. Weasel Tail and Black Looking returned to live in Canada, years later, after the incident had been officially forgotten. Bird Rattler stayed in Montana to become a successful farmer, an honorable tribal judge, and Keeper of the Piegan's sacred Circle Dance Medicine Pipe Bundle until his death in 1939.

The Medicine Tipis
in Our Encampment

The camp was still coming together, and although the big event, the transfer of Horns Society memberships, was still a few days off, there were now already more lodges in the camp than there had been on the final day of last year's encampment.

Sitting out in front of our Yellow-Otter Tipi, we were visiting with Grandma under the large umbrella, looking around the camp circle and talking about our People's tradition of painting some tipis with symbolic designs.

In the long-ago, tipis with painted designs could be found in the camps of most tipi-dwelling people. Such tipis were very personal, expressing the dreams of their owners, and were usually destroyed when the owner died. Among some tribes, painted tipis housed their chief or sacred Bundles, but as these declined, so did designed tipis. Although some tribes have painted their tipis in recent years, these designs usually have no meaning and often bear little resemblance to their traditional counterparts.

Our painted tipis, however, follow a basic style of ancient design, and are easy to recognize and distinguish from the tipis of other tribes. Originally each tipi's painting told a story and accompanied a small sacred Bundle, and while in most cases the stories have been forgotten and the

Bundles lost or sold, the painted designs on our tipis are the same ones our oldest living People saw when they lived in the circle camps as children.

In the days when the first white men came to visit our People, tipis were made of buffalo hides and designs were painted with natural colors, usually various shades of our Mother Earth. From her comes the sacred red paint we apply to our faces, bodies, and holy objects, as well as our tipis. The red paint represents our Earth Mother, the blood within our bodies, and also the color of our Father, Sun, in the morning and evening.

There are many types and shades of red earth, but only two kinds are used for sacred purposes. One is *Nitsisahni*, or "real paint," which is fairly bright red and the most commonly used shade. The other red paint is called the "seventh paint," because it is most often used in Medicine Pipe ceremonies where the number seven is sacred. Darker than real paint, it contains a substance that gives it a greasy feel and a shiny appearance. The Old People say that if sacred paint is not gathered properly with many prayers and good thoughts, it will turn into plain dirt before it can be used.

Other sacred paint colors include black, usually made from powdered charcoal; yellow, made from a clay, though it used to be made from buffalo gallstones; and green, made from a certain type of algae.

In the Old Days, these natural colors were mixed with water and animal fat to form the paint that was applied to tipi covers. Brushes were made from buffalo bones. The bone was cut at one end, so that its pores were exposed to form the tip of the brush. These pores held the thick paint quite well. The natural paints had to be rubbed into the lodge covers very thoroughly, or else they would run with each rainfall. Even so, the natural colors tended to fade very quickly from constant exposure to the elements. Nowadays, we use the somewhat organic combination of oil paint and linseed oil, which has proved to be effective and durable.

Painted tipis are usually given up as an offering whenever a new cover is made, as there should never be two copies of the same cover. The old cover is either offered to the Underwater Spirits by sinking it with rocks into a lake, or offered to Sun by leaving it weighed down by rocks out on the prairie.

Nevertheless, occasionally two or more covers having the same design can be found. In some cases, they represent similar dreams by different people. In other cases, they indicate a design not ceremonially transferred but inherited, and probably looked upon as a family heirloom or coat-of-arms to be reproduced in new tipi covers—usually by younger people unaware that they should not copy the design. And then there are those who know better, yet copy original designs on new covers and sell them to museums and collectors of "Indian relics." Finally, so-called Indian enthusiasts also contribute to the existence of multiple copies of the same design, when they make painstakingly precise but nonspiritual representations of some old design for their own tipis.

The Spirit of the Otter has inspired more designs than any other spiritual power. Our own Otter Tipi was one of four similar ones at last summer's encampment. Four is a sacred number, so it was good to see that many of one tipi design. As all four owners happened to belong to the same part of the camp circle, all the Otter Tipis ended up next to each other.

There are different types of Otter Tipis. All have otters symbolically drawn on their covers. The Yellow Otter Lodge, or Tipi, may have only a small Bundle and a few songs. The Yellow-Otter-Flag has a great many songs and a Bundle that includes the decorated skin of an otter. This skin is known as the flag; it is tied to the end of a pole and suspended over the tipi to wave in the air.

According to our ancient traditions, this is how the very first Otter Tipi came about.

THE OTTER TIPI

Long ago a young man went way up north into a country where our People used to live. He stopped by a lake, perhaps the Great Slave Lake, where he lay down to sleep and seek a vision. No dreams came to him while he slept, so the next day he built himself a raft out of the driftwood littering the lake shore. With a long pole, he pushed the raft away from shore, and then lay down upon it and again fell asleep.

While the young man slept, Wind pushed the raft far out into the lake, where Mink swam up to it. When the young man awoke, Mink said, "I have been sent to bring you to my relative's lodge. Follow me." The young man followed Mink into the water and they swam down to the bottom of the lake. When they reached bottom, the young man saw there a fine lodge, painted yellow with many designs. He heard drumming from within. Mink took him inside and introduced him to his relative, Otter. Otter was lying on a bed of tule reeds (a kind of bulrush or cattail) at the back of his lodge. He offered the young man the seat next to him, saying, "I have heard about you looking for holy Power around this lake. I sent my relative up to get you because

Top left: The four Yellow Otter Lodges during the 1972 encampment. The one on the left belongs to Many Grey Horses; the next one, to Philip Mistaken Chief; the next, to us; and the last, to Mokakin.

Bottom left: Yellow Otter Painted Lodge in 1891; another variation, with a buffalo head painted over the doorway. This one has two stripes painted beneath Night Sky, to represent the Milky Way. The six discs at the top represent the Bunched Stars, or the Pleiades. (R. N. Wilson)

Bottom right: The Yellow Otter Lodge of my family, showing the fallen stars on the prairie, the rounded foothills, the large, symbolic doorway of the otter's den, Night Sky, and Morning Star.

69

I take pity on you and want to give you some of my Power." Then Otter took some sweetgrass and made incense on his altar. He told the young man to listen carefully as he sang a number of songs. The young man listened and learned these words:

Man, he says, my tipi is Powerful.
Woman, she says, my tipi is Powerful.
Rain is my Medicine.
My children, they hear me.
The Earth, below, it is Powerful.

Under water are our tipis.
My tipi, it is Powerful.
My smoking, it is Powerful.

Otter also taught the young man the sacred movements that go along with each song. He gave the young man an otter skin with many fine decorations and taught him how to make otter movements with the skin, and the songs to sing while doing so. He gave the young man a smoking pipe and a drum to use for the otter ceremony. He told him, "When you get back to the camps of your People, you must make all these sacred objects I have shown you, so as to carry on this ceremony properly. You must paint your tipi with the same designs you see on mine. You must make incense often to remind yourself of my holy Power. If you do all these things faithfully, then you may call on my Power whenever you wish." When the young man awoke, he returned to the Blackfoot camps and did as Otter had directed. From that first dream originated all the tipis that now have otter designs.

The sacred Bundle that goes along with an ordinary Otter Tipi (as well as most other painted tipis) contains one or more *Iniskims*—sacred buffalo stones. Iniskims are sacred helpers; they bring good luck. Iniskim songs are sung during the incense and prayer ceremonies. Most families had at least one in their household in the Old Days.

Tough Bread with his wife and their Yellow-Otter-Flag Tipi, in the Blood camp of 1891. The Otter Flag can be seen over the top of the lodge poles. (R. N. Wilson)

The sacred Bundle for an Otter-Flag Tipi contains an otter skin and one or more other animal skins. Bells are suspended from the nose, feet, and tail of the flag itself, although in the past dried deer hooves were used instead of bells. Bands of quillwork or beadwork decorate the neck, paws, and tail, and brass shoe-buttons are sewn on for eyes. The Otter Flag itself is kept in a rawhide case for most of the year. The case is hung out behind the tipi in the daytime, and

70

Top left: Bob Black Plume, or Skunk, places the Otter Tipi Flag on its support during its transfer to the Provincial Museum. Mrs. Henry Standing Alone and Mrs. Bob Black Plume look on.

Top right: Transfer Ceremony of the Otter Tipi Flag. Eric Waterton represented the Provincial Museum at this ceremony. His face has been painted and the sacred skin has been placed over his shoulders to signify that he is the new Owner. On his right is Henry Standing Alone and Willie White Feathers. (Alberta Provincial Archives)

Bottom right: George First Rider sings one of the Otter Tipi Flag songs for the benefit of the Provincial Museum, which paid him for his help. Next to him is Tom Morning Owl, who sold the sacred flag to the Museum. (Alberta Provincial Archives)

taken inside at night. During ceremonies such as the Sun Dance, the Bundle is opened and the flag tied to an extra-long tipi pole so that it hangs high above the doorway. As it waves in the air, the bells jingle, reminding everyone of its presence. Two of the Otter Tipis last summer had Otter Flags flying above their doorways. One belonged to the family of Many Grey Horses, who also owns a Medicine Pipe Bundle. The other one belonged to an old lady named Mrs. White Man Left. The transfer ceremony for an Otter-Flag Tipi used to be very involved and took four days to complete.

OTHER PAINTED TIPI DESIGNS

Let me explain some of the spiritual meanings of tipi designs. Basically, the painting on a tipi is divided into three sections: the band of symbols around the bottom represents Earth; the large area in the center represents Universe; and the section at the top represents Sky.

The bottom band is generally painted black, brown, or red, to represent the color of the Earth, or else it is painted green to represent the grasses and trees. Within this band are usually two rows of discs representing the puffballs that cover the prairies, considered to be the remains of fallen stars. This bottom band can be straight and flat, for the flatness of the plains; topped by semicircles, for the rolling hills; or pointed, for the mountains. In the back, directly opposite the entrance, the bottom band often rises in large square or oval projection, representing the entrance to the animal's den the original owner went to for his dream. In a few cases this large design represents the boulders on which buffalo like to rub themselves when out on the prairie.

The large, central area on the tipi cover usually symbolizes the universe in general, and can also represent the particular element in which the dream animal or bird lives. It is here that the major tipi motifs are depicted. The male symbols will usually appear on the south side of the lodge, the female on the north. Sex is depicted either by sex organs, minor color changes, or by horns. The placement of the sexes on the outside of the tipis is, by custom, opposite that of the persons seated inside, as the place for women seated inside a tipi is on the south, and for men, on the north. Perhaps this originally signified some spiritual relationship between the lodge's spiritual guardians and its occupants. If so, this symbolism was probably lost when the People no longer lived a daily life in harmony with nature.

As few as one pair or as many as four pairs of animals are painted in the center band. The animals usually have "lifelines" representing the major organs. A lifeline begins at the mouth and is drawn in sections of red and green. It runs to the heart, which is painted red. Two green circles toward the animal's rear represent the kidneys.

The basic color of the large central area is most often red or yellow, and less often brown, green, blue, or the basic white of the cover material itself. If the original owner was taken into water during the dream in which he was given the design, the background color is usually yellow. If the dream occurred on land, the color is most often red or brown. Designs given by birds or other Spirits from above most often are white or blue.

Tipis without a symbolic representation of the dream animal's home will have instead one of two other symbols drawn in the back. The most common is a circle for the spiritual center of the universe. Sometimes the symbol is like a bull's-eye, several concentric circles representing Sun, Moon, and Earth.

The area at the top is usually painted black for Night Sky, when dreams are most common. In the back of this part of the tipi, a Maltese cross is usually painted in yellow or orange, representing either Morning Star or a moth. The moth flies at night and is considered to be the bearer of good dreams. To inspire good dreams about buf-

72

Wolverine Tipi Flag on display at the Provincial Museum. The model shows the ancient tipi design and the manner of hanging the flag over it. The tipi and flag were bought from the Bloods. The other objects are also painted tipi decorations, mostly bells.

Shortly after 1900, Clark Wissler, an anthropologist, interviewed the holy leaders of our different divisions to compile a list of all the painted tipi designs among the Bloods. This was not simple to do, because tipis, like most other sacred objects, have always been freely transferred from one division to another. For example, our own all-red Painted-All-Over Tipi, which originated long ago in the dreams of a Blood man, is included in Wissler's list of Blood tipis. Yet, not long after this list was compiled the tipi was transferred to a North Blackfoot man, and remained among them for about thirty-five years. The last Blackfoot owner, a man named Rainy Chief, or Herbert Lawrence, transferred the cover to old Bottle, from our reserve. Bottle didn't use the cover much and later transferred it to his son, Camoose Bottle, who gave it to his brother, Jim. We got it from Jim through a South Piegan man, who was going to have it transferred to himself, but could not gather enough goods for payment. The cover is now very old, so we use it only for special occasions and then only when rain does not threaten —there are many small holes in it.

Although many painted tipis have traveled among our divisions like our All-Over Tipi, Wissler's list includes tipis that were considered distinctly Blood.

1. Big-Striped
2. Mountain Goat
3. Wolverine
4. Bear
5. Fisher
6. Elk
7. Half-Black
8. Bald Eagle
9. All-Over
10. War
11. Crane
12. All-Stars
13. Prairie Chicken
14. Horse

falo hunting or horse raiding, a buffalo or horse tail used to be fastened to the center of the cross and left to flutter in the air. Sometimes a crescent moon appears instead of a Maltese cross.

Large discs are painted on the ear flaps of the tipi, representing the two constellations, Great Bear and Pleiades. On some tipis, lines are painted below Night Sky: different colors represent a rainbow, the symbol of a clearing storm; lines painted in the same color usually represent the paths of the dream animals.

15. Buffalo Hoof
16. Yellow
17. Otter
18. Horse
19. Snake
20. Water-Monster
21. Buffalo Head
22. Skunk
23. Fish
24. Space
25. Center

In 1966, an old Blood man named Joe Gambler gave the Provincial Museum a list of tipis he considered to be traditionally Blood:

1. Buffalo Head
2. Head Down
3. Skunk
4. Half-Black
5. Sheep
6. Prairie Chicken
7. Horse
8. War
9. War (second type)
10. Otter
11. Yellow
12. Hoof (Buffalo)
13. Fish
14. Snake
15. Striped
16. Rib
17. All-Painted
18. Half-Yellow
19. Half-Yellow Otter
20. Gnawed (Ice)
21. Downward Star
22. Across

Red Crow's famous Single-Circle, or Big-Striped, Painted Lodge in 1892. (R. N. Wilson)

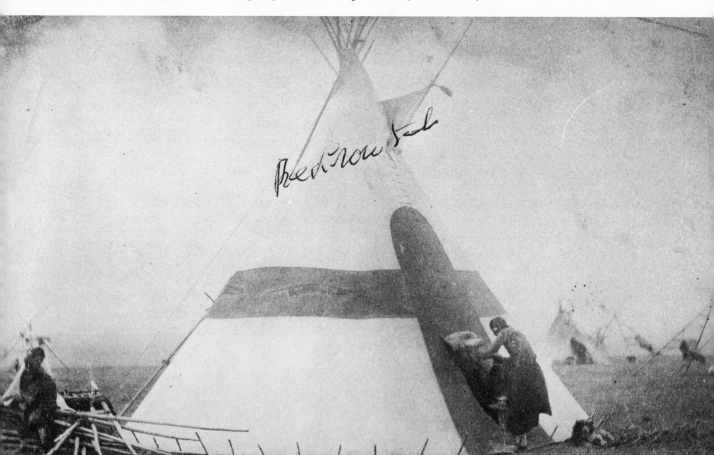

By comparing these two lists you can get some idea of the tipis' varying names and translations, as well as their transfer among our People during the sixty or so years between the lists. An example is the Big-Striped Tipi, in Wissler's list but not in Gambler's. This tipi belonged to our head chief, Red Crow, until his death in 1900. The chief met with his council and his visitors in this very large tipi. On Red Crow's death, the lodge was passed on to his son, Crop-Eared Wolf. Crop-Eared Wolf gave it to his aunt, Red Crow's sister, who was married to a South Piegan named Running Rabbit. The lodge has been among the South Piegans for such a long time that they now consider it one of their old lodges.

The Big-Striped Tipi is also known as the Single-Circle Lodge. A very wide red band with six black otters is painted around it. The otters run from back to front, three on one side and three on the other. A long red oval just below the smokehole represents the otters' home; instead of Morning Star in the back is a green symbol with a narrow yellow border representing Moon, with a horse's tail attached.

Although Wissler lists only one War Tipi, there are traditionally two in our division. When the owner of a War Tipi makes a new cover, he will either copy the adventures painted on the old cover or have someone draw new adventures. One of our War Tipis once showed the war adventures of such men from the past as Natosina (Eagle Plume), Heavy Shield, Eagle Child, Running Sun, and White Wolf. The scenes showed scalps, stolen horses, and captured weapons. When this same War Tipi was repainted a few years ago, it depicted the adventures of men like Shot-on-Both-Sides, Hungry Crow, and Stephen Fox. As the war days were long over, theirs were not war adventures, but scenes showing horses raided from distant ranchers and goods captured from the wagons and cabins of sheepherders and trappers.

For many years the Elk Tipi, which is on Wissler's list, belonged to our head chief, Shot-on-Both-Sides. It now belongs to his son Jim, our present head chief, who stays in it during our Sun Dance Encampments. It is painted blue with two large yellow elk.

The Half-Yellow Tipi, painted half yellow and half red, also was set up at our last Sun Dance gathering. It now belongs to Albert Wolf Child, who plans to transfer it to his son to keep it in the family. Formerly, a variation of it belonged to our Old Man, as well as Mokakin. The Center-of-the-Universe symbol is drawn at the rear of the tipi.

Along with his list, Gambler also recorded his stories of the origin of some designs. Here is his version for the Half-Yellow Otter Tipi.

Oki! The Half-Yellow Otter design—yellow otters around one side and black otters around the other. This tipi was once owned by a man who lived in the water. One day another man sat nearby on a hill; looking down at the river, he suddenly saw tipis emerge from the water. The man from the water told the man on the hill, "This tipi is mine. Jump into the water and go into it. You are having difficult times. I will give you my tipi." The man jumped into the water, entered the tipi, and the transfer ceremony was performed.

Gambler also told this story:

Oki! The Buffalo Head design. A buffalo bull had been killed and all his insides withered away. One time, a man was out on the prairie during a blizzard, so he slept inside the dead buffalo. During his sleep, the man was told, "Don't worry, nothing will happen to you. When you get back to your home draw my head all over your tipi to remind you of the Power that saved you."

In the Old Days, owners were well familiar with the stories and ceremonies for their tipis. This knowledge gave spiritual help and Power to the tipi's inhabitants. They depended on the tipi's Powers to protect them from enemy attacks and from natural harm, such as wind and lightning. The spiritual protection of the tipi meant much more to them than its physical protection as a shelter. After the People no longer lived daily in tipis, the meanings of the tipi stories of origin and ceremonies began to lose importance.

Buffalo Head Tipi, also known as the Upside-Down Buffalo Head Lodge. Sometime after this 1891 scene, this lodge was transferred to old Shot-on-Both-Sides, who gave it to his relatives, Mr. and Mrs. Wadsworth, when they took over the Backside-to-the-Fire Pipe. They later "fed" the lodge to the Crazy Dogs Society, one of whose members, Frank Red Crow, had it transferred to himself. (R. N. Wilson)

The Coyote Lodge. The background is yellow, like the prairie sands; the bottom projections represent mountain peaks. Four stripes represent constellations in the sky.

Atsitsina's Buffalo Painted Lodge a few years ago. In the background is the Striped Lodge and the Deer Lodge with an Otter Flag. This is the Buffalo Lodge of the Bloods; two similar Buffalo Lodges existed among the Piegans, as well.

All-Star Painted Lodge in 1891. (R. N. Wilson)

Antelope Painted Lodge in the Blood Camp in 1891. The background color of this lodge was yellow, to represent the antelope's sandy prairie environment. The stripe around the bottom represents the open plains. At the top is Night Sky with a crescent Moon. The door flap of this tipi was an antelope hide, and dried antelope hooves were strung up and fastened to the smoke flaps and over the doorway, to rattle in the wind. An antelope fawn skin was used as a flag. The tipi's special incense was sweet grass mixed with dried antelope droppings. The figure on the back of the tipi represents its Owner. In one hand he is holding an offering to Sun, and in the other a pipe. The lodge is the home of a distinguished man, because it sits farther inside the camp circle than the others. (R. N. Wilson)

What Has Become of Our Medicines?

Whenever our Old People gather together and discuss things, the question that always arises is, "What has become of our sacred Medicines, our holy things?" We have only four Medicine Pipe Bundles left. The Horns Society is missing some of its original Bundles, as are the Motokiks. Few of our painted tipis still have their sacred Bundles. Where have they all gone?

We revere these things as other devout people may treasure a family Bible, a family rosary or crucifix, or a family Star of David. These things have great meaning when they have been used by generations of parents or relatives; they inspire and reaffirm.

We don't need Medicine Bundles to sing sacred songs and say holy prayers. We don't need them to follow a simple, holy life. But we do need them for the sacred ceremonies that bring our people together and keep alive the Spirit of our Old Ways. Our People used to gather in spring for Medicine Pipe ceremonies; they gathered in summer for Medicine Lodge ceremonies as well as for the ceremonies of the Horns and Motokiks; they gathered during the fall sacred tobacco harvests for the Beaver Bundle ceremonies; and they gathered throughout the year for ceremonies with Insikims, sacred Tipi Bundles, and other Medicines.

Today, there are more sacred Bundles in museum showcases or storage rooms—some as far away as Berlin, Germany—than in the homes of our People. Some of our most sacred Bundles hang on walls as collectors' "Indian artifacts."

I will soon relate how some of our People sold these sacred things to museums and collectors. But to help you understand why they did, I must first explain how ownership and disposition of sacred things is looked upon in our Old Way.

As you may have already gathered, our sacred Bundles are, by tradition, transferred from one person to another by means of songs, ceremonies, paintings, and prayers. In our Old Way, a person who wishes to have the spiritual power of a sacred object need only express his sincerity to the Owner. He does this by offering the Owner a filled pipe and explaining why he wishes to have the Power of the sacred object. If the Owner agrees to the transfer, the person will give him some prized material item, such as a fine horse or favorite rifle, as a further sign of his sincerity. When the sacred object is actually transferred, the new Owner will show additional gratitude with more material sacrifices to the former Owner, the amount depending upon the sacred object. For something so Powerful as a Medicine Pipe Bundle or a Beaver Bundle, it was not unusual for a family to sacrifice all their horses, weapons, and clothing except for those needed to continue their basic daily life. One hundred horses were once given in exchange for a Medicine Pipe. In our Old Ways, these goods were considered sacrifices, material wealth exchanged for spiritual wealth.

Outside influences came to displace this idea of exchange, trading one item for another, and replaced it with the concept of "payment." It wasn't long before most of our People began to apply this payment philosophy to our Old Ways. Some began to regard the sacrifice of exchanging material things for holy things as a form of payment. As the Old Ways eroded, and the spiritual meaning of things like these exchanges became lost, it gradually became fact that our People bought their sacred Bundles by "paying" for them. Some of our People even began to believe that such Power could be bought and sold for payments in goods.

Today, the transfer of our Bundles is often purely a material affair: only the barest ritual is performed to satisfy traditional requirements. Neither the old nor the new owners make any spiritual adjustments in their lives in order to let the Holy Powers help them. The Bundles hang on walls, more as status symbols than as inherited Holy Spirits.

Robert Wilson, the trader, was probably the first to gather a collection of old things from our People, including Medicines. During the years Wilson operated his trading post at Stand Off, it was not unusual for him to accept an old shield, a pair of beaded moccasins, or a pipe and beaded pipe bag in exchange for new blankets or a gun. One man whose family was hungry and had no more food took the sacred Pipestem from his ancient Beaver Bundle and gave it to Wilson in exchange for flour. He replaced the sacred Stem in his Bundle with a broomstick.

Wilson's interest in obtaining the old things was to preserve them as well as to help out his friends on the reserve. He never pressured people to give up their old things. Instead, there were times when he gave the things back. An example

is the sacred Weasel Robe, a red blanket with many decorations that were added by some long-ago person as a result of a dream. Wilson once took the robe in trade. His friend, Black Plume, so admired the robe that Wilson gave it to him. Black Plume later gave it to his son, Dick Soup, who later sold it to the Provincial Museum in Edmonton, where it is now on display.

Most of Wilson's collection is now in the Field Museum of Natural History in Chicago. He owned one of our Black-Covered War Medicine Pipes, given to him by his adopted brother, Mean Bandolier. Wilson kept the sacred Pipe in its wrappings and hung it in a safe place on his wall. He never opened it ceremonially.

Shortly after 1900, Clark Wissler visited the Blood Reserve while making a study of the Old Ways among our South Piegan relatives in Montana. He wrote down several old stories and, using an early graphophone, recorded a number of our ancient holy songs. He bought some "cultural materials," including a few Medicine objects of minor importance.

It was not until the 1930s that we really began to lose our ancient holy things to outside persons. In 1932 Madge Hardin Walters, a wealthy woman from San Diego, California, visited our Sun Dance Encampment. Mrs. Walters was quite impressed by the many fine old "collector's pieces" she saw around the camp. From her home she had brought along some silver and turquoise jewelry and Navajo woven rugs. She found these things to be good conversation pieces and was quickly able to trade them off for some of the more common beadwork. Her new friends invited her to their camps to visit and eat.

"The Indians had become more friendly, and nearly all now smiled and spoke; which attitude I encouraged all I could with tobacco and other gifts to the head men," wrote Mrs. Walters in her later book, *Early Days and Indian Ways*. In the book she also describes her methods of encouraging and conniving people of the Navajo, Sioux, and Blood tribes to sell their ancient things to her. She tells how she traded her Navajo jewelry for old things with "Mrs. Red Crow, Sorrel Horse's sister. . . . This was my introduction to Red Crow and his wife, who became my dear friends and generous, able assistant collectors." This was Frank Red Crow and his earlier wife.

During her visit to the 1932 encampment, Mrs. Walters became well enough acquainted with some of our People to let them know she was willing to spend much money for "Indian articles," even Medicine Bundles. Her daughter later wrote: "From Red Crow and Percy Creighton and Violet Sorrel Horse in Alberta, came clumsily-wrapped brown paper bundles that smelled of smoke and sweetgrass. These packages disclosed treasures of medicine bundles, ceremonial shirts; even a tipi."

By the time Mrs. Walters was finished with us, our People had two fewer Beaver Bundles, three fewer Medicine Pipes, a dozen or so fewer Motokiks Bundles, and so many fewer other ceremonial and society objects that she probably could have started her own Blood tribe in California. At one point, she sent a selection of "her bundles" to the World's Fair in San Francisco, where anthropologist Clark Wissler saw them. He sent her a note of congratulation that said, "I am pleased with your finds." Her finds, unfortunately, were our People's losses.

Mrs. Walters kept a file of notes about her acquisitions, along with copies of the numerous letters written to her by her Blood collectors. Copies of this material are at the Denver Art Museum in Colorado, where part of her collection is, and at the Glenbow Archives in Calgary. The papers speak for themselves. One of the letters is dated "Blood Reserve, Cardston, Alta., May 20th, 1937," and is signed by Frank Red Crow. It reads:

The reason why I did not write to you right away, I was trying to get some things for you and at last have got two things for you. You know a woman makes sun lodge who is honest life trueth to her husband and straight life and she will be aloud by the indians to make the sun lodge, and she buys the holy crown from another woman who had made the sun lodge before and has to pay horses and goods for the crown. I have no idea how long this holy crown since was made quite old. The time you was over here at our sun lodge there is a woman had two holy crowns she sold one that time and a year after she died and left one to her family and I bought this one from them I give two horses for it, the reason why I got this cheap the family all dead just two boys left they will never have a chance to sell it, and boys was glad to get two horses for it. You can pay me any amount you like will be O.K. to me you have so good friend to me. The other thing is a flag used be owned by Calf Robe I got it from that woman on picture with Calf Robe I did buy it she told me to sell it for her she wants $25.00 for it. A teepe painted skunks on round the teepe with the skunk flag. I send the buffalo game bones one is lost I have only three should be four.

I just got done farming and we don't know how it is going be dry or wet. Sorrel Horse went to Browning I told him to call for my package at my sister's. I thank you many thanks for them. I will ask you for a summer coat for my daughter chest 38 in lenth 47 in.

I made a little thing here I send too it is for sewing before the iron came. Good-bye Sincerely Yours

Frank Red Crow

In March, 1939, Mrs. Walters received a package from Percy Creighton, or Little Dog. In it were what Creighton called "very important articles." It was a sacred Tobacco Planting Bundle, one of the few still in use among the Northern Blackfoot People at that time. Creighton added: "They are the main articles used in planting, more important than the [Beaver] bundle itself. A beaver man cannot go without these articles. An old man say I could buy. I took the bundle with a smile. I never thought that I could ever get hold of anything like them. They are the most sacred articles in the big beaver bundles."

Shortly before this, Creighton had bought a Beaver Bundle for $150 from a Blood named Not Good. Creighton sent it to Mrs. Walters and wrote, "There is no longer a beaver bundle in the tribe."

Actually, there were still one or two such Beaver Bundles left on the Blood Reserve at that time. About three years later, Frank Red Crow named the right price to the owner of one Bundle and sent it off to Mrs. Walters in California. On September 16, 1942, he wrote this brief letter:

Dear Friend

I got your letter a few days ago with a great pleasure for the money you send that was alright thank very much. I will go to North Blackfoot Reserve to get you some tobacco planters this will be after the threshing, history and whisel [whistle] I will send all together. First time I see a pipe like that straight stone pipe [referring to an ancient straight bowl that was part of the Beaver Bundle he obtained for her]. I heard that is the way all made like that before the indian ever see a file or iron well anyway before Columbus time. My wife and I sending you best wishes good-by

Yours truly
Frank Red Crow

Among the seven or eight Medicine Pipe Bundles still with our People in the late thirties were two Black-Covered Pipes from the old-time Seizers Society. Frank Red Crow managed to obtain one of these pipes from its Owner, Small Eyes. He wrote: "The pipe bundle is a good one; very old. This man had this pipe 20 years. He was afraid just to sell it to me; he want to sell it as the old Indian fashion way so to get satisfaction, and I have to get it that way and will cost me more."

Mrs. Walters' notes for February 14, 1939: "Red Crow has had medicine pipe transferred to himself and is shipping it." The following week's news: "Pipe bundle arrived. Red Crow says the Indians think it is the oldest bundle in the tribe. He had lots of trouble getting it at all and difficulty getting it across the line [Canadian–U.S. border]."

Mrs. Walters took a special liking to the Motokiks, the Old Women's Society. In the long-ago, that society had about forty Bundle-owning members. As with the Horns Society, each member was required to have a headdress and Bundle. When either was lost, that membership became lost and were not renewable. Thus, as you probably have guessed, Mrs. Walters's interest in the society diminished the society itself.

Mrs. Walters's notes reveal this interesting anecdote about her introduction to the Motokiks Society. She recorded it on June 18, 1936.

When I was there [Sun Dance camp] I was told a headdress of the women's society was for sale, but did not see it and had no idea until I saw the Buffalo Dance how remarkable they were. I have regretted ever since but at the moment I was rather startled by the price of $100 and some Indian promptly bought it.

Mrs. Walters learned quickly. A few years later she wrote:

Our informant states that the total number of Matoki Snake Women was ten. [The society is divided up into groups, each with its own style of headdresses. One of these groups was known as the Snakes.] So far but four of these have been acquired.

There were eight buffalo headdresses in the society at the time. Some of them are mentioned in the various notes:

August 28, 1936. . . . Buffalo headdress from Red Crow with eagle plumes . . . belonged to her mother . . . *Long Time Pipe. She cried and prayed and kissed this headdress before she parted with it.*

September 1, 1936. . . . Buffalo headdress with white beads.

October 4, 1936. . . . Referring to buffalo headdress with feathers . . . Percy Creighton writes . . . I sent you a Matoki H.D. oldest one yet. . . . Owned by old woman—Awl Body. . . . It is called The Bulls Scalp Headdress, because in the first place it belonged to the Bulls, and that society died out, and it was taken into the Woman's Society as far back as I could trace it.

December 24, 1937. . . . Arrival from Little Dog [Percy Creighton] of 3rd buffalo headdress.

January 21, 1938. . . . Little Dog has found the other buffalo headdress.

January 4, 1939. . . . I have been offered two more buffalo headdresses, one of the Mahtokiks that we do not have, a Head Woman.

Mrs. Walters' notes indicate that the Motokiks had one main leader and two secondary leaders, who were the "pipe lighters." The "pipe lighter's outfit" was used to prepare the pipes of all the members. It certainly was a prized possession.

That smoking ceremonial bundle is, I think, rare valuable. My possession of it has been referred to repeatedly by the Indians as if it were decidedly important. I will try to get more information on the Bird Clan. It took over four years of effort and innumberable letters and presents to get a Bird Clan specimen, but now I have two. Same true of Snake Clan.

Ironically, the remaining pipe lighter among the Motokiks was Percy Creighton's wife.

Percy Creighton also obtained for Mrs. Walters one of the last ceremonial necklaces of the ancient Crow Carriers Society, a rattle, and information about the society's history, all for fifty dollars. And of the last remaining war shield on the Blood Reserve, he wrote to Mrs. Walters: "And he told me to send it to you if you want it for $125.00 and also he said the longer he owns this shield, he'll raise the price on it. This man is a rich man. He is not like the others who are hard up for money. I like to know if you are going to buy any more articles or not."

Indeed, the avid lady from California bought many more articles. But these chronicles suffice to show you what happened to many of our ancient Medicines during the ten-year period from 1936 to 1946. Sometime in that period, Walters was stricken with an illness that kept her from making any other visits to the Blood Reserve beyond that first one. By 1946 she had lost her interest in collecting our Old People's things, and began circulating photos and descriptions of her collection to museums and private buyers. Soon her vast collection became scattered. Most of it was sold to the Denver Art Museum in Colorado. There, an anthropologist identified and catalogued the material, with much technical detail and a distinct lack of Spirit. Nevertheless, it at least constitutes an effort to record available knowledge about those old things.

Unfortunately, some years ago the Denver Art Museum found it had more of Mrs. Walters's material than needed. As a result, much of it was traded to other institutions for their surplus material.

After Mrs. Walters, the next major collection of our holy things went to the Glenbow-Alberta Foundation, in Calgary, Alberta. Much of the Blackfoot material was collected by Hugh Dempsey, the foundation's historical director. He was well acquainted with many of our Old People, who named him Putaina, or "Flying Chief."

In the Glenbow collection is a Medicine Pipe Bundle that came from our People; it is described in the museum's records as "the finest one." Hugh Dempsey got it from Steve Oka, who obtained it from his friend Mike Eagle Speaker.

When Steve Oka lost his wife, his outlook on life became very gloomy and he no longer wished to care for his Bundle. He approached Hugh Dempsey and asked $600 for it, claiming he could easily get $500 if he took the Bundle to the South Piegan Reserve and transferred it there. Glenbow paid him only $300, with the proviso that he could buy back his Bundle within one year. Unfortunately, when Steve Oka decided to retrieve it, it was ten years too late.

Meanwhile, a new institution, the Alberta Provincial Museum in Edmonton, went about collecting our holy relics in a significantly less sensitive manner. For one thing, it encouraged the notion that all our religious material would eventually be lost or destroyed unless placed for safekeeping with the museum. Moreover, the museum promised that our People would always have access to their things. This was a convincing offer to our Old People, who were aware that Bundles and other sacred things were often stolen by relatives and sold for drinking money. To these Old People, the Alberta Provincial Museum not only offered protection from such loss, but also asked that the Bundles be transferred to an official of the museum in the traditional way, rather than merely sold. Owners who transferred their Bundles were paid quite handsomely for their cooperation.

Since members of the North Blackfoot Reserve still had many of their Medicine Bundles, the Alberta Provincial people concentrated their first efforts on that reserve. As people gave up their sacred Bundles to the museum, there soon were no more Beaver Bundle or Medicine Pipe ceremonies; the Horns Society and Motokiks no longer held their annual ceremonies, and the Sun Dance gatherings ended. Safekeeping the sacred Bundles did not preserve the religion, the Old People soon learned. Instead, the religion withered. Gone were the physical things that used to inspire religious feelings. The North Blackfoot People wandered about their reserve while the things that inspired their sacred life were on display in glass cases several hundred miles away.

The Alberta Provincial Museum was highly successful in obtaining what it wanted by paying high prices to our People. Bundles once transferred for a few horses and blankets were suddenly "exchanged" for hundreds and thousands of dollars. Sometime in the early 1960s, I was visiting friends on the South Piegan Reserve, where the son of an aging Medicine Pipe Owner told me the exaggerated story about a museum up in Canada offering ten thousand dollars for a Medicine Pipe Bundle.

The following is an account of the Alberta Museum's transactions concerning one of our sacred Bundles. It is perhaps the most notorious acquisition from among the Bloods.

THE SALE OF OUR LONG-TIME PIPE

Most of our Medicine Pipe and Beaver Bundles are very old. No one knows exactly how many years ago they were first made. Among all our divisions, there is one particular Bundle that has been regarded with special awe and respect. This Bundle is so old that even back when our People still knew our ancient legends and histories, no one remembered ever hearing of a time when it was not among us. For that reason the Bundle has always been known as *Mesam-Achkuineman*, or "Long-Time Pipe." Except for a few repairs and additions, this Bundle is without metal or glass objects; nothing is in it that came from a trading post or store. Stories are still told about some of its long-ago Keepers who gave up dogs for transfer payments, because our People were then without horses.

Our sacred Long-Time Pipe was an anthropological prize that lay beyond the hopes of most museums and collectors. Respect for it was shared by virtually all of our People, even the Christianized majority. Its future among the Bloods was believed quite secure, since a number of our People who respected its significance longed to be its Keepers. But that isn't the way it turned out.

Just prior to the Sun Dance Encampment of 1968 we learned that our Long-Time Pipe was to be sold. Its Keeper, John Red Crane, who had only recently taken over the Bundle, had been paid $3,000 by the Provincial Museum of Alberta to transfer the Bundle to them at the encampment. Red Crane invited only the members of his own society, the Red Belts, to the transfer ceremony. Actually, they were paid to attend.

The museum promised that the Bundle would be brought back to the reserve each year to be opened. However, since the Bundle had been transferred to an official of the museum, he became the Bundle's spiritual Owner, thereby giving the museum complete control over it. No ceremony could be held without this official at the place of honor reserved for the Bundles's Keeper. This is somewhat like having a family gathering in memory of a murdered grandparent and being required to give the seat of respect and honor to the murderer.

Shortly after John Red Crane sold the Long-Time Pipe to the museum, he had a strange dream. The Spirit of the Pipe came to him, saying, "Just as you had no pity for me, I will have no pity for you." He told some of his friends about the dream and that he feared for his life. Not long after that, he was taken ill and placed in a hospital. He spent some time there, much of it in pain, before he died. When friends came to visit him during his final weeks, he was unable to speak to them—all he could do was hum parts of the songs for the Long-Time Pipe. He was not at the Bundle's last opening and he never saw the ancient Pipe again after he sold it.

A year after the transfer of the Long-Time Pipe, the museum decided that a complete record of the Bundle's ceremony should be made. Accordingly, $1,800 was spent to sponsor it; all the participants were paid a salary, like movie extras.

A few of the many personal Medicines at the Provincial Museum—skins of a weasel and a muskrat, along with a necklace with deer hooves and sacred bags.

The museum filmed, taped, and photographed the ceremony. Ironically, it may be the best record ever made of a Medicine Pipe ceremony. The salary motivated some people to attend their first ceremony in years. Others came to take this opportunity to again pray with our ancient, holy Pipe. And there were those who were so offended, they passed up this last opportunity altogether.

Our Old Man was at this last ceremony for the Long-Time Pipe. He had once led the ceremony for the Bundle's opening, and knew some of the special songs to be sung at the opening. The museum-official Owner offered him $250 to lead the ceremony. In refusing, the Old Man explained the following to us: "Our holy Pipes are very Powerful. It is very wrong to do something unholy with them. Leading such a ceremony for that white man, and accepting his money for doing it, would be very unholy for me. No one can ever buy my holy life with money." The white man later told people that the Old Man was incompetent and could not have led the ceremony anyway. He eventually recruited another old leader, Brown Chief Calf, to perform the ceremony.

One of the followers of our Old Ways who was most upset by the sale of the Long-Time Pipe was old Many Grey Horses. As a result of some dreams, he and his wife paid a visit to the Pipe's official Keeper. This official recorded the visit and submitted it to his employers as an Ethnological Data Record. This is how it reads in the museum's files:

A GIFT TO A MEDICINE PIPE BUNDLE
AS A RESULT OF A VISITATION
FROM A SUPERNATURAL BEING

On October 9, 1968, I received as visitors, in my home at Cardston, Alberta, two Blood Indians, Mr. & Mrs. Many Grey Horses, who are current owners of a Medicine Pipe Bundle.

They explained to my wife, who acted as interpreter, that their visit was a serious one and not social.

Mr. Many Grey Horses spoke first. He reprimanded my wife for not sitting with me during the recent transfer ceremony of the Long Time Medicine Pipe of which I was the recipient. He said, "When two people are married they must sit together in all holy ceremonies. This is blessing their marriage." He said in the old days, Mrs. Standing Alone, who represented my wife during this ceremony, would have been recognized as my wife. My wife explained that she does not participate in these ceremonies for fear of ridicule. Mr. Many Grey Horses said, "You must not be afraid of that. It is a holy ceremony."

Mr. Many Grey Horses then asked, "Where is the bundle?" [meaning the Long Time Medicine Pipe]. He was told that it was kept in the museum in Edmonton. Then asked how it was stored. Was it covered or open and on display? After being told how it was stored he said that he would explain the reason for their visit. He said that he would speak in old dialect and that his wife (Mrs. Grey Horses) would put it into simpler dialect so that my wife would understand it better and explain it to me in English.

MANY GREY HORSES:

I will tell you why we came. We didn't come to discuss the transfer, we came for a very important thing. My wife had a dream. She has had the same dream 4 times. About two years before any mention of a transfer she had a dream. A man came to her who owned the bundle many years ago. She didn't know the man. He was too far in the past.

The man said that he was being treated very badly and that the people that owned him now were not treating him with respect. My wife told me about her dream next morning. I advised her to go to her father who was a ceremonialist, and explain the dream to him. Her father told her that something was going to happen to the bundle and that he would talk to the owner [John Red Crane] at the next opening ceremony.

Time passed and one day Mr. Red Crane came up to my wife's father and asked him if he would open the Long Time Pipe in the spring. My wife's father said yes.

At the opening ceremony that spring my wife's father asked Mr. Red Crane, "Do you have something important to tell me?" Mr. Red Crane sat for a moment or two and then answered, "Please remember me in your prayers." My wife's father was saddened because he knew that something was not right.

Time passed and my wife had again the same dream, but nothing happened as a result of the dream. Then one day she heard that the Long Time Pipe was to be transferred to you and she was not surprised as she expected something to happen.

My wife had the 3rd dream a year or so later and in this dream the man came up to her and said, "They have done a horrible thing to me. They have laid me out in the open glass case so that people will come in and look at me, and my altar is left standing. Nobody comes to burn sweetgrass any more; and where I am sitting is not holy. Why did they take me away from my own country? It was my home; it is where I originated. It is where I wanted to be until the end."

My wife had the 4th dream a few months ago. In this dream the man came to her with you, and my wife saw the case with the Long Stem Pipe on display. The man said to her, pointing at you, "This is the man that took me. He must be very kind to me and if it so happened that somebody came and asked for me he must not refuse to let me go. I am left uncovered and that is what is making me very sad."

I am very surprised that my wife has had this dream because we never did own the Long Time Pipe. It must be very important or why should she keep having this dream? But it must be because we really believe in this religion and we live accordingly.

So we have come to offer this blanket so that you can take it to Edmonton on your next trip and cover the Long Time Pipe with it. We would be very happy if you would say a few prayers for us and tell the bundle that we have given the blanket as a sacrifice to it.

I bought this blanket in the U.S. and it is the same type that is always used to cover Medicine Pipes.

Mr. Many Grey Horses was undecided as to whether we should take off the old blanket that covers the pipe and give it to him but Mrs. Many Grey Horses said no. She said to place the new blanket over the old one as it was obvious as a result of her dream that one covering was not sufficient.

Mr. Many Grey Horses owns the 4 original drums of the Long Time Medicine Pipe Bundle. When John Red Crane had the Long Time Pipe bundle transferred to him from Stephen Fox he refused the transfer of the drums. Since the

Bundle then had no drums, his friend, Frank Cotton's father, gave him 2 drums and Red Crane's father gave him 2 drums. These drums are not part of the Bundle.

Stephen Fox, who owned the Long Time Medicine Pipe before John Red Crane, still had the original drums, and after the transfer to Red Crane, when Red Crane refused the drums, he consulted Many Grey Horses as to what should be done with the drums since Red Crane had refused them. Many Grey Horses then purchased the drums from Stephen Fox.

Many Grey Horses explained why some people will not attend the transfer ceremonies sponsored by the Provincial Museum. He said that they believe that the ceremony is holy and that the tape recorder is receiving the prayers and not the Creator. He said that when the bundle is taken down the shaman [Medicine Man] smears blood clots all over his body and then takes the bundle down. He then stands and prays for the owner of the bundle, but the tape recorder is "sucking all the prayers" and the owner of the bundle who is being prayed for does not get the full benefit of the prayers and that is not right.

Three years later, in the spring of 1972, SikskiAki and I, with a group of our Old People, visited the Provincial Museum. Upon seeing our ancient Pipe the Old People were moved, but were also dismayed to see it hanging open inside a glass case. The Bundle was not closed and the donated blanket not only was not covering it, it wasn't even there. Museum officials unlocked the case so that we could pray with the Bundle and leave offerings of tobacco in it. Then we asked them to close the Bundle and remove it from display. While they debated our request, they showed us the film of the Bundle's ceremony. Before we left, the museum people assured us that it would no longer be left lying open and that they were prepared to bring the Bundle back to our reserve for a ceremony at any time. This latter assurance was a surprise, because the white-man

Owner, who was no longer on the museum's staff, had told everyone after he left that the museum would no longer cooperate in honoring its claim to make the Bundle available to our People. The white-man Owner had also claimed that all museum materials and papers had become classified to outsiders, including himself.

Although we were pleased to learn we could have the Bundle for ceremonies, we nevertheless began discussing the possibility of taking the Bundle back to the reserve permanently, and selecting a member to act as "new Keeper," or even placing it in the charge of the tribe as a whole. For as we since learned, the former museum official, having divested himself of any responsibility to our artifacts, had been selling our Bundles at even higher prices to collectors of Indian relics. Here is an account of one of his more recent transactions:

This story involves our uncle, Atsitsina, one of our favorite companions. He enjoys staying with us and teaching us the many things that he knows of our Old Ways. Atsitsina was Keeper of two Medicine Pipe Bundles. One was owned before him by his long-gone father, Sun Chief, or Eagle Plume. Atsitsina transferred this sacred Bundle just a few years ago to a young man named Harrison Black Plume. His father, Bob Black Plume, was a leader of our holy ceremonies until recently, when he gave up our Old Ways for the way of the Full Gospel Church. Young Black Plume had vowed to take the Bundle during a family illness, so our uncle did not withhold it. Since Black Plume had little to give in the way of material exchange, Atsitsina offered him the Bundle and told him he would take it back at a later time, after the vow had been fully completed. Meanwhile, the white-man official had already offered Atsitsina a tempting amount of cash for the Bundle. When Atsitsina gave young Black Plume the Bundle, he warned him that under no condition was he to "give the Pipe to that white man." Black Plume gladly acknowledged he would not.

Some time after Atsitsina expected that Black Plume had completed his vows, he went to see him about having the Bundle transferred in return. But Black Plume no longer had the Bundle. Desperate for cash, he had "pawned" it for $900 to the white man. The white man told Black Plume that if the Pipe were not reclaimed within a certain period, he would arrange a ceremony to have it transferred to him, and then make additional payments to Black Plume. The $900 was less than cash value of the horses, blankets, and other goods our People usually pay for the privilege of having such a Bundle. So our uncle put up the $900 and instructed Black Plume to reclaim it.

A short time before all this happened, a Seattle collector of Indian artifacts had been about to pay a South Piegan Owner $4,000 for his ancient Medicine Pipe. The white man had dissuaded this wealthy collector from the purchase, advising him that the Piegan Bundle was "not authentic." This was not true. He had added that a genuine Medicine Pipe would soon be available.

So when young Black Plume went to reclaim the Bundle, the white man told him he had taken it to the Alberta Provincial Museum for safekeeping. A few days later, Black Plume insisted on the return of the Bundle. This time, the white man told him the Bundle had been sent to the National Museum in Ottawa, and that it would take some time to have it returned from there. We checked with both museums, and, as we suspected, neither had ever heard of this Bundle.

After much investigation and many questions (a white friend from Montana and even our uncle directly questioned the white man), and after many more evasive answers and lies, we finally learned for a fact that the Bundle had been sold to the wealthy Seattle collector.

Atsitsina considered taking legal action to retrieve the Bundle. But our People have rarely succeeded in legal situations. Most of us feel the Bundle is lost, and that all those who were involved in losing it will suffer.

Our Beaver Bundles and Their Origin

Beaver Bundles were the holiest of all the holy objects helping our People in their spiritual lives. They were the largest, least common, and most complex of all the Bundles, and required the greatest spiritual devotion of their Keepers.

Almost every bird and animal was represented in the Bundle, either by tanned skins (from animals specially snared to make their deaths quick and clean) or by special songs and movements. In the Old Days, over four hundred songs were sung when the Bundles were opened. The ceremonies were long and complicated. The Keeper trained constantly, all his life, for such occasions.

In 1909 Dr. Clark Wissler published this account of the origin of Beaver Bundles in an issue of the American Museum of Natural History's *Anthropological Papers*. He credited the story to an unidentified Blood man.

Once there was a man and his wife camping alone on the shore of a small lake. [Probably *Saint Mary's Lake in Glacier National Park, Montana.*] This man was a great hunter, and had in his lodge the skins of almost every kind of bird and animal. Among them was the skin of a white Buffalo. Because he was always hunting, his wife was often left alone. One day a Beaver came out of the water and made love to her. This went on for some time, until she finally went away with the Beaver to his home in the water. When the man came home, he looked all about but could not find his wife anywhere. As he walked along the shore of the lake, he saw her trail going down into the water. Then he knew what had happened. He did not break camp, but continued hunting. After four days, the woman came up out of the water and returned to her lodge. She was already heavy with child. When her husband returned that evening, he found her in her usual place and she told him all that had occurred.

In the course of time the woman gave birth to a Beaver. To keep it from dying, she put it in a bowl of water which she kept at the head of her bed. Eventually, her husband became very fond of the young Beaver and played with him every evening.

Now the Beaver down in the water knew everything that was going on in the lodge. He was not angry because he knew that the man was kind to the young Beaver. He took pity on the man. Then the father of the young Beaver resolved to give the man some of his Medicine songs, in exchange for the skins of birds and animals the man had in his lodge. So one day, when the woman went down to the lake for water the Beaver told her he would visit their lodge and ask for some of their things in his songs. He told her to instruct

89

her husband to give the things requested. He also stated the time at which he would come to the lodge to be received by her husband.

At the appointed time the Beaver came out of the lake and appeared before the lodge, but, before he entered, requested that the lodge be purified with incense. Then he entered. They smoked. After a while the Beaver began to sing a song in which he asked for the skin of a certain bird. When he had finished, the man arose and gave him the bird-skin. Then the Beaver sang another song, in which he asked for the skin of another bird, which was given to him. Thus he went on until he had secured all the skins in the man's lodge. In this way the man learned all the songs that belonged to the Beaver's Medicine and also which songs belonged to which skins.

After this time the man got together all the different kinds of bird and animal skins taken by the Beaver, made them up into a Bundle, and kept the Beaver Medicine.

Owners of Beaver Bundles were known as Beaver Men. They were always the learned ones among our People. A Beaver Man had to have a fantastic memory to be able to sing the four hundred or more songs in proper sequence. He had to be a man who lived very much in harmony with nature to know the sounds and actions of the many birds and animals within the Bundle, and to be able to coach the participants to repeat those sounds and actions during the ceremonies. Beaver Men learned all the Ways of nature. The People looked to them for knowledge about weather, seasons, plants, birds and animals, and calendar histories (called winter counts) of the tribe.

In the Old Days, a Beaver Bundle contained examples of the most important parts of all our other sacred Bundles—a Medicine Pipe, a Natoas headdress, a sacred tobacco-planting outfit, as well as all the various skins. As a result, Beaver Men usually knew all the ceremonies for these other Bundles, and, therefore, could give Teachings to the People about them.

If Medicine Pipe Men were considered priests among our long-ago People, the Beaver Men must have been thought of as bishops.

Among all the Blackfoot People, the most notable Beaver Man whose wisdom is still clearly remembered was old White Calf, head chief of the South Piegans. He died in 1903. His companion was Mad Wolf, a minor chief who died about the same time. These two Beaver Men were a Powerful team. White Calf's brother-in-law, old Running Wolf, was the most respected Beaver Man in the recorded history of the Bloods. He and another Beaver Man, old Ki-soum (Sun, or, in Wilson's notes, Old Moon) had also made a Powerful team.

THE 1892 BEAVER BUNDLE CEREMONY

In the Old Days, Beaver Bundles were opened quite often, usually after each new moon. For that reason, when trader Robert Wilson wrote these observations of Beaver Bundle ceremonies, he recorded them under the title *Moon Dances*. Although Wilson saw the ceremonies under the leadership of true Beaver Men, he was too late to see them when the People were fully aware that the long ceremony symbolized every aspect of the Old Way of life in harmony with nature.

A few years ago when I first became interested in the peculiar religious customs of the Bloods, there were two men in camp who were the owners and custodians each of a sacred bundle containing the skins of many animals and birds, as well as a pipe stem and numerous articles, the number and uses of which the following will show. These men are called I-och-Keeme and during the fall, winter, and spring months they conduct a ceremony of a religious nature, generally of nine or ten hours duration, the time oc-

cupied in singing and smoking. The dances are usually held upon the day following the appearance of the new moon, but I have known many to be postponed for different reasons. The tom-tom is not used, rattles and whistles are the musical instruments.

Early in the morning the i-o-kinu sends out a boy or girl, or some member of his household, to invite whoever he wishes to be present. These are generally old and middle-aged men, some of whom bring their wives. At the date of writing I have attended three "moon dances" and remained to the end of each, with book and pencil in hand taking notes from which I hope to faithfully describe what took place and to give as many explanations as I have been able to obtain from the performers. Two of the ceremonies which I have witnessed took place in the home of Running Wolf, one in his house and one in his lodge. The third dance was conducted by Running Wolf in the house of Three Bulls, another I-O-Kunt who assisted. Running Wolf is considered the most proficient of this class in this tribe, but he has a superior in the person of the Blackfoot [North Blackfoot] "Owl Child" who was master of ceremonies upon the occasion that I saw the dance in Running Wolf's lodge. This superiority consists simply in a good memory [Wilson had a tendency to draw conclusions from outward appearances, not from deep understanding]; 1st in being able to lead their peculiar ritual all day long without making errors, and 2nd, in being able to begin without delay each song in its correct place. When we remember the length of time the I-O-Keeme sings, and that the songs are about one hundred in number, nearly all of which are never used upon any other occasions than "moon dances," the use of a good memory is evident. [It is likely that only one hundred songs were sung at the ceremonies witnessed by Wilson. Even old White Calf did not know all the songs. However, due to some taboo, Beaver Men never allowed anyone to count the songs; if they saw someone

Ki-soum, or "Sun," the holy man who was also called Moon. (Glenbow Archives)

counting, they would sometimes mix up their songs to confuse the counter.] Running Wolf and Old Moon have been for years the only two I-O-Keeme in this tribe. [This statement depends on one's definition of Beaver Man. There were then a number of Blood men who knew Beaver Bundle songs and were learning to lead the ceremonies.] Last summer "Three Bulls" purchased a third outfit from a Blackfoot but during last Winter "Old Moon" sold his to a S. Pegan [South Piegan]. These transfers are made by a payment of horses, and a ceremony of installment as is made in all religious regalia so acquired and disposed of. An Indian buys the regalia in fulfillment of a vow or promise made in time of sickness. [This transfer of Beaver Bundles is thought to

91

Running Wolf, the holy man and ceremonial leader, in 1913. He was also known as Everyone Talks About. Behind him is his son Cross Guns, or Tom Daly. Next to Cross Guns is his wife, who was the old Mrs. Jim White Bull. On Cross Gun's right is Tom Many Feathers. Sitting next to Running Wolf is his head wife, Nice Owl Woman. (Glenbow Archives)

have originated after the Old Days. Originally, a Beaver Man kept his Bundle for most of his lifetime. He usually had one or more students to whom he passed on his Teachings over a long period of time. His Beaver Bundle generally passed on to one of these students, who then became the active Beaver Man.]

MOON DANCE, FEB. 3RD 1892, 11:30 A.M.
I will now describe in detail the last dance I witnessed. Three Bulls house is a big building about 20 feet square, the door and window faces the South. When I entered, there were present 17 men and 8 women. Opposite the entrance was a space on the north side, against the wall, where laid the mysterious bundle as yet unrolled. Running Wolf sat next to it on the east. Three Bulls upon the left of Running Wolf and next to him was Old Moon; the other men sat against the wall side by side reaching along the east wall to the door. Upon the right, on west side, sat the squaws, the wife of Three Bulls being next to the bundle and the wives of the other two medicine men, right of her; the other squaws sat in a row against the wall thus leaving a space for dancing in the middle of the room. Near the door, in front of a stove, were several pots of rice, stewed beef tongues and tea. "Running Wolf" began the opening songs with gestures and was assisted by the other men near him.

A long, slender, forked willow was passed around the room from right to left; each person as he or she received it, held it up to the cheek and murmured a prayer. This implement is used to carry coals from fire to altar as I will show. When the stick came back to Running Wolf he made a long prayer and put it down in front of him. In front of the sacred bundle was the altar, a pyramid of clay about 6 inches in height, flattened on top [to represent a Beaver's home]. Running Wolf now handed a squaw the willow fork, who extracted from the fire a red coal which she deposited upon the pyramid. He next gave her a little piece of wool or hair which she placed upon the fork and stood waiting near the stove; Running Wolf was all this time singing. At end of the song the door was quickly opened by a woman sitting near it; the wool was cast from the fork into the fire and Running Wolf sprinkled incense upon the coal and he and all those present made signs of chasing something out of the door.

Singing renewed at once [with] gestures as if to receive something from the entrance which they placed upon their breasts. [This is sometimes referred to as the "receiving sign," the People showing that they take into their hearts whatever is being sung or prayed about.] Many of the songs were started while all the singers placed ends of their fingers to the floor. [These songs referred to our Earth Mother.] A man took the forked stick and brought a coal from the fire to the altar upon which incense was then made with sweet-grass. A song in the meantime being sung. Gesture in this was shading the eyes with hands, and searching for something on the ground. [This gesture illustrated the words in one of the opening songs, in which the Beaver says, "When spring comes I look outside, and if I see any enemies I dive back down under the water."] Running Wolf ended that song with a prayer.

Singing was at once renewed. R Wolf and Three Bulls' wife, who were the persons nearest to the bundle, now turned in their seats towards it. The woman took up the bundle and held it up a foot or so from the cushion and towards the altar; it being rather heavy she was assisted by the woman next to her. R Wolf took up a roll of raw hides and rattles and held them also towards the altar. Three Bulls held up a bag containing rattles and then several songs were sung at conclusions as the articles were set down again. After another song Three Bulls' wife unrolled the bundle, while the men spread a tanned beef hide on the floor, hair side down. . . . Continuing his songs, Running Wolf took the bag of rattles and distributed them to the musicians. [A special rawhide was spread over the tanned hide. The rattles from the Bundle may be beaten only on this rawhide.]

In next song, each musician took up one rattle and held it with handle resting on floor, and ended the song by imitating the caw of the crow. . . .

3 songs came next, rattle held as before; at end of each song they cawed, struck the upturned bottom of rattle with ends of fingers of right hand, thus mimicking very nicely the picking and cawing of the crow. Next was a song during which they all took up rattles and beat slowly a few times on the hides in front of them and ended the song by striking some quick and strong blows,

at the same time yelling in low voices. [More songs.] The two wives of the priests took a bundle of sticks from the sacred bundle and swung them to and from the altar, keeping time. [The cawing and pecking were actually imitations of ravens, not crows. The rattles were usually made either from buffalo rawhide or from scrotums of buffalo. While pecking on the rattles of buffalo skin, the ravens sang, "The wind is our Medicine—Powerful dead buffalo we want," referring to the buffalo carcasses ravens feasted upon after hunters finished butchering them. When the singers first took up the rattles and beat them on the rawhide, they sang, "My rattles are Powerful." The sticks the women took were probably extra incense tongs, which were kept with every Beaver Bundle.]

In fourth song the two squaws got up and danced around the room, one holding a root digger, a stick sharpened at one end and one edge; this was painted red as were all the implements. Whistles were produced and tooted during the following songs. After three more were sung, Running Wolf took a pipe-stem and got down upon his knees and bobbed about in which performance he was soon joined by his wife and Three Bulls' wife. With their blankets drawn up around their heads, they kept up those singular antics, working their hands in imitation of the beaver. That ended by all three people, 3 times lowering their heads to the sacred bundle and grunting several times, and then they took hold of the outside covers and shook them as if to frighten away a spirit. During all this time, "Moons" wife, who is a great wag, was cracking jokes and making fun of almost every movement of Running Wolf. [This part of the ceremony, taken with light spirit, often evokes laughter when the Old People leading the ceremony try to imitate small animals at work. The amount of fun-making at our holy ceremonies would probably amaze a visitor. But our ceremonies are meant to bring happiness and harmony, not gloominess and fear. When someone is praying, however, there is always silence and respect.]

Running Wolf and the two women, singing as they did so, now proceeded to unroll the pipe from its coverings, which were four in number, the outside one being of red stroud and the others ordinary calico. Outside of each cover was wound a long strand of buckskin, painted red. Singing ceased long before the unwrapping was finished. At 1:10, rattles and songs were renewed, but a man from the number sitting in the house brought a common pipe ready for lighting and kneeled in a most solemn manner in front of R Wolf and presented it to him. The latter dropped his rattles and took the pipe. When the singing ceased, he held the pipe with stem to the altar and made a long prayer, at the conclusion of which all responded and the pipe was handed back to the still kneeling man who returned with it to the other men, who at once lit it and passed it around to all the men.

This pipe had a stem too long for one man to light and smoke at the same time. One man applied the match, while another used the mouthpiece. [This is the proper way of lighting a pipe, even if it has a short stem. One man has the duty of "cutting the tobacco." He sits before the cutting board, mixes the smoking herbs, fills the pipe, and lights it for the first smoker.] A three-pound [a carrot, or bundle of rolled and twisted tobacco leaves] of tobacco was now divided into many pieces by the two squaws above mentioned and a portion given to each person present. The women near the door now busied themselves with serving out stewed tongues into many little pans and bowls; each singer held up a rattle while Running Wolf sang, and Moon prayed loudly 7 times. Each man and woman present was handed a single dried sarvisberry which was held waiting for the proper time to eat it. R Wolf in next song held his berry to the altar and then put it in his mouth, all doing likewise. At once he and the other musicians took up one rattle each and poked it with fingers of other hand at same time

cawing like a crow. R Wolf then took a piece of meat from the stewed tongues, a dish of which had by that time been placed in front of each person, and after praying to the earth, shoved the meat between the cracks of the floor in front of him. All the others prayed and did likewise and the feast began. [Before we eat a ceremonial meal we always break off a piece of meat and hold it up toward the Spirits of the Universe, while giving a prayer of thanks. At the end of the prayer we say, "Oki, this piece is for you, Spirits of the Earth," thus symbolizing our request that our Earth Mother share her food with us.]

Singing was renewed at 1:40. Two little sacks containing red and black paint were taken from the outfit, and R Wolf extracted a particle of the Red Paint and held it towards the altar as he sang. Next he put a small bunch of wool in left hand, poised the paint with right, and finally placed paint with the wool rolled both together and deposited them upon the altar. The same was done with the black paint, after which the squaws painted a child's face red and black. One of the men present (Cut Face) brought his child, a boy, and kneeled in front of R Wolf, laid a dollar bill at the latter's feet and waited while the child's face was painted as follows. Running Wolf continued singing with the other musicians who all rattled; covering the palms of both hands with a mixture of red paint and grease, after many waves to and from the altar, he applied the paint all over the face of the now kicking and struggling child who tried in vain to free himself from the grasp of his father who held him throughout. At the end of his process Running Wolf made a long prayer and then rubbed the stuff off his hands.

Renewing his singing, he mixed the black in same way and after striping the boy's face [painting a black stripe over the red paint], indulged in a 2nd elaborate prayer; he also painted a black ring around each wrist. The striping of the face consisted in a single black stripe down the middle of the face from forehead, at base of hair, to chin, over the nose and mouth. He finished the boy by waving the pipestem from altar to the child's body, passing it down each side . . . at last placing the mouth-piece to the boy's lips, he dismissed him with a prayer.

While her husband was thus engaged, R Wolf's wife painted three other children with many prayers, flourishes, and incantations. The prayers being to Sun, that the children may have good health and live long lives. Two little boys walked up and laid some old garments at the feet of R Wolf who painted them as before, and a baby was operated on [not surgically, of course, but ceremonially painted] by his wife, who put mouth-piece of pipe-stem to the little one's lips at the finish. Painting of the seven children was finished at 2:15. The father of the first boy I mentioned had his own face coloured red when he entered. To this Running Wolf added 4 black spots, 1 on each cheek, 1 on chin, 1 on center of forehead.

The next movement was the production from the sacred package of some dried buffalo bladders which were painted red by 3 Bulls, his hand being guided in this operation by R Wolf who held his wrist. Singing all the time without rattles Running Wolf and his wife guided the hand of 3 Bull's wife as she painted two more bladders. All four of those people now grasped at the same time a painted bladder which they brought with a solemn wave or flourish to 3 Bull's head and thence to his feet. A second bladder was used likewise. . . . Incense was then made. . . . An old woman presented herself for decoration and was followed by a squaw bearing a child, all of whom were painted. A white man's squaw [Lee's] dressed in civilized garb and carrying in her arms a white baby, was the next and last applicant. Mother, child, and some of the others, were given four daubs of dark red on cheeks, chin and forehead. Backs of their hands and wrists were also red. . . .

Running Wolf would sometimes forget the required song and at such times he would sit quite still with eyes closed searching his mind for the tune. I saw him in this perplexity cause an old man to bring a coal of fire to the altar upon which he [Running Wolf] made incense and then passed his hands through the smoke and to his head. . . . After a delay of 5 minutes his wife found the song and hummed it for him, at which he at once remembered it all and went on. . . . He and 3 Bulls took the floor dancing and whistling; one holding a pipe-stem, the other a buffalo's tail. These articles they would exchange with each other from time to time throughout the dance. They danced around to the altar and finished by handing the pipe-stem to 2 Bulls, who put it to his lips and prayed and then handed it to R Wolf. . . . And thus it was passed around the house from right to left, each person as he or she received it prayed with the mouthpiece to the lips. It took 20 minutes to complete this circle, the music was renewed as soon as the pipe reached the women, at end of which incense was made again. When the pipe-stem returned to the woman who had started it, she gave up a long prayer and laid it in its place.

Many of the Indians prayed at me although not to me of course; they wished their diety to give me a better heart, to make me more liberal; some prayed that they and I should always be as good friends as in the past. R Wolf held up the front of the hide covering the bundle to hide his actions from view and soon the sound of a bull keeping time with the rattles was heard. At 3:30 R Wolf, after 10 minutes of antics such as poking up the nose or head of the animal, exposed the article he had been hiding, which was a large otter skin decorated with a scalp tied to the nose, and bells upon the legs. The head was only stuffed. This object he lifted up and rising to his feet danced around the room to the women and handed it to them. She prayed as usual and set it in place. Running Wolf returned and went through the same performance with a large dried Beaver skin with tail and claws on.

During the next song the two women got

down upon their knees and Running Wolf's wife, dancing in that position, held her blanket in such a way as to catch one of her husband's rattles which he threw into it, at which the squaws both took to their feet and danced around the room. At 3:45, soda biscuits were passed around to the men; like all the food, this was sent around the room in the course of the sun, that which reached those men sitting near the entrance made a complete circuit. As usual a small bit was broken off a biscuit by each man and put upon the ground with a short prayer, but in this case it was done by the singers only. The women were also helped to biscuits, and Moon's wife alone made offering to the earth and prayed a lot of nonsense "at me." Running Wolf exhibited a duck skin, and holding it up, he sang 4 songs, ending each with an imitation of a Duck's call; the rattles were not used during those 4 songs. 4 squaws and Running Wolf got down on their knees and with their hands and arms over their heads, resembling antlers, they made gestures of deer, while dancing in front of the altar; at the end of each song, they turned about without altering their body configuration; all got up at the end of the fourth song.

In the following, Running Wolf's wife took a large beaver skin, and placing it on her back, she danced around; three women followed suit. . . . These hides were several times changed about among the 4 women who danced completely around the room several times, imitating the motions of beaver. . . .

At 4:20 incense was made; the assistant who brought the coal of fire for the altar, this time accidentally dropt it on the floor half way between the fire and altar; it was brushed to one side and a fresh one obtained. 3 Bulls, I noticed, all day was chewing the bark of red willow, which he bit from willow sticks he had. The fossil songs were now commenced, during which a fossil [an Iniskim] was produced by Running Wolf from the outfit. At end of one song he held it to his lips and prayed. . . . Incense. . . . The fossil was passed around and prayed to by all. . . . Incense . . . . The common pipe was filled and handed to Front Horn who pointed the stem to the Sun and made an elaborate prayer. . . . Incense. . . . Then came a song in which the rattles were used in a different manner. Each musician held up one above his head at arms length, shaking to keep time; then, all were lowered with handles touching the floor and the cawing of crows imitated. Incense. . . . The event next in order was a feast of boiled rice which was handed around and eaten without prayers or offering [because it did not represent a traditional food]. . . . Incense . . . numerous songs and prayers. . . . Tea was given out in cups, bowls, and tin pans; the squaws continued dancing. A rattle, made by stringing a number of buffalo toes to a stick by means of holes bored in the points of the toes and leather streamers through the holes, was thrown by Running Wolf into the lap of one of the dancing women. The dancer was free to throw it to anyone, who then must get up and dance with it, and, in turn, throw it to some other person, always of the opposite sex. The woman threw it to "Moon," who got up, and after dancing around a few times, threw it to Running Wolf's wife, who responded and danced near me and threw the rattle to me. Not caring to join the festivities to such an extent, I threw it to an Indian near me, who took the floor and threw the rattle to the woman who had it first, who, in turn, deposited it on the knees of Spotted Bull, who was still dancing with it when music stopped, which seemed to cause much merriment. Incense 7:25. Song and prayer by R Wolf. More songs and dance by woman. Each rattler, holding up a single rattle, all sang the closing songs from 7:30 to 7:35. Two women faced the door and danced during these songs; at the 4th part, the door was thrown open and they danced out. The musicians knocked rattles together in the air to close off the last song.

BUNDLE CONTENTS

As Beaver Bundles were most sacred and scarce, one can imagine that collector Mrs. Walters was most interested in acquiring them. Here is what she says about them in her notes:

The beaver bundle seems to serve general rather than specific purposes. Yet anyone in trouble may make a vow to give a berry soup or feast for the beaver men. At the proper time, a horse, blankets or other property are given to the owner of a bundle who carries the ceremony and all pray for him. The beaver bundle is not carried to the war, but it is opened at tobacco planting time and again at the tobacco harvest and, furthermore, the ritual is connected with the Sun Dance bundle in whose ceremonials it performs an important part.

And acquire them she did. Regarding one of the Bundles she bought for $150, Mrs. Walters includes the following comments by Creighton:

"This bundle is not very well recorded because it came from the North Piegans. It was known as the Elk Tongue bundle. It belonged to a man whose name was Elk Tongue who had it for years then it was transferred to a Blood man named Not Good, and he had it for ten years and transferred it to a man, Scraping White [the Old Man's stepfather], and he had it several years and he gave it to Wolf Bull, he had it for eight years and Not Good wanted it back and he had it for sixteen years and now he sold it. .... You can hang it on the wall."

Also among Mrs. Walters's notes is an itemized contents list of what she identifies as "Second Beaver Bundle." She also had a "first" Beaver Bundle, which she got from our People. Elsewhere in her notes, she refers to this first one as Blackfoot Beaver Bundle and auxiliary bundle. The "auxiliary bundle" is actually a set of bags containing accessories used during the ceremony. We do not consider this a "Bundle."

Here is the list of what she found in the main Blackfoot Bundle:

Outer wrapping—red painted skin. Inner wrapping—buffalo hide. Thong for tying bundle. "Buffalo rock" [Iniskim]. Buffalo skin wrap for rock. Buffalo rib. 4 sticks about 10 inches long. 6 bladder bags tied together. 32 bird and animal skins. Awl. Bladder bag (inside of animal skin). Bladder bag (inside of same skin), contains— Sandstone pipe bowl. Beaded fur charm (inside of same skin).

And in the "auxiliary bundle":

Nez Perce bag [the large, walletlike bags woven from corn husk strands by the Nez Perce People, obtained by trade and long-favored for holding rattles and other accessories of Beaver Bundles]. 11 rawhide rattles. Rattle of thong-tied Elk hooves. 8 smooth sticks, 8 inches long. 2 braids of sweetgrass. 2 skin bags tied together, red paint and black paint. Skin bag, containing two buffalo rocks. Feather and weazel-trimmed pipe stem in red "stroud" [coarse blanket] case. Long slender stick. Piece of broomstick in red stroud case [to replace a missing second sacred Pipe]. Rectangle of painted raw-hide.

The missing Pipestem might have been worn out, broken, lost, stolen, or buried with a previous Owner. In the Old Days the missing Stem would have been remade. That only thirty-two skins were left with the main Bundle in 1939 gives some indication that Beaver Bundles were then no longer kept up. Long ago, many more skins would have been included. It is possible that the missing skins were not replaced because their songs had been forgotten, making them unnecessary in the ceremony, or because people were uncertain which skins were missing or how to replace them. Clearly, the People no longer had the intimate knowledge of nature that had been required of Beaver Men in the long-ago.

Mrs. Walters itemizes the "bird and animal skins" of the main Bundle:

Crow—whole skin—somewhat decayed—identified.

Common loon—whole skin, stuffed slightly

Common loon—whole skin, stuffed slightly, possibly male and female

Western grebe [a type of water bird]

Western grebe—with blue beads for eyes

Little brown crane. Some stuffing in body. Not in good repair.

Sand hill crane—bad repair—some stuffing in head and body—legs missing

American merganza [merganser]—whole skin

Whistling swan—complete skin

Eastern kittiwake [a type of gull]

Eastern hairy woodpecker, male, very fragmentary

Head of male ruddy duck, sewn to body of a western grebe, curious bag-like body—made by sewing into grebe skin a piece of cloth (in breast)

Buffalo head duck—entire

Part—skin of ruddy duck—male—as bag for tobacco—or to be slipped over hand

Composite pigeon skin—body well stuffed and head missing

Head of western grebe

Head of heron or horned grebe, identification not possible, rose colored globular beads for eyes.

Hybrid red-shafted flicker, eyes of blue beads —repairs with cloth and thongs

Foot of western grebe

Part of pin tail duck—no head—fragmentary condition

Ground squirrel, not clearly identified
   "   "   "   "   "
Muskrat—whole skin, not stuffed
   "   "   "   "   "
Muskrat—fore part of skin—like pouch

Muskrat—whole skin, not stuffed

Ground squirrel—a mere fragment

Pine squirrel—skin remains whole

Long-tailed weasel

Fawn skin—whole skin—open at neck and rear—a cloth bag inserted probably for tobacco, but no indication of such use.

Beaver skin—whole skin and tail—adult—thong in nose

Beaver skin—whole skin and tail—not stuffed (young)

Mink skin—whole—rose colored beads for eyes

Piece of buffalo skin—hair on—skin side red. Listed as wrapping for buffalo rock

Buffalo rib—rubbed with red paint—shows polish on midsection where edge is sharp, as if used for scraper. [It was used to stir the sacred soup for ceremonies.]

Skin of a young badger—body drawn out at the neck—to form bag. Part of the breast and tail reinforced with red strouding.

Straight sandstone pipe—grey

Bladder with handful of dried berries, probably service-berries. One large berry was found in the bowl of the pipe.

A typical bone awl from deer leg. Painted red—probably used as a pipe stoker, but not blackened by use.

Charm of badger fur, a beaded top piece, with short strip of weasel tail as a base setting, a thong for suspension.

Following this list were these notes:

In skinning animals and birds for Beaver Bundles, the idea seems to be to pull the body out through the neck or the rectum area. This enables the skin to be stuffed and, in some cases, a cloth bag or poke inserted for tobacco and other ob-

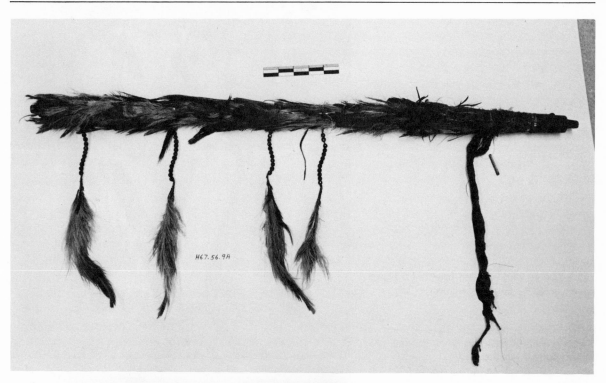

Top: The sacred Pipestem from the Beaver Bundle that once belonged to Eagle Ribs.

Left: Sacred objects from a Beaver Bundle. The rawhide bowl has a willow hoop around its opening. It was used to serve the sacred soup during the planting ceremonies of the sacred tobacco, which Beaver Men used to lead. In the bowl are a bunch of dried serviceberries. The two digging sticks were used to make the holes for the sacred seeds. Offerings of tiny moccasins are tied to one stick for the Tobacco Spirits. The Iniskim, or sacred stone, at the right, was often left nearby the sacred plants for protection. Sacred Tobacco was last planted by the Bloods around 1871.

Right: Calling Last, seated in front of his Beaver Bundle in 1958. (Glenbow Archives)

Bottom: Calling Last dancing with the sacred Pipe from his Beaver Bundle. He is blowing on the eaglebone whistle in time to his dancing. (Alberta Provincial Museum)

jects. Now and then, the neck and head and even the body cavity is stuffed with rags, or cotton to fill up space. In a few examples we have found sweet grass, etc. thrust into the cavity.

When the skin begins to fall apart, especially in case of birds when legs, wings, and head begin to separate, crude attempts may be made to fasten them together. Not always is good knowledge of specimen characters shown; as when a duck head is fastened to the body of a grebe.

Finally as to the peculiar sandstone pipe bowl. It shows signs of weathering like an archeological specimen. It has not been handled much, with no signs of use in smoking. It does not fit the stem of decorated pipe accompanying the bundle [though it might have fit the missing Stem].

OUR LAST BEAVER BUNDLES

The Beaver Bundle ceremony began to lose its spiritual meaning when our People, settled down on the reserve, no longer lived closely with the birds and animals. The North Blackfoot People were the last to use Beaver Bundles as part of the traditional planting ceremonies of the sacred tobacco. These were continued until a few years ago, although no sacred tobacco had been grown among the Bloods and Piegans for a very long time.

Percy Creighton was incorrect in 1939 when he wrote Mrs. Walters, "There is no longer a beaver bundle in the tribe." There were still more than half a dozen at that time. But by 1965 there remained only two Beaver Bundles on the Blood Reserve. One belonged to Stealing-Different-Things-Woman, the old widow of Rides-at-the-Door, and our last holy woman. This Bundle was scorched a few years ago when the house it was kept in burned down. The old lady managed to escape the fire safely with her sacred Natoas Bundle, her holy woman's headdress, and, somehow, the Beaver Bundle. She and her husband had re-

ceived it from a South Piegan family to whom they had transferred a Natoas Bundle during a Piegan Medicine Lodge ceremony. This Beaver Bundle was last opened by old Calling Last.

Calling Last was our last Beaver Man. He owned the other Beaver Bundle still with us in 1965. It had been transferred to him many years before by a Blood man named Calling at Night. It was this Bundle that Calling Last sold to the Alberta Provincial Museum, and the one used in the transfer ceremony the museum recorded.

Although our People find it difficult to pray sincerely and communicate with the Spirit World in the presence of such physical distractions as cameras and nonbelieving persons, perhaps the Old People permitted this filming and recording because they were told that without such a record, young Bloods might never again see Beaver Bundle and Medicine Pipe ceremonies performed properly.

In justifying the filming, Calling Last told the People, "The white men bought the Bundle. It's theirs. It belongs to them, if they want to take pictures."

Understandably, this recording of the museum's is regarded with mixed feelings by our People. Although it was simple for the recorder to pick up the words of the ritual, and later for someone to translate and write them down, how could a machine possibly absorb the true spiritual meanings of the ceremony? How could such a transcription really succeed, when there were numbers of outsiders, along with technicians adjusting lights, microphones, and cameras? And when the sacred place of honor, where the Beaver Man was supposed to sit, was occupied by an anthropologist representing the museum? Nevertheless, while this ceremony was almost totally without the Spirit of life in harmony with nature, we are fortunate to have a complete record of it. As things turned out, it was the last Beaver Bundle ceremony ever celebrated. Calling Last died shortly after this.

101

Woman doing a sacred Beaver Bundle Dance. (Alberta Provincial Museum)

Mrs. Rides-at-the-Door, or Stealing-Different-Things Woman, hands one of the sacred skins to a representative of the museum, while Mrs. White-Man-Left continues to dance with a sacred skin. (Alberta Provincial Museum)

Praying with offerings from the sacred berry soup. From left to right: Calling Last; Bob Black Plume; Joe Gambler; and Albert Chief Calf. (Alberta Provincial Museum)

Building the Beaver Lodge, the Beavers sing: "In the spring, when I come out, I look around; if I see any enemies I dive back down." (Alberta Provincial Museum)

Mrs. Rides-at-the-Door and Mrs. White-Man-Left imitate buffalo while shaking bunches of buffalo hooves from the Beaver Bundle. (Alberta Provincial Museum)

The Fourth Morning in Camp

Like everyone else, we awoke late on the fourth day. That morning no bright light from Sun heated up the walls of our tipi. I got dressed and looked outside the door: a solid bank of fog shut off the view beyond the edge of the campground. Sun was hidden by the cold drops of mist that filled the air. The fogbank looked like the front of a prairie fire—something greatly feared by the People when they camp out on the dry summer prairie. More than once, the People have hurriedly taken down their camps while wind-blown flames raced toward them.

The origin of the name *Blackfoot* probably came from such prairie fires. The forest and mountain-dwelling neighbors of our long-ago People called the prairie dwellers Blackfeet because their moccasins were always black from walking through scorched areas of their country. Another story has it that our People's moccasins were blackened by the dark soil of our former northern country. Both explanations were probably true, at different times.

There are also two possible origins of our own tribal name, *Blood*. One common explanation is our ancestors' custom of keeping their face and clothes covered with sacred red paint. Or the name could have come from the time some of our People wiped out a camp of Kutenai People and returned home with blood smeared all over themselves. Whatever the origin, our People do not refer to themselves by this name when speaking in Blackfoot. Our own name is *Kainah*, "Many Chiefs." It is said that some of our People were always bragging about their accomplishments, so that the other divisions said of us, "Those People certainly must have many chiefs." Our name is described in sign language by drawing the forefinger across the mouth from one side of the face to the other, symbolic of a common method of face painting in the Old Days.

The Piegans are known as *Pikunni* in Blackfoot language. It refers to a People who wear scabby robes. The wives of the long-ago Piegans were thought to have been lazy, so that their buffalo robes were often poorly tanned with hard, or scabby, spots on them. In sign language, we refer to the Piegans by rubbing a closed fist in a small circle over one of the cheekbones. This symbolizes a custom among the Piegans of painting their cheeks with sacred red paint. For some years the Piegans have formed two of our four divisions; one lives north and the other, south.

The word for Blackfoot is *Siksika*, and the sign is made by drawing the hand over the foot, from toe to ankle, and pointing to something black. In our language this refers to our northernmost division only.

As we ate breakfast on this foggy morning,

our door curtain was quietly lifted from the outside and a blanket-covered figure quickly stepped inside. The mysterious visitor was our favorite uncle, Atsitsina. Sitting down at my left, he let the blanket drop to his waist. He watched the door, saying to us, "I'm scared they might catch me, you know! That's why I haven't been staying with you at the camp. The Horns don't have enough members and they might grab me and make me join with them. Some of them are pretty close friends of mine."

When a younger society takes over the Horns, it must have enough members of its own to fill all the memberships of the Horns. If not, the new members will recruit additional, and occasionally unwilling, members. The recruiters wear blankets over their heads and carry a filled pipe as they approach the home of the intended captive member. If they can catch him inside and touch him with the pipe, he must smoke it, thereby agreeing to join the group. This can be done anytime during the year, but is most common while the People are gathered at the Sun Dance Camp. It is a well-known tradition all our People respect. However, as Atsitsina was over seventy years old, and the average age of new Horns members less than forty, it was unlikely he would be called on in this manner.

"Well, they might not try to catch me," Atsitsina admitted, "but I'm scared to join them, so I don't want to take any chances. You know," he went on, "my brother, Ksachkom ["Earth," or Fred Eagle Plume] is joining, and he still needs to find a partner. Everybody knows that I never did join the Horns, so they might try to get me now."

I asked why he had never joined, since most of his friends had been members several times. He replied, "Well, you know that I've always been with Medicine Pipes. I never thought that I could devote myself to both these things properly, so I just took part in one."

I waited for him to go on. When he didn't I asked, "How come your dad, Natosina, was able to take care of both things properly—besides learning other holy Ways?"

He replied, "You know we don't talk about the Horns Society if we don't belong to it. There is a lot of Power and secrets with that society. I've always been scared of their Power and I don't like to have anything to do with secrets. Maybe I couldn't keep secrets good enough. I always got enough Power from my Medicine Pipes. And I didn't have to keep any secrets with them."

Then he told us about the time he was almost captured to join the Horns:

"Back in the thirties, I was trying to live like a white man. I went to the Catholic church on Sundays, and I worked on my farm all week long. I was a pretty good farmer. I had cattle and horses and farming equipment, and a lot of acres to work. I didn't even go to the Sun Dance Camps because that was during the busiest time of the farming season. Well, this one summer, I was cutting my hay, while most of the People were camped up here at the Buttes. I was at home, my wife was feeding me some dinner, when we saw a car drive up. I recognized the car from a distance; it belonged to a friend of mine. I got up and walked to the door to say hello to him. But before I opened the door my wife called, 'Wait, don't open the door. There's some men getting out of that car and they got blankets on!' I looked through the curtain just when one of them was taking a pipe from the car seat and hiding it under his blanket. I knew right away what they came for, so I ran to the back of the house and jumped out through an open window. I left my saddle horse just standing there by the house. I ran all the way back to where I was haying. My wife told them that I was working somewhere in the fields, so they left and drove to somebody else's house to try their luck. Gosh, if they had caught me, I would have had to quit my farming right then and move up to the camps. And I would have had to give up most of my horses to

105

pay for my membership. Maybe I wouldn't have had enough horses left to keep on farming. That's what happened to some others who joined."

Our uncle was born in about 1900 to Sikski-Aki and Natosina. His mother became old. Later, her name was given to the infant girl who was to become my wife. Before SikskiAki, his father had a first wife called Marmot Woman; and before Natosina, his mother had been married to Low Horn, who was killed on his way to the Sun Dance Encampment of 1898.

Our uncle's dad, Natosina, was best known by the name Eagle Plume; and our uncle himself is officially registered as Willie Eagle Plume. At one time he was known as Big Snake, the name of his father's brother. And now, as we fed him breakfast, he told us he had taken a new name, this one from his father's half-brother, Aukitsikin-nih, "Bad Moccasin." But he is best known as Atsitsina. It was a childhood name that remained with him throughout his life.

At first many of our People receive a baby name referring to a personal characteristic. Later, as they grow into childhood, they are given a childhood name, usually in honor of an ancestor or other successful person. Then, upon a first war-raid or distant journey, a person may take an adult name for himself, or be given one by others. Finally, in old age, many give up their names to some favored young relative and take on their final name. A person might also change his name for other reasons, such as being inspired by dreams.

I used to think that our uncle's name was Glove Man, the literal translation of the word *Atsitsina*. But just recently I learned that his name is actually understood to mean "Prairie Owl Man." He explained how this happened:

"Oki, the reason my name is Atsitsina—I'll tell you the story. My father's sister, her name was Three Owl Woman, and her husband, his name was Sits-With-His-Chest-Out, they had two children. Their youngest child was a little older than

me. He was very attached to me from the time I was born. I probably had an infant's name, but I don't know what it was.

"One time, that little boy came running into our lodge because he heard my crying. He looked at me and he said, 'That little child is very cute. He looks just like an atsisi.' Those are the birds that make their homes in the ground on the prairie. Some kinds stay in the woods, but this kind stays on the prairie; and we call it a prairie owl.

"Those Atsisi are really cute. They are really small. If a person sees them, they look like an owl. They have big eyes, but they are small, about the size of a pigeon, at the largest. Long ago, an Old Man said not to kill them. He said, 'If you call them they will listen to you and you will be able to pick them up and you can look at them.' And that's true—I know—when you see one you just call to it, *At-see-tsee, at-see-tsee*, and you go toward it, slowly. It will just look at you. *At-see-tsee, at-see-tsee*; you don't hurry it, you just go slowly. You go easy. *At-see-tsee.* You wear a glove to pick them up. That's why they're called *atsitsi* ["glove"].

"Oki, so that boy said, 'He looks like an at-sitsi,' and they added *ninna* [man] to make it *Atsitsi-na*. My brother [the boy who gave him the name; cousins are called brothers among the Blackfeet], he was Little Buttocks. Later he became On-the-Edge-Piegan. He's been dead for a long time. I became well known as Atsitsina, and they are still calling me by that name."

SMOKING PIPES

Atsitsina usually sang our Bundle's songs whenever he visited us, but this time he was afraid his familiar voice could be easily heard around the early-morning camp. He asked that we postpone the songs and help him with a task.

"I came to ask, could you put a hole through this pipestem? I must make some pipes. Some of

Atsitsina.

the new Horns came to see me already. They all want new pipes. Could you help me make them?"

Each member of the Horns Society must have his own smoking pipe. It should be of our traditional style, with a black stone bowl. There are very few such pipes left among our People. Most of them have been buried with their owners or sold to collectors and museums.

Atsitsina went on: "Used to be lots of men here that could make pipes, but not any more. My dad made lots of pipes. All the time he worked on one or two, when he wasn't busy doctoring or leading ceremonies. He used to get a good horse for just one pipe. I think he was the last one that made pipes in the really old way [using the elements of hot and cold to chip the stone into shape]. I never learned how to do it that way. Only way I can make them is with a hacksaw and a file and a hand drill."

I saw evidence of Atsitsina's skill and popularity as a pipemaker when he and I were visiting the Provincial Museum in Edmonton. Eric Waterton took us down to the museum's storage area and showed us the large number of pipes they had collected over the years. Atsitsina and I were looking for ideas for future bowls that we would make. Every time I picked up a pipe and said, "Say, here's a nice one," he would look at it carefully, smile in recognition, and reply, "Yeah, I made that one for so-and-so about so-many years ago."

As we sat in the tipi and talked, I took two of my pipestem cleaning rods and stuck them into the midst of our fire to heat them up. The rods consist of straightened coat hangers with one end bent into a handle and the other sharpened to a point with a file. Traditionally, one asks a person living a straight life to burn the hole through a pipestem, so that the hole will go straight through and bring good luck to the smoker. I considered it an honor that Atsitsina had asked me to perform this duty.

After the rod ends turned red from the heat, I took one in my right hand and held the stem in

107

my left. The stem was made from a branch of silverberry willow, a popular wood for making pipestems. However, the most popular pipestem wood is a species of ash that has a nice-looking straight grain, found in the country of the Crow and Sioux People. In the Old Days it was brought back to Blackfoot country by members of war parties. Today it is obtained by trade or gift, or else our People cut it themselves while visiting in that country for a powwow encampment.

Before beginning the hole, I prayed that I would continue to live a straight life and that the hole in this pipestem should be evidence of whether or not I would do so successfully. If the hole should come out through the side of the stem, it would be a bad sign for me and my family. I made three passes toward the spot and then pressed the heated point against the core of the stem. As the first wire cooled off, I placed it back into the fire and took up the other one. In this way, the soft core of the stem was easy to burn through. Slowly, I turned the stem in my hand to make sure that the hot wire would burn a hole straight through.

Atsitsina described how holes were put through pipestems in the Old Days: "My dad said that ever since he could remember there had always been some wire around the camps, but he told me that they used to use long twigs of hardwood the same way that we use wire. Before that, in the long-ago, they must have made their pipestems the same way that I showed you to make a pipestem on a war trail—just cut a dry stick from a rose bush, or something similar, and split it in half with a knife. When it's split that way, then you can scrape the stuff out of the middle. When you put it back together, you can seal it shut with pitch or with that glue they used to make by boiling hooves, and then you can wrap wet sinew or thin buckskin all along it."

A little puff of smoke from the other end of the stem signaled my success at burning through a straight hole. As soon as the stem had cooled,

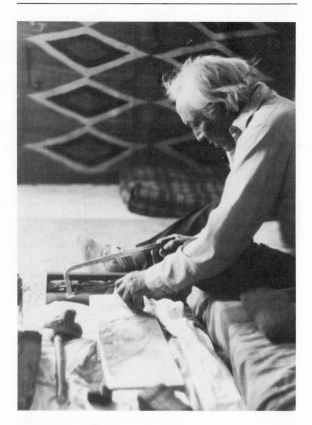

Atsitsina at work on pipes.

Atsitsina took his pocket-knife and began scraping off the bark. We leave the bark on until the hole is finished; that keeps the heat from splitting the stem.

Let me tell you something of our black stone pipe bowls. They are basically acorn-shaped and rest on a rectangular base. Atsitsina thinks that the shape of our pipe bowls was not so ornate before the introduction of metal tools, about two hundred years ago. Before that time, pipemakers used sharpened pieces of flint or quartzite to drill their bowls. They made what we call "straight-pipe" bowls, in the shape of a tube, like a thick cigarette-holder. A few of these ancient bowls sur-

A drilled pipe-bowl, ready for final shaping and sanding.

vived as contents of Medicine Pipe and Beaver Bundles.

The inverted-T-shaped "peace pipe" bowl, common among most of the Plains tribes, was sometimes obtained by our People in trade or as gifts. The red stone, catlinite, that these bowls are made of, is not found anywhere in our Blackfoot country. A Gros Ventre man once gave Atsitsina a block of this stone, from which he carved a couple of small bowls. Our traditions do not allow the use of red-colored bowls during ceremonies, as the red pipe represents the bowl style of our traditional enemies. Such pipes should be used only for personal and social smoking. In spite of this, a few of our sacred Pipes have had red bowls (including ours), and an occasional participant brings a red pipe to use in a holy ceremony, perhaps without being aware of this long-ago tradition.

Blood pipemakers have always obtained their stone from the same ancient quarry. It is on a cutbank along the Belly River, just at the edge of the city of Lethbridge, Alberta. The dark-gray stone sticks out of the loose soil in thin layers that run along the face of the cutbank. We dig out the stone from beneath the surface, so that it will not be dried hard. Then we throw the chunks as forcefully as we can down the hill. At the bottom of the hill we gather up the pieces that did not break. As an additional test of strength, we may strike together two doubtful stones. Some take the stones home and soak them in water, then lay them under their beds overnight. Good stones will be dry by the next day, while the bad ones will have wet lines wherever there are cracks.

After we select a good stone, we study it so that its natural shape can be best utilized in the shaping of the bowl. The outline of the bowl is then scratched into the stone. With a hacksaw the stone is sawed into an inverted-T-shape, following the scratched outline. A brace and bit are used to drill holes into two ends of the T-shape until they meet in an L-shape. These holes are about the thickness of a little finger. With a screwdriver, or similar tool, the hole into which the tobacco will be placed is now enlarged until it suits the maker. Sometimes it is large enough for a thumb to be inserted. The acorn shape of the bowl is started by sawing with a hacksaw small pieces off the stone at the top and bottom. After this, the bowl is roughly oval-shaped, but the sawing leaves sharp edges. These sharp edges are removed with a file. Two narrow pieces are often sawed off from the base so that a boatlike keel will be left on the bottom of the finished bowl. To complete the bowl, a great deal of filing and sanding must be done. A rasp is first used, then a smoother file, and finally various grades of sandpaper. The bowl is worked in this way until it is smooth and its appearance pleases its maker.

The holes are always drilled before the finishing work is begun because the drilling is difficult and risky. I have cracked several promising bowls because I put too much pressure on the brace or used a stone that was too weak. Besides, it is easier to shape the bowl around the holes than it is to drill the holes according to a specific shape.

After the bowl is shaped, it must be blackened. Atsitsina taught me the method of blackening shown to him by old Natosina, his dad. He made me promise to preserve the knowledge as a "family secret," for that was how his dad had kept it. Since most pipemakers use variations of the same method, I will tell you some that have been used.

A brief study of Blackfoot pipes, published in the American Museum of Natural History's Anthropological Papers of 1963, comments on two Blood pipemakers interviewed in 1947 by an anthropologist named John Ewers. Both Blood pipemakers were also Beaver Bundle Owners. One of them was Small-Back-Sides, better known by his other name, Not Good. He was seventy-two years old at that time. Ewers had this to say about his pipemaking:

Small-Back-Sides' simple hand tools differed from those used by other pipemakers. He employed a hand drill, composed of a narrow V-shaped metal shaft, set in a wooden cross-handle. Holding this tool . . . he drilled the stem hole first, and then the bowl hole. He enlarged the latter with a flattened, sharp-sided screwdriver. He shaped the outside of the bowl with a rasp, then erased the tool marks with commercial sandpaper.

Small-Back-Sides said that he usually drilled and shaped his pipe bowls during the winter months. When cottonwoods were in bud the following spring he blackened the pipe bowls by rubbing the surfaces with sticky cottonwood buds, covering them with grease, and holding them over a fire of buckbrush. Finally he polished the blackened pipes with a cloth.

Old Iron, father of Ponah and Mrs. Red Crow, was the other pipemaker interviewed in 1947. He had owned Medicine Pipes nine times during his lifetime. Ewers describes his pipemaking methods:

Although the Blood Indian, Iron, was reputed to have been 89 years of age in 1947, he told me that he had been making pipes for only 2 years. He used a black stone which he picked up here and there beside rivers and which did not require blackening.

Iron took the stone home and boiled it for a short time to soften it. He worked at his pipemaking for short, intermittent periods, sometimes laying the work aside for several days before returning to it. Before each work session he boiled the stone. He drilled the bowl and the stem hole before shaping the outside with a file. He removed the file marks with commercial sandpaper.

Iron's stone appeared to be inferior and his method of boiling it to soften it was unique among modern Blackfoot pipemakers. He acknowledged that if he boiled it too long it would crack. He also was afraid to exert much pressure in drilling holes for fear of cracking the stone. His pipes were relatively small in size.

Pipemakers went to different places to gather the materials with which to blacken their completed bowls. Because a man was once seen blackening his new pipe bowl on top of a hill about five miles southeast of Cardston, that hill is still known as Burning the Pipe Black on Top of the Hill.

In recent years a few people have tried to make copies of old-time pipes to sell to collectors of such things. Some examples I have seen would have been used for slingshot ammunition by the Old People. One maker, whose lack of skill was outrageous, admitted using black shoe polish in an effort to duplicate the old-style black gloss. He hurriedly produced it to satisfy an American collector who was in the area to buy "relics from the Old People."

When it was time for Atsitsina to leave, he apparently forgot his fears of being tapped by the new Horns members. I walked him to the door, where a relative was waiting to take him by car. He left openly, saying he would return in a few days to take me to another part of the Belly Buttes to collect some plants and teach me about them.

As he left, Atsitsina said, "I sure would like to pray with my old Pipe when they open it. You go and pray for me, huh?" He was referring to the Backside-to-the-Fire Medicine Pipe, which he had twice kept in the past. We knew that Jim Twig, the present Owner, was going to transfer it after the opening ceremony, but Atsitsina was again afraid to be so easily accessible to recruiters for the Horns.

Sun had burned off most of the fog by this time. We could see the Motokiks walking in a line toward the east, just outside the camp circle.

MOTOKIKS: THE WOMEN'S SOCIETY

The Motokiks had put up their lodge on the evening of the third night in camp. It was not big. They had begun to put it up as we started our supper, and as we finished, so were they. Their lodge looked like a small Medicine Lodge without any coverings or boughs. The framework was covered with tipi linings around the sides and tipi covers over the top. A long tipi pole, donated by someone in camp, was used as the Center Pole, and stuck out far above the top of the lodge. Just above where the roof poles intersected the Center Pole, a small stick was tied firmly, crosswise and at a slight angle, making it look something like a Christian cross. Its purpose is not known and is probably one of the secret traditions of the society.

The Horns and the Motokiks are companion societies. Some parts of their ceremonies are pub-lic, and other parts are so sacred they are performed only before members and explained and passed on only to members. The following is a fairly brief but accurate description of the society, published by the American Museum of Natural History over fifty years ago.

Some specimens were collected [from the Motokiks Society]. However, some secrecy was maintained as to details, and the writer gained the impression from Blood informants, that the awe in which the Matoki was held was secondary to the Horns. He was told that as a rule, the wives of Horn Society men were also members of the Matoki. This was explained as proving that the great prestige of the Horns gave one the social level desirable for Matoki membership. According to the recollection of my informant the leading woman in the Matoki was usually the wife of the leader of the Horns.

The members of the Motokiks Society are divided into four groups, all under the leadership of the head woman known as the Pole Owner. Her annual duty is to obtain a new Center Pole and to attend to its ceremony when it is erected. The Center Pole is always left as an offering after the ceremony each year. One woman was a Pole Owner for fifty-four years, according to Percy Creighton. Her name was Pretty Wolverine Woman. When she gave up her rights, she was succeeded by Moccasin Woman.

Each member cares for a sacred Bundle, kept in a rawhide container. The main contents are headdresses and sacred paints. Anyone in camp may see the members dressed in their headdresses and paints, so I can tell you more about them.

Traditionally, the Motokiks are divided into the Snakes, the Birds, the Bulls, and the Scabby Bulls. Much of the following information comes from the notes of Mrs. Walters, who took such an interest in the Motokiks she tried to buy all their Bundles for her collection. Although she didn't get them all, she got many, mostly from Percy Creighton, whose wife was one of the leading members.

An important member of the Motokiks is the pipe lighter. She takes the smoking pipes to the society lodge fire and lights them whenever they are to be smoked. The last pipe lighter was Spear Woman, who died of old age while visiting in Browning in 1934. Percy Creighton obtained her Pipe Lighter's Bundle for Mrs. Walters. Only the assistant pipe lighter could then fulfill the duties of pipe lighting. The assistant happened to be Percy Creighton's wife.

Mrs. Walters comments that in 1939 there were fifteen active members during the Motokiks ceremonies; in 1946 there were sixteen. During our recent encampment only eight women took part in the ceremonies, led by Mrs. Laurie Plume, the Pole Owner.

In 1936 Percy Creighton asked the oldest man on the reserve, who was ninety-four years old, if he had ever heard about the time when the Motokiks were first organized. Creighton wrote Mrs. Walters that the old man "in his boyhood days . . . saw the society dancing, and he don't know when this society formed together." We know that the Motokiks had been formed at least as early as 1832, when most of the Bulls Society members, very old men who had been outstanding chiefs and warriors, died in a smallpox epidemic. After the epidemic, the Bulls Society ceased to function and the surviving members gave all the society's ancient headdresses to the Horns and Motokiks.

Some of the Motokiks Bundles Mrs. Walters bought contained Bulls headdresses. Her notes, which follow, describe a Snake headdress and the contents of a Bundle whose former Owner was Small-Faced Woman.

The Bundle was kept in a cylindrical rawhide case for protection. The case had "fringe on side —triangular painted design—green and red— much worn and warped." The contents included the following:

one unused clam shell and one clam shell used to mix green paint in, along with a mixing stick, all wrapped in a bladder and kept inside a small bag of cheesecloth.

one buffalo skin bag of sacred red paint, wrapped in a piece of canvas and tied with a thong.

a bundle of sweetgrass braids wrapped in calico cloth.

a large bundle with calico cloth around it, containing the headdress parts, which were only assembled when it was used; the parts included the snake, made of stuffed, yellow-painted buckskin with a zigzag line beaded along its body, beads and bells to be attached at several points, and three plumes, consisting of many small feathers attached to three main shafts, to be attached to the snake to complete the headdress.

a batch of small feathers, some red and some natural white, in a paper wrapping.

a bone whistle, also kept inside this part of the Bundle, each member wearing such a whistle during the ceremony.

The main Bundle also contained a "loose bead trimmed pendant"; a tiny cloth bag, inside of which was a bladder filled with some kind of roots; and a small "accessory" bundle of paint bags, more roots and painting shells, and some ancient cloth and scarf wrappings.

Robert Wilson was probably the first person to photograph members of the Motokiks wearing their headdresses and putting up their lodge. In those days, the lodge was still constructed with a framework of travois. To accompany Wilson's photographs of 1892 scenes, let us read some excerpts from the 1905 notes of David Duvall, a South Piegan man who collected traditional information for the anthropologist Clark Wissler. These notes are now in the American Museum of Natural History. Duvall got most of his information from an old member who was the wife of Heavy Runner.

Top: Women of the Motokiks Society tying their travois together to make the frame for their lodge during the 1892 encampment. (R. N. Wilson)

Center: Motokiks putting up the walls of their lodge. (R. N. Wilson)

Bottom: Lodge of the Motokiks Society with the two front doors open toward the east. (R. N. Wilson)

The ma'toki dance but once a year when the camp circle is formed. Their ceremony lasts four days. First they make a shelter somewhat like the one used for a sun dance. A tipi pole is set up in the center, with a peculiar cross piece near the top. A number of travois are set up in a circle around this pole and joined together by tipi poles tied along the top, making a single railing all the way around. . . . On the sides and over the top are stretched tipi covers. At the bottom they are weighted with stones. Along the sides within blankets are suspended. . . . Near the cross piece on the pole are four transverse black bands about a hand apart. . . . The members bring their bedding and occupy their respective places during the entire four days.

There are six men attached to the society, but all the other members are women. Four of these do the singing. The remaining pair act as messengers and attendants. . . . Each woman has a red-painted backrest stick planted before her seat to support her headdress. When they sleep they lie with their feet toward the center. Just to the west side of the center pole is a fire. When food is brought in and handed to members, they pass what is given them to members on the opposite side. Each member has an individual smudge altar before her seat. . . . Along the sides next to the sitter are rows of buffalo chips covered with sage grass. Sweetgrass is used for smudge. The headdresses must always be smudged four times before they are placed on the head.

Men, women, and children go in to be painted, taking with them sun offerings of cloth, etc., which are tied to the base of the center pole. The faces of these donors are painted over with red and a blue mark made down the forehead and nose with a fork at the top . . . to symbolize the tipi pole in the center and spoken of as the tipi pole paint.

The ceremonial shelter has two doors, one at the northeast and one at the southeast. In going out members use the nearest door but return by

114

Headdress of a Bull member of the Motokiks Society, on display at the Glenbow Museum.

Headdress of a Bird member of the Motokiks Society, on display at the Alberta Provincial Museum.

Headdress of a Snake member of the Motokiks Society, on display at the Alberta Provincial Museum.

the other. The four singers use rattles and a rawhide of the same type as accompanies the beaver bundle. They sit west of the fireplace. [Spiritually, it is thought that Beaver Men in the long-ago contributed their rawhide and rattles to the society, just as they contributed the Natoas headdress to the Medicine Lodge and the sacred Pipe-stem to the Medicine Pipe Bundles.]

All the women wear bone whistles suspended by neck cords and upon these they blow while they dance. They do not all dance at once, but by groups. Thus, the four scabby bulls rise and dance. When they sit again, the feather bonnets [the Birds group] take a turn, etc. In all movements the owner of the tipi pole has absolute authority. . . . She wears a buckskin dress and a snake bonnet and sits to the right of the other snake bonnet wearers. . . . The feather bonnets

are covered over the crowns with a mass of soft bird feathers. They have tail pieces falling down on the shoulders and bearing transverse rows of small wing and tail feathers. . . . The scabby bulls wear war bonnets with horns and robes of cowskin, hair side out. They dance in single file, circling the Pole. First they rise and dance in their tracks, then move to the south side of the fire and dance, then to the west and then to the north. Next the snake bonnets rise with the tipi pole owner in the lead and dance in the same way. Next come the feather bonnets and finally the buffalo wool bonnets.

It is customary for persons who have made vows or pledges during the year, if their prayers be granted, to provide a feast of berry soup for the ma'toki. At various times during the ceremonies a pledger brings in a kettle of soup and some tobacco which is offered to the tipi pole owner with an announcement of the circumstances. Then the soup is dished out to the members and each and all pray for the pledger.

On the morning of the last day, before sunrise, the ma'toki forms in procession and imitates buffalo going to water. They seek out some depression or low place in the prairie. As they drift along they segregate, as they do in the dance. At a place designated by the leader they all lie down like buffalo.

Now, it is customary for a man or a boy to have made a vow that he will "drive in the ma'toki" at their next ceremony. His sacrifice must be a horse and many presents to the owner of the tipi pole. This man then rides out as if looking for a buffalo. When he finds them, he builds a fire with cow dung to windward. As soon as the ma'toki smell the smoke, they rise. The driver then mounts and rides toward them, at which they start for their shelter. As they proceed, he rides on their flank. They trot to the shelter, but the four scabby bulls trail slowly in the rear. When the members get inside the shelter they run around the inside sun-wise until one by one

An old woman named Maka, or "Shorty," wearing her Motokik's Bull headdress. Her face is painted for her office, and she has her society whistle in her mouth. (Edward Curtis)

Opposite page: Scabby Bull headdress of the Motokiks Society. The lady's name was Snake People Woman. (National Museum of Canada)

Some members of the Motokiks Society in 1892. The sacred headdresses belong to the groups known as the Birds and the Snakes. (R. N. Wilson)

some person lays hold of them and leads them to a seat. Two of the snake bonnets run around in the reverse way. The four bulls come in last and walk slowly around until pulled into their seats.

Like the horns and other societies the members sell, or transfer to others, usually all transferring at the same time. The ceremony seems to require four days and nights, during which time they are not supposed to sleep. . . . It is said that the entire night is given to hilarity. Joke and jest reign supreme. Some dress like men and act out the part, give orders to a wife, etc. Some roll up blankets like medicine bundles and hold mock ceremonies. . . .

The fees for buying a membership are a horse, a gun, and other property. The most expensive place is that of the tipi pole owner for which twelve horses and a proportionate amount of other property are required.

118

Shortly after Atsitsina left, we went outside our tipi to watch the Motokiks. They were already beyond the camp circle, walking in single file from east to west, along the south side of the circle. We saw Mokakin take down a spare lodge pole leaning against the back of his tipi. An offering made of willow sticks, sage grass, and cloth was fastened to the pole. Mokakin had put the offering on the lodge pole before Sunrise, so that Sun could see where it came from.

The women sat down on the ground outside the south end of camp. Mokakin untied the offering and gave it to his son Charlie, along with a filled pipe and a bunch of sage grass, to bring to the women. Charlie presented these things to one of the members and knelt before her to receive her prayer. Then she lit the pipe and passed it around. After it was smoked out, she returned it to him. The women got up and, single file, moved on to the west side of camp, where they again sat down to await anyone who wished to make offerings. They repeated this at the north and east ends, then returned to their lodge.

The next morning, people would have another opportunity to approach the Motokiks for prayers and blessings, this time in their lodge. There, the prayer seekers would be painted with the Center Pole design. We wished to have Mrs. Red Crow, the society's only remaining Scabby Bull, paint our son Wolf Child, so that he could add this blessing to his young life.

MINIPOKAIKS: THE FAVORITE CHILDREN

That evening, after the camp quieted down, we went next door again to visit Mokakin and Ponah. Eagle Ribs is always happy to entertain his guests with stories and talk. One of that night's subjects was *minipokaiks*—"favorite children." It was a tradition among our People for parents or grandparents to select a child as a favorite, one who showed particular promise to succeed in our Ways, given proper care and Teaching. If the parents of a minipoka went to many ceremonies, the child was likely to grow up to become a ceremonial leader. If the parents went to many social functions, the child was likely to learn much about leadership. Other minipokaiks, however, were simply spoiled and pampered so that they grew up expecting others to help them at the first sign of difficulty. Mokakin told us this legend, The Story of the Abandoned Children, about one minipoka of the long-ago.

This happened a long time ago. I don't know how long. I heard the story told by others when I was young.

Members of the Motokiks Society in 1972, making a ceremonial round of the camp early in the morning.

Wolf Child, after receiving a face painting and blessing from Mrs. Red Crow, during the ceremonies of the Motokiks.

119

Some children were playing in the bushes by the camp. One of the children was a minipoka. His father was the head chief. Everybody was afraid of this chief; sometimes he got a bad temper, but he was Powerful and a good leader.

Oki, the kids were playing in the bushes. The minipoka had to go to the toilet, so he went away from the kids where they could not see him. But the other kids, they wanted to know how a minipoka would take care of himself. So they watched through the bushes. When they looked at him, their eyes got big. What fell to the ground was a big pile of pretty shells, the kind Medicine Pipe Owners wear as a necklace. The children ran out from the bushes and grabbed the shells. They were so excited that they knocked the minipoka down and took all the shells. When he got up, all the shells were gone and the kids ran off through the bushes with them, singing and laughing.

The minipoka started to cry and ran home to his father. When he told his father what happened the chief became angry. Right away, he gave the order for camp to be moved and for no one to call home their children. The People had to do what the chief ordered. By the time the children were finished playing and got back to the camp, all they saw were the smoldering fires where their tipis used to be. They all sat down and cried because they knew that they had been abandoned.

One of our Old People was raised as a minipoka by his influential father. His parents located a young girl from a good family to become his wife, even though he was still a boy and living at home. He became a member of the Horns Society when he was only about twelve or fourteen, which is very unusual. The Old People say that even now he still acts like a minipoka and likes to see things done to suit himself.

While we talked about minipokaiks, Ponah admitted she had been the minipoka of her father, Iron. She said that they had a painted Medicine Tipi transferred to her. When I asked what a little girl did with a painted lodge of her own, she told us:

"It wasn't a big tipi. It was just a little tipi for kids to play in. My mother made it for me to play in with my friends. My sister and I, we went to boarding school. My mother, she put up the tipi right by the school, and nobody bothered it. She put in a panichtan [lining], and she tanned some little animals and put the skins around the inside for rugs. She even made little bags from rawhide [parfleches] and put them all around the inside. When my mother came to visit us, she stopped on the way at Long-Nosed Crow's [Wilson's Trading Post] and bought a lot of groceries. Then she told me to invite all my friends to the tipi and we had a big dinner. Even the nuns sometimes came over to sit in the little tipi with us."

Ponah said that the design painted on the tipi had been dreamed of by somebody and was actually transferred to her. The tipi was painted yellow, with four lines of stars going from top to bottom, one line at each of the four directions.

Our conversation wandered on to other things, and of course, Mokakin told us more old Napi stories.

ANOTHER NAPI ADVENTURE

One time, Napi came out from a forest and found a bunch of Gophers playing in a meadow. This was how they played: One of them would lie down in an old fireplace and the others would cover him up with earth and then build a fire on top of him. As soon as the fire got too hot, the buried one would call out, "Tsst, Tsst!" Napi asked the Gophers if he could play, and they told him he could. So he lay down in the fireplace and the Gophers put earth over him and built a fire on top of it. As he got warm, he called out, "Tsst, Tsst!" The Gophers uncovered him. Soon it was Napi's turn to build the fire.

Napi said to the Gophers, "I think it's easier

if I cover up all of you at one time." The Gophers all climbed into the fireplace, except one because she was pregnant. Napi made a hill over them and then built a big, hot fire on top of the hill. Soon he heard sizzling and popping and he knew that the Gophers were roasting. When the pregnant Gopher saw what was happening, she ran away. From her came all the Gophers that are living today.

After the fire burned out, Napi took out the roasted Gophers. He was hungry, so he ate lots of them. But soon he was full, and there were many roasted Gophers left. He decided to take a nap, and then he would be able to eat more. Before he went to sleep he looked down at his rear end and he said, "If anybody comes and tries to steal these Gophers, you make a noise so that I will wake up." Then he went to sleep.

Soon his rear end was thinking, "What will happen if I make a noise?" So it made a little noise, and Napi jumped up right away. When he looked around, he saw there was no trouble, so he went back to sleep. His rear end thought that was funny, so it did the same thing again, only it made a little bigger noise. Napi jumped up, and again seeing nothing, lay down back to sleep. This happened a few more times until Napi fell fast asleep.

After a while a Bobcat came along and found the roasted Gophers next to Napi. Bobcat saw Napi asleep and began to eat his Gophers. Napi's rear end tried to wake him up. It made loud noises at first, then really awful noises. Napi didn't wake up, but Bobcat became so disgusted that he picked up all the Gophers and took off.

When Napi finally woke up he saw that all of his Gophers were gone. He became angry at his rear end for not waking him. He took a hot coal of silverberry wood from the ashes in the fireplace and tortured his rear end with it. That's the reason we don't use silverberry wood in our fires. It smells so bad we call it stinkwood.

As sometimes happens after the laughter of an amusing story, our minds became relaxed and it was easy for us not to say anything. Our eyes became fixed on the ancient process of fire turning wood into ashes. A breeze softly flagged the canvas lodge cover against the tipi poles. The gentle sounds of evening activity seemed distant. Mokakin began to speak. "Day after tomorrow, my grandson is going to take our old holy Pipe."

Our Medicine Pipe Bundles

Mokakin's remark reminded me of the rumor that the Backside-to-the-Fire Pipe was going to be transferred during the encampment. And during the previous winter we heard that a vow had been made for "Laurie Plume's grandchildren to take a Pipe." Now, as Mokakin spoke, I began to realize there was a connection between the two rumors.

A vow is made for a grandchild to be Owner of a Bundle so that the entire family can benefit from it spiritually. In recent years, some of our Old People who felt they could no longer properly care for such a Bundle vowed for their grandchildren to take it and share its responsibilities, in this way keeping its holy Power in the family. Unfortunately, the generation gap causes as much problem among our People as among others. As a result, some families who take over sacred Bundles are only caretakers; they make no effort to learn the Teachings that make Bundle ownership a way of life.

Fred Weaselhead was going to be the new Owner of the Backside-to-the-Fire Pipe. I was surprised to learn that Jim Twig was transferring it, since he had been its Owner for only a short time. But I suppose he was quite busy with the Horns, his own family, his cattle ranch, and his schoolbus service.

"That's going to be the fifth time that Pipe is in the Weaselhead family," Mokakin said proudly. "We had it three times; our boy Frank had it not long ago, and now our grandson, he's going to have it too. It's sure different today from the time we first got it."

By this Mokakin meant that the Spirit for our Old Ways has changed a great deal since that same Bundle was first transferred to himself and Ponah forty years ago, when the transfer ceremony used to take four days. Although our People still show all the traditional respect for our Medicine Pipe Bundles and their Owners, it is often without spiritual meaning.

NINAMSKANIKS: MEDICINE PIPE PEOPLE

"Now that you are Ninamskaniks," the Old Man had said to SikskiAki and me, "you must learn to have holy thoughts all the time, so that you will inspire others to think of holy things. You must set good examples, so that others can learn your holy Ways. Leave behind your bad thoughts. Pray for those who are evil, but remain on your own good path. Have good hearts toward others and help them when in need. I will teach you what I know, but always remember to pray. Pray often and your dreams will be good. . . ."

And so, with the Old Man's guidance and

Teachings, SikskiAki and I became *Ninamska-niks*, "Medicine Pipe Owners."

Each article in our Medicine Pipe Bundle is there to inspire holy thoughts about the element of nature it represents. Under the Bundle's plaid shawl covering are several dozen ceremonial objects—decorated sacred Pipestems, a rattle, whistle, sacred paints, shells and beads, and the skins of birds and animals—each with its own song and place in the ceremony.

Our sacred Pipe Bundles mean to us what the sacred tablets, Koran, Bible, or rosary, mean to others. They are sacred objects we pray with in our tipi-temples and in our Church of the Great Outdoors. We do not pray to the objects in the Bundles; we pray to the Holy Spirits they represent.

Our grandfather, our Old Man, was Keeper of our sacred Pipe Bundle for ten years. During that time, the Bundle hung over his bed, as it now hangs over ours; it heard his songs, felt his prayers, and bathed in his sweet-smelling incense. When I lean my head against the Bundle and close my eyes, I can see his smile and hear the deep and flowing sound of his voice, and I forget my discouragements and discomforts. We are indeed fortunate, SikskiAki and I, that as we live by his Teachings, his Spirit surrounds us all the time, everywhere. As I tell you about some of the Teachings of our Medicine Pipe Bundles, perhaps then you will understand this special feeling we have for our Old Man and how he helped us to learn so much more about life in harmony with nature.

I'll begin by telling you the ancient legend, as I learned it, about how our People were first given a Medicine Pipe Bundle.

THE ORIGIN OF OUR MEDICINE PIPE BUNDLES

Oki, this story took place very long ago, when our People were able to communicate with all the Powers of the Universe. In the camps there lived a beautiful girl who was the only child of her parents. Many young men sent her presents and wished to have her for a wife, but she refused them all. She preferred to remain and help her parents, who were old and poor.

One day a young man came to her and demanded to know why she had refused to accept his courting. When her reply did not satisfy him, he became angry and shouted at the girl, "Do you think that you are too good to marry any of us?" The girl cried as she replied, "I will stay with my parents until I am married to Thunder!"

Not long after, the girl was out gathering firewood. Suddenly a man stepped out from the bushes and stood in front of the girl. He was a fine-looking young man in handsome buckskin clothes. The man said to her, "I have come for you." The girl was frightened and replied, "I cannot go anywhere with you. You are a stranger." The man smiled and said to her, "My name is Thunder, and I have come for you because I heard you telling the People that you would marry me." The girl remembered her statement and knew she had no choice but to go with her new husband.

Thunder took the girl up to his home in the Sky. She stayed with him there, all spring and summer. He was very kind to her and she was happy to be his wife. However, she was lonely for her parents back on Earth. Thunder noticed this and told her, "I know that you are longing to be with your parents and I wish to see you happy. Soon I must go away from here to my winter home. At that time I will send you back to stay with your parents. But I wish to send a present of gratitude to them, and I must first teach you the songs and ceremony to go with it. I will be sending them the most sacred thing I own, my Pipe. It is such a Powerful Pipe that it must be kept covered at all times. It must be taken outside every day so that all the Spirits in the Universe can see it. Its ownership must be shared by your parents, for it is my present to both of them."

Thunder then spent the next seven days in-

123

structing his wife in the Powers of his Pipe. Each day he taught her one of the songs he sang whenever he took the Pipe from its coverings. Finally he told her, "Each spring I will return for you. My arrival will mean the end of winter's hardships for your People and the beginning of the seasons of plenty. When I announce my arrival, your People must prepare themselves by holding the ceremony that I have taught you with my Pipe."

The girl went back home and gave Thunder's Pipe to her parents. Ever since that time our Medicine Pipes have been thought of as Thunder Pipes, and our People have celebrated the annual return of Thunder in the spring by holding the Pipe ceremonies.

In time, others were instructed to make sacred Pipes similar to the first one given by Thunder. These instructions came through Powerful dreams that were carefully interpreted before being acted upon. Only a man who had great spiritual power would make up a sacred Pipe, and only after he was convinced that his dream gave him positive approval. And the man who was selected to construct the Pipe worked under the direction of the original dreamer. Some people were also taught new songs to sing in addition to the original seven. One by one, the Spirits of different birds and animals also came to the People in dreams and asked to be remembered during the annual celebrations for the coming of the seasons of plenty. Each one offered his skin and his medicine song to be included in the ceremony. That is how our People came to believe in the spirits of sacred Medicine Pipe Bundles.

BUNDLE CONTENTS AND THEIR OWNERS

Unlike the Medicine Bundles of many other People, the contents of ours are not secret; we can discuss them as well as their spiritual powers. We keep the sacred objects bundled up so that their spiritual powers will only be used in the proper sacred way.

The main object in every Medicine Pipe Bundle is the sacred Stem. Like exceptionally long regular pipestems, they have a straight hole beginning at the carved mouthpiece and ending at the carved bowl-fitting. Sacred Pipes are very handsomely decorated, with many black-and-white ermine tails, black-and-white eagle feathers, eagle plumes, other feathers, and beads, bells, and porcupine quills. They are kept in long, tubular cases of red, blue, or black wool stroud cloth, the kind with the white selvedges brought to our People by traders of the long-ago. These cloth covers replaced the original buckskin covers as they wore out.

Spiritually, the sacred Stems represent all the Holy Powers of the Universe. They were first given by Thunder, who embodies the rain-water that helps to make everything grow. The wood stems represent all the plants that grow upon Earth; the eagle tailfeathers represent all the Above Powers, including all the birds, the eagle being the most Powerful among them; the ermine skins stand for all the Below Powers, including the animals that walk on Earth; and the beads and bells symbolize all the goodness and beauty of the Universe. The sacred Stems are attached to stone bowls that represent the strength of our Earth Mother. Her Spirit travels in the form of smoke along the long and straight path of the sacred Stem, into the body of the smoker, and as he exhales it, up into the air that flows throughout the Universe. The physical appearance of a sacred Pipe represents all the holy beauty that can be found if one lives by its holy Ways.

No one knows exactly how many sacred Pipes were made among our People throughout the ages, but there were probably no more than a few dozen. Shortly after 1900, Clark Wissler made an extensive study and concluded that there were "something more than seventeen" Medicine

Pipes among all four divisions of our People. Since there were almost that many remaining among all our People less than twenty years ago, his estimate may be low. But it does give some idea of how many there were among a tribe of over ten thousand registered members. Today there are twelve Medicine Pipes left on the four reserves of our People.

The sacred Stem constitutes the "main" Pipe in a Bundle. There is also another long Pipestem, which we call the secondary Pipe. This second Stem is not included in all the Bundles, and its original purpose has been forgotten. Its stem is flat, not round like the main Pipe's, and it is only sparsely decorated. It is kept in a cloth cover similar to the one for the main Pipe. These two sacred Stems are like father and mother to the other contents in the Bundles.

The skins of birds and animals vary according to the origins and later dreams accompanying each Bundle. Each skin represents not only its own species but also that element of nature in which it lives most successfully; this is usually mentioned in the song for that bird or animal.

Every Medicine Pipe Bundle contains the skin of an owl, representing night. Owls have the Power to succeed then, when others are handicapped. Another important skin is that of the loon, which represents the element of water. The loon has the Power of Water, where it swims and finds its food and raises its children. The skins of hawks and eagles are important because they represent the element of air, the Power to fly in the sky. The skins of antelopes and deer symbolize the element of Earth and the Power to live on the prairies and in the forests. The skin of a marmot stands for the Power to live in the high mountains; the squirrel, the Power to live in open land. A rattle of buffalo hide represents the Power of the Old People's most important source of food. Dried berries (served in a sacred soup during the Thunder ceremony) are testaments of the Powers of plants, as well as another of our Old People's

source of food. A whistle makes the sounds for the winds and all the birds that fly in the air. Pouches of sacred Earth paints represent our Earth Mother. Sweet pine needles, used for incense, speak for all that is sweet and holy. The tanned elk hide wrapped around the Bundle testifies to the majesty of that animal. The tanned skin of a black bear, wrapped around the elk hide, represents the physical power of bears and gives the Bundle strength and protection. A plaid shawl draped over all of these things gives the Bundle privacy and symbolizes the Power of the changes that have come to our Old Ways.

Sacred Pipes are smoked only during Medicine Lodge ceremonies, and not at any other time —not even during Medicine Pipe Bundle-Opening ceremonies. When taken out of their Bundles, they are not smoked but danced with. Dancing is so important that many refer to our Medicine Pipe ceremonies by the Blackfoot term *Ninamska-Paskan*—Medicine Pipe Dance.

In the Old Days, when the People lived together in lodges, the Medicine Pipe Bundle was opened on the first day Thunder was heard in the spring. When this happened and it was confirmed in the home of a Bundle Owner that the opening ceremony would be held, the wife immediately began preparing the berry soup. Owner and wife would then change into their best dress and straighten out their lodge, which soon filled with relatives, friends, and all nearby Medicine Pipe People. If the Owner was not properly educated to open his own Bundle, he asked a former Owner to lead the ceremony.

Each Bundle had its own group of followers. Those who formerly owned the Bundle always attended all its ceremonies. Close relatives of the present Owner came, and the ones who helped with the transfer payments were given spiritual rights to parts of the Bundle. Others came because they were interested in the special Powers of the Bundle.

In the Old Days, members of a band transferred ownership within their own group. When the People moved on to the reserve, they settled there according to their bands. Thus, some of our Old People knew quite well the histories of the Bundles among their own band, while they knew little about other Bundles.

Bundles are the spiritual property of their Keeper, or Owner. Our People used to live with the fact that owned property could be reclaimed at any time by nature, through loss, damage, or death. They believed that owning something meant caring for it until it was claimed by a stronger Power.

TWO MEDICINE PIPE
TRANSFERS: 1890s

Many firsthand narratives of long-ago Medicine Pipe ceremonies are available among the Piegans, but not so many among our People, the Bloods. The oldest record among the few comes from the papers of Robert Wilson in the 1890s. Those who took part in the ceremonies he witnessed still practiced their Old Ways daily, but even then were no longer totally dependent on nature in their way of life, so that they could not fully relate to the representations of nature inside the Bundles.

Although Wilson was not always aware of the meanings of the symbols he saw, I will pass on to you what he wrote.

Sacred pipe holders are easily distinguished by the free use of red paint on their person, having it rubbed all over their white blanket or coat and also over the leggings and moccasins, their wives painted the same. A pipe-holder wears upon each wrist a blue bead tied with a buckskin strand, (the wife also; or, if man does not wear beads upon wrist, he will have one bead and a shell strung upon a buckskin string on his neck.) [The Owner and his wife wear both necklaces and wristlets during the ceremony.] *Children*

who have been painted during [the] *ceremony of transfer also wear the beads. It sometimes happens that an Indian does not keep the pipe the alotted four years* [as was common for some Medicine Pipe Bundles and society memberships in the Old Days]; *a sick person's relatives may ask him for it inside of a few months of his possession of it.*

A sick man often declares that he will take [the] *pipe if he recovers, or will take it to recover. Upon* [such] *declaration he sometimes goes to lodge of owner, and pipe is unrolled and laid against his shoulders, chest, head, and wounds, with prayers all over his person. He takes it and pressing his lips against* [the] *pipe, prays for health.*

The Sacred pipe has always a recognized value in horses, and the candidate knows how many cayuses [ponies] *were paid by present owner of pipe and that he must pay a like number.* [To pay less] *would be considered an insult to the pipe and would deserve punishment in shape of bad luck.*

Value of pipes run from 3 to 25 horses [amongst] *the Bloods; these horses need not all be paid by the candidate; his friends, relatives and comrades may help him by donating a horse or two and there are generally enough willing ones for two reasons, e.g., a person paying one horse at a friend's initiation is entitled to have a child decorated at the ceremony of transferring the pipe and said child will bear more or less of a charmed life. And when his friend disposes of the pipe at end of four years or longer, his horse can be returned to him out of those paid by last purchaser. It is, therefore, a mutual advantage, for without friends so inclined the intending pipe holders might not be able to get the high priced article.* [Wilson's statements are basically correct, but the helping friends and relatives were also motivated to have the Bundle in their area of the camps. The requirement for "payments" did not limit Bundle ownership to "wealthy" persons in the Old Days, only to ambitious persons. Anyone not wealthy but who had enough ambition and spiritual power could go out on a raid and bring home enough horses to take care of the physical sacrifice.]

"High sleeper" paid sixteen out of his twenty-one horses. He had lost all his relations but one and bought the pipe to change his luck. I witnessed the ceremony of his purchase which took place in the lodge of Crop Eared Wolf [the adopted son of Head Chief Red Crow, who later became his successor], who had owned the pipe for ten years. I also was present at the transfer of a pipe from "Roach Mane" [the young-man name of Ponah's father, Iron] to "Brave Bear."

The following description I write after being present at four Thunder dances:

Inside the lodge, directly opposite the entrance, is a space occupied by a cushion to receive the pipe which was now outside, where it always stands in fine weather during the day, leaning on two sticks against the west side of the lodge. On each side of this space and extending around the lodge to the entrance in two half circles are arranged blankets and quilts for seats for the visitors who soon begin to arrive; the host (who is seated with the cushion at his left hand) tells each person where to sit; four or five men, who are good singers and know the songs used on these occasions, are told to take their places on the left of the entrance and are given tom-toms.

The Master of Ceremonies, or Priest, of the occasion, who is never the host but someone who knows all the songs of the pipe, of which there are a great many, and who is well versed in the mystic rites or functions in connection with the sacred pipes, takes his place next to space for pipe, sitting opposite to host, the cushion space being between them.

In front of cushion, between it and the fire, is a square hole dug in the ground, size about 9 or 10 inches square, and two or three inches deep; its sides being at right angles with the cushion. Upon

entrance the assembled guests sit smoking and chatting upon all topics.

Host's wife presently brings in the Sacred bundle and ties it to the lodge poles directly over the cushion. Bundle is covered with a red shawl and consists of a Bear Skin rolled around twenty or so skins of animals and birds, some of the latter stuffed, among which is an owl. In centre of bundle are several red cloth bags containing the Sacred Pipe, its two stems, a long wooden whistle, rattles and a number of articles the uses of which I will presently show.

Between the cushion and hole before mentioned is now placed a live coal from the fire. The priest places an open bag of sweet grass [actually, sweet pine] on the ground and taking right hand of host in his right hand, he guides host's hand to bag and extracts therefrom a pinch of the powderized sweet grass, while both are muttering a prayer. [The incense] is sprinkled upon the coal of fire with a spiral motion of the hand, causing a sweet odour to fill the lodge. The bundle is now taken down and waved towards this altar four times before it is set down upon the cushion. [Wilson fails to mention that the series of Medicine Pipe songs is begun before the incense is made. The singing goes on while the Bundle is taken down and placed between its Owner and the leader of the ceremony.]

Bowls and pans are now produced and the squaws bring in pails of berry broth and rice, which is served unto all present, myself among the rest, though the stuff was not very tempting to look at. I managed to make away with part of my share as my right hand neighbor said it was not good to refuse. Before eating, the oldest man present picked one berry from his dish and holding it above at arm's length began an elaborate prayer to the sun thanking him for past blessings, for his old age (70 years), and soliciting future favours for himself and host. He had hardly started before the other old men followed suit and before they had concluded, every male [and female] in the lodge was praying in the same manner, some to the sun, some to the moon, birds, stars, eniskims [Iniskims, or sacred stones] and all their numerous deities, each person concluding his prayer by placing the morsel, which he had been holding up, upon the ground and rubbing it through the grass into the earth saying: "Earth persons, I give this to you." After they had done all this, the host held up some of his food and prayed as follows:

"Oh Sun! Oh Sun, pity me, Oh Sun, pity me, pity me that my children may grow up to be men and women. Pity me, that I may be a good man with a good heart, that my horses may increase and not get stolen. Pity me, that I may not die when sick, that I may escape all danger when I travel from home. I am happy to be able to see my family around me. I am glad to be able to look at my horses, I am glad that I can move around this summer in health, I am glad that things are as they are and hope that I am to be so blessed a long time."

[At this point the food was eaten, although Wilson does not mention this.]

Priest now takes tallow and red paint and paints his hands and face, holds his hands over incense and passes them over his legs, breast, arms and head [actually, in reverse order, symbolically cleansing the evil downward from his body], praying as he does so. Host does same, but does not paint himself. They now sing a number of songs, making gestures as they sing. . . . Priest now paints the South half of the square hole in the ground Red, and the North half, Black. Priest and host and wife now proceed to unroll the pipe by untying the numerous strings; each string as it becomes disengaged is waved towards incense and then put away. From bundle is taken four plumes, two are painted Red and two Black. Host now takes a pointed red stick and makes three feints to stick it into the ground at S.E. corner of hole and at the fourth does so, making a little hole in which a Red plume is placed. Same is

done at S.W. where the other red plume is placed, then N.W. and N.E. corners [in] which are stuck the black plumes. Two small willow sticks painted red, about 2 feet long, [are] stuck upright in the ground in front of and close to the bundle, a third is tied across horizontally near tops of them, four waves being made to altar before each stick is placed in position. The mouth ends of the two pipestems are placed resting upon this crosspiece, a stuffed owl is laid with it, head also upon the crosspiece end of long wood. A quantity of tobacco, generally a 3 lb. carrot of H.B.C. [Hudson's Bay Company, which was often supplied by Wilson from his trading post] tobacco, is now divided up by host and a piece given to priest who, breaking off a small particle, holds it out in front of him and, often giving a short prayer to the earth, pushes the balance into the earth. One of the old men present counts a couple of coups which are loudly applauded. Four children, or as many as the host has, or any child relative whose parents wish it to be painted, are brought forward, and painted by Priest. All is now ready for dancing which is started by Priest, who takes some article from the Sacred Outfit, generally the fancy stem of pipe, and dances around the lodge and out through the entrance. He often has in one hand this whistle which he points up to the sun and earth, blowing as he dances, and shaking the pipestem which has a great many bells on it. After turning around outside he dances back through lodge and having danced four times, hands articles to host, who prays to them [or with them, as I have said] and puts them in their place. After some chatting, the drums start up again and sing three songs and at the fourth, one of those men present who have owned a Sacred Pipe gets up and dances around the lodge, dancing towards the pipe three times, holding out his hands as if he would take it; the fourth time he takes it and often one of the other articles and dances with them in his hands. Each man dances to four songs [actually one song, sung four times], then gives the articles to host as before. Sometimes 2 or 3 will be on the floor at same time. One may have owl, or rattle alone; they can suit themselves and take whatever they like. [Not exactly. Past and present Medicine Pipe Owners may select anything from the Bundle, but some persons who have never owned a Bundle may have had the rights to certain objects within a Bundle transferred to them. They can then always dance with those objects but not with any other.] When using the whistle they begin at a high note and descend the scale with a continuous toot, toot, toot.

In making the first three feints to take the pipe, the dancer often retreats, dancing back around the lodge making the sign to kill (as if stabbing with a knife). [This preliminary dancing Wilson describes is no longer done at all. Today, when a man gets up to dance he takes the selected object, prays, and dances four times.] They nearly all dance the same step in this ceremony, a slow, regular, vigorous jump with both of the knees bent; the tunes and songs used upon these occasions are not sung at any other time; the step in dancing is also peculiar to Calumet [Pipe] men. There is a preference shown for the owl, which is most often taken up and almost always prayed to by the dancer as he takes it in his hands, or the host when it is handed back to him. [According to our traditions, the dead come back to visit the living in the bodies of owls. For that reason owls are respected as being very Powerful, and many participants desire the spiritual strength they get by dancing with one.] At one of these dances, while one of the dancers had the owl in his hands, I was amused to see a claw and leg of the bird fall to the ground, at which all present put on a very long face, thinking it a bad omen, and it is a strange fact that the owner of the pipe and host on that occasion died before the summer was out, his Calumet was buried with him, the stems lying on his breast. [Any accident that occurs during a sacred ceremony is con-

sidered to be a bad sign. A piece falling from a sacred object, an error made in the singing, a rattle or drumstick dropped, or a person falling down, particularly if caused by the negligence of the participant, will cause the marked person to immediately ask some old man to call out four brave deeds, in the hope that the old man's powers in times of danger will help prevent possible misfortune as a result of the accident.]

Sometimes a woman is allowed to take the pipe at these dances and clumsily dances [this is a gross interpretation of the smooth dancing done by women; an ideal woman remains very dignified during social occasions and does not dance with the glamour and obvious enthusiasm shown by the men], facing a minute to each of the five points of the compass [actually, four]. There are generally some extra moves in the ceremony of unrolling the Calumet peculiar to each pipe; for instance in one case, before dancing, a squaw takes a drum stick and strikes two blows on each of the lodge poles that the entrance is between [the spiritual purpose of this to notify the sacred lodge that loud noise, in the form of drumming, is about to commence], in another case a forked stick is used to rest the head of the stuffed owl upon, this stick stuck upright between the other red willows.

The following narrative is also from Wilson's notebook of the 1890s. He calls this story a "Calumet Transfer."

When an Indian has once said that he will take the Sacred Pipe, he must not fail to keep his promise, for he is sure to be visited with misfortune should he so trifle with the Sacred. Nowadays a man names the day that he will pay the horses and be initiated. Formerly, it was customary to leave that to the owner and priests who would take him by surprise the night before the transfer was due to take place. The pipe is unrolled with the same ceremony as in Thunder

Dance, and the assembled men spend the night singing and feasting and dancing. At the first sign of daybreak five or six of them take the stem and pipe and the owl and silently go to the lodge of the sleeping candidate, taking with them a stroud blanket or robe upon which they place the man. Putting into his hands the stem and owl, they then seize the corners of blanket and lift the man bodily off the ground and carry him out and off to the lodge of the owner of pipe where the ceremony is to take place. They there deposit him upon the right of the Sacred outfit, which [place] is vacated by the host who takes very little part in what follows. While they are carrying their prisoner from one lodge to the other, a great deal of shouting is done by themselves and those in the other lodges. [This shouting is in the form of cheers honoring the candidate.] The candidate, when seated, places the things he has been carrying in their places. Singing and dancing is now indulged in for about two hours, during which the guests slip out one by one and go home and wash and put on their good clothes, as they are looking rather tough after the night's sleepless feasting. Finally a couple of priests of the occasion chew sweet grass [again, sweet pine, the Medicine Pipe incense] and prepare to do the decorating. A boy is decorated, his friends having paid two horses for the privilege. First a red ring is painted around the candidate's face and around each wrist, and from there around to tips of fingers; a spot is painted, one on each shoulder, and feet are also painted red. Priest's hands are waved four times to incense before he does the painting; he now takes a sheep skin band, hair outside, painted red and blue, and puts it on man's head, hand waved four times to incense; a feather is stuck through hair at top of head, from right to left, and boy is fixed up same way. Some other children are now painted.

The vendor's wives now paint candidate's wives and hold up a blanket, curtaining off that portion of the lodge where they sit and dress them completely in new clothes which they, the vendor's wives, supply. Vendor's wives chew sweetgrass while they are dressing others. When they are through the blanket is taken down. The candidate is dressed completely in a new suit of clothes by vendor; this is done before his wives are dressed. Each garment is waved four times to incense before being put on. Candidate now gets up and, passing behind pipe with fire stick in hand walks out, stepping on four bundles of sage the first four steps. A painted white horse is waiting outside which he mounts, and there is handed him the fancy pipestem, which he holds in his arms. A priest leads off the horse, singing, to candidate lodge which the latter enters [candidate enters his lodge]; a squaw brings back the horse, and priest returns with stem and owl [to vendor's lodge]; 2 Priests and 2 others go outside [vendor's lodge] having in their hands both pipestems, owl, rattle, and whistles, they stand in a line and sing while the four drummers form another line behind and they all move off, singing, to lodge of candidate; front line dancing and singing forwards and backwards, at times facing around when they at last arrive at candidate's lodge. Front line goes in, drummers at once return [to vendor's lodge], candidate at once comes out [from his own lodge] and, mounting horse which had been brought around again, he comes back to [vendor's] lodge and enters. As he enters, the drummers all take hold of a common pipestem and bow their heads low, still waiting, until he passes in, when they lift their heads and go to work at their drums.

Now there is dancing for an hour, very much like Thunder Dance, but more of it, there sometimes being four up at once. Head bands and feathers are taken off. A blanket is now held up as a curtain, closing from view the man and boy. The two priests take the front locks of hair of each [the man and boy] and form a top-knot by braiding out one braid in front and doubling it back upon itself and tying it with buckskin; a long strip of otter skin is wrapped around [the braided lock], making a long roll sticking out over the face; while this is being done a third priest stands outside holding the fancy stem towards middle of blanket to time of slow beat of drums.

A blue bead and shell is tied on each top knot; the priests again chew sweetgrass, spit on their hands and rub them over heads of man and boy after they have fixed the hair; head bands and feathers are now replaced. One priest now gets up with man and boy, man with fancy stem in his hand; all face South then West then North and dance a minute to slow time in each direction, at which there is great applause. [In the form of shouts and war cries. We clap our hands only to accent our talking, not to applaud. The "applause" is to cheer the new Medicine Pipe Man during his first ceremonial act as Owner.] Women do same, that is, candidate's wives and two other women. All morning, relations of candidate have been bringing in household articles such as dishes, fry pans, cups and saucers, pails, also blankets, guns, and etc. and piling them up at the entrance. These are now distributed by vendor and his wife to their relations, probably giving those who contributed when they were buying the pipe years ago.

Pipe is now rolled up and the newly made medicine man's wife carries it home on her back.

Wilson learned the Ways of the Medicine Pipe ceremonies quite well, although, as indicated by my parenthetical comments, he occasionally made a mistake, or misinterpreted. The following story, told by our uncle, Atsitsina, illustrates how well Wilson knew these ceremonies. The story takes place during the Sun Dance Encampment at the Belly Buttes in the 1920s.

I will tell you the story of Long-Nosed Crow. His name was Bob Wilson. He was just like an Indian. He spoke the Blackfoot language just as I am speaking it now. Everybody knew him. He knew me and my father very well.

One time, when this big-shot from the States called Schultz [James Willard Schultz, the author of many books about our Old Ways] *was visiting the Bloods, they went together to a Medicine Pipe Dance. It was for the opening of Big Sorrel Horse's Pipe, the Backside-to-the-Fire Pipe. Wilson told Schultz, "I believe in the Indian religion. I have my reasons. When they have Big Smoke ceremonies, I always help them. I bring them tobacco and stuff to make soup with. I can go in and have my face painted. They pray hard. Their prayers help me good."*

Many White Horses was opening the Bundle; he was called by his nickname, Bachkseene [closest English translation is "bungling idiot"]. We watched as Bachkseene opened the Bundle, then danced with the Stem. After that, they sang two "rest songs," then danced, one after another, without rest songs in between.

After the ceremony, Wilson came over to us and said in fluent Blackfoot, "Hai-Yah, now you are walking lost, the way you were opening that Bundle. The ceremony was mixed up. In the Old Days, when the leader finished opening the Bundle, he would dance twice and go outside with the Pipe and pray. Then he would come back in and dance two more times and give the Pipe to the main Owner to pray with. Then the leader would tell the drummers to sing four resting songs and then tell whoever wants to dance to get up and dance, and that person would get the sweet pine and put it on his feet and pray with it and he would dance. He would dance four times. Then he would give the thing he danced with to the NinamskAki [Medicine Pipe Woman] and she would pray with it and give it back to the Bundle. Then they'd sing four more rest songs and then dance again. You're all mixed up now. The songs you sing are correct, but the way you do it is wrong."

Wilson was pretty smart. He knew a lot about the Old Ways.

BACKSIDE-TO-THE-FIRE PIPE
OPENING CEREMONY: 1972

NinnaOnesta—Albert Chief Calf—was the crier on the morning of the Backside-to-the-Fire Pipe ceremony. He came around early, announcing that Jim Twig was going to open his Medicine Pipe. Not yet having fulfilled his annual obligation of having the Bundle opened, Jim Twig wanted to do this before starting the Bundle's transfer ceremony. All past and present Medicine Pipe Owners were invited, according to custom.

NinnaOnesta wore a black cowboy hat with a red-dyed eagle plume fastened to one side, and a pink scarf around his neck. He had on his ever-present sunglasses, and in one hand carried a cane. At the age of seventy-seven he was still a sturdy and strong-voiced man. Here is what we heard him say: "Hurry up! Hurry up, all of you people who want to see the Medicine Pipe Dance. [Jim Twig] is going to open his sacred Pipe today. He wants to get started early so that we can finish before dark. Oki, all of you Akai-Namskaniks [past Medicine Pipe Men], all of you Ninamskaniks, you are invited. Bring your bowls. All of you people who want to see the ceremony, you are invited to come to the yellow-painted Elk Tipi. Hurry Up!"

We got up and made our incense. SikskiAki no longer took our Bundle outside to hang over the doorway during the day. The Old Man told us that there were too many casual visitors now in camp who had no idea how to show proper respect for such a sacred thing. As we made our incense, we prayed for our success with the Spirit of the Old Ways; we dwelled on good thoughts about our own life.

We were about to eat breakfast when Mrs. Stabs Down came in. Our Bundle had last been kept by her and her husband for the benefit of their children, who had been initiated as Owners. By tradition she is now our "Mother." She had come to ask for some sacred yellow paint, knowing that I use that color as part of my personal Medicine. She said that the old Horns wished to buy some for use in the upcoming Horns Society transfer. Her husband was giving up his membership, while her brother was going to join. I told her I would donate some to the Horns. Then she declined our invitation to visit and quickly left to help the Horns in their many preparations for the transfer.

We had just finished breakfast when another visitor arrived. This time it was Ksachkom ("Earth"), or Fred Eagle Plume, Atsitsina's brother, who, in his seventies, was the oldest man to become a new member of the Horns during this transfer. He was joining to fulfill a vow that he had made some time ago. He came to borrow my pipe bag. He said that Atsitsina had loaned him a pipe, but that he must have a bag for it during the transfer ceremonies. I said nothing, knowing that tradition would not allow me to ask for the bag's return if he did not bring it back on his own. The soft deerhide from which the bag is made was the last one tanned long ago by my "grandma" who lives in the south. I could never replace it. In addition, the bag is beautifully decorated with SikskiAki's beadwork. Since I did not care to lend it, I remained silent to his request. Knowing the reason for my silence, Ksachkom explained that a new bag was being made for him by some woman relative, and that he only needed mine because his was not yet ready for use. Then I agreed to let him use the bag. It is a custom that Medicine Pipe Owners do not lend out their belongings, but give them away if someone is really in need of them. If they do lend anything, then it must be returned within four days. After that they can neither ask for it nor expect to take it back if it is brought.

Sun let us know early that it was going to be very hot that day. It is easier for the body to sit through a long ceremony in the spring, after the first sound of Thunder, than in the middle of a hot summer. We knew that we would not be very comfortable after wrapping our wool blankets around ourselves. Tradition requires participants in holy ceremonies to cover themselves with a robe or blanket to show modesty and respect before the Holy Spirits. At most Medicine Pipe ceremonies, this tradition is mainly followed by current Medicine Pipe Owners and by the leader of the ceremony. Others wear blankets only while dancing with one of the sacred objects from the Bundle. However, a few people ignore tradition and go without their blankets altogether.

To complete our preparations for the ceremony, we took the shell necklaces and bead bracelets from the rawhide paint-and-accessory bag of our Bundle and put them on. Medicine Pipe Owners and their families used to wear these symbols all the time. Now most people wear them only to ceremonies. They serve as a constant reminder of the main elements of nature: shells to represent water; blue beads to represent the sky; thongs to represent animals; and a coating of sacred red paint to represent Earth.

We heard the voice of NinnaOnesta again, announcing that the ceremony was about to begin. We wrapped ourselves in our blankets (Wolf Child and me; women generally wear theirs over their shoulders) and immediately we became very hot! How it must have been in the Old Days when many of our People dressed like that every day, wearing a buffalo robe or wool blanket as outer garments and buckskin or wool clothing underneath! They had deep convictions in our customs to find happiness despite physical discomfort.

The Elk Tipi was a large yellow-painted lodge with the head and horns of a buffalo painted over the front doorway. Hoof tracks decorated both sides. The tipi belonged to Richard Little Dog, who led Medicine Pipe ceremonies among the South Piegans in Montana. Jim Twig borrowed this tipi for his ceremony, because it could accommodate many people. A second tipi

cover was stretched over a framework erected to lean against the east side of the main tipi, thus forming a sort of patio. Friends and relatives of the Owner crowded into this secondary tipi and watched the ceremony through the open front of the main tipi. The cover of the secondary tipi was rolled up so that others could watch from outside.

We always enter our tipis from the east side, from the direction Sun's first rays of light announce the start of another day. Some women and children were already seated within the secondary tipi; the main tipi was about half full when we entered it. We stood in the doorway, waiting to be received by host Jim Twig, who sat beneath the Bundle. His wife sat on his right. Someone called out for him to hear, "Oki, here are some Medicine Pipe Owners." Jim looked, smiled at us, and then pointed to a place next to Emonissi (an old man also known as Laurie Plume), who was going to lead the ceremony. I went to the place I was shown, while SikskiAki occupied the matching place on the women's side.

One other Medicine Pipe Owner was already sitting in the main tipi. He was an older South Piegan named Charlie Horn. His wife inherited her aging parents' Bundle, which they now take care of at their home in Browning. Theirs is one of five Medicine Pipe Bundles still left on that reservation. Medicine Pipe ceremonies are usually held in the houses down there. While our Pipes are usually brought out only in the spring, theirs are brought out whenever anyone makes a vow to sponsor the ceremony.

Shortly after we sat in place, visitors from our other divisions arrived. First came old Makes Summer (Joseph Young Eagle Child), my Weather Dancing instructor during the last Medicine Lodge ceremony among the South Piegans. Then came Ben Calf Robe, a man in his late eighties and a former Medicine Pipe Owner among the North Blackfoot People. They were shown seats up front, the place for honored guests. Old Charlie Horn, a quiet and humble man, sat halfway back instead of way up front where all Medicine Pipe Owners are supposed to sit.

One more drummer was needed to start the ceremony. Our Old Man, sitting by the doorway, volunteered to fill the vacancy. The physical efforts required of drummers would strain his old body. He knew that, but he wanted to help get the ceremony started. I helped him move over to sit on the first of the cushions arranged for the drummers in an east-west line.

Just before the ceremony actually began, old NinnaOnesta showed up. Once the ceremony begins, it is not proper to rearrange anything, but there was still time to have the physically stronger NinnaOnesta replace the Old Man.

The ceremony went like any other, with the incense, praying, singing, and untying of the Bundle. In the Old days, at least seven sets of seven songs would have been sung. But no one knows all seven sets anymore. Today, usually the first set of seven is sung, and then part of the second set.

After the Bundle was opened, we ate the sacred meal of fresh berry soup, as well as boiled meat and eggs, crackers and cookies, and oranges and apples.

This pause lasted for about twenty minutes; then the ceremony continued with dancing done in time to drumming and singing. During this part, participants were given an opportunity to express their own spiritual feelings about the Bundle. Anyone who had been initiated into the Spirit of our Medicine Pipes could get up and dance with an object from the Bundle.

The custom of dancing is different with this particular Bundle, the Backside-to-the-Fire Pipe. With other Bundles, only the men dance, while their female relatives may dance in place to accompany them. Then, women dance with the sacred objects only to fulfill vows, standing next to the leader and bouncing lightly up and down; relatives accompany them, dancing in place four

times, facing each of the four directions. The dancing party stands on a walkway made up of blankets, quilts, and pieces of material given to the Bundle's Owner afterwards. However, for this Bundle, both men and women dance, one encouraging the other.

Before the dancing began, Emonissi took the sacred Pipe outside the main tipi and prayed to the Powers of the Universe. He returned and laid the sacred Stem on a rack, made up of three sticks like a miniature goal post. The drummers began the introductory turn for the Medicine Pipe Dance. All the songs, or chants, were accompanied by hard-soft, hard-soft beats on the rawhide-covered hand drums. The four drums used to be among the accessories of a Bundle, but no longer. Today, drums are usually borrowed.

During the introductory song, Mokakin got up and prepared to be the first dancer. He went up front and took a pinch of sweet pine needles from the pouch next to the altar. Putting the needles in his mouth, he chewed them, then spit a bit of them in his right hand, which he brushed down the left side of his body. He did the same with his left hand. Then he repeated the whole ceremony. Finally, he spit some of the incense in his hands, rubbed his palms together, then rubbed the soles of his moccasins a total of four times. He was now symbolically purified and ready to handle the sacred objects from within the Bundle.

One of the two Pipestems was very simply decorated, while the other was more fully decorated with the eagle tailfeather fan. The simple pipe looked like the secondary Pipe and the latter looked like the main Pipe, except for one feature. The secondary Pipe is usually more recently made; but here this simple pipe was very ancient compared to the one with the eagle tailfeathers. And indeed, Mokakin selected the much older, more simple Pipe, which was this Bundle's main Pipe.

Mokakin prayed aloud, holding up the sacred

Stem. He gave thanks to be able to pray with his old Pipe once again and he asked for strength so that he could pray with it again next year. He asked the Spirits of the sacred Bundle to continue sharing their power with him and his family and all past and future Keepers of the Bundle.

After the prayer, Mokakin hummed a few notes and the drummers took up the rhythm of the song. Like other Pipe Owners, Mokakin had his own special song for dancing; these songs come either from Teachers or from dreams.

Mokakin is a dramatic and spirited dancer. His basic style is to bend forward at the hips, loosen his knees, then take short jumps with both feet. With each jump forward, he turns a bit to the right or left. His left hand rests on his hip, while his right hand is extended before him, holding the sacred Stem.

As he danced by the others, he held the Stem towards them, giving its blessing. Some responded by reaching out with their hands, symbolically grasping the Holy Power, then holding it to their hearts.

Meanwhile, Ponah bounced enthusiastically to her husband's dancing, holding a corner of her shawl in each hand of her outstretched arms. As she bounced, she turned from side to side, and occasionally burst forth in the high-pitched tremolo of a woman's victory cry.

Each time the singing stopped, Mokakin straightened up, waiting for the next song. As he waited he caressed the Pipe and straightened out any tangled ribbons and feathers.

When the fourth song was over, Mokakin walked over to the doorway of the main tipi and handed the sacred Stem to his daugher, Theresa. Because the topknot from this Bundle had once been transferred to her while her parents were the Bundle's Owners, she had the right to handle the Pipe. Mokakin reached into his pocket and took out a couple of dollar bills, which he handed to two male visitors. This was to show his generosity and inspire good thoughts in the recipients.

Ponah did the same thing to two women visitors. Then Mokakin went up and took from the Bundle the secondary Pipe. He carried it, dancing, behind his daughter, who was holding the main Pipe. Ponah again kept time, and when the dance was over, all three again gave gifts to the visitors.

Theresa gave the sacred Pipe to her brother Frank, also a former Owner. They danced side by side around the fire while their father followed with the secondary Pipe. This time Mokakin also carried the sacred rattle, shaking it and keeping time to the beat.

After more gifts to the visitors, the sacred Pipe was handed to someone else. And so it went, the Pipe and dancing alternating among the men and women until it was handed to one of the drummers, who asked someone else to drum in his place as he danced. When he finished dancing his four rounds, he unexpectedly brought the Pipe over to its Owner. According to tradition, the dancing was over, even though only half of the participants had been given a chance to dance.

Jim Twig then got up to begin the final part of the ceremony. First, he gave each participant a piece of old-fashioned twist tobacco. Each person removed a pinch and held it aloft, while Emonissi began a prayer. Everyone joined the prayer and then offered the pinch of tobacco to Earth. Next, Jim Twig passed out packages of tobacco and rolled cigarettes to all present. In the Old Days he would have handed out sacred tobacco, harvested during the previous summer, dried in the fall, and kept all winter inside some of the skins within the Medicine Pipe Bundle. When his supply was exhausted, he returned to his seat, ending the ceremony.

People picked up their blankets, gathered their eating bowls and bags of food, and left the tipi. Emonissi and Jim Twig stayed seated, so that they could tie the Bundle back up. For this, no ceremony was required.

135

Later on the Fourth Day

Back at our tipi, we put away our blankets and other things, lay down in the shade, fanned ourselves, and drank lots of cool water. Getting water to the Sun Dance Camps used to be quite a chore in the Old Days, as there was no accessible water source in the Belly Buttes. Nowadays, a truck with a full tank of cold well-water drives around the camp circle every evening so that people can fill their containers.

It was a clear, calm, middle-of-summer day; the temperature must have been at least a hundred. We heard someone singing. The song was to honor the wife of Harry Shade, about to become a member of the Motokiks. Although it is traditional for this society to transfer memberships as a group, a woman may make a vow to join if she learns that a present member is willing to part with her Society Bundle. As in this case, Noyiss, the wife of Henry Standing Alone, had agreed to transfer her membership. We looked toward the Motokik's lodge, where we saw someone leading a fine horse with a pile of beautiful blankets on its back—all representing payments for the new membership.

Part of the Motokiks' transfer ceremony is public and part is closed. We walked over to the lodge to join a crowd of others to see what we could through the two doorways and the lodge covers, which were opened for all to see. Inside, three women were dancing in place. They wore Snake headdresses, whistles on leather thongs around their necks, and shawls over their shoulders. The feather plumes of their headdresses waved in the air as they danced. Each of the women tooted on small whistles made from eagle bones. The women's faces were completely covered with sacred yellow paint, which looked greenish in the subdued lighting of the lodge. Thin red lines were drawn from the corners of their eyes and mouths.

Four of the older men did the singing—Joe Sun, Albert Wolf Child, Mark Old Shoes, and Fred Weasel Fat—all former members of the Horns Society. They sat in a row, facing east, each beating the song's rhythm with a rawhide rattle on a sheet of rawhide spread before them on the ground.

The members' beds were lined head to foot around the lodge wall. Members who were not dancing sat quietly on their beds. Before each bed, a piece of earth was cleared. This was the altar where the incense was made. Just beyond the altar, toward the center of the lodge, a short, upright stick had been firmly planted in the ground. Tied to each stick was a decorated rawhide container. This was where the sacred headdresses were kept when not worn.

Soon the doors of the lodge were closed, shutting us from the mystery of the ceremony within.

136

Since there were no other activities on the afternoon of this fourth day in camp, we took the opportunity to return to our house, along the Bullhorn Coulee. I wanted to pick up some yellow paint for the Horns and to water our horses and fill up their trough. And SikskiAki and I were looking forward to a refreshing bath in our private swimming hole.

When we got home that's the first thing we did. A few cattle ranches between our place and the mountains keep us from drinking the otherwise clear water, but they sure don't keep us from lying in the cool flow of the river. Then we relaxed quietly on a blanket in the warmth of Sun.

We enjoyed the privacy not possible at the campground. There, unexpected visitors can drop by at any time. In the Old Days, visitors were probably reassuring in the northern plains, vast and lurking with danger and enemy. But even then, men sometimes went on the warpath to "get away from it all." On the warpath they had the opportunity to reevaluate themselves and family and friends. When they returned, they could be assured of a change in routine, with new adventures to talk about, new horses to train and ride, and new possessions to admire and share.

Women seldom had the opportunity for privacy, except when they went down to the river for water or to the woods for fuel. Only a few husbands allowed their wives to share in the adventures of hunting and horse raiding. Most were confined to the daily chores of child care and housekeeping.

Sun was low in the sky, an evening ember still shooting its rays across to us, as we drove back to the camp in the east. There, the Buttes looked like flaming sentinels watching over the flat where the camp was. Just before dipping below the horizon, Sun's last rays bathed the Buttes in orange colors, leaving the edges of the fissures and caves outlined in red, their insides already black with darkness.

The road between the Buttes and the reserve is unmarked, but we all know it as the Belly Buttes Road. We turned off this road and followed the old wagon trail downhill to the edge of the camp's flat. The trail wound its way over ruts, past gullies, past abandoned badger and fox holes. A lone cottonwood post, forked at the top and surrounded by a few smaller posts, outlined the shape of a Medicine Lodge from a past holy gathering. The missing posts had either been carried off by families in need of firewood during our cold winters (which can go to fifty below!) or else were eaten by a pack of hungry porcupines.

Back at camp, we entered our tipi somewhat anxiously. Every time we leave our Bundle we fear it might be stolen. Yes, stolen! Right there in the Sun Dance Encampment. Not stolen by a thief, although that possibility exists, but stolen by one of our own People who might still believe in the Old Ways. You see, there is a custom among our People that helps anyone who wants to obtain the Power of a holy Bundle without having to ask for it or offer the Owner reasons why the Bundle is needed. If such an individual has the property necessary for the transfer, he can find a Bundle in the home of an absent Owner and then sneak in and steal it.

To steal a sacred Bundle, a person must be a previous Owner, preferably of the Bundle he is about to steal. He must make incense, say a prayer for success, and then call out four coups before he can take the Bundle out of the lodge. If the person is not qualified to do this, he may enlist the help of some older man. Once the Bundle is stolen, the person must still satisfy the Owner with payments.

For a stolen Bundle, the paymens are expected to be about twice what they would normally have been. I will give you an example of this custom later on.

My Teachers had warned me that our Bundle could be stolen. They pointed out that one respected Medicine Pipe Owner with the same fears as ours took his Bundle back home, while the other Owners never even brought theirs to camp. During the Piegan Sun Dance earlier that summer, I asked a Medicine Pipe Owner where his Bundle was. "In a bank vault," he replied. "That's where I always take it when I go away from home." He told me that several people wished to have his Bundle, but he did not feel they were spiritually sincere in their desires. He knew that one of them would steal it, if given the opportunity. SikskiAki and I felt that our sacred Bundle should be present at the annual holy gathering of our People, despite the risks. However, we generally try not to leave it.

We were relieved to find our Bundle hanging in its sacred place when we returned to our tipi. We made a small fire to have a coal for incense.

HOW OUR FAMILY GOT ITS PIPE

In the Old Days, the custom for some Medicine Pipe Bundles required that they change Owners every four years. If no one vowed to take the Bundle after that time, the Owner selected someone who was spiritually deserving and had enough property to make the physical sacrifice. In some cases, the Owners waived the payments of property and simply gave the Pipe to a worthy person, usually a relative, often a child.

The Owner did not announce the person he chose until the day of the transfer. Those men who felt they were eligible but did not wish the responsibility left camp with their blankets as soon as they heard the opening songs, and they stayed away the entire night. Early the next morning, while the camp was still asleep, the Owner and his party would go to the tipi of the selected man. One of the party carried along the owl from the Bundle, giving them the Power to silently approach their "quarry" in the dark. Then the Owner, with the sacred Stem, would touch the candidate, who was obliged to accept his new duty.

In every transfer ceremony, the new Owner is symbolically "captured," even when the candidate willingly vows to take the Pipe. Let me tell you how we were "captured" when we took our Pipe.

The Owner of our Pipe was Stabs Down. Our camp, consisting of our old Painted-All-Over Tipi and a canvas wall tent, which served as a cookhouse for the ceremony, was set up near Stabs Down's tipi. But it was so windy during the night that we didn't hear the singing when they opened the Bundle.

Our uncle, Atsitsina, who camped with us and served as our advisor, woke us early on the morning of the transfer. He was the go-between for Stabs Down and us to make sure that we were all prepared for the transfer. He made a final check to see that our blankets were properly fastened, then told us to wait quietly for the arrival of the capturing party, which, according to custom, we weren't supposed to expect. In the Old Days, we wouldn't even have known the day of the transfer.

Nevertheless, after all the months of learning, planning, and saving, and after the early trials and disappointments, we found it impossible to pretend that we were not moments away from taking on the most sacred duty in the Old Ways of our People. After all the listening and reading about the sacred Pipes of our People, we would soon begin living within the holiness and honor of our own Pipe.

We prayed and cried as the wind whistled through the top of our tipi and flapped the faded red cover.

While we prayed, the capture party arrived. From Stabs Down's tipi we could just barely hear the sounds of drumming. We had no idea who was gathered there.

Before us was White Horn, a relative of ours also known as John Many Chiefs. The Owner had chosen him to lead the ceremony. He wore a striped blanket across his left shoulder, holding out the sacred Pipestem in his free right hand as he danced toward us. White Horn was once Keeper of this Pipe, and its Spirit was with him as he danced. He handed the sacred Stem to me, then stepped aside, permitting the man behind him to dance before us. This man carried the secondary Pipe, which he gave to me. The third man in line gave me the wrapped owl skin; the fourth man handed me the decorated whistle and rawhide rattle.

The capture party spread out a blanket and instructed me to sit on it, holding these sacred objects next to my body. With the help of two young men, they all picked up the blanket, lifting me into the air. They carried me out toward Stabs Down's tipi, SikskiAki and Wolf Child following behind.

Atsitsina walked along, singing the ancient honoring song of our family's band, the Many Children. He preceded each song by calling, in a loud, sing-song fashion, "Natosina, Ah-hey . . . SikskiAki, Ah-hey . . . Makwi Poka, Ah-hey," and then he sang, announcing the sacred duty we were about to assume.

I could hear the Old Man's voice, booming above the other drummers, singing in Stabs Down's white tipi as we approached it. On the way, the party stopped four times and gently lowered me to the ground. They carried me into the tipi as Sun moves, from east to west around the fire. The Owner's seat was vacant, south of the opened Bundle. SikskiAki and Wolf Child sat at my right. The leader sat to my left; he instructed me to replace the sacred objects in the opened Bundle between us.

The Old Man was very proud that his "grandchildren" sat in the place of honor next to the sacred Bundle that had so long been his. He sang a rousing honoring song that silenced everyone in the lodge. When he finished he took up his drum and beat a rolling introduction with his drumstick.

The drummers began one of the Medicine Pipe dance songs and the four members of the capturing party danced with the sacred objects. White Horn led the group, which included Arthur Healy and Jim Red Crow, both of whom were former Owners of this Bundle, and Henry Standing Alone, who once owned the Bloods' Long-Time Pipe. Each of the dancers demonstrated his spiritual enthusiasm in his own way as he danced the four rounds. Then the men handed the sacred objects to SikskiAki, who accepted their Spirit by brushing them over her body four times. The objects were then brushed over Wolf Child and me and were replaced in the Bundle.

The transfer ceremony ends when the retiring Owner dances four rounds with the sacred Pipe. During the dance, he goes outside to inspect the goods offered as material payments for the Bundle. If he accepts them, he gives the Pipe to the new Owner. If he does not, he may either sing a song, specifically requesting something the new Owner should sacrifice, or he may instruct the leader to close up the Bundle and call off the transfer. He would do the latter only if the prospective Owner's lack of material sacrifice was a mockery. No one remembers such an occurrence in recent times. However, there was once an incident when specific horses were requested by the retiring Owner of our People's Long-time Pipe.

Old Stabs Down is often considered the previous Owner of our sacred Bundle. He is a man in his mid-seventies, although he appears much younger. He speaks very little English and he is among the more traditional of our People. But he likes to point out that some people mistake him for a non-Indian because of his light features. Unlike others who prefer the Old Ways, his herds of cattle and horses make him one of the reserve's most successful ranchers, and in his house he has one of the few color television sets among our People.

The real Owner of our Bundle was Stabs Down's teenage son, Wallace. He was the one to dance outside and inspect the goods we offered. Wearing a striped Hudson's Bay blanket and holding the sacred Pipe, he danced the first two rounds of the "inspection song." During the second round he danced outside where our relatives stood with some of the goods we were giving up. Our main payment was to have been seven horses; several we owned, the others we would buy. Due to a misfortune in his family, however, Stabs Down sent word to us sometime before the transfer that he would rather have the money for those horses we hadn't yet bought. So we offered a thoroughbred quarter horse and a good mare with a colt. Instead of the other four horses, we offered a large number of twenty-dollar bills sewn to a large Hudson's Bay blanket, according to custom, and also a large pile of blankets, clothes, and dry goods.

SikskiAki and I held our breaths, hoping that all our spiritual hope and enthusiasm would not be let down for insufficient material payments. It had taken us some time to gather what we offered. After a brief look at our things, the Owner turned slowly and danced toward us as the drummers took up the inspection dance song again. At the end of the song, young Wallace stopped before us and handed the sacred Pipe to me, saying, "You got yourself this holy Pipe." Then he turned around and walked to his seat by the doorway.

With that simple gesture we were given the key to our long-time dreams. We now had the right to learn the sacred songs and Teachings of the Medicine Pipes and to use them whenever we wished to have their Power.

During the ceremony that followed, we were all painted in the style of Medicine Pipe People. My family was given new blankets and shell necklaces and bead wristlets to wear. White fur headbands were placed on Wolf Child and me.

A transfer within the transfer took place when the little granddaughter of Mokakin and Ponah gave up her rights to wear the sacred topknot from our Bundle, which is a strip of otter skin. While the topknot song was sung, the fur strip was wrapped in a spiral around a small, doubled-over braid that SikskiAki had fixed over Wolf Child's forehead. In our language, he became a Medicine Pipe Child. We gave up a quarter horse yearling, another pile of blankets, dry goods, and moccasins in payment for this.

Back in the Old Days, most Medicine Pipe Owners wore topknots to identify themselves. The origin for this has been forgotten. In recent times most men cut their hair too short to wear topknots, which is probably why the rights to these topknots are transferred to some child. The parents make sacrifices, offering nearly as much as given for the Bundle itself. Usually the Bundle belongs to their own parents or a relative.

The Fifth Day

THE BACKSIDE-TO-THE-FIRE PIPE TRANSFER CEREMONY

The main event of this day in camp was to be the Backside-to-the-Fire Pipe Transfer. The ceremony itself had actually begun the night before, with a preliminary opening of the Bundle in Jim Twig's tipi, where he and former Medicine Pipe Owners had gathered. (This opening is not to be confused with the annual opening Jim Twig had had earlier.) After the Bundle had been ceremonially opened, and the guests fed, the group dispersed, leaving the Bundle untied for the rest of the night in the tipi.

White Horn was to be the leader at the transfer ceremony on this day—the same White Horn who had officiated at our own transfer. He carried the sacred Pipe under his white blanket, leading the capturing party toward a white tipi. There the future Owner waited with two of his sisters, one to be his partner, in place of his wife, and the other to accept the Bundle's topknot. This was a common arrangement among Old People who made the vow for a young person to take a Pipe.

Mokakin sang an honoring song for his grandson. Two other grandparents, Ponah and Emonissi, also sang their own rendition. The tiny bells on the sacred Pipestems jingled with the leader's movements.

After the sacred objects were replaced in the Bundle, the singers began the inspection dance song. Jim Twig took the sacred Pipe and danced outside to see the payments. To make their grandson's transfer successful, both grandparents had amassed four nice horses, a new Winchester rifle, a couple of blankets covered with bills, and a huge pile of blankets and dry goods. When Jim Twig came back inside, he danced up to young Weaselhead, handed him the sacred Pipe, and said, "Oki, here is your holy Pipe."

The transfer is completed after the new Owners have had their faces painted. Two men held up a large blanket to shield the painting from the view of others. The drummers sang while Henry Standing Alone stood outside the blanket and held the main Pipe over the blanket, jingling its tiny bells above the head of the new Owner. The topknot and headbands were fastened on by the leader and his wife. Then the leader and his wife exchanged new clothes with the new Owners, to symbolize the rebirth of the Owner and his wife. In the Old Days, these new clothes would have been made of finely decorated buckskin. Today, except for handmade moccasins, the new clothes are store-bought and are seldom worn at the exchange. Often, only blankets are actually exchanged and worn.

After the blanket was taken away, the ceremony continued. A procession of people came into the tipi to take turns dancing in place with the sacred Pipe. These were people who wished to share the Pipe's spiritual powers; and for the privilege of dancing with the Pipe, they contributed some blankets and dry goods. The first group was young Weaselhead's relatives. They placed the blankets and dry goods around the fireplace in a semi-circle, dancing on them and facing the four directions. After each dance, the material was given to the former Owner and considered part of the payment.

After the relatives, some members of the Magpie Society came in. Fred's late father (Pat Weaselhead, Junior, son of Mokakin and Ponah) had been a member of the Magpies. Upon his death, his comrades had taken his son into their society as a junior member, as was the custom. For ceremony, they danced and then gave their walkway of blankets and dry goods to the Bundle's former Owner. The last group to come in and dance in the same way were members of young Weaselhead's social society, the Kaispaiks, or Grass Dancers.

After the last dancer, the Bundle was folded up, but not tied, and taken to the new Owner's tipi for the remainder of the ceremony. The woman has the honor of caring for the Bundle, not only at home but also when moving it. She carries the closed Bundle on her back, following the leader and her husband.

Due to the uncomfortable heat that day, a pause was taken until later in the afternoon, when the mountain breezes would blow across the campground. We went back to our own lodge to rest and relax.

It was almost suppertime when the crier came around to announce that the Bundle would be closed up. He reminded the participants to bring along their bowls to share in the meal the new Keeper's family would provide. The new Keeper's tipi was soon filled with visitors, most of them former Medicine Pipe People. Berry soup and other foods were dished out, prayed with, and eaten. The atmosphere was now very relaxed. It

was after dark when the last person danced with the sacred Pipe and returned it to the new Owner, bringing the transfer ceremony to a close.

HISTORY OF THE BACKSIDE-TO-THE-FIRE PIPE

Part of the Spirit dwelling within each sacred Bundle is the history of the Bundle and of those who formerly owned it and prayed with it. What I know of this Pipe I learned from my two Teachers, Atsitsina and Mokakin, each of whom had already kept that Bundle.

It is called the Backside-to-the-Fire Pipe because the sacred Stems are placed within the Bundle in the direction opposite that of Pipes in other Bundles. Our other sacred Pipe Bundles must always hang on a west wall, facing Sun's first light from the east, and the Pipestems must be placed in the Bundle so that the mouthpieces point to the south, where the lodge fire is. But the tradition of the Backside Bundle calls for the mouthpieces to point North; thus the "backside" of the Pipes face the fire. This is according to spiritual directions given to the Pipe's first Keeper.

White Horn, an uncle of the ceremony's present leader, had been the first Blood man to own this Pipe. He had it transferred to him by Drum, a member of the Sarsi tribe. Although the Sarsi People belong to a different language group, they share a long alliance and dependence with our People, and have adopted most of our religious and cultural customs. Thus, their Medicine Pipe Bundles are similar to ours. The main Stem of the Bundle looks like a Medicine Pipe from the Crow People, so the Bundle may originally have come from them.

White Horn had the Bundle for many years, and because he was so fond of it his family decided to bury it with him when he died. Before the burial, one of our head men, Day Chief, was instructed in a dream to take the main Pipe from the Bundle. Day Chief, with the help of another head man, Blackfoot Old Woman, made a new secondary Pipe and gathered the other objects required to make up a Bundle. That is why the main Pipe today looks very ancient and the rest of the Bundle looks more recent. All this occurred some years before Day Chief's death in 1907.

Mokakin recited the names of all the Blood Owners of that Pipe Bundle.

1. White Horn
2. Day Chief
3. Carries a Knife
4. Last Dressed
5. Crazy Crow
6. Many Mules
7. Calf Robe
8. Headdress
9. Calf Robe
10. Pete Heavy Shield
11. Big Sorrel Horse
12. Antelope Whistler
13. Bob Plaited Hair
14. Jack Low Horn
15. Alec Stevens
16. Willy Wadsworth
17. Ben Strangling Wolf
18. Black Sleeps
19. Shot-on-Both-Sides
20. Black Forehead
21. Pat Weaselhead (Mokakin)
22. Charlie Panther Bone
23. Day Rider
24. Pat Weaselhead (Mokakin)
25. Fred Weaselfat
26. Willie Eagle Plume (Atsitsina)
27. John Day Rider
28. Willie Eagle Plume (Atsitsina)
29. Mrs. Day Rider
30. Pat Weaselhead (Mokakin)
31. Frank Weaselhead
32. Jim Twig
33. Fred Weaselhead

Day Chief in 1895. He was also known as Thunder Chief. (Steele & Co.)

Antelope Whistler, son of Blackfoot Old Woman and brother of Mike Yellow Bull. He was a former Owner of the Backside-to-the-Fire Pipe. (Clark Wissler)

Right: Charlie Panther Bone and his first wife, around 1900.

Mokakin was proud to be able to recall all Owners of his old Pipe. He made us all laugh when he reached the end of the list: "Oki, then my boy, Frank, he give to Jimmy Twig . . . and that's where I lost it. I can't remember who got it next."

This Pipe had been the first Atsitsina had ever owned. Here is his story of how he got it.

Oki, I am going to tell you about the way Backside-to-the-Fire Pipe was transferred to me. I had that Pipe twice; I also had another Pipe, later.

Oki, my wife was very sick and I was wonder-

ing what I could do for her; how I could help her have life again. I was very confused. I didn't know what to do, so I asked my relative, Crow Tail-feathers [Alex Fox], to take me to Jacob's [a white rancher who raised grain on leased land]. I told him, "I've got some money there. I want to get it."

So we went to the white man's house and he gave me the money. On our way back Crow Tail-feathers asked me how my wife was. I told him, "She is very ill. I think she is in bad shape." He said, "You should help her. You believe in the Indian religion, you should use it!" I told him, "Oki, I will become a Ninamskan. I will take one

144

of those holy Pipes and learn how to live with it." In those days my life was good. I had a lot of horses. I had everything and I wasn't in need.

When I came home, my brother, Doesn't Own Nice Horses [Jack Low Horn], was at my house. I came in and I hugged my wife and I told her, "Oki, Last Badger Face, so that you will become healthy again, we will become Ninamskaniks." My brother was surprised and said, "That is a good thing you are doing. You are taking refuge in our holy Ways. My old Pipe, Backside-to-the-Fire, you go and take it." I agreed, and I told him I would go right away to the present Owner and offer to take it.

I filled my smoking pipe and we started out in our wagon to the home of White Badger Face [Fred Weaselfat]. We went inside and I gave him my pipe. I said, "Here, smoke this. I am asking for your holy Pipe. I am coming to your Pipe so that my wife will get better again." He just said, "Ah," which meant yes to me. Then he took my pipe and he prayed with it. I told him, "I just bought two good horses and will give them to you to show that I meant what I said." He told me, "Well, you got yourself a Pipe. You can have it transferred to you anytime you want."

On the way back home, Jack said, "Oki, in the summer it will be transferred to you." He told me it would be too much trouble to start making a new tipi, with my wife still sick. He said, "Buy a white tipi. But it will not look right just to have a plain white one. My wife, Cuts Her Hair, still has the Buffalo Tipi. We will paint it on your white tipi."

I bought the white tipi from an old lady, Yellow Star. I asked her, "Old Lady, why don't you give me your tipi?" She said, "Yes, I have no use for it. Take it, and pay me whatever you want."

As soon as it was summer I told my brother, "I am going to go to Bald Head's [a white Rancher named Ryere]. I will sell my hay to him so that I will have the money for the transfer."

We painted the tipi. My brother, Ksachkom [Fred Eagle Plume] drew the buffalo on it. They told me when the Sun Dance started they would go there and set it up. I started bringing my hay to Bald Head. I worked hard and saved up nine hundred dollars. Then word came that they had set up the tipi and that we should come to the Sun Dance Encampment.

I got my money and bought the things for payments. The next day I went to camp. In the distance I could see the tipi. When I got there I moved right into it. The next day we went to get the horses I was going to give for payment. They were in the pasture of Camoose, my brother-in-law.

First we had to transfer the Buffalo Tipi to me. Calling Last painted me for the tipi transfer and led the ceremony. My relatives got out four eagle headdresses. My brother said, "You will get painted for these. They will be transferred to you."

The next morning Heavy Head and Speaks-in-the-Middle [Iron] came with some others to capture me. They took me to the tipi where the Bundle was transferred. On the way, we stopped four times; each time there was a headdress for the Owner.

When they finished transferring the Bundle we brought it home, and I asked Heavy Head if he would finish the ceremony in my lodge. So we had a dance with the Pipe. Then Heavy Head initiated me to step over a dog, so that I would be allowed to step over dogs from then on. They brought a dog over in front of our tipi. Somebody brought out a hot coal and placed it by the dog. Heavy Head made incense with sweet pine and held each of my feet over it four times. The fourth time he told me to step over the dog. He said, "Now you will not get hurt by touching a dog or by being around one." But he said that dogs must never come into a tipi or house where a Medicine Pipe is. That's the Old Way.

The next morning Heavy Head woke me up and gave me the right to get up. I was just like a

Atsitsina holding his holy Backside-to-the-Fire Pipe while a Horn member smokes from it. The Pipe's sacred opening ceremony at a Sun Dance is the only time a Medicine Pipe is brought out to be smoked.

child that was being taught how to do everything the first time, my wife, too. He gave me the right to smoke, then told me to go outside and look around. I tried to look three times; the fourth time I put my hand above my eyes and I looked all around. That was to start out my first day as a Ninamskan.

Heavy Head told me, "When you get home from the Sun Dance you will make a sweat for me and I will transfer to you the rights that I haven't transferred yet." As soon as I got home, I built the sweat lodge. After the sweat, Heavy Head asked me to have a horse tied up so that he could give me the right to get on a horse. I borrowed my brother's [SikskiAki's father's] horse. Heavy Head told brother that the horse must never carry meat

after the initiation; he was going to be a holy horse and would go lame if he carried meat. He made incense and we did it the same way as with the dog. Then he gave me the right to butcher meat. He gave me the rights to do all the important things in the Old Way of life.

Atsitsina also told an interesting story about this Pipe Bundle, involving the father and grandfather of our present head chief, Jim Shot-on-Both-Sides.

Oki, I will tell you a story about Backside-to-the-Fire Pipe. It must be a very Powerful Pipe, because it is still here, among our People. Even our Long-Time Pipe is not here anymore. It was

146

taken north and now it is a white man's Pipe. But my old Pipe, it has a lot of Spirits; I'm sure that it hears me talking about it right now.

That Pipe belonged to me two times. The first time it was transferred to me. The second time, it was returned to me after the death of the person I transferred it to. We went to his mother [old Mrs. Day Rider] to pay our respects. She is a relative of ours. Mrs. Day Rider came over and kissed me, and she was crying. She said, "Oki, Big Snake, go get your Pipe. You don't have to pay on it, just get painted for it again." I didn't say anything. I just looked at her. My brothers, Jack and Jim Low Horn, they told me, "Why aren't you talking? It's your Pipe. Take it. It won't be good for it to be around a sad place."

After the funeral I went to her house. She was walking outside, crying. She just pointed to the house. I went inside and I hugged my Pipe. I told it that a sad thing happened to it because its Owner died. I took it and started home. That's why I had it a second time.

THE LONG-TIME PIPE

Some of our People think that the Long-Time Pipe was in the Bundle originally given by Thunder. They call the Long-Time Medicine Pipe *Mesam-Achkuineman.* Our People hold that Bundle in special reverence; its Owners are often chiefs.

The earliest-known Owner of the Long-Time Pipe was Grey Broad Head. He was remembered by a much later Owner, Stephen Fox, who died not long ago near the age of one hundred. Stephen Fox was still a young man when he met Grey Broad Head, who was then about one hundred himself. This man attributed his old age to the Power he got while keeping the Long-Time Pipe. He told Stephen Fox that his payments for the Pipe included fifty dogs. That was back when our People relied on dogs for help in moving camp and packing meat.

Stephen Fox in his old age. He is praying and calling out four coups for the leader of the Horns Society, during our Sun Dance Encampment a few years ago. He holds the leader's swan-skin-wrapped staff. Stephen Fox lived to be almost a hundred, and remained very active until his death, at which time he was survived by many children—some of them older men and some still quite small.

In later years, the Pipe was owned in succession by Owns No Fancy Horses, Eagle Head, Heavy Shield, Old Man, Sleeps on Top, who was Stephen Fox's father, and Crop-Eared Wolf, our head chief after Red Crow's death. Crop-Eared Wolf gave one hundred horses as a sacrifice for the Pipe. This was back in the days when he was known by the name Many Horses. The Buffalo Days were ended by that time.

Crop-Eared Wolf had the Pipe for a number of years. He gave it to Wolf Chief, also known as Big Wolf. Big Wolf had a fifteen-year-old daughter named Ambush Woman, who was his mini-poka. She married a young man by the name of Parted Hair and her father gave his new son-in-

147

Bobtail Chief, also known as Lone Medicine Pipe Owner and Apikunni, in 1958, shortly before his death. He was a former Owner of the Long-Time Pipe and the last man who could open the Bundle properly. His father was a non-Indian trader, but he chose to follow the life of his mother's People. (Glenbow Archives)

law the Long-Time Pipe. In addition, he gave thirty horses to the groom's parents. They, in turn, are said to have sent fifty horses and their own Medicine Pipe to Big Wolf in honor of the marriage.

The next Owner of the Long-Time Pipe was Shot-on-Both-Sides, who was our head chief for almost fifty years. His wife became known as Long-Time-Pipe-Woman. He kept the Pipe for thirty-four years before he transferred it to Big Sorrel Horse.

Big Sorrel Horse transferred the Pipe to old Weaselhead, also known as Chief-in-Timber, who was Mokakin's stepfather. When he transferred the Pipe to old Bobtail Chief, also called Lone Medicine Pipe Owner, old Weaselhead kept the

Bundle's blue-bead wristlets. The wristlets for the Long-Time Pipe stayed in Weaselhead's family for many years. The original drums from the Bundle are now owned by Many Grey Horses. They are often used at the opening ceremonies of our remaining sacred Pipes.

Bobtail Chief transferred the Long-Time Pipe to Stephen Fox, who vowed to take it during an illness. Stephen Fox was a successful rancher who owned many horses. Bobtail Chief did not think that enough of those horses were being sacrificed for something so Powerful as our Long-Time Pipe. During the transfer ceremony, after he had looked outside at the payments, he came back in and told the drummers to sing a special song in which he said, "I do not see that fine gray team among your payments." Stephen Fox quickly sent someone after the matched team, which he had hoped not to lose.

Stephen Fox was known by the name White-Plastering-His-Home until he became Owner of the Long-Time Pipe. During the transfer, he took on the name Big Eagle. This was in keeping with our tradition, which allows a person to take a new name for noteworthy accomplishment: a first coup, a long-distance journey, or a major role within our tribe.

Stephen Fox left behind a large family when he died a few years ago. Some of them are well known in reserve politics, business, social affairs, and news media. He got the Fox name when, as a young boy, he was sent to school with his sister. The teachers did not care to learn the students' traditional names, so they decided to give them all "proper" names. Because his sister's name was Medicine Fox Woman, they were both given the last name of Fox.

Calling First wanted to have the Long-Time Pipe, even though Stephen Fox did not wish to give it up so soon. So he decided to make sure of a transfer by stealing the Pipe from Stephen Fox. Fifty-two horses were among the payments made during that transfer. Calling First had the distinc-

tion of having been married to a ten-year-old girl when he was only twelve. The marriage was arranged by their parents. It is said that Calling First used to have his mother watch his wife while he went out to play with his friends.

During the 1930s our next-door neighbor, old Dick Soup, made a vow to take the Long-Time Pipe for his son, Arthur, who was then in a hospital. The following year Arthur returned home, and the Pipe was transferred to him. Old Bird Rattler called out the necessary coups while Soup was given the right to mount a horse (by tradition this required a man to relate how he had rescued a friend during battle) and to dismount (for which the coup had to be about an enemy who was pulled from his horse). Of course, no one today has such deeds among his record of accomplishments.

The next Owner of the Long-Time Pipe was Henry Standing Alone, also known as Folded Intestine. He and his wife were well-liked participants in our holy ceremonies. Unfortunately, they were killed recently in a tragic auto accident. Around 1939, Folded Intestine's daughter was very ill and he became depressed and lost his faith in our Old Ways. He wondered why his little girl had to suffer so much instead of him. But his daughter recovered and then he became critically ill. It took three months for him to get well again. While almost dead, he had a dream in which he was told that if he vowed to accept the duties of a Medicine Pipe Bundle, he would recover. He related his dream to two older relatives, Heavy Head and Cross Child, both former Medicine Pipe Keepers. They offered to help him fulfill his vow if he wished to follow their advice. They told him that since no particular Bundle had been mentioned in the dream, he might just as well vow the Powerful Long-Time Pipe. The Bundle was transferred to him during the next Sun Dance Encampment.

Standing Alone transferred the Long-Time Pipe to his sister and her husband, John Red

Crane, also called Black Bachelor. After them the next Owner was Charlie Davis, another successful rancher following the Old Ways, like his friend Dick Soup. While Charlie Davis was on his deathbed, John Red Crane took the Pipe back, and later had it transferred to himself a second time.

Not long after Red Crane took the Pipe over that second time, he sold it to the Provincial Museum. And that's where it is now.

SCENES FROM THE CEREMONY WITH THE LONG-TIME PIPE— BLOOD RESERVE: 1968

(Photos from Alberta Provincial Museum)

Accessories for the Long-Time Pipe: a rawhide bag for paints and necklaces; an eagle-wing fan for the Owner; a braided rawhide rope for the Owner to use when horse raiding; and the wooden tripod to hang the Bundle *on*.

Brown Chief Calf, the leader, praying with the Long-Time Pipe.

150

Sacred berry soup being served to participants of the ceremony. This is a typical scene at all Medicine Pipe ceremonies. Most Owners and former Owners follow the custom of bringing wooden bowls to eat from, while others bring whatever containers they have available.

The drummers and singers of the Long-Time Pipe ceremony. From front to back: Willie White Feathers; Albert Chief Calf; Atsitsina; and Mark Old Shoes.

Participants praying with offerings of tobacco at the end of the ceremony.

Wolf Old Man with the secondary Pipe. The Old Man was then over ninety.

Opposite page, top: Pat Weaselhead (Mokakin), pausing at the beginning of his dance song. He is holding the Long-Time Pipe and the secondary Pipe.

Opposite page, bottom left: Giving encouragement to Mokakin during his dance is his wife, Ponah, and her sister, Mrs. Red Crow.

Opposite page, bottom right: Mokakin's sacred dance. Joe Young Pine stands in back.

Frank Red Crow, dancing with the sacred rattle. He is being helped by his wife and by Mokakin, who holds the owl skin. The Red Crows bought new Hudson's Bay striped blankets to wear for this ceremony.

Frank Red Crow, or Close Shooter, during the ceremony. On his right is Bob Plaited Hair.

Henry Standing Alone bids farewell to the sacred Pipe that he and his wife once owned. The Bundle was sold by his sister and brother-in-law.

OUR FAMILY'S MEDICINE PIPE

Of the four Medicine Pipe Bundles that remain among our People, ours is the only one that has no name suggesting its origin. It has been called "Pipe with a horse-head bowl," or is referred to by the name of one of its notable past Owners. None of our present Old People have ever heard of it coming from somewhere else. It may have originated in the dreams of some long-ago Blood.

There is one brief, old story that concerns the mysterious Powers of our Bundle. Now, the bowl for the sacred Pipe is made of red pipestone, carved in the shape of a horse's head. It is very old, similar in appearance to those made by the Sioux People and some of their eastern neighbors. In the Old Days the People of those tribes had sacred Pipes but without the accompanying Bundles. The bowl might have come with the sacred Stem from one of these tribes. More likely, the original Blood Owner obtained the bowl through trade.

During a long-ago opening ceremony, this horse-head bowl was somehow broken in two. The People were quite concerned about what might happen as a result of this accident. The Owner, whose name has been forgotten, put the two pieces back together, very slowly, and wrapped them up with buckskin. Then he placed them back into the Bundle. Atsitsina continues the story:

"The next spring the Bundle was opened, as always. The Owner told the leader of the ceremony, 'Be careful, don't move the bowl around. It's broken.' The leader said, 'Which one is broken?' 'The one for the main Pipe,' the Owner told him. 'It broke last time when we danced with the Pipe.' The leader was curious so he took off its wrappings. 'Sah,' he said, 'No, it isn't broken. You must be mistaken, because it was never broken anywhere.' He was holding up the bowl and looking it over very carefully. 'Ha—Ayah!' the Owner cried out, 'It sure was broken last year. Everyone saw it. But now it doesn't look like it was broken.' That is a very strange thing about this Pipe that my children have, here. It was broken, but when they opened the Bundle again, it was all right. That's very strange."

Running Wolf and Heavy Shield are remembered as Owners of our Pipe during the Old Days. One of its former Owners, White Horn, John Many Chiefs, gave me the following list of the Bundle's Owners as far back as he knew them:

1. Lizard Shoulder
2. Eagle Arrow
3. Frank Red Crow
4. Red Beads
5. John Cotton
6. Red Leggings
7. Bumble Bee
8. Arthur Healy
9. Wings
10. Bob Black Plume
11. Crow-Spreads-His-Wings
12. John Many Chiefs
13. Laurie Plume
14. Willie Scraping White (Wolf Old Man)
15. Bob First Charger
16. Frank Red Crow
17. Jim Red Crow
18. Stabs Down
19. Adolf Hungry Wolf

Arthur Healy is the earliest Owner still living. He was just a young man when he received the Bundle. It was a gift when he married the daughter of its former Owner, old Bumble Bee. Healy transferred the Bundle to old Wings, who died not long ago.

Wings took over our Bundle sometime in the 1920s. The minipoka of his father, Day Old Man, he joined the Pigeon Society when he was only ten years old. At fifteen he became a member of

Eagle Arrow. The eagle-bone whistle and the feathers are his Medicine. (Glacier Studio)

the Brave Dogs. At the age of thirty-five he joined the Horns.

For several years Wings worked on his brother's farm and then on the reserve's agency farm. Because the agent liked Wings, he was often given pleasant jobs like driving to town in a buggy to pick up mail and groceries. Eventually the agent decided to set up Wings on a farm of his own. Wings chose a vacant piece of land on the reserve and became a "homesteader" (an option still open to members of the band). The agent loaned him eight good horses, a wagon, a six-strip canvas tent (many of our People still lived year-around in tents and tipis back then), a plow, and enough food to get him started.

By the time Wings vowed to take our sacred Pipe, his farm was operating well, and he had already paid off the agent's loan. But after he made his payments for the Bundle, he didn't have enough horses left to haul a wagon. Besides, the wagon itself had been included as part of the payment. For him, the sacrifice had been considerable.

The next Owner of our Bundle was Bob Black Plume, also known as Apikayi, or "Skunk." He was given the name by his grandmother, who used the Power of that animal in her doctoring. He was a regular leader of our sacred ceremonies until recently, when he decided to give all his devotion to the Full Gospel Church.

Bobtail Chief was the leader of the ceremony during which our Pipe was transferred from Laurie Plume, or Otter, to our Old Man. The Old Man kept it for ten years, then gave it as a present to his son-in-law, Bob First Charger. The Old Man was then mourning the death of his wife.

SikskiAki was first in the presence of the Pipe when our Old Man had it. She was just a little girl when Grandma AnadaAki and her husband, Ben Strangling Wolf, took her along to the Old Man's spring Thunder ceremony. Although Sikski-Aki was then quite young, her memories add to the spirit the Bundle now has for us.

THE DIFFERENT-PEOPLE PIPE

One of our remaining Medicine Pipe Bundles has been with our People since the year 1833. Some ethnologists have called this Bundle the Gros Ventre Pipe and even the Long-Time Pipe. Among our People it is known as *NamaTappi-Achkuineman*, or the "Different-People Pipe." It was brought here from the Mandan tribe.

Our head chief at the end of the Buffalo

Days was Red Crow. Before him our head chief was Red Crow's uncle, Pinukwiim, or "Seen-From-Afar." He was so named because he often traveled great distances to visit people of other tribes. There is a story that he led a party of men as far south as Mexico, a journey that took about a year. Pinukwiim brought back the Different-People Pipe from one of his visits to the Mandan People, who lived far to the east in the area of present-day North Dakota.

Pinukwiim and his wife boarded a keel-boat belonging to the American Fur Company for part of their trip east. They left Fort McKenzie in present-day northern Montana, in the spring of 1833, after the ice broke up in the Missouri River. The company was shipping its winter trade of hides and furs and was eager to have the trade of the Blackfoot divisions, in whose country Fort McKenzie was located. It was to the company's advantage to have an influential man like Pinukwiim riding one of their boats.

They passed through the dangerous country of the Assiniboine tribe in order to reach the fur company's Fort Union at the junction of the Missouri and Yellowstone rivers. Our people and the Assiniboines are traditional enemies, but a brief peace had been brought about by the fur company before Pinukwiim's journey.

At Fort Union, Pinukwiim and his wife met a party of Mandan People, who invited them to their earth lodge village. They were treated with honor and respect during their stay. The Mandans gave them each a Powerful holy Bundle when they prepared to return home. His wife was given a sacred buffalo headdress from a Mandan women's society. This headdress was later taken into our own Motokiks Society. Pinukwiim was given the sacred Pipe we now call the Different-People Pipe in memory of the Mandans and their earth lodges.

The return trip took thirty-four days. The German explorer Prince Maximilian noted in his journal that he saw the Blood couple in a Hidatsa earth lodge village earlier in the summer, and that "the man was well made and both were very neatly dressed."

About twenty years later Pinukwiim again visited the Mandans. By then he was head chief of the Bloods. A trader recorded in his journal that he was "splendidly dressed (in) a magnificent bonnet of war-eagle feathers falling to his feet." He must have been a most courageous man to wander in such style through the country of his enemies.

After Pinukwiim, the earliest Owner we can recall is Old Spear Chief. He transferred the Pipe to old Long-Time Squirrel and his son, Many Grey Horses. From them the Pipe went to Steel, then to Weasel Moccasin, and then to old Plume. Long-Time Squirrel took the Pipe for a second time, before it went to Mark Old Shoes in 1950. He transferred the Pipe to Jim White Man Left, who then transferred it to the Old Man's later partner and roommate, Big Nose. At the Sun Dance Camp the Bundle was ceremonially stolen from Big Nose's lodge while no one was there. It was transferred to the children of Many Grey Horses, who still own it.

THE CREE MEDICINE PIPE

Another of our remaining Medicine Pipe Bundles is known as *Assinai-Achkuineman*, or "Cree Medicine Pipe." The sacred Pipe in that Bundle was captured from a camp of Cree People during a battle. That battle took place sometime around 1880 and was one of the last fought between the Crees and our People. This is the way it happened:

After a Cree raid on Blood camps, One Spotted Horse led a war party of Bloods and Piegans in retaliation. He is remembered today by the name One Spot.

Some distance east of the present-day city of Edmonton, the war party located a small Cree camp and attacked in broad daylight, overpowering the Crees. Those who escaped sought shelter in the nearby coulee and river bottom. They left everything behind in their camp except their women and children.

The invaders rounded up the Cree horses and looted the camp. One Spot's partner, Many Mules, saw the sacred Pipe wrapped up and hanging from a tripod. As he approached it, One Spot called out, "My friend, don't touch that sacred thing. Those Crees have a lot of Power that may kill you if you take their Medicine." Startled, Many Mules left the Pipe and went on to look for other trophies. Then One Spot went over to it, said a prayer and took the sacred Pipe for himself, calling out, "I am One Spot of the Bloods."

The war party had captured many horses, clothing, and other goods. A large victory dance was held when the party returned. They had not lost a single member. One Spot cradled the sacred Pipe in his arms while others danced with their captured goods. But he left the Pipe on a tripod outside of his tipi; he did not want to risk the safety of his family by bringing the Cree Medicine inside.

A few days later, One Spot asked several holy men, old Medicine Pipe Owners and Beaver Men, what he should do with his new sacred Pipe. They advised him to go through a purifying ceremony to remove any bad Spirit the Crees might have cast upon it from a distance. A bunch of sage was gathered and mixed with buffalo meat, a traditional sacrament believed to have the Power to remove bad Spirits from anything. The sacrament was rubbed all over the Pipestem and One Spot's body while all the Old Men prayed. After that, One Spot kept the Pipe inside his tipi.

In order to take this sacred Pipe into our Medicine Pipe Ways, it was necessary to have it transferred to an Owner. Because One Spot had fulfilled his purpose by capturing the Pipe and bringing the party safely back home, he decided to give it to Many Mules. The basic materials for a Medicine Pipe Bundle were collected, and Old People made up the accessories and prepared the skins. Since no one knew the Pipe's Cree songs, our own Medicine Pipe songs were used for the traditional Blood ceremony. People who in the past had been given the rights for such sacred objects as topknots, tripods, Owner's necklaces, and so forth, were called upon to transfer those rights to the new Owner and his wife.

It has been said of the Cree Pipe that new Owners were never captured with it, and that the Pipe was always taken to fulfill vows. Because some of our People never lost their fear of the Power of the Crees, the Cree Pipe was not transferred often. The sacrifice payments were always less than for our other Pipes.

A history of its past Keepers is not well known. One former Owner was Round Nose, who transferred it to Joe Young Pine. After him, it went to Charlie Wolf Plume. Among recent Owners were Jack Hind Bull, then Jim White Bull, and then Hind Bull's daughter, Mrs. Bill Heavy Runner. She gave the Pipe to old Bob First Charger. After his death it was transferred to the partnership of young Joe Chief Body and his adopted daughter, the present Owners.

Around 1910 several Bloods, including Dog Child and Sun Calf, came upon a Cree camp. They asked the Crees if anything was known about their old Pipe. One of them, Shot Many Times, spoke Blackfoot fairly well and was familiar with the Pipe. He said that his People received their first sacred Pipe from Sun. He had only heard about a few such Pipes, and their Owners were always brave men and holy leaders. At times their duty required them to unwrap the sacred Stem and walk between the lines of a battle in order to offer the symbolic "Pipe of Peace" to the two fighting groups. Many bloody battles were ended this way, but an occasional Pipe-bearer did not live to see the peace.

Shot Many Times also described some Cree customs with sacred Pipes. In daytime the Pipes were hung outside on tripods, and daily incense

A typical Cree camp, along the Sasketchewan River, in 1871. The painted lodge in the foreground has a tipi flag hanging over it and a Medicine Pipe Bundle hanging on a tripod behind it. (Charles Horestsky)

was made for them. The Owners ate from wooden bowls and were treated with special respect by their People. When the sacred Pipe was smoked—before a war party left on a dangerous mission, or when an offering of peace was being made—each smoker took only four whiffs, even if the tobacco was no longer lit.

Shot Many Times sang a few Cree songs for the Pipe. The Bloods found them to be much different from our own Medicine Pipe songs. One of the war songs included these words: "I sing to the Sun. Give me a man of honor to kill."

In 1916 an anthropologist named Alanson Skinner studied the Crees and wrote about their sacred Pipes: "There have been three pipes among the Cree, but there are only two now, as the Qu'Apelle River band (some ways east of Edmonton) sent theirs to the Bloods to make peace, and the latter still have it." This statement indicates that there was probably either a great misunderstanding, or else wishful thinking on the part of the Cree who gave the information to Skinner.

THE CHILDREN'S MEDICINE PIPE

Besides the four Medicine Pipes we open every spring to celebrate the return of Thunder and the good seasons that follow, there is one more Medicine Pipe Bundle, which is rarely opened. Keepers used to carry this Bundle's Pipe to war so that its Spirit would give them the Power of success. Since the end of the war days, the Bundle has been transferred to the children of those who wanted its Power. Thus, it became known as the Children's Medicine Pipe Bundle.

159

This Bundle has the distinction that its sacred Pipe, though fully decorated, is only the length of a normal pipestem. In the Old Days, there were several short Pipes, but only two remain today among all our divisions, and only this one is considered to have been a true war Pipe, the other having never been to war. Originally, seven songs were sung for the opening. But during recent transfer ceremonies, only two of the original songs were sung; the others had been forgotten and were replaced by our usual Medicine Pipe songs.

George First Rider said that some of the Pipe's wartime Owners included Atsitsina's father, Natosina; Over-Designed Tipi; Striped Bear; and Big Wolf. From them he learned this story of its origin:

A man had only two wives. He was successful, but he didn't have many horses. He had one real good horse for buffalo hunts. When he went on a buffalo hunt, he killed many and gave much meat to the People. If he was asked for something he would give it. His name was gradually putting him into higher rank because he was very generous. But he didn't gain anything of real value from his raids on the warpath.

One time when it was raining continually and the wood piles were all soaked, he went on a buffalo hunt. To enjoy the adventure of the hunt more, he didn't join hunting parties but went alone. When he brought home his meat, he was all soaked. He told his wives, "Don't bring the meat inside; unload it outside and give some to the People." Then the wives brought in the meat they were going to keep. They brought it in to dry. It is usual to dry the meat a little, so that when it is sliced it will not slip out of your hand. Fresh meat is slippery, and would cause the women to cut themselves with their knives. And the meat is tasty when it is cut dried. If the meat is sliced fresh, the flavor seeps all out.

Now he told his wives, "Build a fire with that big-sized wood. I am tired from riding and drowsy

from being wet. Take the children out. Go someplace so I can sleep. So they built a fire and laid some bigger wood on top. A half-dried wood was laid right on top. The women went out and they weighed down the door flap with a log so that nobody would go in, knowing that the door was shut.

As he was dozing off, he heard a voice singing. After a moment he heard it again and sat up. He saw the fire was burning low, so he raked up the fireplace and rekindled it. There was a lot of half-dried wood that was not yet burned and he pushed it into the fire. Then he lay down, facing the wall as before. Again, he heard the voice singing. There were words in the song, but he didn't get the words. He sat up and listened, but when he looked about, no one was singing. He opened the door slightly and looked out, but no one was there, either. He went back and raked all the unburned wood into the fire and as he lay down the voice sang. This time he could make out the words. He had never heard the song before. "My Pipe is holy. My Pipe hears me. My Pipe is my Medicine."

The voice was singing in the fireplace, so he sat up and looked at the fireplace. The voice sang, "My Pipe I give you. My Pipe I now give you."

As he looked, a Worm stuck its head out from the half-dried wood. Worm was wiggling because the fire was burning the wood toward where he was. "This is the one that is singing," the man said to himself.

After a while, Worm said to the man, "I am giving you my Pipe." The man replied to Worm, "Why are you worried? Nothing is going to happen to you." Then the man picked up the wood with Worm on it and he went out. As it had rained for a considerable time, there was water in hollow places. He doused the wood in the water and went south along the river. When he came to an opening in the forest he found a good spot in a growth of big trees. He stuck the wood into a pile of dead trees and gave the wood some of his fine-cut tobacco. "Oki, here is a smoke," he told Worm, and went home.

When his wives returned, they found weapons and moccasins but not their husband. In earlier times, if a person went out to look after his horses on a rainy day, he went barefoot so as not to spoil his moccasins. The wives said, "Here are his moccasins, and here is his knife, and he didn't take his bow and arrow. Maybe he went out for a while."

Soon the man returned and told his wives, "I am tired. I will sleep here alone and tomorrow we will invite some people."

In the morning his wives boiled some meat and he went out and invited seven Old People. They came in, they sat down, and they ate. When they got through, he told them, "Oki, you Old Men, I will tell you a story and you will tell me what is to be done."

The man then told his story of how Worm had sung to him and given him a Pipe. He told them, "Last night I slept alone. I burned incense. As I slept I saw the Pipe. It was given to me and I heard the songs clearly. It was an ordinary smoking pipe, only it was decorated with feathers at the bud. Oki, Old Men, make your decisions on what is to be done."

So the Old Men thought. After a time, each one said, "Let it be done this way," or "Let it be done that way." One of the men was an important Medicine Pipe Man. He advised, "This pipe will be decorated at the bud with flared feathers strung together and then it will be a Medicine Pipe. But it will not be taken as the regular Medicine Pipes are taken."

The first person to take the Pipe wasn't the man who had the vision. A young married man took it first. The man who had the vision knew the songs, so he transferred them to the first Owner of the Small Medicine Pipe. The young married man provided food and the Small Medicine Pipe was transferred to him.

The young man didn't have his Pipe very long when the man who had the vision stole it and went on the warpath with it. When he returned successfully with it, another young man took the Small Medicine Pipe in a transfer. After that, it was regularly stolen to be taken on the warpath. When they returned they brought it home with something stolen in the raid—a horse or a rifle.

So that is how our sacred Bundle was used.

It is believed that no one who wore the sacred Pipe on the warpath was ever injured. It was taken along in its cloth covering. Just before the start of a battle, or before the bearer went into an enemy camp, it was taken out of its covering and those who were in its company prayed and sang with it. The bearer then tied the sacred Stem in his hair.

The Children's Pipe has had many Keepers since the end of the war days. Most recently, it was transferred from the children of Stabs Down to the children of Adam Delaney, who is the new leader of the Horns Society.

ANOTHER SMALL MEDICINE PIPE

At one time there were at least three Small Medicine Pipes among our People. The Children's Medicine Pipe is still with the Bloods, and another Small Pipe is now among the North Piegans. The third one was obtained and sold by Mrs. Walters to some museum in the United States in 1941. Atsitsina remembers this story of its origin:

There was a Blackfoot by the name of Middle Calf. He was so brave and Powerful that he always went on war raids by himself. One time, he was coming back home with a bunch of stolen horses when he had a dream. In his dream an Old Man told him, "I am the one who has been giving you Power. I am now going to give you my strongest Medicine. It will allow you to reach very old age. You must give it to your children to take care of, so that they can grow old too."

161

Then the Old Man showed Middle Calf how to make the small Medicine Pipe.

When Middle Calf got back home he made a stem just like for a regular pipe and he made it look fancy with eagle feathers and beads and arrowheads. He coated it with incense and with real paint, and he painted his children for it.

They used to take this Pipe to war, just like the Children's Pipe. Only they sold this Pipe to the white People down in the States.

In the notes of Mrs. Walters is a letter Percy Creighton wrote her dated July 24, 1941:

At the Sun Dance saw a head dress, Buffalo with trailer, also a 'war pipe.' There are two small pipe bundles on Blood Reserve—used on war trails carried 'tied at back of head.'

A regular pipe bundle is about 3–4 feet long; these little ones about 14 inches. With it is a bag of paint, charming medicine, 4 eagle feathers quilled, a string of 'pony' beads, at the end a flint arrow head, 2 eagle claws fringed between, and beaded pipe stem covered with buffalo hide and quilled on 3 sides, the lower handle is covered with muskrat fur—bound with mixed feathers—[the Bundle includes] owl, coopers hawk, falcon feathers, a pair of blue bead bracelets, small bag of incense, a deer hoof rattle, a bone flute, smudge stick, and case of rawhide fringed.

In 1906 the anthropologist Clark Wissler made this comment about the Small Pipe:

There is a small pipe among the Blood, regarded as very powerful in war. It has four songs, one of which is a typical medicine-pipe song while the others are quite different. In the presence of the enemy this pipe was smoked by the party carrying it, the songs sung, and the pipe tied in the owner's hair. The first Blood to own it received it by transfer from a North Blackfoot. Recently [1903] it changed hands for six horses and other property.

162

Wissler also mentions in a footnote to that story that the Dakota (Sioux) "had similar pipes for the same purpose."

SOME OTHER MEDICINE PIPES WE USED TO HAVE

As late as 1960 there were still ten Medicine Pipes on the Blood Reserve. Half have since been sold to museums and private collectors. Although our Pipes are much sought after with large sums of money, the collectors show little interest in the spiritual history of these Bundles. When they display the Bundles, any accompanying information is generally anthropological in nature and often spiritually misleading. In one case, a sacred Stem is displayed next to a collection of regular pipes inside a glass case labeled Indian Pipes.

The Alberta Provincial Museum has seven or more Medicine Pipe Bundles, none accompanied by thorough documentation that might give future students an idea of the true Spirit which once was with them. Some are accompanied by no more information than the last Owner's name.

To complete my words about our sacred Pipes, I will tell you what I have learned about some of those that no longer belong to our People.

OUR UNCLE'S PIPE

Just a few years ago, our uncle, Atsitsina, became a Medicine Pipe Owner, perhaps for the last time. He had hoped to keep the Bundle for many years, but someone made a vow to take it. Atsitsina arranged to take it back after the vow was fulfilled, but the last Owner quietly sold it and it was quickly taken far from our reserve.

This particular Bundle, which never had a distinct name, had been owned by Atsitsina's dad, Natosina, for many years during the Buffalo Days. Natosina stole the Pipe from old Iron, who took it back again after Natosina's term was over.

Later, it belonged to Grey Broad Head, who once owned the Long-Time Pipe as well. Next in line was his brother, Running Antelope, then Charlie Eagle Speaker, and then Harry Spear Chief. Albert Chief Calf, who is known by his father's name, NinnaOnesta, or Chief Calf, had the Bundle for a long time. After NinnaOnesta, the Bundle went to Jack Eagle Bear, from whom Atsitsina stole it in the Old Way. He told us the story of how he stole it:

Oki, my brother, Jim Low Horn, and I went to Lethbridge one time to buy groceries, and to get some intestinal meats from the butcher there. As we drove along I asked him, "In the Old Days, how did people steal Medicine Pipes?"

He said he knew exactly how it was done. He said, "I won't tell you how it was done. I will show you. You have been wanting a Medicine Pipe in your old age, so we will just go and get the one that used to belong to your father."

He told me to drive to Jack Eagle Bear's house, where my dad's Pipe was. When we got there all we saw was just a bunch of kids playing. Jim asked them, "Where is Long Mane?" That was Eagle Bear's other name. They said, "He went to Stand Off. He just left. He will be gone for some time."

We went into Long Mane's house. The Pipe was hanging up in there. The children all came and looked. There was a place for incense, and the sweet pine needles were there. Jim told me, "Take some of those pine needles. Use them on your feet and rub your body with them and put them in your pockets and put some in your mouth and spray them on the Pipe." I did what he said, then I took down the Pipe. The children were all just looking at us. Jim told me, "Go and put it in the car." Then he told the children not to tell their father who took the Pipe.

When we got back home my brother said, "That is how it is done. Now you have stolen a Pipe. Very few people have done that. They were scared to steal Pipes." He told me that I

would be brought to trial before the Owner and his society. He said that I would have to pay a lot more on the Pipe because I had stolen it.

Some time passed and I heard people say that Long Mane's Pipe was stolen. They didn't know yet who it was. Then Bob Black Plume came to my house, and he told me, "They have found out you stole that Pipe."

Then Long Mane sent word for me to go to his house. When I got there, he said, "You stole my Pipe. In the spring we will have your trial. You set the date when you will be prepared for the trial." I said, "I am ready to take it any time. I have all my payments ready." Then he asked me, "How do you stand? How much do you intend to give me so that I will let you out of the trial?" My brother had given me five ten-dollar bills. I gave them to Long Mane and he said, "That will do for a start." Then he measured my feet and my wife's for the moccasins they would make for us. He said, "Just say when, so I can tell my comrades, the Crazy Dogs, because it's their Pipe too." [They had helped with the payments during his transfer.]

As soon as the days were nice, I sent word to him to come up and transfer the Pipe to me. When the day came he set up his tipi by my house. I had my Pipe transferred to me at my home. That's the right way if the transfer is not during the Sun Dance. All the Crazy Dogs came. Laurie Plume led the transfer ceremony. I paid really good on the Pipe. All my relatives came and helped me.

So that is how I stole my Pipe. I'm the only one still living who stole a holy Pipe; just me, Willie Eagle Plume.

STEVE OKA'S PIPE

While mourning over the loss of his wife, Steve Oka found no comfort in the Medicine Pipe their friend Mike Eagle Speaker had given the couple as a present a long time before. No one from the reserve made any effort to claim the Pipe. (Sacred Bundles are usually cared for by someone else when there is a death in the Owner's family. Often a former Owner takes the Bundle back and later has it transferred to himself.) So Steve Oka sold the Bundle to Hugh Dempsey for three hundred dollars. Dempsey took it for the Blackfoot collection in the then-new Glenbow Museum in Calgary.

The Bundle's former Owner, Mike Eagle Speaker, was one of the first from the Blood Reserve to obtain a college degree. He once told me that he originally got the Bundle because of a vow made during a time of need in his family. Because the Power of the Bundle helped his family overcome their trial, Mike felt he had been repaid for his material investment, and for that reason had given the Pipe to its next Owner, accepting no payments.

Mokakin said that this Pipe originally came from the North Blackfoot People. The first Blood man to own it was Sun Calf, a partner of old Red Crow. After him the Owners were Hungry Crow; Rides-at-the-Door (the holy woman and her late husband); Gordon Bird; Morning Bird; Camoose Bottle; Joe Eagle Ribs; Mike Eagle Speaker; and then Steve Oka.

WILLIE MILLS'S PIPE

One of our former Medicine Pipe Bundles is listed in the collection of the Provincial Museum as the "Willie Mills Pipe." Mills was the grandson of the Negro interpreter, Dave Mills (Young Scabby Bull). Like Steve Oka, Mills sold his Pipe while mourning the loss of his wife. He sold it in 1966 to the white man of the Alberta Provincial Museum.

Mokakin and Atsitsina, both of whom had sacred Pipes at that time, told me that they used to dread this white man's visits. Mokakin said, "That guy, he never takes no for an answer. He come back and he come back, no matter what I tell him, he always come in with his big smile. Even nobody trusts him with it. He smile, and

pretty soon he don't smile no more when I tell him I'm not interested in his money. As soon as he knows something is wrong in our house, he comes again."

When his offer to buy sacred Pipes was first accepted by old Willie Mills, the white man wrote to his superior at the Provincial Museum:

Among the Indians, when ownership of the bundle is transferred, payment is made to the amount of $1,000 to $1,500. There are very few of these and they are difficult to obtain as the Plains Indians consider them to be sacred and extremely valuable. . . . Today there remains only 5 on The Reservations in Canada and the United States, and 6 in museum collections in the U.S. and Canada [far from true; there were many more]. . . . These bundles are very old and valuable, the originals are never duplicated and vary in age from 80 to 200 years. The market price for this type of bundle is $1,000 if complete. This particular sacred pipe bundle . . . is approximately 150 years old . . . contains 105 items.

The "market price" he lists was set by himself and, like the value of all good investments, it rose rapidly after he wrote his letter. He was able to buy the Bundle for $700, which he thought was quite a deal, since Willie Mills gave "goods to the value of $1,100 for this bundle when ownership was transferred to him in 1953." Mills had gotten the Bundle from his father, Harry Mills, who had been its previous Owner. Before him it was owned by Nelson Rabbit; Brown Chief Calf; Mark Wolf Child; Big Sorrel Horse; Iron; and Calf Shirt, who had the Power with Rattlesnakes.

A BAD MEDICINE PIPE BUNDLE

One of the Bundles that our Old People actually remember being made up during their lifetime is the one that Lone Invitation Caller was directed to make. That Bundle became known as the Bad

Medicine Pipe Bundle. George First Rider's father, Dog Child, had this Pipe for a short time, and of course, George has a story to tell about it.

This Pipe was a man-made Pipe. It was constructed by Lone Invitation Caller. It was a Black-Covered Pipe, constructed in a different way, like a Water Bundle Pipe [a Beaver Bundle Pipe]. Eagle tailfeathers strung together like a fan were attached to the Pipe. [The war Pipes that we call Black-Covered Pipes are basically like Beaver Pipes; neither has a fan of eagle feathers and both have Stems covered all over with eagle plumes. This Bad Medicine Pipe had a fan of eagle feathers and was placed inside a black covering.]

But the Pipe was useless. It was then called the Hairlock Pipe.

After Lone Invitation Caller had constructed the Pipe, he gave it to his friend Bull Limper (Spear Chief). Lone Invitation Caller didn't perform a miracle with the Pipe, he just transferred the Pipe at the home of Spear Chief. It takes four days to transfer a Medicine Pipe, but Lone Invitation Caller didn't transfer his Pipe in the proper manner.

Before winter came, Spear Chief's wife died. Then he realized that the Pipe was a fake, so he cut the tails from the beaver pelts and sold them. A little while later Spear Chief died, and his son, White Leggings (Harry Spear Chief), kept the Pipe. White Leggings took sick and he almost died. Then he gave it to Little White Weasel Calf [Dog Child, George's father]. But I told him, "Put that Pipe away, it's a fake!"

So the Pipe was taken across the U.S. border, and it was there for a year. Nobody ever bought the Pipe because it was newly made. Then it was brought back and Little White Weasel Calf gave it to Little Eagle Ribs [Joe Eagle Ribs]. Right after Little Eagle Ribs took the Pipe, Little White Weasel Calf's wife died, and pretty soon he did, too. Little Eagle Ribs took the Pipe, and before it was transferred to him, he died. His stepson [Sam Hairy Bull, who sold Eagle Ribs' Beaver Bundle to Edmonton] took the Pipe. The boy got drunk and gave the Pipe to Calling Last for some liquor. Calling Last found out that the Pipe was a fake, so he went and sold it in Browning, Montana. And that was the end of it.

A BAD PIPE FROM THE GHOSTS

Our People fear the mystery of ghosts. They believe that ghosts are able to make living souls go along with them to the Sandhills, where all ghosts of Blood People are thought to dwell. One Blood man went with the ghosts and returned with a Medicine Pipe they had given him. This story has become a popular legend among our People. Here is Mokakin's version:

This Medicine Pipe had the name Shaggy Medicine Pipe because it was all covered with eagle plumes that stuck way out. The Pipe was so new, the plumes weren't flattened from being wrapped for a long time.

Oki, this took place a long time ago—I don't know how many years. A man came back home from his war trail and found that his wife was already dead and buried. He had loved her very much and he became very lonely for her. Every night he went up on a hill and cried and mourned. One night a ghost came and spoke to him. "If you want to visit your wife I can take you to her. You've got to bring some tobacco for an offering. But don't bring any weapons or anything made out of metal." Ghosts don't like metal. The man went home and took off his knife and his rings and he picked up some tobacco. Then he went back up the hill.

The ghost took the man a long ways through the dark, over hills and across rivers. Finally they came to a big open place where there was a big tipi camp. The ghost stopped in front of one of the tipis and told the man to go inside and wait. Inside, another ghost was sitting at the back. The ghost told him, "Yes, you will see your wife, but don't touch her or even kiss her."

The man was told to look outside the tipi, where he saw his wife walking. He wanted to go over to her, but the ghost told him he could only look. When daylight came everything disappeared and he was alone sitting in a field. He felt pretty lonesome. Then he remembered his offering of Kinnikinnick, so he took it out and said, "Here is your smoke." Something grabbed the pouch from his hand and soon he saw a cloud of smoke next to him. The smoke gradually began to outline people and the tipi in which they were sitting.

After the ghost-man finished his smoke he said, "Man, I have pity for you, so I am going to help you. First, I'm going to let you take your wife back home with you. But you've got to remember four things when you take her. First, don't look back when you leave here; second, don't ask her any questions; third, don't touch her until you take four sweat baths with her; and fourth, never call her a ghost. The man remembered what they told him. Then the ghost-man said, "Now, I'm also going to give you my Medicine Pipe. We're going to open it for you right now and you are going to see it and learn the ceremony." So the man watched and listened to what they did.

When the man left the ghost camp, his woman walked behind him. He didn't look back or say anything to her. After a little while he built a sweat lodge and they both went in it. He saw that his wife's body was just a skeleton.

They went on and on, and then the man built another sweat lodge. This time he saw the outline of his wife's body, but it was all covered with maggots.

On and on they went some more, then he built a sweat lodge for the third time. This time he could recognize his wife's body, but there were still maggots crawling on it.

When they got on top of the hill by their camp, where he first saw the ghost, he built a sweat lodge for the fourth time. When it was finished his wife's body sat up and she came back to life. They held each other and he kissed her.

After the man and his wife were home for a while he began to make up the Medicine Pipe that the ghost gave him. For several years his wife took care of the Pipe and they lived pretty good. The man was happy to have his wife back and he treated her very well. Then, one night they had a lot of guests in their tipi and his wife was cooking some food. Just when it was ready to eat, she knocked it over and spilled it all in the fire. The man lost his temper and shouted at her, "What's the matter—can't you do anything right, you ghost woman!" His wife jumped back on her bed and covered up her head with her shawl. The man told her to get up and clean the spilled food. When she didn't get up, he went over and pulled her shawl off. Underneath the shawl there was only the skeleton of his wife.

Not long after that the man gave up his Shaggy Pipe to somebody else. Then he died. The one he gave the Pipe to also died. Some more people had the Pipe, and each time they died when they got it or soon after they gave it up. Finally a chief took it to see what he could do. When he died, the People said, "This Pipe came from the ghosts and everybody that has it becomes a ghost, so we better give it back to the ghosts." So they buried the Shaggy Pipe with the chief and they never made it up again. Everybody talks about it since then.

THE BLACK-COVERED PIPES

There was once another kind of Medicine Pipe. These were covered with dark-colored cloth and accompanied by a few accessories in a rawhide bag. They were used to inspire spiritual power for an individual or for a society in times of war. The People did not look to these Pipes or their Owners for everyday spiritual help.

There used to be many of these Black-Covered Pipes, but none remain with us today. Most of their individual origins and ceremonies have been forgotten, but we can surmise that they originated either in the dreams of men who were successful on the war trails or were captured in battle from enemy tribes, most commonly Crees, Crows, Gros Ventres, and Assiniboines.

Atsitsina told me this story about one that was captured by a Blood man:

Oki this story is about a Black-Covered Pipe. My father's friend, Crow-Parts-His-Hair, captured it. My dad and his friend went on a raid against the Eastern Crees. [The term used here by Atsitsina was Pinapasinai, *literally, "downstream People." It could mean the Assiniboine, Hidatsa, or some other tribe to the east of us.] They went into the enemy camp at night to look for horses when Crow-Parts-His-Hair saw it hanging above a tipi door. He cut the thongs and took it down. Then they got some horses and returned home safely with the Pipe. All different kinds of fine people [successful people] had it. We don't know where it finally went to.*

These war Pipes were kept covered with black cloth so that they would not reflect Sun's light and reveal the Owner out on the war path. At one time, buckskin coated with sacred black paint was used to cover them. Among the Pipe's accessories were one or more *Iniskims*, sacred stones, fixed up in such a way that they could be tied into a person's hair. Such Iniskims were worn in battle either by the Owner or by someone who had borrowed the Pipe for battle. The Pipes were usually carried on the bearer's back, suspended from a belt worn over both shoulders. Sweetgrass was used for incense. The few Black-Covered Pipes that survived past the war days were treated like simple versions of our regular Medicine Pipes; they were transferred and opened to the same ceremonies, but without the many details of the Bundles.

One of the last Black-Covered Pipes was transferred to Frank Red Crow in 1939, so that he could sell it to Mrs. Walters. For twenty years it had belonged to a man named Small Eyes, or Gros Ventre Boy, as he was also known.

According to Mrs. Walters's notes, this Bundle contained no bird or animal skins. Its main contents were the sacred Pipe wrapped in cloth and a rawhide bag filled with paints and other accessories. Part of a red shawl covered these things. The sacred Pipe was "covered with beads, furs, and feathers." Its mouthpiece was bare of decoration and showed the careful work and smooth, glossy finish it received from its maker. Most of the Stem was fully covered with fluffy eagle plumes. A number of spiritual decorations were suspended from the Stem. Most outstanding of these was a "layer of eagle feathers, each quill reinforced with a strip of rawhide, wrapped with quills, and tipped with a bit of weasel fur and human hair." A tiny Iniskim was attached to the base of these feathers with a thong. Fastened securely at another point along the Stem was a tiny bead-edged sack, probably containing some previous Owner's personal Medicine. Six bunches of fluffy eagle plumes hung from the Stem by strands of blue-green beads. Also attached to the Stem was a buffalo tail, decorated with strips of weasel skin, pieces of red cloth and porcupine quills, and a long tassel of horse hair, decorated in the same way.

The rawhide case was made of elk hide in the old-style boat shape. It was rectangular and its upper corners ended in angular peaks similar to the forward point of a boat. The bag contained a calf skin with the hair still on. Wrapped in a bed of shedded buffalo hair in the calf skin were nine Iniskims. One Iniskim had been carved to look like a man. Also in the bag were the remains of a feather originally worn by the Owners, a wrapped-up Iniskim taken on war trails, a bag of black paint and a paint stick, a bag of red paint, two pieces of stone remnants of former Pipe-bowls, and a rawhide-covered piperest. This piperest was about four inches in diameter and contained part of a buffalo chip. It was covered with five rows of old pony beads and sacred paint. The bowl of the ordinary smoking pipe, which was used during the ceremony, always rested on this chip.

Another Pipe once belonged to the Catcher's Society. It was last owned by the Old Man's step-father, old Scraping White. It was inherited by his son, Harold Chief Moon, who sold the Pipe to a collector from the States.

A Black-Covered Pipe from the Seizers Society was sold to Mrs. Walters by Percy Creighton. He sent this note along with it:

The pipe belongs to a man named Never Sits Down, the same man who made the Never Sits Down shield [the most famous shield among our People—several variations of it have been made over the ages, and we will see one of them later]; he was a great medicine man. He made this pipe and carried it when on the war path. When the enemy is in sight, he takes his pipe, and makes ceremony with it. That allures the enemy from their watchouts, and it's easy for him. With all his undertakings [he] always gets away with plenty of horses from his enemy. When he died, his friends of the same age put the pipe as the head article of this Society, called the Seizer's, and the pipe is called the "Seizer's pipe." Now the society is done away with.

Seizers Society Pipe on display at the Alberta Provincial Museum. It formerly belonged to the Bloods.

Iniskims:
The Sacred Buffalo-Stones

In the Old Days, there was a sacred article sure to be found in every household, which everyone learned the songs and simple ceremony for in early childhood. This sacred object was called the *Iniskim*, the sacred buffalo-stone.

Iniskims are stones whose odd shapes help to inspire thoughts about the Powers of the Universe. A man preparing to go on a hunt or a woman in need of spiritual support would take the Iniskim and, holding it between the palms, pray to Earth and other Spirits of nature the sacred rock represents. Some of us still pray with Iniskims.

Any stone kept in a sacred way can be an Iniskim. Odd-shaped stones and fossils are the most common. The odd-shaped stones usually resemble persons or buffalo; the fossilized shells inspire thoughts about the Holy Power of the Universe. The latter took on special significance when our People learned that the vast prairies were once under water.

The Iniskims in Beaver Bundles, Medicine Pipe Bundles, and sacred Tipi Bundles were collected by our People in the very long ago. Some of these old Iniskims were passed along with their Bundles or separately, and are still among us today. The Iniskims kept on the family altar or worn on a necklace are not so old. Most have been found recently by members of the family.

Few old Iniskims of this kind still exist, as they are usually buried with the persons who find them.

When a spiritual-looking stone was found, it was brought to a holy man or woman, who blessed it with a covering of sacred paint, sang the ceremonial songs, and, after thus endowing it, awarded this new Iniskim to the finder.

Iniskim necklaces were commonly worn, especially by children. At ceremonies, our Old Man wore a bead-decorated one given to him in childhood by his grandfather, Owl Boy. He instructed us to keep Iniskims on our altar at camp, and while traveling to wrap them up in a layer of matted buffalo hair and keep them inside a rawhide bag. Such bags are usually square, with long fringes of buckskin along the sides, and decorations of colored geometric designs. These bags are usually large enough to hold most of a family's sacred articles—incense, paints, necklaces, feathers, smoking mixtures.

The Old Man used to keep at his house a little earth-filled box that sat between his stove and rear wall. It was his altar for making incense. Inside it were several small Iniskims, each resting on a little cushion of buffalo hair. Some of the stones looked like standing persons; others resembled buffalo. One was simply a smooth, round pebble. All were covered with sacred red paint.

169

Let me tell you the ancient story about Iniskims as I learned it from the Old Man.

THE FIRST INISKIM

In the long-ago, before the People had horses, they sometimes starved when they were unable to move their camps fast enough to keep up with the moving buffalo herds. This story takes place during such a famine.

Three sisters were married to the same man. One day they were out gathering firewood. The youngest sister was carrying a large load of wood when her carrying strap broke. Each time she stopped to fix the strap it broke again. Her sisters went back to their lodge while she tried to fix her strap for the fourth time. As she bent over to fix the strap, she thought she heard a voice singing. She looked around but could see no one. Yet the voice seemed to be coming from very near by. She became frightened and got up to leave, but the voice called out to her. Then she noticed in the direction of the voice an unusual-looking stone sitting up on the ground near her pile of wood. She went over to take a closer look and saw that the stone was sitting on a little bunch of buffalo hair. The voice began to sing again; it came from the stone:

You—woman—will you take me?

I am Powerful!

Buffalo is our Medicine.

The young woman reached down and picked up the stone. In those days the People had no pockets, and she was not carrying her miscellaneous pouch. She put the stone beneath her belt next to her skin and she went home. She did not tell anyone what had happened.

That night, she had a dream. The stone came to her and sang its song again. Then it told her, "I have come to you and your People because I pity you. My Power is able to communicate with the buffalo and bring them here. I have chosen you to bring me to camp because you are humble and I know your thoughts are good. You

must ask your husband to invite all the holy men to your lodge tomorrow night. I will teach you some songs and a ceremony which you must show them. If you do this then I will have my Power bring back the buffalo. But you must warn your People: my Power is always announced by a strong storm, and when it first arrives it will look like a buffalo, a lone bull. You must tell your People not to harm him. The rest of the herd will follow as soon as he has passed safely through the camp.

During her dream the woman was taught several songs she had never heard before. The Iniskim told her that he had many relatives about the prairie, and that all of them were in contact with the same Power as he. He told her that any of the People who wished to have good fortune from this Power should look for one of his relatives and bring them home and treat them with respect.

When the young woman woke up she wondered what to do about her dream, for she was quite shy of her husband. Only the sits-beside wife takes part in the husband's ceremonial functions, never the wife who sleeps closest to the door. When the husband went outside, the young wife told her older sister about the stone and the dream. The sister said, "I will tell our man what you just told me. If your dream comes true, then you may have my seat next to him. But if not, I will only pity you for what you will have to suffer."

When the husband learned of the matter, he immediately sent out invitations to the camp's holy men. In a short while, they gathered in the home of the young woman and were served a small portion of berries, and broth made from scraps of leather. They were excited when they heard why they were invited, although one or two got up and left. Our Old People were always skeptical of someone who claimed to have been called upon in a dream and given a Power.

With the approval of the holy men who remained, the husband asked his young wife to sit at the head of the tipi and lead the ceremony that had been shown to her. She had a tiny piece of fat, which she mixed with sacred paint in the palms of her hands. While she covered the stone with the sacred paint she sang one of the songs:

Iniskim, he says: buffalo is my Medicine.

Iniskim, he is saying: I am Powerful!

The men then knew that it was not an ordinary stone, but a sacred stone. They were anxious to see if it really had any Power. The woman then rubbed the Iniskim over her body four times and prayed at great length. Then she sang another song:

This Iniskim, my man, it is Powerful!

During the song she handed the Iniskim to her husband, sitting beside her. He rubbed his body with it and prayed, while his wife continued to sing the sacred songs. The ceremony went on in that way until the Iniskim had gone all the way around the gathered company. By that time most of the men were able to sing one or two of the songs.

Before they left, the woman told them about the warning in the dream. A crier was sent around the camp telling the People to tie down their lodges and prepare for a big storm. They were also told not to harm the single bull that was to show up in the camp after the storm. Most of the People followed the advice, but a few laughed and said it was only the crazy dream of a woman.

It was long after dark when the weather began to change. Most of the People had gone to sleep. Only the husband, his wife, and some of the holy men stayed up and continued to sing the Iniskim songs. A breeze started to blow, rustling the covers of the tipis. Before long the breeze turned into a wind, and the tipi covers flapped loudly against their poles. The wind continued to get stronger, and suddenly the People were all awakened by the cracking sounds of a big cottonwood tree as it was blown down. The unfastened tipis of those who disbelieved the woman were blown down and their contents hurled away. While the People prayed for safety, they heard loud hoofbeats and heavy breathing in the darkened camp. It was the lone bull wandering through the camp. No one dared to harm him.

In the morning the storm stopped and there was a large herd of buffalo grazing beside the camp. The People were able to bring down as many as they needed, for the animals just wandered around without alarm. The People cried with happiness for having real food again. They were anxious to replace their worn-out bedding and robes, and to fix the holes in their tipis and moccasins. Everyone paid their respects to the young wife, who now occupied the place next to her husband at the head of the tipi. Everyone brought a tiny offering of buffalo meat or fat and placed it before the sacred Iniskim, which was sitting on a little pile of fur inside of the cleared-earth altar at the back of the tipi.

Ever since then our People have had the Power of the Iniskims.

Matted buffalo hair wrapper containing the many Iniskims for the ancient Black-Buffalo Painted Lodge, at rest in the Provincial Museum.

The Old Ways of Doctoring

You can get some idea of our Old Ways of doctoring from this brief account of an actual case, taken from the writings of Joe Beebe.

The most peculiar thing I ever witnessed in the way of Indian witchery was when an old Medicine-man used the Weasel Test on a very sick man to find out if he was going to die or pull through. The sick man was near the end. He had quit eating for two days and could not turn in bed without the help of his wife. The official Doctor of the Reserve said there was no hope, and the patient should not live many days longer.

This man was lying on his bed, his head was on high pillows and his legs straight out under covers. The Medicine-man turned over the bed covers enough to expose the whole of the left leg of the patient, and he sang a very weird song. Then, out of his medicine-bag he took a skin of a small weasel, and a twisted buckskin cord, about two feet in length, heavily daubed in red earth.

The medicine-man placed the pelt lengthwise on the exposed lap of the sick man; the head of the pelt rested on the man's knee. Then, taking the buckskin cord, he bound the weasel skin securely to the man's leg, tight enough, but not uncomfortable. He tipped the ends of two fingers in a small bag of red earth and made imprints, tracks like the weasel makes, from the weasel's head on the patient's knee; down his leg to his foot, about six inches apart. Putting back the covers on the leg, he faced the patient and said: "This is going to decide if that White Man's words are going to be so, or not. If you are to be on your feet again, this weasel ought to free itself from the binding and follow its tracks; if not, it is too bad. Now just lay still; I will go in the other room and have a smoke."

In about a half hour, the medicine man came back in to take his seat at the left of the patient. It was a very trying moment for the sick man. The covers were removed from the leg, and by some strange phenomenon the lifeless thing was out of its binding and was well past the patient's foot, as if it had crawled there, to the utter surprise of the patient and his wife. The old Indian picked up his weasel and undid the cord, which was still securely tied. Putting back his things in his bag, the Indian Doctor said: "You are not going to die just yet; you will be up on your feet again in just four days." And very true.

This happened about fifteen years ago. The very sick man the white Doctor had no hope for is still alive, and he happens to be your humble servant, Red Tail Feathers [Joe Beebe's other name].

Now, I am a christian and do not believe in superstitions, whatever. But this unaccountable thing we saw, I and my wife, is still a puzzle to us. However, seeing is believing, they say.

This Medicine-Man's name was Getting Wood at Night. He died last winter.

The term *Medicine Man,* or *Medicine Woman,* describes anyone who has knowledge of the spiritual world. But among our People, such knowledge can be possessed by different individuals whom we do not necessarily refer to as Medicine Men or Women, even though they are in that category. We prefer to refer to them more specifically—holy people, doctors, or ceremonial leaders.

Early white visitors learned that the People seemed to believe in the Powers of holy and medicinal things. These visitors used the term *Medicine* in their journals to describe these mysterious Powers. Thus, those called upon for help with the mysterious Powers became known as Medicine Men. A Medicine Man or Woman of the doctoring order did not necessarily belong to the Holy Order, although many belonged to both. Holy men and women inspired others to find happiness through good thoughts and a holy way of living; they offered spiritual advice and prayers. A person became a member of the Holy Order only after many years of study with older holy people. The Power of Medicine Men to doctor came only through dreams. This Power was seldom told to others and could never be transferred to anyone else. People respected the Medicine Man for all the good things he could do, but they also feared him, because they saw many times that he had Power over life and death. It was a rare thing for one of our doctors to use his Power for evil purposes, whereas it was common among the doctors of our neighbors, such as the Crees.

Young people who were interested usually learned the uses of common plants, which we call "everybody's medicines," from older relatives. If the relative was an experienced doctor, this might inspire the young person to dream of specific uses for the plants. The dream would usually include songs and ceremonies necessary to call on the Power of the plants. Most doctors had a good knowledge of plants and herbs, but their special Powers in curing were with the things they had dreamed about. The older the doctor, the more specialized dreams he was likely to have. Many old doctors had quite a lot of Power in this Way.

During the 1930s, when many of our People still followed the Old Ways, there were several well-known doctors administering to their ailments. In 1939, a woman named Esther Goldfrank came to us from New York to study personal relations among the Bloods. In her records, she included some information about Blood doctors. Among these doctors was Knife, uncle of Sorrel Horse, who gave this information to Goldfrank.

Knife first got his Power to doctor when he went to a bear's den to seek a vision. The den was located near Hill Spring, not far from the town of Cardston. Although it was an abandoned den, Knife heard bear sounds his first two nights there. The third night, the bear's Spirit came to him and taught him how to heal. He was told to take a bear's claw, tie certain shells to it, and wear it as a necklace. In addition, he was instructed to always grab his patients and treat them as though they were bears. Knife later gave the necklace to his son, Two Guns, who had dreams of his own with it. Two Guns dreamed that he should wear a certain kind of stone on a necklace slung over one shoulder, so that he would be able to doctor hemorrhages. He was best known for this last specialty. Sometimes his grateful patients paid two or three horses for his doctoring.

The white woman's notes also mention Heavy Head, who was a doctor as well as a holy man. He received his first Powers to doctor while fasting in the Belly Buttes prior to his self-torture at the Sun Dance of 1889. After Gets Wood at

Mrs. Mountain Horse, or Homeward Offering, at home with her herbs and doctoring supplies.

Night (who had doctored Joe Beebe) died, sometime in the 1930s, Heavy Head began dreaming about the way that doctor had used a weasel skin. Gets Wood at Night spoke to Heavy Head and taught him in his dreams how to use his weasel and earth. At first Heavy Head was afraid to try this Power, but the dreams persisted until he put the methods to use. He was a very successful doctor.

Heavy Head's student of holy Ways was also a recognized doctor. This, of course, was our Old Man. Though our Old Man was known for curing a variety of ailments, including hemorrhages and sinus problems, we know very little about his doctoring Powers. One of his wives was a popular doctor for pregnant women, according to Percy Creighton, who had called on her to help his own wife during the 1930s. The Old Man's brother, Crow-Spreads-His-Wings, was also a doctor, as was the older of the Old Man's wives, who specialized in treating fevers.

Another well-known doctor during the thirties was Dog Child. Esther Goldfrank described him in her notes as "a Medicine Man and lady fancier," after he had put his arm around her and laid his hand on her breast when she asked to have her picture taken with him. Dog Child doctored until his death in 1948.

Until recently, there was a little old lady named Mrs. Mountain Horse who was called on for herbal brews and medicines somewhat like a pharmacist, rather than for physical doctoring. Better known as Homeward Offering among our People, she specialized in medicinal brews and decoctions. Under her iron-frame bed were many bags and sacks filled with all sorts of plants and roots, and her little one-room house was never without the pungent odor of drying herbs and boiling medicines. People came to her every day with their glass jars and containers, preferring her natural remedies to those the drug stores in town disguised with colorful capsules. A blanket or some dry goods and a couple of dollar bills were usually left on her bed by grateful visitors. Her sweet, shy smile accompanied each potion of medicine, and her continuous prayers helped to give it spiritual strength.

Because the Powers to doctor are personal, I am not able to tell you much more about doctors. It would be disrespectful for me to ask about their Ways and it would be a breach of their trust if I wrote what they have told me. Let me only say that we have sought advice from Mokakin, and we have gone to the old lady for her medicines when we were ill. We were well satisfied with both. But the Old Ways are so nearly gone that we would have to follow the Old Man's advice if we became seriously ill. Once he said this to us: "I am quite old now, barely able to keep myself well. I will continue to help those who have been coming to me for most of their lives. But when they are seriously ill, I tell them, as I now tell you: It is better to go to a hospital where they have much modern knowledge against which

174

my skills are often as nothing. The world has changed so much that many of my natural medicines have no Power over the new illnesses which the People often seem to suffer. Some persons claim to have instant remedies for all sorts of complicated ailments, but I know from experience that successful doctoring comes only after much knowledge and devotion. Unless the doctor and patient both live in the same Ways, it is hard to cure with prayers if those prayers are only words which pass from one to the other. There must be a strong understanding. That is why I only doctor our Old People anymore."

GEORGE FIRST RIDER

In a modern pink house just outside the town of Cardston, Alberta, lives a controversial man named George First Rider. George was the only child of the famed doctor and Horns priest, Dog Child. Dog Child was proud of his only son and taught him everything he knew. He gave presents to the old, knowledgeable men so they would teach his son. Unusually intelligent, George learned the many songs and stories quite well. He asked his Teachers to explain many things other students simply accepted and memorized. He was interested in a holy life beyond being able to repeat ancient rituals.

George First Rider is now in his seventies and still very active. He has short gray hair, very light skin, and blue eyes—rather startling for the son of two full-blooded parents. He drives a shiny pickup truck with a camper and often wears a suit and tie, which add to his white appearance. George is a minister in the local chapter of the Full Gospel Church. Although he actually understands English quite well, like many of our Old People he often refuses to speak it because of pride and fear of making mistakes.

George's intelligence and appearance have always caused him difficulty. Long ago, when he tried to join the Horns Society, the man whose Bundle he wanted told him, "I'm not giving up my membership to no white man!" Through a more sympathetic member, he was able to join the Horns. But others resented him because he dared to question things they had simply accepted. In the Old Days his aggressive character would have helped him become a powerful leader; but in the twentieth century most of our People have been mainly interested in quietly carrying on the remnants of our Old Ways. George's efforts to accomplish what might have helped continue the Old Ways were casually ignored by some and harshly rejected by others.

For many years, George countered his social failures with alcohol and stealing. Though he knew as much as anyone about the Old Ways, he felt that he was not living the successful life he deserved from all his years of learning and devotion. A few years ago he began embracing his new religion, which gave him the strength to give up evil ways. A sticker on the back of his truck reads: JESUS LOVED THE DEVIL OUT OF ME. To him the devil now includes many of our Old Ways, as well as his own ways with liquor and theft. Although his lifetime of leadership training helped him become a minister of his new religion, all the specific Indian Teachings were of no use to him "after he became a white man" as his wife says. But George's knowledge has not gone to waste.

Not long ago, the Alberta Provincial Museum and Archives realized that the knowledge and customs among our People would be lost forever unless they were recorded. This would be difficult, however, as the Blood People have long been known for their unwillingness to talk to outsiders about our Old Ways; some subjects, such as the Horns Society and the Motokiks, are never discussed at all. This was no problem for George First Rider. He had the knowledge of the Old Ways and no longer felt restricted to talk about them. Moreover, he felt he deserved some compensation for all the payments made to his Teachers and all the years devoted to learning the

Old Ways. So, for what he considered such a return from the museum, George began to pour out his knowledge into four different tape recorders supplied to him at his house by the archives and museum library. The archives employed Dave Melting Tallow from the North Blackfoot Reserve to interpret George's information into English. George filled so many tapes that the interpreter, who has already been at work for several years, will require several more years to complete all the translating.

George's recordings of the Horns Society's secret ceremonies will not be repeated here. But I hope the stories that are will never be used as an exclusive source for learning about the many Blood People he tells about.

The stories George tells cover many different subjects. The two we will hear now concern our Ways of doctoring.

DOG CHILD'S DOCTORING POWERS

I am First Rider. This is the Duck Moon [March]; it is the twenty-third day. I will tell a story of my father, Dog Child, and how he knows about doctoring.

There are two sharp-peaked mountains behind Chief Mountain. On one of the sharp peaks there was a bald eagle's nest. When my father was very young, he had a dream where he was told, "A man has invited you to go to him," meaning to go over to Chief Mountain. But my father didn't go. Many years later, when he was still a young man, about twenty years or younger, he dreamed again that a man was asking him to come to him at Chief Mountain. So my father went and slept there, and when he slept, the man told him, "I have sent for you so that you can watch me. This is the way I cure." The man showed him what to do and taught him the song to cure with. This was the song of the bald eagle. The song began with a spoken prayer: "HiYo, bird, help us. Now you are going to look for your meal. Help us that we may have something to eat this night and this

day." Then came the song, which consisted entirely of these words: "May I eat all that flies. May I eat a fish."

My father would start to sing this song himself, beating his drum, and then another person, his assistant, would take over the drumming and begin singing also, as my father began the curing, inspired by the supernatural powers of the Bald Eagle.

My father also had supernatural powers from a bear who lived at the Belly Buttes. This bear was sketched on one of my father's drums.

Willie White Feather's father, Morning Writing, slept at the Belly Buttes and the bear told him, "Give me a woman and I will have pity on you." But we were never sure if he succeeded in bringing a woman from the camp circle to sleep up at the Belly Buttes.

My father cures with the claw of the bear. The bear also sang; he sang this song: "I am the dream bear. The dream bear, it pitied me."

I knew all my father's songs. I used to drum for him during his curings.

My father licked red-hot stones with the help of the powers of that bear. He would stick his forefinger in boiling water, then put his finger on the red-hot rock, and then touch his finger to the sick person's body. My father did that to me once. I was having a headache. He licked the rock, heated red-hot; then he licked me on my temple. His tongue was so hot I felt the heat as it went through my head.

My father would paint his bare right foot with sacred Earth and put his painted foot in boiling water, next put it on the red-hot rock and then put his foot down on where the pain hurts the sick person. If the person was dying, even if he was barely breathing and couldn't move anymore, when my father touched his foot on the person, the person would jump up.

Sometimes my father used the bear claw to dig out Indian turnips [camas]. He chewed the turnip and sprayed the person with it.

Dog Child in 1939. (Esther Goldfrank)

A DOCTOR NAMED BEAR HAT

Bear Hat had two sacred helpers. They were curlews—large, long-legged birds with big beaks. The curlews were not alive; they were stuffed curlews, stuffed with very dry ground dung and painted with sacred yellow paint. Bear Hat kept these curlews, some yellow paint, and some sweetgrass in his sacred bag.

Bear Hat was wounded in a battle the day after a night when horses were stolen from the camps. This is how it happened:

The People felt they were being watched, so they had been on the alert. They kept their horses close to the camps by tying their legs together. The legs of two gentle horses were tied together —the right leg of one horse tied with a long rope to a picket. Some were hobbled. When there was no danger, a horse was hobbled in a way so that it could walk while grazing, but not go astray.

Four aggressive young men were called to watch the horses. They hid behind woodpiles. It is strange how they did not see the horses herded away, but it was said that it was raining, and the young men might have curled up in their blankets and slept.

When the young men woke up with birds singing in the morning, they looked around and saw that one of the horses tied to a picket was missing. They examined the rawhide rope that had tied the horses and saw it was cut with a knife. They called out, "Horses are taken!" The People awoke and scrambled out to discover that some of their horses were missing.

Immediately, they began tracking the thieves. As they followed the trail, they discovered horse dung, which was still warm. So they knew the thieves were not far ahead.

Today, the new generation would say that it is midday or noon, but the People of the past would say, "Sun has laid still." It was at this time that the pursuers came upon the thieves, sitting at a fresh fire by the river bottom. They were

Crees and they were panic-stricken. They ran into the bushes, leaving the stolen horses behind. In the chase one of the Crees fired at Bear Hat and shot him in the chest.

After the Crees were massacred, the pursuers found Bear Hat, blood coming from his mouth, slumped over on his horse. "I am hurt," he told them. Some rode quickly back to camp, announcing the victory over the thieves and that the horses were recaptured, and reporting that Bear Hat was injured. They brought a travois to carry Bear Hat back to camp, and when they returned, the People, seeing Bear Hat's condition, did not celebrate their victory dance. But Bear Hat insisted. "Nothing has happened to me yet. I am not dying. So have your victory dance."

And so the victory dance was celebrated, with the scalps and the hands and feet that the pursuers had cut off the Crees in the massacre. The People sang: "My wounds . . . I don't feel them."

Even Bear Hat, the bullets still in his body, joined in with these words.

Night came, and then morning, and Bear Hat was still alive. His wife took the curlews from the sacred bag and faced them toward the wall, away from where Bear Hat lay. She then asked among the People for seven men and seven married women still without child, all singers with good voices. The men sat in a row toward the center of the lodge, facing north, and the women sat behind them. The man sitting at the head took Bear Hat's yellow-painted drum with the curlew picture drawn on it. Drums having supernatural powers were offered by the People to the six other men.

The wife then pulled Bear Hat to the center of the lodge, leaving him on the bare ground, his feet toward the fireplace. She took the two curlews in her arms, and after walking around the lodge, clockwise, in the direction Sun travels, she put them down on their bellies facing Bear Hat and covered them with a yellow-painted cloth.

Hanging a yellow-painted whistle around her neck, she then took from the sacred bag some yellow paint in her palms and spit on it. She daubed her forehead with it and rubbed some on the back of her hands. Bear Hat lay on his back, the blood dried on his exposed wound. His wife told the People, "Bear Hat told me something might happen in times to come. You will do as I have told you and you will revive him."

Taking the yellow-painted drum from the lead singer, she sat by the doorway, beating very fast on the drum and blowing on her whistle four quick, loud whistles at a time. After four quick beats on the drum, she began to beat slowly on the rim, singing her song with no words. The men and women singers, who had never heard this song before, learned it quickly. She returned the drum to the lead singer, and they all sang as one voice. The women especially sang with skilled voices, just like coyotes.

The wife was wearing a yellow-painted robe with loops at the corners. She stuck her hands in the loops, and spreading out her robe with her arms, she made as if she were flapping wings, all the while blowing her whistle. Then she let the whistle drop from her mouth, and she put words to her song: "Man, sit up. Man, sit up."

Again, she blew on the whistle, as she moved slowly toward the covered curlews. Suddenly, she pulled the cover off the stuffed birds. The stuffed birds got up on their feet and spread their wings, making four trumpetlike sounds. The curlews staggered and then ran, flapping their wings; one ran around the north side, the other around the south, meeting on the chest of the wounded Bear Hat.

As Bear Hat began to rise upward into a sitting position, the curlews suddenly no longer seemed lifelike, and reverted to stuffed skins. When Bear Hat sat up, a cloth band was securely wrapped around his chest. Then a drink was prepared for him. Water was poured into a wooden bowl, and the yellow paint was added, which the wife stirred with her finger. When the water turned yellow, Bear Hat drank it. Next, his wife cooked some raw-dried meat—half dry and half raw—over a fire. She sprayed yellow paint on the meat as it cooked. It was mostly still raw when she served it to Bear Hat. The meat still had some blood in it to refill Bear Hat of the blood he lost.

The wound healed in four days. Bear Hat's curlew skins had cured him.

Then there came a time when a boy was ac- cidentally shot while on a hunt. He was shot in the ribs and the bullet came out his back up near the shoulder. When the hunters returned to camp with the wounded boy, they called for Bear Hat. And just as Bear Hat had taught his wife—with the curlews, yellow paint, seven men and seven childless women, the yellow robe and drums and whistle, and the yellow-paint brew and half-dried meat—so Bear Hat cured the boy.

That is how Bear Hat got the name Curlew.

Teachings of Nature

One day during the Sun Dance Encampment, Atsitsina and I went north of the camp to where the Buttes dip down close to the brush and the tree-lined Belly River. He had said that we would find there a variety of plants and that we would see many birds and animals.

Atsitsina told me he could remember many plants his father had used as a doctor. I, too, could recall Mokakin and our Old Man using various plants to doctor people successfully. As is the case with our sacred Bundles, these men received their doctoring Ways through dreams. However, there are many plants that we call "everybody's medicines," which are used in daily life and do not require dreams or special Teachings to be effective.

Unfortunately, much of the old-time knowledge has been lost since the time our People lived completely in harmony with nature. Many of our Old People, however, still are familiar with the ancient names of birds and animals, and know how to recognize them by sound and sight; and they know the names of certain stars and constellations, and the ancient legends surrounding them. And so, those of us who wish to follow these Ways are thankful for the knowledge that does remain.

EDIBLE PLANTS

Unlike many other tribes, our People never practiced any form of agriculture other than the cere-monial raising of sacred tobacco. After our People settled on the Blood Reserve, however, they soon learned to raise potatoes, turnips, carrots, and some other vegetables. Before that, vegetable foods had been used only for a change in diet, or as an addition to our Old People's basic diet of meat.

None of our People today were raised without such products as flour, tea, and sugar. But over the past fifty years their basic diets have changed tremendously, from natural meats and vegetables to commercial beef and many starches, fats, and sweets. According to the Old People, bodies were much stronger in the Old Days. The Old Man, as a doctor, had this view of the diet changes among our People:

When I was young I was taught that the good foods were meat and berries. My parents were just learning to raise a garden when I was born, so they didn't know much about the white man's vegetables. The meat we had came from animals that ate nothing but natural growths and water. Even our cattle lived just as though they were wild. Today our meat often comes from animals that are fed white man's invented foods, and they are given strange materials through injections with needles. Even their manure often does not smell natural. In the past, all the animals we ate just lived on grass and plants and water—all that was clean. We used to eat our meat with plenty of fat on it. That gave us the strength to

Typical Blood boys in 1885, at the end of the old war days. The older boys have on blanket coats, while the younger one has a shirt made from a flour sack. His leggings are of wool trade cloth. They all have children's bows and arrows without metal tips. These boys were the Old Man's contemporaries. (Boorne & May)

live outdoors, especially when it was cold. Every morning we went swimming in water, even during the winter. If the water was frozen we rolled in the snow and covered ourselves with it. That made our bodies strong. An old relative of mine, Star Chief, often came with us kids to make sure there were no cowards. Our mothers followed behind and brought us our blankets. That old man always told me, "This is going to make your bodies good and strong and you will live to old age." And he was right.

Today, when the People take baths they just use warm water. The meat that we get tastes funny. When the People eat fat it just makes them fat, because they just sit around all day. That meat is flabby and our bodies don't have to work hard to make it go through, so we don't build up any strength. That's why our bodies get sick when we eat all those strange white man's foods, because they don't have to build up any strength to put them through. I don't doctor the People anymore because they have such strange illnesses.

The Old Man preferred a simple diet of meat, boiled or roasted, and homemade bread. For dessert he liked berries—raw or boiled into a soup with water, flour for thickening, and a little sweetening. He liked to drink mint and rose hips tea. He preceded every meal with a prayer and a cup of cold water, saying that the cold water helped to get the stomach into action so that it would properly digest the food. He finished his meals with cold water also. His personal Medicine did not allow him to be disturbed while eating. Thus, he kept a cup of water by his plate—if anyone got up or came into the room during his meal, he quickly took a drink to keep from choking on his food. When we took him to eat in a restaurant, he always tried to get a table at the rear, or at least with his back to the door so that he could not see people coming and going.

Most of the plants our Old People kept for winter were dried before being stored in bags of rawhide and tanned hide. Some people made food storage bags by sewing together two or more skinned heads of deer, moose, or elk. The noses were cut off and covered with rawhide; the necks formed the tops of the bags, closed with buckskin thongs. Bags were made for keeping berries, turnips, fats, and dried meats. Wild mint was often included to flavor and help preserve the contents. Instead of cookie jars, kids raided these storage bags for treats whenever mother or grandmother was gone from the tipi. Wintertime guests would be treated to a handful of assorted dried foods from the storage bags. They would spear them with a sharpened green stick and eat them raw or roast them over the fire.

Edible plants were gathered during two seasons. Spring was the time to collect the roots of prairie turnips, bitterroots, and camas. Fall was the time to gather serviceberries, bullberries, and chokecherries. Bitterroots and camas were found in the Rocky Mountain regions, while others appeared all over the nearby country. Berries were either eaten fresh or prepared for storage by spreading them on a hide or blanket to dry beneath Sun. Chokecherries were pounded with a stone hammer until the seeds were sufficiently ground up so that they could be eaten. Roots were baked, boiled, and dried for different uses.

Let me tell you a little about each of our more important edible plants, starting with the berries.

SASKATOON BERRY (*Amelanchier alnifolia*): Also known as the serviceberry, our People call this the "real berry," which will give you some idea of its significance. It is traditionally the most important berry among our People, and it is still served at most of our ceremonies. These berries grow in abundance on tall and dense bushes. They ripen during the middle of summer, about the time of the Sun Dance, into round, purple, juicy fruits.

Serviceberries are excellent fresh. The results of overeating are horrible stomachaches and diarrhea. They will keep for several years if thoroughly dried and properly stored.

Pemmican is made by mixing dried serviceberries with ground-up dried meat and melted grease. The mixture is shaped into cakes and stored in rawhide containers to use during the winter.

Berry soup is served as a sacred meal during ceremonies such as our annual Medicine Pipe Bundle openings. Fresh or dried berries are boiled in water, then made into a soup by adding flour and sugar. Pieces of bitterroots, meat, or fat may be added to the soup.

CHOKECHERRY (*Prunus virginiana*): Our People call this the "crushed berry" because of the way it is prepared. Chokecherries grow on trees and ripen in early fall. They are not good to eat before fully ripe. When fresh, they are boiled with water or fat and sweetened to make a soup. If the stones are swallowed they will cause constipation. For storage they are dried after being crushed with stones. The crushed cherries are formed into small cakes, like cookies, which are placed on small sticks or turned over regularly to keep them from spoiling on one side while drying.

Preparing chokecherries properly is quite an art. If they are not crushed sufficiently, the unground stones, or pits, will make them difficult to eat. Grease must be mixed with the ground cherries to keep them from drying too hard. They are stored in a bag made from a small animal skin whose open legs have been stuffed with wild mint; this keeps the cherries from falling out and allows a little air to enter, preventing the contents from becoming moldy.

Pemmican can be made by breaking up dried cherry cakes and soaking them in a bowl of water. When the cherries become soft, the water is strained out. This water, known as chokecherry brew, is a popular drink, especially in wintertime. The soaked cherries are then mixed with fat (backfat is popular because it does not cake up easily) and pounded some more. The mixture is then kneaded into small balls and served, or placed into rawhide containers to be taken along on hunting or war trips, as was the case in the Old Days.

Chokecherry stems are used in a variety of ways. Thin ones can be stuck into a roasting piece of meat to add flavor. Bark scrapings are steeped to make a tea. Stems are also used for tipi pins or "buttons." Most bows and arrows were made of chokecherry wood. Medicine Pipestems, tripods for sacred Bundles, and root-digging sticks are all made from the branches. The wood is so hard and tough that it will not soak up water, and so is an excellent fire-starting wood after a hard rain.

ROSEBERRY (*Rosa acicularis*): The red pods on wild rose bushes, also known as rose hips, are "wild tomatoes" to our People. They are usually gathered after the first frost. They can be eaten fresh from the bush and were commonly used as an emergency food, since they remain on the bushes through most of the winter. Eating the seeds, however, causes an itchy rectum.

Rose hips meal can be made by boiling fresh fruits, crushing them with fat, and cooking the mixture on a black plate (frying pan). The meal is then sweetened and eaten. They can also be boiled with a mixture of flour and sweetening to make a soup. Occasionally, they were used in place of other berries for making pemmican. They make an excellent tea, which provides a good winter source for vitamin C.

Other berries used by our People in the past include strawberries, raspberries, and thimbleberries, all of which were eaten raw or used fresh in soups and stews. Gooseberries, known as "punctured berries," were either eaten raw after they ripened and turned purple or were cooked into soups; their green leaves were boiled in sweetened water to make a drink that was a favorite of children. Oregon grapes, "blueberries," were eaten fresh, but only in small quantities due to their strong, acidlike taste; they were sometimes boiled and then dried for winter use. Silverberries were sour and not popular for eating, but became a bit sweeter during the winter. Because they stay on their bushes so long, they also served as an emergency winter food; the inner layer of bark from these willow bushes could be chopped up and eaten. Bearberries were another emergency winter food; they could either be eaten raw or mashed with fat and sweetened to be fried in round cakes.

Now let us talk about edible roots.

CAMAS (*Camassia quamash*): Due to the appearance of these roots, this plant is called *mississa*, or "excrement." The stem and leaves rise one to two feet above the bulb. Found in moist meadows near the mountains, the plant is dug in the fall after its blue flowers have fallen off.

In the Old Days, camas was prepared for eating and storage by being baked in a pit. After the pit was dug it was lined with flat stones and a fire built over it. When the stones became hot, the coals and ashes were removed and replaced with grass, and the camas bulbs were piled on the grass. The bulbs were then covered with more grass, a layer of twigs, and a cover of earth, about four inches deep. On top of all this a fire was burned for two or three days, depending upon the quantity of camas in the pit.

When the pit was reopened, children gathered the twigs to suck the sweet juices of the roasted bulbs. The roasted bulbs were dried beneath Sun and placed in storage bags. It is said that they tasted like roasted chestnuts. Sometimes they were pounded with serviceberries before being dried.

WILD PARSLEY (*Lomatium simplex*): This wild turnip, which grows deep and is hard to unearth, is known as the "big turnip." Its Plant grows one to two feet high and has yellow flowers. The roots used to be dug up with digging sticks made of oiled, fire-hardened, and dried berry sticks or birchwood. The ends of the sticks were held against a piece of rawhide to protect the digger's stomach as she pushed the stick into the ground with the weight of her body. After they were gathered and peeled, these turnips were eaten raw or roasted, or Sun-dried for storage.

SQUAWROOT (*Perideria gairdneri*): Known as the "double root," this plant grows from one to three feet tall and has small, white flowers. Like other roots, it could be eaten fresh, after boiling, or dried for winter storage. A common way to prepare it for eating was to boil

it in animal blood and then add sweetening.

BITTERROOT (*Lewisia pygmaea*): Called "looks like a white stick," this root is most commonly found on the other side of the mountains from our country. The Old People considered this root to be very healthy, in spite of its terribly bitter taste. It was dug up in the spring, as soon as the flower buds appeared. The slender white roots were peeled and dried. It was steamed if fresh, or boiled and cooked in soups if dried.

INDIAN BREADROOT (*Psoralea esculenta*): This root was the main turnip used by our Old People, which is why they called it *mahss*, or "turnip"; but it is also known as "elk food." It grows all over our old country. These turnips, which have a very pleasant taste, were gathered shortly before the flowers dropped off. They were peeled and eaten raw, or roasted either over an open fire or directly in the coals. For storage, they were peeled and strung up to dry beneath Sun, and then often coated with fat so that they would not become too hard during storage.

COW PARSNIP (*Heracleum lanatum*): This plant, known to us as "wild rhubarb," grows up to eight feet in height. The stalks were gathered and eaten in the spring, while they were tender. Our Old People thought of the immature flower stalks as the "man stalk," and simply peeled and roasted them for eating. The leaf stalks were called the "she stalks"; these were peeled and split before being roasted and eaten.

Roots of the wild rhubarb were split, cut up, and dried for winter use. Sometimes they were dipped in animal blood before being dried. When prepared for meals, they were boiled and sweetened.

CANADIAN MILK VETCH (*Astragalus canadensis*): Known as "tender root" because its roots were commonly eaten raw, this root was especially liked by children. The roots were also dried for winter, when they were boiled in blood or broth.

SPRING BEAUTY (*Claytonia lanceolata*): Because of its potatolike root, this plant is known as "lumpy head." Two short and narrow leaves and white-pink flowers grow up from the root. Found on the prairies and in the foothills, these roots were dug up in spring and eaten fresh, boiled, or roasted.

NATURAL MEDICINES

Many plants are gathered for medical use. Here is Atsitsina's introduction to his Teachings of these plants:

Oki, I will tell you a little story of how my father, Natosina, used to get his doctoring medicines together.

For instance, If someone was hemorrhaging from the mouth, he would use a combination of Gros Ventre scent (western meadow rue), sweetgrass, and white clay. The Gros Ventre scent had to be still green. My mother would put these plants in the oven for a long time, feeling and checking them every once in a while. When they were very soft she would take them out and crumble them onto a piece of buckskin. When she was finished, they looked like black pepper.

There was this white man we called Mountain Chief. He was spitting blood and he asked my father to make a brew for him. My father made a small brew and prayed while he boiled it. Then he told the man to drink it with the leaves in it. He told him, "Don't lie to me. Tell me the truth if you like it and if it works for you." He drank it. A couple days later he was much better. That man gave my father a horse, some cash, and other things for curing him.

When I used to ride horses, one time a horse fell on me. My knee swelled up. My father told my mother to get some thorns from a rose bush

and bake them. She baked them. He pushed some hot thorns into my injured leg. I thought my leg was going to break! He put a long stick into the fire, and while it was burning he painted the thorns with sacred yellow paint and sacred black paint. Then he took the glowing red stick and heated the thorns, which burned right down to my skin. My leg felt like it was being held by something Powerful. I couldn't move it at all. The next day I was able to move my leg, but my father said, "Today we will have the treatment one more time." After the second treatment, the swelling went down and I was able to walk. I guess that was a form of what they call today acupuncture.

Oki, now let me tell you about some of the different things that grow. For instance, the "man-sage" [prairie sage] is used by men, the "woman-sage" [pasture sage] by women.

If a man has any kind of bad luck, he will use the prairie sage to cleanse the evil from his body. If a relative dies, a man will make incense with the prairie sage and rub it over himself to cleanse his body. They are pure growths from nature, so they can clean away unpure things. If a man is going to have a sweat lodge, he will sit on the man-sage and he will chew some. This will purify him.

Oki, there are all kinds of uses for this man-sage. When they went on war raids they would carry some leaves to chew on, so they wouldn't get out of breath. They chewed it for the same reason when swimming. If a man has smelly feet he will put some leaves in his moccasins to make the smell go away. He will boil some and wash his hair in it. If his nose is bleeding, he will chew it and put it in his nose to stop the blood. If he has body odor, he will put some under his arms and between his legs and the smell will go away. If he has the itch, he will boil some and put it on whatever place is itching. A man will put in a few leaves of man-sage in any kind of curing brew to purify it. In the Old Days, men put bunches of man-sage in the nose and mouth of their kill to purify. That makes the meat taste good. Any offering we make to Sun includes man-sage.

Oki, a woman uses woman-sage in the same way. A handsome woman will bathe with it and use it in her hair. For an easy birth, she will chew on it. She will use it for perfume and to keep herself from sickness.

Oki, my father always prayed while picking medicine plants. He kept all his curing medicines tied up in little buckskin pouches. There was no writing on them; he used different-colored beads to tell apart the few bags he didn't know by the way they looked and smelled. Sometimes he would show them to me and say, "I will use this for coughing, and this for hemorrhaging, and this for swelling." He put sage in with them to keep them pure. My father taught me a lot of his medicines, but I have lost most of them. Nobody was interested, so I have lost [forgotten] many of them.

The following list will tell you about some of the plants used as natural medicines by our People. The given uses were commonly known in the past, and are still relied on, at times, today. Many more uses were known only by certain persons in the Old Days.

ALUMROOT (*Heuchera americana*): A plant with blue flowers and many roots, it's called "dry root" by our Old People. It used to have a number of medicinal uses.

The roots could be boiled and drunk hot for stomachaches, cramps, diarrhea, and sore throats. Cooled, the brew served as a wash for sore eyes. The leaves themselves could be chewed and applied to sores and swollen places.

Even horses benefited from its curing powers. A horse with a cough would be thrown down and tied, and the root-brew poured into a tube stuck into its mouth. To treat their saddle sores, the plant leaves

would be mixed with fat and boiled in water.

BANEBERRY (*Actaea rubra*): There are two species of this plant; one bears red berries, the other, white. Both types of berries are poisonous. But the roots, known as "black roots," were prepared to make a potent brew for coughs and colds.

BEARDTONGUE (*Penstemon*): Because of its flavor, this plant has come to be known as "tastes like fire." Its brew was used to treat stomachaches and cramps, as well as vomiting.

BEAR GRASS (*Yucca glauca*): Also known as yucca and soapweed, our People call this plant "sharp vine." The roots were boiled in water and used as a hair wash in ceremonies of tribes in the south. Physical breaks and sprains were bathed in the steam of grated roots boiling in water. The roots were also used as an antiseptic on cuts.

BERRIES: Some of the same berries used for food were also used for medicine. Serviceberries, for instance, were brewed to doctor people with stomachaches and liver troubles, even though too many serviceberries in one sitting could create stomach problems in themselves! The juice of ripe berries is still good for bloodshot eyes and flushing out foreign particles in eyes.

Chokecherry twigs were chewed to eliminate one's desire to smoke.

Gooseberry roots, gathered and boiled into a solution, treated various body odors— bad-smelling hair, stinky feet and armpits, and even bad-smelling ears. The offensive area was simply washed with the solution.

Strawberry leaves were brewed to be used as a wash for sore eyes.

Oregon grapes were boiled into a brew for sore kidneys. The bark of the root was used in a decoction for stomach troubles, mountain fever, kidney aches, and sometimes hemorrhages.

Rose hips, soaked in warm water, were

applied as a poultice to boils. Covered with a bandage, the seeds dried up the boil, which pulled off when the bandage was removed. The roots of the rose bush could be brewed into a bitter, red-colored drink to treat diarrhea.

CUT-LEAVED ANEMONE (*Anemone multifida*): This plant is called "looks-like-a-plume," because of the wooly tops of its fruiting heads. This wooly material was burned on a hot coal and inhaled for headaches.

INDIAN HEMP (*Apocynum cannabinum*): Known as "little blanket" or "many spears," this plant is usually found in dense brush and on high cliffs. The roots were brewed to make a laxative or a hair wash. The dried leaves were sometimes smoked.

LARKSPUR (*Delphinium*): Known as "blue leaves," the leaves were brewed for kidney troubles; the brew also made a good eyewash.

LOCOWEED (*Oxytropis*): These plants are known as "rattle sounds," because the ripe seeds inside the pods rattle in the wind. The leaves were chewed and the juice swallowed for sore throats and for coughing spasms in children. A brew was also made to treat sores on the head.

MINT (*Mentha arvensis*): The leaves of wild mint, or "strong smell," are still brewed into a popular tea, which is especially good for upset stomachs. When chewed and swallowed, the leaves are effective for chest pains.

OWL CLOVER (*Orthocarpus luteus*): These plants were given the name "dye" because they were boiled with porcupine quills, feathers, and skins to dye them red. The blue seed pods that form after the yellow leaves fall off were boiled into a drink and given to adults with chest pains and to children with constipation.

PRAIRIE CROCUS (*Anemone patens*): This plant came to be known as "early old man," because it matures and dries up quickly. The small root of the plant is still brewed and

drunk to ease delivery at birth or to bring on an abortion. The crushed leaves used to be bound to itchy parts of the body.

PRAIRIE SMOKE (*Geum triflorum*): Called "lying on its belly" because its roots grow along close to the ground, it is still dug up, scraped, washed, and then crushed and boiled to treat sore throats, as well as sore, swollen, or snow-blinded eyes. The roots can be crushed and mixed with melted grease to treat sore gums, or mixed with melted kidney fat as a drink to treat ulcers. This kidney fat mixture can be applied to body sores such as chapped lips, blisters from riding, and sore nipples from nursing. The leaves are also brewed for a person spitting blood. Finally, ripe seeds gathered from the white flowers can be crushed to make a perfume.

PUFFBALLS: Known as "dusty stars," these fungi are thought to be the remnants of fallen stars, which dot the Prairies. The puffy substance, used to catch sparks, was an essential part of fire-making kits. Puffballs were also held against bleeding noses to stop the flow, and applied to cuts on horses. The yellow contents were brewed for a drink to treat hemorrhage. They were also used as a compress for hemorrhoids, and by women while menstruating.

SAGE (*Artemisia gnaphalodes*): "Man-sage" had many uses in addition to those already cited by Atsitsina. The basis of a decoction for treating coughs, its leaves could be chewed to stimulate appetite. It was also a main source of "toilet paper" in the Old Days. Burning leaves created a smudge to drive away flies and mosquitoes; soft leaves placed in nostrils checked bleeding. And it sometimes was added to dried meat for seasoning, although it was not actually eaten.

SAGE (*Artemisia frigida*): "Woman-sage," which grows together with man-sage, was used by women in the same way men used man-sage, except that women used it additionally as padding during menstruation; it was said to keep the skin from chafing.

Horses with back sores can often be seen rolling in patches of sage to treat themselves. Tops of this sage used to be brewed to treat heartburn and mountain fever.

SILVERWEED (*Potentilla anserina*): The roots of this vinelike plant, known as "garters," were chewed and applied to sores on children's bodies, after swimming. When the children dried off, the sores also dried, and the scabs could be brushed off.

SILVERY LUPINE (*Lupinus argenteus*): This plant, called "wolf turnip," has mildly hairy leaves that were used in several ways. They were brewed and drunk for coughs and for gas pains, causing the stomach to expel the gas. A person with painful hiccups can be given a mouthful to swallow while stretching the neck and plugging up the ears. The leaves are boiled and sprayed on horses' sores where flies gather.

SNOWBERRY (*Symphoricarpos occidentalis*): A common shrub with white berries called "white weasel eyes," this plant's yellow roots were the base of a decoction made to stop the heavy flow of a menstruating woman.

SQUAWROOT (*Perideridia gairdneri*): The "double root" was used for medicine as well as for food. It was chewed and swallowed for sore throats. A strong brew, made for kidney ailments, could also be poured into the nostrils of people and horses to treat catarrh. The chewed root also lent itself as a poultice for swollen parts of the body.

SWEET CICELY (*Osmorhiza chilensis*): Known as "smell root" and similar names, this plant's brew treated coughs, colds, and pneumonia. It was force-fed to mares in winter to prepare them for foaling.

SWEETGRASS (*Hierochloe odorata*): We call this plant *sepatsemo*, or "fragrant smell." This, our most common incense, was added to many medicine mixtures because of its sacredness. Boiled in water, it made a hair wash; chewed, it would be applied to swellings. It looks much like other grasses, but can be distinguished by the reddish color near its base.

VIOLET (*Viola adunca*): Called "blue mouth," its leaves were chewed and used as a poultice; it could also be made into a brew for a child having difficulty breathing.

WESTERN MEADOW RUE (*Thalictrum occidentale*): This plant was named "Gros Ventre scent" because it was most commonly found in the country of that tribe. Used as a perfume, the leaves could also be powdered and placed in horses' noses to make them long-winded.

WESTERN WILD PARSLEY (*Lomatium simplex*): This is the "big turnip" that was used mostly as food. As a medicine, the root was chewed and placed as a poultice with a heated cloth on bloodshot eyes. This poultice also treated sores in the mouth and ears, as well as earaches and swollen ears. A brew was made from it for chest pains.

WHITLOW GRASS (*Draba verna*): Because the stem of this plant rises from a circle of small leaves, it is called "center grass." The roots of this plant were made into a bitter drink to bring on abortion.

WILD BERGAMOT (*Monarda fistulosa*): This plant is called "singly young man." The blossoms could be brewed to make an eyewash, or else both leaves and blossoms were brewed together for stomachaches.

WILLOW (*Salix*): The great variety of willows are generally called "what they bring," referring to their ceremonial use during the Medicine Lodge sweat baths. The deep roots of these bushes were cut into pieces and dried, and from that a brew was made for hemorrhage, difficult breathing, dandruff, and bloodshot eyes in people and horses. Boiled with kidney fat, the mixture was used as a wash by people with curly and kinky hair to cure what they considered their undesirable appearance.

YARROW (*Achillea millefolium*): This plant was also called "having a pine stem." Chewed white flowers were used to poultice swellings, including mumps. Leaves were brewed for liver ailments and hemorrhages, and horses with sore eyes. Several cups of the brew were said to help speed up labor during childbirth. The leaves were sometimes used for a special incense during Beaver Bundle transfer ceremonies.

OTHER USES OF PLANTS

Besides food and medicine, our Old People found many day-to-day uses for various parts of plants.

TOBACCO that our Old People smoked was a mixture of commercial tobacco and the leaves of the bearberry plant (*Arctostaphylos uvaursi*). This plant was also called *kinniki-nick*, "that which is mixed." Although it grows on the prairies, only the mountain variety is used for smoking; the prairie kind smells like grass when it is burned.

Bearberry leaves can be picked from their low-growing shrub throughout the year. The leaves are separated from the stems, and then dried, crushed, and mixed for smoking. They are more properly prepared by first washing, to remove the bitter taste, then greased with kidney fat and placed in an oven to dry. This is called "frying your kin-nikinick." The fried leaves are placed in a cloth bag and crushed into smaller pieces, which are then stored in special bags made from the skins of unborn fawns and buffalo calves.

BEADS were made from the dried fruits of a number of plants, including silverberries, rose hips, and juniper berries. These beads were once used to decorate buckskin clothing, before traders brought glass beads to our People. Berries, too, were often strung to make necklaces and wristlets. They were made in this way: A fire was started with dry wood, then grease was dropped on the wood. The necklaces and wristlets were held in the greasy smoke until they were covered with an even layer of dark grease. Then they were polished with a soft piece of buckskin to a very pleasant finish.

Berry stones were also placed inside raw-hide rattles.

DYES were made from a number of plants: owl clover made red; violet flowers made blue; some lichens were used to make green; and the roots of the Oregon grape, yellow.

Plants also provided stuffing for pillows and saddles, and carpeting inside of tipis. Uses for their various woods ranged from fire fuel and holding up lodge covers to making bows, arrows, and traps.

BIRDS AND ANIMALS

Because the Old People lived their days with the birds and animals, the names they called them generally summarized an outstanding trait or characteristic. Some birds and animals are named for their similarity to others, often indicated by the prefix *big*.

This first list concerns the names of birds.

BIRD: The general word for bird is *piksi*, although the exact meaning has been lost. Small birds are *sistsi*; very small birds are *poksistsi*.

EAGLE: There are two kinds, the golden eagle and the bald-headed eagle. *Pitai* designates the golden eagle; *ksikichkinni*, or "white head," the bald eagle.

HAWK: The hawks as a group are *aiinnimai-aks*, or "seizers." The large rough-legged

189

hawk is *ishpochsoatsis*, or "used as a tail-feather," because its tailfeathers resemble the larger ones of the golden eagle and were used at the back of headdresses when there were not enough real eagle feathers. Hawk skin was included in Medicine Pipe Bundles, along with the skins of the various eagles. This hawk is also called "little eagle" and is sometimes mistaken by hunters for a real eagle.

The small sparrow hawk is known by the ancient *pispski*, which means something like "very high"; the sharp-shinned hawk is "big pispsksi"; the swainson's hawk, *sikpuitapanikim*, or "dark greasy feathers"; the red-tail hawk, *otachkuisoatsis*, or "yellow tail-feathers." The osprey is known as *pachtsiksistsikum*, or "mistaken for thunder," because of the noise its feathers make when diving.

OWL: *Sepisto*, or "night crier." The large horned owl is *kakanotstoki*, or "hollow ear," an important part of Medicine Pipe Bundles. The long-eared owl is *pachtsisepisto*, or "mistaken for owl," because it looks like a small horned owl. The burrowing owl is *matasi*, or "hollowed-out rectum," because of the shape of its nesting holes.

SWAN: *Ksikomachkaii*, or "white going home," it was usually seen only when it was migrating.

GOOSE: *Apspini*, or "white cheeks"; the snow goose is *einochksikanikim*, or "dark-tipped feathers."

DUCK: *Meksikatsi*, or "red feet." The larger ducks have the name prefixed with "big," and the small ducks with "little"; ducks such as the merganser that remain in our country far into the winter are called *miseeh*; the first syllable means "hardy," while *seeh* is another general term for ducks.

PELICAN: *Sochkaukomi*, or "big throat."

GREBE: *Miksksistaii*, or "fine diver," because

it could go under water; its skin was common in Medicine Pipe Bundles.

LOON: *Matsiisaipi*, or "handsome charger," because when it skimmed across water, it reminded our Old People of a proud warrior charging into battle; the loon is the second most important bird in Medicine Pipe Bundles, after the owl.

CROW: *Maisto* is its Indian name, but the origin has been lost.

RAVEN: *Omachkaisto*, or "big crow," which the Old People considered the wisest of birds. Men on the war or hunting trail always looked for and followed it because success was sure to await the party in the direction the raven flew. Two restless ravens in the path of a war party indicated enemies ahead. A raven circling slowly over a camp meant that some news was forthcoming.

WOODPECKER: *Pachpakskskissi*, or "pounding its nose." The red-headed woodpecker, whose cry is said to sound like the Blackfoot expression "stick your heads out so that I can eat you," is *mikimita*, which means "fire-reddened breast," or *ekotsotokan*, which means "red head." Lewis's woodpecker is known as "big mikimita." The pileolated woodpecker is called *sikskikunnikesuyi*, said to mean "flashes black feathers," although the term also suggests flashing something more vulgar than feathers.

MAGPIE: *Mamiatskikim*, or "has a body like a fish," because of its long tail. Its cry resembles a slumber song old women sing for little children: "Long tails—fly ahead and stab your provision bag at my door." It refers to the way they stab their beaks at whatever they can find.

CATBIRD: *Pokah*, or "child," because its cry resembles a baby calling *Na-ah*, or "Mama."

MEADOWLARK: *Otachkuikaii*, or "yellow breast." To the Old People, spring arrived at the first sign of a meadowlark. They

190

also believed the presence of meadowlarks to mean that all was well in the camp.

KINGBIRD: *Sikiminiwanyeh*, or "Stingy with berries," it makes a great ruckus if anyone picks berries where it is feeding.

WATER OUZEL: *Iksisakum*, or "meat"; it will dip its head in response to hearing its name called aloud.

ROCKY MOUNTAIN JAY: *Apiakunski*, or "white forehead."

STELLER'S JAY: *Omachkutskuisistsi*, or "big blue bird."

WAXWING: *Simitsima*, or "main lodge pole," for the pointed crest on its head.

DOVE: *Kuko*, referring to the domestic pigeon; the old-time Kukoiks Society members are called Doves or Pigeons.

GROUSE: *Kitoki*, or "prairie chicken"; the sage hen is "big kitoki" and the ptarmigan is "white kitoki." Grouse are also called *kitssitsum*, or "looking like smoke." The Franklin grouse is called the *matsapsi*, or crazy kitssitsum, because it is so stupid it can be approached and killed with a stick. Another grouse is called *apaskau*, or dancing kitssitsum, because of its mating dance.

The long-ago names of other birds have been forgotten. In the old days, only devoted Beaver Men and Medicine Pipe Keepers knew more than the names of the most common birds. Because so many birds are hard to approach, most of our People could only give general identifications of many species, and therefore the birds were named by their most obvious characteristics—big, small, blue, yellow, and so on.

Before our list of Blackfoot animal names, I would like to explain a little about our relationship to those animals around us.

Until the coming of trappers and traders, our People rarely killed anything they could not use. Buffalo and deer were hunted for meat, hides, and other parts. Fur-bearing animals were hunted and trapped with snares and deadfalls for their skins, which were used for clothing and sacred articles. They were seldom eaten. Animals and birds that spent most or all of their time in water were almost never eaten. Spiritually, they were thought to belong to the *SoyeTuppi*, the Underwater People. Fish were never eaten, except by a few. Before entering any body of water, most people gave an offering of tobacco or beads in recognition of the Powers of Water.

Even back when our People lived in harmony with nature, it could not be said that they never wasted anything. A spiritual person offered to Sun whatever he could not use of his kill. Men on war parties often shot buffalo for food, but could not eat or take back home most of the animal. When our People drove buffalo over cliffs, the ancient manner of hunting that was used until around 1850, they killed many more buffalo than necessary. About that time, buffalo were killed more for their hides than for food. Even our own People began trading buffalo hides and furs they had trapped for goods at the trading post. Thus began the end of our way of life.

Compiling the following list of Indian names and identifying their meanings was difficult, as the Blackfoot language has changed a great deal since the Old Days. Word definitions varied depending on precisely how a person was taught to use the word. In each case I have chosen the definition most often given, or the Old Man's definition.

DOG: *Imitai*; its meaning has been lost. Before horses, dogs were used to pack loads and move camps. The dog of the Old Days looked like a large gray wolf and could drag up to seventy-five pounds on a travois. The average family had about twelve dogs; there were several hundred in a camp. At times they could be quite unmanageable; they

191

would fight, chase wild animals, or run into water, even when loaded with packs and travois.

HORSE: The first horses our Old People saw resembled elks but were used like dogs. Thus the name *ponokamitai*, or "elk dog." Horses first came to the Bloods from neighboring tribes sometime around 1750, before the Bloods had seen their first white man. By a century later, our People's whole way of life had changed. By then they owned about eight horses per lodge. Our head chief, Pinu-kwiim, owned about a hundred horses before his death in 1870. Many horse-poor people borrowed some from the chief to pack their belongings whenever camp was moved.

The original horse we used was known as the "Indian pony." It is now almost extinct due to the government's efforts to interbreed it with the larger "white man's horses," more practical for farm and ranch use. Compared with today's horses, the old pony was smaller and better suited for rough traveling, requiring little food and water.

Horses, like dogs, were eaten only in times of great hunger. Their hides were popular for drumheads.

BUFFALO: *Einiua*, the most important source of food for our Old People. The name is said to refer to the animal's black horns. Spiritually, buffalo are still very important, although their scarcity has made it necessary to substitute beef in most ceremonies. Hides and dried meat, however, are occasionally available.

ELK: *Ponokau* refers to the animal's long legs. Elk were so commonplace in the Old Days, our Old People easily hunted them whenever buffalo herds could not be found. All parts of the elk were used.

Tanned elk hides made robes that holy women wore throughout the hot summer days of the Medicine Lodge ceremony. Skinned elk heads or leg hides were sewn together as berry bags. The long, smooth elk ribs made excellent runners for children's sleds. An elk's canine teeth, easy to remove because they do not grow into the jawbone, were highly valued decorations for women's dresses, men's vests, and necklaces. They are still valuable today.

A delicacy among our People was elk's rectum. Unlike many other animals, the elk has a very clean rectum. Before cooking, it was washed and stuffed with serviceberries and fat. Then the top ashes in the fireplace were scraped away and the stuffed rectum placed over the bottom layer of coals. When the top ashes were replaced, a small fire was built over the ashes. The man of the household would invite distinguished guests to share the delicacy with him. The end was cut off and given to the dogs; the rest was sliced up into small pieces for the People. This greasy, sweet, and spicy delicacy was considered "a meal for a chief."

MOOSE: *Sixtsi-sou*. The first part of the name refers to the animal's basic black color; the second part connotes "coming through," referring to the moose's characteristic charge, even through brush and trees, when disturbed or angry. Our Old People did not often venture into country where moose were found.

Moose nose was another culinary delicacy. In addition, large moose antlers were used to make bowls, and emergency moccasins could be fashioned from the peeled-off skin of moose hocks.

MULE DEER: *Is-sikotuye*, or "black-tipped tail."

WHITE-TAILED DEER: *Auwah-tuye*, or "waving the tail from side to side." This ancient name originally meant something like "waving their tails like dogs."

CARIBOO: *Omach-tsistsini*, or "big hoof." It

192

was rarely seen by our People, and then only in the mountains.

MOUNTAIN SHEEP: *Mistaks-omach-kskinnae*, meaning "mountain big horn." *Omach-kskinna* refers to domestic sheep, as well.

MOUNTAIN GOAT: *Ap-omach-kskinnae*, meaning "white big horn" or "white sheep."

ANTELOPE: *Saki-auwakahsi*, or "prairie deer." The name connotes shuffling or trotting out on the prairie. This animal, fast and difficult to hunt, was very common in the country of our Old People.

GRIZZLY BEAR: *Omach-ku-kyaio*, or "big bear." Bears in general are *kyaio*, referring to the head and neck. Their Powers, especially that of the grizzly bear, were feared by our People; only the bravest men would hunt or attempt to kill such an animal. In the past, bear was never eaten and bear skins were never used for anything except religious purposes. Hunters gave the skins as offerings to the Holy Powers, and proudly wore the claws around their necks. Medicine Pipe Owners will never say the animal's name, nor will they touch any part of it, except for the black bear skin in their Bundle.

BLACK BEAR: *Sikoch-kyaio*, which means "black bear."

BROWN BEAR: *Apoch-kyaio*, which means "brown bear."

TIMBER WOLF: *Omachka-apeesee*, or "big wolf." The general name is *makwi*, which connotes one who gets and eats plenty. Another name for wolf is *apeesee*, suggesting that they are wild relations to dogs. *Makwi* refers specifically to wolves, while *apeesee* also refers to bush wolves, technically considered coyotes.

COYOTE: *Ksino-au*, which refers to the way they can sneak around without being seen. This name is mainly for the small prairie coyote.

BOBCAT: *Atayo*, which refers to the bobcat's scream; it was also known as *suapit*, or "fringes on the legs."

LYNX: *Sok-atayo*, or "heavy bobcat."

MOUNTAIN LION: *Omachk-atayo*, or "big bobcat."

KIT FOX: *Sinopah*, which means something like "he has arrows"; it suggests the fox's ability to strike swiftly and unexpectedly.

RED FOX: *Otatoye*; means something like "distant Medicine robe," referring to the ancient custom of using a red fox skin in place of cloth when making an offering to Sun.

WOLVERINE: *Issistsi*; means either "claws shaped like hooves" or "carrying its young."

FISHER: *Pinutuye*; refers to the way the hair on its tail stands straight out, as though it had been clipped.

OTTER: *Emonissi*; refers to the way it slides around and is difficult to approach when it is on land.

BEAVER: *Ksisstukki*; means something like "cutting trees with his teeth." Beaver skins are tanned, complete with tails; the fat is removed and the tails are stuffed with crushed perfume plants and sewn shut. Beaver skins were commonly worn for winter clothing, especially leggings, with the hair outside to repel snow and water. Large beaver skins made popular saddle blankets. Some people made necklaces with the front teeth, and the claws from the hind feet were strung as wristlets. Beaver bile was placed on wounds that would not heal. Beaver castor made a popular perfume, among our People as well as many others.

MUSKRAT: *Misochpski*, or "hard-puffed face."

MARTEN: *Asinnatuye*, which means something like "young cropped tail" or "young fisher."

WEASEL: *Otao* is the summer weasel, referring to its brown coat. The winter weasel, or ermine, is called *Apao*, referring to its white coat. The winter skin is symbolic of life and death, day and night, and good and bad. For that reason it was favored for decorating all sorts of things. Our people tended to use these skins in place of the black and white eagle feathers used by other tribes.

Ermines were snared with sinew loops. The skin, simply peeled off the body, was stretched with willow sticks, and left to dry that way. The skin was "tanned" by rubbing it vigorously between the hands until it was soft.

BLACKFOOT FERRET: *Omachk-apao*, or "big weasel," so called because it was similar to ermine.

MINK: *Soyekaye*, meaning something like "wet back" or "water on its back."

SKUNK: *Apikayi*, or "white along its back." One way the Old People got skunks not to spray was to smoke them out of hiding places with a fire covered with plenty of sage. The smoke was said to blind the animal and confuse its sense of smell, so that it could be quickly dispatched with a club.

RACCOON: *Siksikishzip-otatoye*, or "black-striped red fox."

BADGER: *Misinskiyo*, meaning something like "sharply-pointed nose."

PORCUPINE: *Kaiskachp*, referring to the way the porcupine bristles its quills when threatened. Porcupines served as an emergency food, especially for men on the warpath who had lost their weapons. Since porcupines do not run away they could be clubbed with a stick. The tails would be skinned and resewn over a thick stick. As the skin dried, it tightened around the stick. A piece of buckskin was sewn over the tail in a way that left the tip protruding. When this tip was evenly trimmed, it could be made into a hairbrush or doctor's instrument. Sore muscles and joints were treated with rapid up-and-down stabs of the hairbrush. This did not puncture the skin, but stimulated the sore area.

JACKRABBIT: *Ahtsista*, the common name for all rabbits; it refers to the way the animal crouches down with its hind end.

SNOWSHOE RABBIT: *Mistaki-ahtsista*, or "mountain rabbit."

COTTONTAIL RABBIT: *Sik-ahtsista*, or "black rabbit."

PRAIRIE DOG: *Omachk-okatta*. The first part means "big"; the second refers to the way these animals were captured by children. A loop of sinew laid over the animal's hole snared it when it stuck its head out. The same name now also refers to gophers.

MARMOT: *Omachk-sikitsis-omachk-okatta*, meaning something like "big-toothed, big-snared."

MOUSE: *Kahnesskiena*, meaning something like "old face."

WOOD RAT: *Omachs-kahnesskiena*, or "big mouse."

SHREW: *Pokak-kaisksisi-kahnesskiena*, or "small, long-pointed-nosed mouse."

CHIPMUNK: *Miatsikaye*, or "striped back."

SQUIRREL: *Eekaiiseah*, referring to the animal's warning cry.

FLYING SQUIRREL: *Apastoksi-eekaiiseah*, or "white-faced squirrel."

BAT: *Motaienstami*, meaning something like "owner of many lodge poles." When a bat's wings are spread out, they look like lodge covers with many lodge poles, or small bones, underneath.

SEASONS AND STARS

The way in which our Old People kept track of the changing times was a reflection of their life in harmony with nature. They considered the year to be divided into two seasons—summer and winter. The year ended when summer was over, after the hunting and gathering of food supplies, sometimes around October or November. The new year began with the trials of winter, and reached its peak with the Sun Dance celebration in mid-summer.

The two seasons were further divided into moons, seven moons to each season. That is why the number seven is sacred in our ceremonies. The names for each of the moons varied, and sometimes the same name did not always mean the same moon to two different groups of People. Nevertheless, here is a list of the months as they are written on calendars and the corresponding names used by our Old People.

OCTOBER—When Winter Starts; First Big Storm; When Leaves Fall Off.

NOVEMBER—When Winter Starts; When Geese Fly South; When Big Winds Blow.

DECEMBER—When Rivers Freeze; When Big Storm Comes and Is Followed by Quiet; and, more recently, Big Holy Day Moon, for Christmas.

JANUARY—When the Heavy Snows Fall; Helping To Eat (because the cold used to keep the People from hunting and forced them to share their food supplies); and, more recently, Kissing Holy Day Moon, for the white man's New Year's Day.

FEBRUARY—Eagle Moon; Unpredictable Moon; More Big Storms; Big Chinook; and Short Moon, because the moon only stays dark two nights.

MARCH—Geese Coming Back; Time for Sore Eyes (from snowblindness).

APRIL—Ice Breaking Up; Long-Time Rain.

MAY—Leaves Coming Out; Last Snow Storm (which often brings deep snows and used to cause a lot of buffalo to fall off the snow-covered cutbanks and die).

JUNE—Green Grass; Time of High Waters; Frog Moon.

JULY—Flower Moon; Thunder Moon.

AUGUST—Berry Moon; Moon of the Medicine Lodge.

SEPTEMBER—Chokecherry Moon; Long-Time Rain; Leaves Blown from Trees by Winds; End of Summer Moon.

As you can see from the list, there are twelve moons, each having several names. When our people came under the influence of the white man's calendar, the multiple names of the original fourteen moons probably were gradually redistributed among the twelve months. No one remembers the names of the original fourteen moons.

There are four days between each "moon" when the moon does not show. Our Old People called this four-day period the "opening," as when a Medicine Pipe Bundle is opened inside the lodge before it is taken out for all to view. Some say that the moon then lasts for twenty-six days, and some say that it lasts for thirty, which may also be an adaptation to the modern calendar. Our Old People broke the moons down into nights, rather than days. The term "sleeps" was used to signify the passing of time, as in "we traveled three sleeps to get here."

At night the question How is the last brother pointing? meant "What time is it?" This referred to the position of the seven stars (Ursa Major) which, according to legend, were originally seven brothers.

Certain people, especially Beaver Men, kept track of the seasons and moons. They cut fourteen fresh buckskin strings at the beginning of the new year (winter) and kept these at the top of the sacred Bundle. Each evening, while making incense, a knot was tied in the buckskin string for that moon. The twenty-six or thirty knots were tied in sequence; the four "opening nights" knots were tied as a group a short distance away. The moon of each string could be further identified with special colorings or beads. Sometimes carved sticks were used instead of strings. More often, the sticks represented a whole month, a whole season, or even a whole year. Since the strings or sticks were handled every night, the Keeper had no trouble remembering the meaning of each thing on them.

The Keepers of these calendars also remembered special events, such as the death of a relative or chief, a notable war raid, or a famine. These events were marked by a double knot tied in the string. The meaning of the double knot was recorded in the memory of the Keeper and his wife. Each full year was recorded in this way and designated by the title of the year's major event, rather than by a number. In my calendar, for instance, 1972 was the Year of the Piegan Sun Dance, since it had been the first one in many years. Such yearly records are commonly known as "winter counts."

BAD HEAD'S CALENDAR, OR WINTER COUNT

PakapOtokan, or Bad Head, was a wise man who was interested in the history of his People. Chief

Fourteen counting sticks from an ancient Beaver Bundle. They were used to count the seven moons during the two annual seasons—summer and winter.

of the Buffalo Followers band, he signed both the Lame Bull Treaty of 1855 and the 1877 Treaty Number Seven. His other name was Father of Many Children. He kept in his memory an ancient winter count for the Bloods. Hugh Dempsey (Flying Chief) of the Glenbow Foundation located three different written copies of this winter count and combined them in one of Glenbow's little *Occasional Papers*. This information about Bad Head comes from it.

Two of these versions of Bad Head's winter count were collected from unknown Bloods, one by Robert Wilson and the other by the Oblate Father Emile Legal. The third version was written in a school scribbler by someone who learned the records in 1906 from Owl Chief and Ermine Horse. Bad Head had recited the winter counts to each of them sometime earlier.

The years and their important events were recorded by Dempsey with the help of his father-in-law, Senator Gladstone. Year numbers refer to the traditional year, from summer to summer.

> 1810: "Cropped tails—when they came." This is said to refer to the crop-tailed horses ridden by the members of the Astoria Expedition who came near this country in the summer of 1811.
>
> 1811: "Crying Bear—when he was destroyed." A Blood warrior killed by the Crees.
>
> 1812: "Gambler—killed by Flathead Indian." The Flatheads used newly acquired guns to win several victories over the Blackfoot people during this time.
>
> 1813: "When many of us went to war." The Crows were heavily raided by Bloods that year.
>
> 1814: "Top Knot—when he was killed." One of the Bloods who didn't make it back from the Crows.
>
> 1815: "Mad Child—when he was destroyed." He was killed when the Crees attacked a camp of twenty Blood and Sarsi lodges near the Belly Buttes.

1816: "Asekarsin—when he was killed," by another Blood.

1817: "Buffalo Paunch—when he was killed," by his brother.

1818: "Winter Sun Dance"; a winter camp on Sheep River was threatened by an attack from Crees, so a holy woman vowed an immediate Sun Dance to help her People. The attack did not come, but the sacred ceremony was held anyway.

1819: "Coughing epidemic"; one-third of our People died during an epidemic.

1820: "Four Horns—when he was killed," by a Pend d'Oreille Indian.

1821: "No Top Knot—he died."

1822: "Limping—when he first came here, where the rivers meet"; an unidentified white trader.

1823: "Long Hair—when he died."

1824: "Crows—when we drove them."

1825: "Many—when they made a peace treaty"; a representative of the Hudson's Bay Company, while traveling with a large party of Flathead People, recorded making a treaty with a two-hundred-lodge camp of Bloods, Piegans, and Gros Ventres.

1826: "Strong Goose Neck—when we made a big steal—Crows"; the Crows were raided while camped near present-day Belt, Montana.

1827: "Many died."

1828: "Crowfoot—when he was killed"; Crowfoot led a peace party that was attacked and destroyed on the way to the Shoshoni People. His name was later taken by the famous North Blackfoot chief.

1829: "Seven Persons—have been destroyed." Hugh Dempsey recorded the following incident with this year's count: "In 1829, seven Crows were killed near Buffalo Horn Butte, a short distance West of Chinook, Montana. The Bloods were led by Spotted Bear who captured a pipe-hatchet. The latter event is recorded in the White Bull winter count for 1870, and Seven Persons Creek, in southeastern Alberta, is named for the incident."

1830: "When we were freezing"; many people died from the cold while on a war raid.

1831: "Kipp—when he lived here, where the rivers meet"; James Kipp built Fort Piegan at the junction of the Missouri and Marias Rivers.

1832: "When he was camped there—Big Knife—where he wintered." The year that Fort McKenzie was built in Montana.

1833: "Stars—when they fell"; Dempsey says, "This meteoric shower was seen throughout much of North America on the night of Nov. 12, 1833, and is recorded in the winter counts of other plains tribes. The Bloods were camped on the Highwood River at the time."

1834: "Crows—when we laid in wait."

1835: "When they were killed in the water—Piegans, two."

1836: "Children—when they had strangulation of the throat"; a diphtheria epidemic.

1837: "Smallpox"; two-thirds of our People were wiped out.

1838: "Calf Chief—when he was killed"; a white trader killed him.

1839: "Meeting Someone—when she was killed"; she was mysteriously killed.

1840: "Hind Face—she was killed"; a drunken Blood killed her.

1841: "Walking Crow—when he was killed"; attacked by a Crow war party.

1842: "When at Women's Buffalo Jump—many in one camp."

1843: "Big-mouthed gun—Blackfoot—hunted by white man"; most of the party of North Blackfeet who came to trade at Fort McKenzie were killed when the fort's cannon was fired at them.

1844: "Separated—when we went to trade"; half the Bloods traded with the Hudson's Bay Company at Rocky Mountain House;

the rest traded with the Americans in Montana.

1845: "When he crawled under—Going to the Sun"; he crawled in a hole to hide from the Crees.

1846: "Came in front to steal—Crows"; a crow war party stole horses from in front of their owners' lodges.

1847: "Not a Favorite Child—when he was defeated, by the Assiniboines."

1848: "Winter—started to move with our camps."

1849: "Fifty—when they were killed—Assiniboines"; killed by the Blackfeet.

1850: "Eagle Calf—when he was killed"; the Crees killed him.

1851: "Winter floods."

1852: "Went north where he wintered—Father of Many Children."

1853: "When he made a shelter of branches—Assiniboine—abandoned camp."

1854: "When we ate dogs"; extreme hunger and no food.

1855: "When we were first paid—soldiers"; the Lame Bull Treaty in Montana.

1856: "When we were slipping"; an unusually icy winter.

1857: "Prairie White Man—killed—Pend d'Oreille Indian"; a white man was killed by an Indian.

1858: "We made a big sweat lodge."

1859: "When they killed each other—Hind Bull and Fish Child"; Dempsey writes, "These two brothers were chiefs of the Many Fat Horses band. While drinking near Rocky Mountain House, Hind Bull took his daugther away from her husband and Fish Child objected. In the argument that followed, Hind Bull shot Fish Child but, before dying, the latter stabbed his brother to death."

1860: "Pend d'Oreilles—when their horses were taken—Assiniboines"; the Piegans

came to the aid of the Pend d'Oreilles after most of their horses were captured and several people killed, and saved them from being wiped out.

1861: "When he got there—Medicine Prairie Chicken"; a visit from the half-Piegan head chief of the Crows to the Blood camps.

1862: "Tartowa—when he was killed"; a Blood who went insane and finally had to be killed by his brothers for the camp's safety.

1863: "Four enemy in a camp—when they were destroyed"; four lodges of Gros Ventres were wiped out by Piegans, while they were part of the Blood camp led by Blackfoot Old Woman.

1864: "Black smallpox"; scarlet fever killed over one thousand of our People.

1865: "We waited a long time"; the traders didn't come for some time because they were afraid they would be blamed for bringing in the earlier disease.

1866: "We were captured by hand"; many were killed attacking a large Cree camp, thinking it was only a small one.

1867: "Plenty trade—on trading expedition"; because of the new repeating rifles, our People slaughtered buffalo to trade the hides.

1868: "Bear People—shot at People"; members of this band got drunk and rode through the camps killing several people.

1869: "Smallpox"; again it was brought in with goods from the white People. Over two thousand of our People were lost.

1870: "Assiniboines—when we defeated them —Fort Whoop-Up"; a massive party of Crees and Assiniboines attacked the smallpox-weakened Blood camps along Belly River, not knowing that most of the Piegans were camped nearby. Many Crees were wiped out.

1871: "Highwood River—white men settled there"; they sold whiskey and guns.

1872: "They wintered there—Highwood River
—white men"; another trading post built
along this river in southern Alberta.

1873: "Calf Shirt—when he was killed"; a
minor chief, known for his strength and
brutality, was killed by a trader.

1874: "Police—when they came—Fort Mac-
Leod"; the Northwest Mounted Police.

1875: "When it was finished—whiskey"; the
Mounties got their men.

1876: "When there were plenty of buffalo";
despite the regular slaughter, there still
appeared to be many buffalo.

1877: "When we had a bad spring."

1878: "Mild winter."

1879: "When first—no more buffalo"; our
People could not find any buffalo in their
usual hunting grounds, so they went south
to Montana, where there were still many.

1880: "When we all moved camp"; by 1881
all of our People returned along the Belly
River, since the buffalo in the south had
become scarce there also.

1881: "Queen Victoria—her son-in-law—when
he came"; the Marquis of Lorne, who was
the governor-general of Canada, visited our
People at Fort MacLeod in 1881.

1882: "Red Crow—when he was robbed"; the
Crees stole eighty horses from Red Crow.
The thieves were not caught, but many
Blood parties went out in retaliation and
recaptured some of the horses. Our Cree
Medicine Pipe was captured on one of
these raids.

1883: "Fire wagon—when it arrived"; the
Canadian Pacific Railway reached the
Rocky Mountains that year.

Bad Head died in 1884, a nearly blind and
helpless old man.

TELLING FUTURE WEATHER

Our Old People had ways of foretelling weather
conditions by observing the many signs of nature.
An upcoming winter, a new spring, or even future
events could be prepared for by making certain
observations.

If muskrats built their houses close to shore,
the People expected a mild winter, and if houses
were built some distance from shore, they expected an average winter. If the muskrats built
out toward the middle of a pond or slough, however, the People prepared for a tough winter.

If migrating geese were flying high, that
was also a sign for a mild winter. If the geese flew
low, the Old People would say, "The geese are
close to the ground. We had better look for lots
of supplies for the upcoming winter."

The pelts of animals were checked for thickness to learn how to prepare for winter; the
thicker the pelts, the more severe the winter
would be.

The color of rabbits indicated how soon
winter would arrive and how soon it would be
leaving. As winter approached, they would turn
white; toward spring, they'd turn brown again.

Winter was expected to come early and
strong if curlews stopped singing early in summer,
if meadowlarks left the area before the berries got
ripe, and if songbirds were seen gathering in
flocks early.

During the winter, the People would watch
for the spectacular northern lights, the aurora
borealis. They believed the lights came from the
"Woods White Men," who were having a dance.
If the lights were bright, a big storm was expected
within two days. If the lights were not very
bright, a mild storm was expected, probably just a
wind storm.

At the end of winter, the People watched
gophers digging their holes. A lot of dirt outside
the hole meant the gophers were digging deep

and that the grass would not grow very well. People then said the buffalo flowers would not grow tall and the buffalo would not be fat. Buffalo were said to get good and fat on the buffalo flowers.

When Sun paints both of his cheeks (when two Sun Dogs, or halos, show) the weather will turn very bad. When Sun paints his forehead and his chin as well as his cheeks (four Sun Dogs), it is a sign that a great man is going to die.

A rainbow during a storm meant that Thunder was roping the rain clouds and taking them somewhere else, so that the storm would soon be over.

Today the Old People say that signs of nature are difficult to read because of the ways that man has changed nature around. Atsitsina gives this example:

Oki, I used to hear the Old People say that when Night Light [Moon] is lying on her back that she is resting and that the weather will be good. My father would say, "She is lying back like a bowl and holding in all the rain water. When she is finished resting, she will make it cold or rain again."

When Night Light is standing all the way up, the Old People will say that she is mad. You better dress warm because it is going to get cold.

Now it is all different. These white men, they are bad. They fly to the moon and they have moved it. All things have changed. The weather is not like it used to be. The things that my father taught to me don't always work right anymore because things change in strange ways. That is not how things were made to be.

THE SEVEN BROTHERS

Our Old People thought of stars as the spirits of legendary People, and the names they endowed them with suggest these origins. Most of these legends have been forgotten, but three are still quite well known. Two concern the two groups of stars that are symbolically represented by circles on the smoke flaps of most of our painted Medicine Tipis.

One legend tells of that part of the Great Bear commonly called the Big Dipper. We call it the Seven Brothers.

In the long-ago there was a widowed man who had nine children: six grown sons, a small son, and two daughters, the younger of whom cared for the little boy. To keep the family supplied with food he and his six grown sons went out hunting nearly every morning. As soon as the hunters left, the grown daughter would immediately go off to gather firewood.

As time went by, the younger daughter began to wonder why her older sister always spent so much time gathering firewood, and why she went to do it only while the men were away. So one day she followed her sister into the brush. She was much surprised to see her older sister meeting with a large bear and making love with him for some time. She hurried home, much confused by what she had seen.

When her father and brothers returned that evening, the young girl told them about her discovery. They were quite insulted, as not only had the older sister embarrassed the family by turning down several good men who wished her for a wife, but now she had an illicit husband who was a bear. They immediately gathered their weapons and went after the bear and killed him.

When the older sister learned what had happened to her lover, she was greatly upset. She went to the body of the bear and took from it a part, which she wrapped up and carried next to her own body.

The People in the camp learned about the incident and ridiculed the girl until she became very angry. She prayed to the Spirit of her lover for help, and all at once she turned into a huge bear. She ran through the camp and tore down the lodges and killed most of the People, before the Power left her and she again became herself.

The younger sister saw this and became greatly frightened. She put her little brother on her back and ran into the woods to hide. There she encountered her returning brothers, who were in mourning because their father had been killed in an accident while hunting. When they heard what had happened at the camp they were even more grieved. They told their young sister to go back home and secretly gather up spare moccasins and food so that they would be equipped to travel to some distant place together. They told her that they would place cactus thorns in front of the tipi door, leaving a narrow path for her to cross over and making it difficult for their older sister to follow.

The little sister and her brother returned to the tipi and quietly gathered the supplies. But soon the older sister realized what was going on and began to get very angry. The little girl quickly put her brother on her back, grabbed the provisions and ran out the door, carefully avoiding the cactus thorns as she ran. The older sister chased after them but her feet became covered with the thorns. As she hollered in pain, she again got her lover's Power and turned into a bear. At that she chased after the others.

Now one of the brothers had a lot of Power of his own. When he saw that the bear was about to catch up to them he spit over his shoulders, and right away a lake formed behind them. The bear was delayed in going around this water. As she started to catch up again, the Powerful brother took his porcupine tail hairbrush and threw it behind him. Right away a dense thicket was formed, and the bear had a difficult time getting through it. As the bear began to catch up to them once again, they decided to climb a large tree. The bear stood at the bottom and said, "Well, now I will kill you for sure." The Powerful brother took out his bow and arrows while the bear began to shake the tree. Four of the brothers fell out of the branches; but before the bear could do anything to them, it was struck by an arrow between the eyes. Right away the bear turned back into their sister, but she was dead.

The Powerful brother felt sad for having killed his own sister. He said to the others, "Well, we have no one left here on Earth now, so we might as well go somewhere else." The others agreed and asked where they might go. He told them to close their eyes, and then he shot an arrow far into the sky. When they opened their eyes they were all floating in the sky.

Thus was formed the Big Dipper, or Ursa Major. The four brothers who fell from the tree are the four lowest stars in the group, while the other brothers form the remaining three. Some say that the small star to one side of the handle is the little sister, while others say that she married one of the stars of the Little Dipper, and that she is the North Star, or Pole Star. Our People, who call this "the star that never moves," used it as a nighttime compass in the Old Days.

Another nighttime compass our Old People used was Morning Star, which the Old People called *Ipisoachs*. In our legends, he is the son of Sun and Moon, which is why he shines during the time between night and day. Like his father, he comes from the east, indicating the arrival of morning.

There is another star that is not quite so bright and comes up before Morning Star; this was called Mistaken Morning Star, for obvious reasons.

The other group of stars usually represented on the smoke flaps of our sacred tipis are commonly known as the Pleiades, but we call them the Poor Children.

THE POOR CHILDREN

In the camps of the long-ago there was a poor family with six boys. They were always dressed shabbily. It was early in the summer season, when men went out every day to hunt and replenish the supply of meat and hides that had been used up during the winter. This was the time most children received from their parents new robes made from the soft hides of calves. But the six poor boys continued wearing their old scabby robes because their father was too poor to hunt for any calf skins.

The other children made fun of the old hides worn by the poor boys. The boys were too ashamed to play with the other children and felt that their parents did not care for them. The poor boys wandered away from the camps and were soon lost out on the prairie. The Spirits of the Sky felt sorry for them and invited them to come and live up there. So that is where they went. It is said that they still hide out of shame during the time when buffalo calves are hunted for their skins. That is why they cannot be seen at that time of the season.

The Pleiades, incidentally, are made up of seven stars, but only six can normally be seen with the eye.

Our Old People gave Mars the name Big-Fire Star, because of its red color. Mistaken Morning Star, or Venus, was also called Day Star, because it can sometimes be seen in the middle of the day. Morning Star, by the way, is known today as Jupiter.

THE PERSON'S HAND

This legend is about the constellation known as Lynx. Our People knew this group of stars as the Person's Hand.

Two friends were out hunting buffalo, long ago. When they located a small herd, they separated so that they would have a better chance of success in case the herd moved away from them. One of the men shot a cow; the other one got nothing. The one who got nothing came up to his friend who was busy butchering his kill, saying, "Well, friend, I got nothing, so why don't you give me the kidney from your cow." The other said, "No, you scared the herd away. I was lucky to get this one." At that point they began to argue, and the unsuccessful hunter attempted to reach into the cow and grab the kidney for himself. The man became angry, took his knife and slashed off his friend's hand and threw it up into the sky, where it remained to become the Person's Hand. In retaliation, the wounded man cut off his friend's hand, and from then on the People found a section of the buffalo's stomach that they called a person's hand.

And that is all I know and was able to learn about stars.

End of First Week

For many people in our encampment, the most important ceremonies involved the Horns Society and their transfer of memberships. These ceremonies were to be the last major event of the encampment, which, incidentally, it has always been their duty to organize. Although many aspects of the Horns' activities are too esoteric for anyone who has not been initiated to understand, the public parts of their ceremonies are for the benefit of all the People.

The Horns Society

Officially, the Horns Society ceremonies could not begin until the Motokiks had finished theirs. On the fourth morning after the women had put up their lodge they took it down, signifying the end of their celebration. A few husbands helped with the dismantling. In a short time only the Center Pole remained standing, an offering to the Holy Powers. The women gathered around it and raised their headdress sticks toward the top. They prayed and sang and no doubt asked for strength and good luck so that they might all join together again the next summer. Then they left their sticks tied to the bottom of the Center Pole, along with cloth offerings for the Spirits that had been with them during their ceremonies.

With the Motokiks' lodge down, our attention turned to the Horns Society's. It had been made with two tipi covers. Two frames had been set up very close to one another so that the tipis seemed to intersect, one opening into the other. Actually, the poles that would have intersected had been left out of the structure, making one oblong frame over which were spread the two tipi covers. One of the covers was white; the other was partly painted with red symbols.

Not far from the lodge of the Horns was a large white tipi in which those members of the Magpie Society who were to become Horns were holding their meetings.

That night, not long after Sunset, we heard the Horns singing for the first time during the

The Motokiks gather around their sacred Center Pole for one last prayer and blessing, before hanging up their Bundles for the year.

encampment. At the start, several hand drums beat in unison a steady rhythm to accompany the men and women singing the comrade songs of their society. We all listened quietly and respectfully. The singing continued late into the night, a spiritual form of entertainment that was to be repeated during the next few nights.

The members of the Horns Society slept in their double lodge during the nights of their ceremonies. Food was cooked in other tipis and brought to them at mealtimes. Every morning the members brought out their ancient sacred bags and Bundles and hung them from several long wooden tripods set up behind their lodge, to the west.

SOCIETY TRANSFER CEREMONY: 1891

As a non-member, it would be improper for me to say much about the activities of the Horns during our encampment. However, Robert Wilson recorded the public activities of the Horns Society transfer ceremony of 1891. The events he witnessed were basically the same as those that took place in our camp.

An enclosure had been built in the middle of the space inside the large circular camp. This enclosure was round and about 40 feet in diameter. It was constructed of travoix, lodge poles and lodge canvas. The travoix, 18 in number, were set up in pairs resting together at the top. These nine pairs were placed at equal distances from each other in a circle and between each pair was tied horizontally a single lodge pole. The poles were about 3½ feet from the ground and over them was thrown lodge canvas thus making a continuous wall or shelter for the inmates who had spent one night there. Between the two most easterly pairs of travoix, the pole and canvas had been omitted which left a means of egress and exit for the crowd of men, women and horses that thronged the place.

Sitting with their backs to the wall inside the shelter, and forming except at the entrance an unbroken circle of men, sat the 18 old members of the Society in company with their assistants [called Partners], and some old men who acted as instructors. In front of each old member a staff was stuck upright in the ground. Nine of these were long poles, 10 feet or thereabouts, with 10

inches of their upper ends bent down almost in a perfect half-circle and tied in that position by a leather strand. This gave the 9 large staffs a striking resemblance to the crooks of ancient shepards. A 10th man had stuck in front of him a 10 foot spear with an iron head, and all of the others had simply a short plain stick about 4 feet in height. Upon each of these upright staffs were tied one or more of the long painted and fringed raw-hide bags always seen hanging upon a tripod at the back or west side of an Indian house or lodge. In front of each staff sat the candidate for membership and his assistant. The relatives and friends of candidates were busy bringing in horses, guns, and great quantities of lodge goods, as well as numerous blankets and articles of mens clothing, etc. These were the payments for membership which were laid down near the groups about the staffs, and were then taken possession of and carried away by wives, daughters or other relatives of the old members.

Property changed hands in a lively manner for over an hour. When all the necessary and voluntary payments had been made and the space in the centre of the enclosure was clear, the ceremonies of initiation and installment were prepared for. First of all a small fire was built in the centre, for red-hot coals were necessary to make incense. When the fire had burnt down sufficiently for the purpose, each candidate, or his assistant, went to it and took upon a forked stick, a single coal which he carried with great care to his altar, which was a spot 12 or 14 inches square between the staff and where each candidate and companion sat.

These altars were made as the Indians usually make them, simply by cutting and scraping away the sod to the depth of an inch or more. An Indian standing near me remarked that should one of the men have dropped to the ground the coal he was carrying between the fire and the altar, it would have been considered a bad omen.

The 18 coals were all safely deposited at the

centre of the 18 altars, and the old members made incense by sprinkling upon them a small quantity of dried grass. Each old member next made four passes with his hands from incense to the bag on the staff and then untied it and after passing it [four times to the altar] he laid it upon the ground. The bags were at once opened and the head dresses etc., which they contained were taken out and exposed to view. Each candidate was now painted by the old member whose regalia and position in the Society he was about to acquire. Some were painted red, others yellow; in all cases they were painted from head to foot. Some had their faces painted jet black and a red stripe from ear to ear across the eyes and another red stripe across the mouth. In the meantime, the wives of 4 of those who sat behind the short staffs were putting together 4 large war bonnets which they stuck upon the staffs. A number of dark clouds from the north were at this time overshadowing the camp and from them a few drops of rain were falling, the appearance in fact was in favour of a rainy afternoon. Running Wolf, two other men and Running Wolf's wife stood up in a row facing the entrance and behind them stood an old man who in a loud voice prayed that the rain storm should pass to one side or the other and not interfere with the sacred proceedings. He prayed 4 times with a pause between each.

White Calf now took down, or rather pulled up, Running Wolf's staff and held it horizontally over the altar. In a loud voice he made a prayer, and when near the end of it, he put a daub or two of red earth paint upon it. At the conclusion of the prayer he covered the pole from one end to the other with the red earth which was mixed with grease and of a pink shade. When White Calf had finished, all the other poles were taken up by the instructor of old members and painted in the same manner, but all the short staffs and some of the long ones were yellow. From each of the bags before mentioned, was taken a long strip of fur with which to wrap the long staffs from end to end. With slow and deliberate motions this part was performed. Gathering up the whole strip in a bunch in his hand, the old instructor passed it 4 times to the altar and then tied one end securely to the extremity of the crook. He then proceeded to wind the fur spirally and closely down the length of the staff covering the wood completely. None of the fur was allowed to touch the ground during the operation. At the lower end, 4 foot of the pole, the wrapping was fastened again, and against it was bound some braided and dried grass used by this Society for incense and a dried bladder bag of the buffalo.

Running Wolf's crook was wrapped with white swan's skin, the others with otter. All the fur was about one inch in width. All of the long staffs and the spear were wrapped as described, each with the grass and bladders at the bottom. At the end of each crook and at three places down its length was tied a bunch of two eagle feathers, the spear alone had a 4 or 5 inch strip of black and white cotton tied loosely to its full length. The wife of the chief of the outgoing members now took the swan-covered staff, and wearing a small horned head dress also of white swan skin, she walked over and took up a position near the entrance but facing inwards. She also carried in her arms a bundle of clothing rolled in a blanket. Bear Back Bone next got up, wearing nothing but a breech cloth and moccasins, and stooping low, with a slow and solemn pace, he approached the woman; close behind him walked Running Wolf, also stooping or rather hiding behind the others. When Bear Back Bone [the name was actually Bear Shin Bone] reached the squaw, he straightened up to his height and, after reverently passing his hands from the top of her head to the shoulders, he kissed her upon the left cheek. She then handed him the pole and headdress. Running Wolf next lifted his head up and with same solemn pass with the hands also kissed her and received from her the bundle of clothing. They slowly returned to their place in the circle,

205

stooping as before, the squaw bringing up the rear.

The same ceremony was gone through with the 4 large war bonnets, but the latter moved in a direction contrary to the course of the Sun while the others followed it. The candidates were at once dressed in their new clothing and Running Wolf, Bear Back Bone and another stood up in a row as before, while White Calf 4 times prayed aloud that the rain should not fall. The blanket Bear Back Bone had received was folded up and laid upon the ground. Its owner took a kneeling position, facing it. White Calf made a pass with both hands from the altar to Bear Back Bone's head, one to his shoulder, a 3rd to his waist and the 4th to his hips, giving this time a gentle push at which Bear Back Bone jumped nimbly over the blanket without altering his stooping position. He sat upon the blanket while Running Wolf was put through the same maneuver, then all ditto.

This finished the installment of the new members and now they prepared for the dance. Four drums we brought in and deposited at the middle of the circle, and the head-dresses were all placed upon their new owners. An old Chief "Morning Paper" [Morning Writing] counted 4 coups, and the drummers struck up at once. All the staffs were pulled up and all the men, new members, old, and instructors, jumped to their feet and the dance began. The step was one peculiar to the Society, and a rather lively one for some of the older men to perform. They held their poles in front, lowering the tops to about an angle of 45 degrees. At intervals they would reverse all together and dance facing the low wall of the enclosure. They all made a continual peculiar sound, something between a coo and a low shout and in time to the drums. The dance lasted about 4 minutes, during which they reversed 4 or 5 times. Next they formed a procession, led by one wearing a large war bonnet which had an arrow sticking in head piece. They danced towards the entrance. As many times as the leader reversed, all

followed suit; after many times turning about, they approached the entrance and the leader went out and the procession followed in the form of one irregular column with the squaws bringing up the rear, carrying the short staff. They danced towards the east and between the lodges until, when quite outside of the camp, a halt was made and the procession reformed. Running Wolf mounted a white horse and the second leader of the Horns mounted a dark one. These two riders took positions far in the lead, about one hundred yards ahead, and the same distance from each other. Fifteen of the others formed a line; behind them walked the 4 drummers in a second line, and the women as before brought up the rear in a third line. Midway between the line of men and each rider was a dismounted man; one of them had in his hand an Indian standard, an otter skin [actually a fisher skin] decorated with beads and bells. They marched in this way around to the Southern side of the camp, the drums beating time but not loudly. When about ¼ the distance around the camp had been made, or when they were opposite the South side, they halted and danced a few minutes. The mounted men dismounted and danced where they stood, their horses being held by boys. The march was renewed as before. A second halt and dance at the West, a 3rd at the north and a 4th at the East, the spot where they had first formed a line, completed the outside of the camp march and they prepared to reenter the camp by taking the same positions and formation as when they came out. Dancing all together, the tom-toms beating loudly, they returned to the centre of the camp space.

Their enclosure had in the meantime been taken down and carried away, but they all sat down near where it had been and in about the same positions that they had held inside of it. The 4 large war bonnet wearers took them off and hung them up upon their short staffs. When they had been sitting, resting for half an hour, a woman appeared and stood about 50 yards to the East of them, holding in her hands a bowl of water. Two of the dancers got up and slowly walked towards her, as before stooping low, one behind the other. The leading man kissed her, in the same solemn fashion as before, received from her the water, some of which he drank and after passing the bowl to his companion, who had in the meantime also kissed the squaw, he handed her a small bundle of clothing. The other man now finished drinking and deposited the empty bowl upside down upon the ground at the feet of the woman. They now returned, as they came, to their places and the squaw picked up the bowl and went home. Two other women brought water for the thirsty and the same performance was gone through. In one case three men came out instead of two. These squaws were the wives of late members of the Society, and considered that they were doing a very sacred duty in allowing

Members of the Horns Society around 1920. The leader's Swan Staff is the third one from the left, next to the bannerlike one of the secondary leader. The man holding the fifth staff from the right is the head chief, Shot-on-Both-Sides. The three men in the straight-up headdresses are Wings, Willie White Feathers, and Weasel Moccasin. On the chief's right is Laurie Plume. Second after him is Mokakin. (Glenbow Archives)

A headdress of the Horns Society on display at the Alberta Provincial Museum.

A horned Medicine headdress on display at the Alberta Provincial Museum.

themselves to be publicly kissed. In fact there was not a smile upon the face of any of the actors, nothing to suggest anything other than a religious duty, but I could not restrain a smile as I saw Spotted Bull, who is a notorious wag, solemnly kissing the wife of Mas-tak-ath who is one of the most handsome women in the tribe. White Calf stood behind two men and a woman, facing the East, and shouted aloud a prayer. They then faced the South, he prayed again; changing to the West again, he called out a prayer and finally repeating with faces to the North they all sat down.

A group of women and old people, not members of the Society, were sitting near the circle of dancers, for the purpose of having prayers shouted over them. The dancers stood close to these sitting people and facing them always so that they had to move in a circle themselves in facing the 4 different directions. This performance was repeated by two other parties of four persons each. Next a dance was indulged in. The main party danced in a circle around those sitting on the ground, being led by one with the arrow in his war bonnet. The other three with large headdresses danced outside of the rest and circled in the opposite direction, and against the Sun. The speed was increased to a fast hop and then the leader stopped suddenly and without turning hopped backwards 5 or 6 times for perhaps half of the circle, during which they reversed as often as they halted. After a brief pause the dance was repeated and, in all, it was done 4 times; then all sat down. Running Wolf's crook was carried over to some old men who sat about 50 yards to the north of the party; one of these took Running Wolf's crook and counted 4 coups. The drummers beat an applause or response after each coup and the crook was carried back to its owner. The same was done for the second leader.

After a rather extended rest, they all got up and the closing dance was performed. "Little Shield," the wearer of the war bonnet with the arrow in it, not being an active man, handed his

Horns Society members, around 1920. Left: Long-Time Squirrel. Center: Head Chief Shot-on-Both-Sides, wearing the Opposite-Dance Headdress. Right: Rough Hair, holding the fisher skin. (Glenbow Archives)

Members of the Horns Society around 1920. Standing, from left to right: Bob Riding Black Horses; old Chief Calf (supposedly), wearing the Headdress-with-a-Red-Plume; Weasel Calf; SweetGrass; and Crazy Crow with the arrow in front. In the foreground, wearing the straight-up headdresses: Mike Oka; Not Good; and Weasel Moccasin.

head-dress to Spotted Bull, because the final dance had to be led by the regalia. Around the circle they rapidly hopped. The Leader was closely followed by two of the other large war bonnets, the 4th one along circling in the opposite direction and outside the rest.

A dense crowd had gathered about the dance by this time. After dancing around the circle several times, the leader made a feint to go through the crowds of people at the east and each time he came around he danced a little closer, being driven back through by the boys and young men who shook their blankets at him as they would at an animal. Someone handed Spotted Bull a rifle and the next time he came around to the East, he, still hopping, charged right at the people. Blankets were shaken in his face and the crowd did not give way for him until he fired a shot over their heads, at which all fell back allowing the procession to dance out into the open ground. The assembled crowd now dispersed.

The Society returned to where they had been sitting and waited there until the lodges of two of their members were taken down in the camp and moved over to them by the women. The members then took charge of the material of the two lodges and out of it constructed one big oblong lodge into which they entered. This was their permanent abode for the remainder of the time the Bloods were in camp. This society did not dance again, but religious duties and the rites were performed by them every day afterwards. Such is the dance of the mysterious order of Atskiniax, about whose sacred rites the middle-aged will talk in whispers to you, telling you every few minutes that it is very dangerous to talk about it at all.

OUR OWN HORNS TRANSFER

The new Horns have made a concerted effort to regain the respect of the People and to learn as much about the Ways of their society as they can from former members who are still living. They have carefully traced the disposition of all the missing society Bundles, locating ten of them, and, as of this writing, are negotiating for their return to the society.

For some time before last summer's Horns membership transfer ceremony, families of the new members went around the camp circle, one at a time, displaying their payments for the membership. Old People walked ahead of each procession, calling out the name of the new member and singing words of praise for him. Mokakin was the most popular man in camp for this duty, and before long his voice was so hoarse and broken he could barely be heard. Among the processions he led was one for Ponah's nephew, Cyril Red Crow. To help him with his payments, his sister and her husband, Stabs Down, paid the quarter horse we had given to them some time earlier when we took our Medicine Pipe. Most of the horses shown as payments were covered with fine blankets, while those who led them wore buckskin suits and eagle feather headdresses. All these goods were to be given as payments.

The transfer ceremony was held inside a fenced circular enclosure. Spectators crowded outside to see functions similar to those described by Wilson. Within the enclosure was a large crowd of old members, new members, and former members, all with their wives. The former members served as advisors to both old and new members. A couple of the retiring members were South Piegans who had come up for the occasion from Montana.

When the new members had made their rounds outside the camp circle, they were preceded by their leaders, one on a black horse and one on a white, just as Wilson observed. The dance leader wore the ancient headdress with a feather stuck in the front to represent the arrow once shot into the forehead of a long-ago, similarly headdressed dance leader. The original arrow remained lodged in its place while the wearer of the headdress led his party of Bloods to a victory against the enemy. This battle and victory are re-

Atsitsina and relatives displaying the saddle horse, shawl, and headdress being paid by Fred Eagle Plume for his membership in the Horns.

enacted during each summer's dance, the symbolic battle ending when the leader fires his gun into the air and charges through the crowd of children, who are the "enemy."

As part of their performance, the Horns gave away rations of food to all the adults in the crowd. At the same time, the staffs of the two leaders were blessed by two old men who each called out four brave deeds. The leader's Swan Staff was brought to our Old Man; it had once been his, when he had been leader of the Horns. He called out four exploits of horse raiding, and said a prayer. The other staff was taken to Ben Calf Robe, the old man who had come down to visit the encampment from his home on the North Blackfoot Reserve. He had also been a member of the Horns Society, which is now inactive there.

A 1935 ACCOUNT: GEORGE FIRST RIDER

To complete this story, here is an excerpt from George First Rider's narrative of a past Horns Society.

During the winter in the year 1935, the Horns Society started to collect. My partner, Elk Bear, was given the authority to hold the collections. He said, "My friend First Rider will hold the money collections." The Horns members all agreed for me to hold the money. That day my life was still bad, [because of] my drinking, stealing, and all the bad habits in my life. But still I was given the job to be the treasurer. At pay days [when the People received treaty payments], I collected the money. I even had a secretary to keep the files. I had come to think of the job as religious, so I thought I'd stand good on it. . . .

So, the Horns Society collected $500—and I held the money. The Horns members said, "We will give $250 to the one that is going to sponsor an Okan so she can use the money to buy what she needs." Then the Horns Society members selected the major Bundle Owners [of Society Bundles]: four men were selected, I was one of them, and two of us went east on the reserve, two to the west, to tell all the Blood People of the coming assembly. . . .

In two days the Blood Indians were all at the circle camp. Two days after that, the Horns Society went around visiting the women that could sponsor Holy Lodges, but none volunteered. Since no one volunteered, we invited the owner of the Motokiks Center Pole [the leader of that society] to sit outside our tipi. She couldn't come inside because only members and their wives are allowed in the double-lodge of the Horns. She was told to erect her lodge. She was given $100 to put up her Motokiks lodge. We kept the other $400. At this point she assembled the Motokiks. . . .

On the night of the fourth day at the camps,

211

the Horns Society members and the Motokiks assembled, standing in a line outside the Horns lodge, and chanted a song. Then came an announcement. Low Horn spoke: "Okaha-aaai! In the coming morning the Horns are going to have a dance. This coming morning the Motokiks will build their lodge. Medicine Pipe Owners, Beaver Bundle Owners, Pigeons, and All Brave Dogs— get yourselves ready to beat your livers! [An ancient expression which meant to have an exciting dance.]

In the morning I took my team and my wagon and with some members and another, empty wagon, we all went to Cree Speaker at Stand Off. [Cree Speaker was a white man named McNeill who could speak the Cree language. He had a general store and post office on the west side of the Belly River, at Stand Off.] The monies were $400, so we took some grub with $100, then we drove back. The place where we were going to have our dance was already staked out, so the grub was unloaded there and the wagons were taken away.

Then we went inside the Horns lodge. There, we untied our Society Bundles and painted all the Staffs. . . . We bound them, fixed up our headdresses, and painted our faces with yellow paint. . . . I painted my face with yellow paint and with red painted streaks across my face.

The drummers came in and sat inside the door. They sat with their backs to the fireplace [because they were not current members] and then they sang. . . . As they sang we danced out the door and formed a line outside. . . . We danced forward four times and then we danced to the east exit of the camp circle. With the black horse on the outside and the white horse on the inside toward the camp circle, the riders mounted and we went forward. . . .

The leader walked on the South side, behind the rider. He owns the headdress that was shot in the forehead. [This is the dance leader, not the society leader.] The White-Arch-Staff owner rode in front. [This is the staff wrapped with a white swan skin and carried by the society's leader.] The owner of the Arm Band rode across behind. [This is the secondary leader of the society.] The riders dismounted and we all danced. . . .

The riders walked their horses real fast. The drummers walked behind. Behind the drummers are the Horn Society women [wives of the members] on foot. Behind them are more riders; they are just mounted spectators. . . .

When we got all the way around the camp circle we danced back in at the east side. The leader danced in front. We danced four by four. We got up to the double-lodge on the fourth song, and the singing stopped. We stood in order. We all had tipi pegs and an oblong stone ready. Everyone was hammering pegs into the ground [to make holes] and then we all stuck the arch staffs into the holes. . . . We all put our robes behind the staffs and everybody sat down in order. The women sat in the centre.

Now the grub. There was a cow that was slaughtered, and some berry soups, and there were some white-man fruits to make puddings. The Horns distributed the food, and after everyone ate we got up and danced. The People who made vows to dance with Horns Society staffs danced with a staff. The Horns danced four times and they stopped dancing, and then they gave away the things that they received. [A person who vows to dance with a certain staff will give its owner some kind of payment for getting to share the Power of that staff.] After we gave away the stuff, the staff owners pulled out their staffs and pegs. When a staff is pulled out, a pinch of tobacco is put in the hole and then the hole is tamped shut. . . .

Next, we went outside where a crowd of spectators formed around in a circle to watch the dancing. The leader led us around in the dance. There were a lot of girls and boys standing, watching on the east side. This is the time when the

212

leader took a rifle. Nobody saw it. It was wrapped; it was hidden. . . .

On the fourth dance [each dance consists of four rounds within the circle] we all stood in line. . . . During the start of this fourth and final dance, the leader danced in zigzag motion; he danced just like as if he was dodging enemy arrows. The children, boys and girls, threw manure at him. The leader continued dancing in zigzag motion, dodging from side to side, and the dancers behind him performed in the same manner. . . . Our leader was Low Horn. He danced just like as if he [was] going to charge. He danced a little ways out and then he turned and retreated. Then he danced right into the midst of the children before he was forced to turn back. The boys and girls were throwing manure at him. He was moving his head from side to side so that the manure would not hit him on the face. The manure was not thrown with full force.

Low Horn danced around again, holding the rifle in front of him, pointed up. . . . As the children were screaming, he danced right into the midst of them. He fired a shot and the children all fell down just as though they were killed.

The Horns members walked through the fallen children to the lodge, where we stuck our staffs into the ground, and then we wiped off our facial paints.

OTHER SOCIETIES

Today the Horns and Motokiks are the only traditional societies still active among our People. We don't know that any other women's society ever existed, but men used to have several to join, according to their age group and their experiences as warriors and leaders. Let me give you a brief Teaching about these societies so that you will understand how our People were motivated to form them and why they have respect for them.

Mountain Horse, standing before a gathering of the Horns Society, in 1910. (Glenbow Archives)

213

Societies were formed to give members spiritual strength as they faced, often alone, the many physical challenges of daily life. This reassured the People of the tribe that organized groups of able men were always prepared to give assistance and protection.

Members of societies belonged to various bands within a tribe, and therefore were not able to meet as a complete group during most of the year. Yet as each member went about his daily life, hunting and raiding with his family or others, he was strengthened spiritually, knowing that his comrades were near and far. He took pride in wearing his society's symbols and regalia, whether he was dancing in the camp circle or making a stand against an enemy party, and he knew that the Spirits of his fellow members were with him. If he happened to be in battle alone, he might cheer himself on by loudly announcing his membership in an ancient society whose members were known for bravery.

Men's societies often acted as the People's militias and policemen. It was their duty to carry out the chief's orders during tribal functions, so that harmony would be preserved among everyone. When camp was moved, society members rode along the outskirts of the caravan to defend it from enemy attacks. They helped stragglers and scouted the trail ahead. During communal hunts, society members kept the hunters together so that none got too eager to move ahead of the others, alarming the buffalo herds. (They punished such offenders by seizing and destroying their property. Thus, in our Old Ways, a policeman is called a "seizer.")

During the annual Sun Dance Encampments, members of some societies acted as seizers. The head chief and his council of band chiefs made up the orders for the camp, and criers announced the orders to the People. The societies whose members would enforce the orders and keep peace in the camp set up their lodges inside the camp circle, near the lodges of the chiefs, so that they could observe what was going on all

Members of a young men's society, possibly the Pigeons, outside a Medicine Lodge around 1880. The tipi in the background has a Medicine Pipe Bundle tied over its doorway. (Ernest Brown)

around them. The societies for older men were chosen for these duties.

There were seven men's societies in the Old Days. Together, all their members were known as *Ichkunakatsiiks*, or "All-Comrades." These societies included the Mosquitoes, Braves, Crow-Carriers, Brave Dogs, Horns, Black Soldiers (or Black Seizers), and Bulls. In later years of the Old Days, the Bulls Society became extinct, while the Pigeon Society formed in its place. The youngest groups were the Pigeons and Mosquitoes; the oldest were the Horns, Black Soldiers, and Bulls. The ultimate in a warrior's life was to have been a member of all the societies.

The younger societies were mainly social. The Pigeons were originally boys who had not gone on any war raids. By the time they had been on a few, they usually became members of the Mosquito Society.

The Mosquitoes are said to have originated in the dream of a man who lay naked out on the prairie and let swarms of mosquitoes suck blood from him. While he was unconscious afterward, a mosquito came to him and gave him the society for his generosity. Each member would wear an eagle claw upon each wrist, to represent the mosquito's bill. During ceremonies, the members would use the claw to scratch those who got in their way. Anyone who resisted their symbolic scratches would be fallen upon by all the members and severely scratched.

Each society had a ceremonial dance, during which the members had their faces and bodies painted and wore their society insignias. The significant part of the Braves' ceremonial dance was the end, when all the members ran north out of the camp circle and threw their moccasins into the air to symbolize the discovery of a buffalo herd. It is said that one time the barefoot members suddenly noticed they were facing a large enemy war party that had concealed itself near the camp. The Braves, carrying only their spears, stood little chance in a direct encounter, so the society leader ordered the members to resume dancing. The performance so impressed the enemy that they retreated.

Within these societies were usually two members known as Bears. These Bears had the publicly accepted right to appropriate food from someone for the use of all the members. If they saw a successful hunter returning home they could demand a portion of his meat to be used as a meal for the society. The Bears could be identified by their painting, clothing, and other insignias, especially a headdress made from a strip of bear fur with two claws attached to resemble small horns on the wearer's head. Percy Creighton bought one of these headdresses from old Gambler and sold it to Mrs. Walters for forty-five dollars. It had belonged to the Brave Dogs Society.

Some of our older men are still members of the now-inactive Brave Dogs Society, as it is known among our division. The Piegans call the same group the Crazy Dogs Society. Meetings of one group may be attended by members from other divisions. They can often be recognized during our social dances, or powwows, by their membership insignias—individually painted rawhide rattles, which they carry suspended from their wrists by fur straps. Traditionally, each member painted his face according to the design on his rattle.

Social societies of male contemporaries are still formed among our People. Today there are the Red Belts, the Magpies, and the Parted-Hairs. One group, called the Baggy Underwears, is making an effort to take on a new name.

Blood members of the Braves Society at Lethbridge in 1886. In the foreground are three of the society's four lance-bearers. Most of the members carry spears and paint their bodies symbolically. The Bear Braves are standing at the back (there seem to be five, although there should only be four). (Glenbow Archives)

Dance of the Pigeon Society (or Doves) as seen in 1907. The members are dancing in a circle. Each one carries a bow and arrows, and his body is painted. The photographer's feet can be seen in the foreground; he took these photos without permission while lying down as a spectator. (Glenbow Archives)

Mountain Horse, leader of the Crow Carriers Society, dressed for battle. He wears a Medicine headdress, as well as a weasel-tail suit of shirt and leggings. Each of these articles was transferred ceremonially. Symbols of scalps he has taken are tied to his rifle. The hand on his horse represents an enemy he killed in a hand-to-hand encounter; the two large spots represent places where horses he was riding were shot in battle. On the horse behind him is old Bumble Bee, who is holding a staff of the Crow Carrier's Society. Bumble Bee enlisted in the armed forces at the same time as did several of Mountain Horse's sons. However, he could speak no English and refused to cut his hair, so he was sent back home. Before he left he is said to have told the other Blood soldiers: "Don't be foolish like these white soldiers. They call off the war every day at mealtime. You boys want to keep on shooting, even if you see them sitting down to eat." (Glenbow Archives)

Bear Braves of the Pigeon Society at Fort MacLeod in 1924. On the left is Rough Hair. The other two men are North Piegan Bear Braves, wearing belts and arm bands of bear skin. Their hair is tied back and bear ears are fastened on top of their heads. All three members carry bows and arrows, and robes. (Glenbow Archives)

Joe Healy, or Flying Chief, dressed in the regalia of a Bear Brave of the Pigeon Society, in 1886. (Russell)

Grass Dancing

Our People have always been willing to accept the Ways of other People if they could be fit into our traditions. In that manner we adopted the Grass Dance, traditionally an important function among the Omaha People, apparently celebrated by their Central Plains neighbors for many years. A ceremonial dance with many symbolic details, its purpose was to spiritually encourage the prairie grass to grow tall, which would mean more food for the buffalo. That's why it became known as the Grass Dance. The dance was eagerly adopted by other tribes, including the Crow, Sioux, and the Assiniboine (from whom our People obtained it).

During the final years of the war days, a Blood man named Sitting Bull led a party to the east to raid the Assiniboine People. The Assiniboines are relatives of the Sioux, or Dakota, People, whom we commonly call Parted-Hairs, due to their custom of parting their hair down the middle. They hid themselves in the brush on top of a nearby hill, watching the camp through Sitting Bull's field glasses to decide on a strategy to raid it.

When evening came, the Assiniboines did not go into their lodges, but instead gathered in a circle inside their encampment. One man went out behind a lodge and took down from a tripod a large drum, around which several men gathered. They began by beating a fast, steady rhythm. Soon dancers emerged from the lodges. Their dress and actions reminded the Bloods of prairie chickens during mating season: they stooped low and shuffled their feet quickly, while swaying their bodies slowly from side to side. In this manner they approached the drum from all directions. When they had gathered around the drum, the drummers began a slower beat, to which they sang a pleasant song.

Sitting Bull and his party watched and listened all night long. By the time the dance was over it was too late for the party to attempt to raid the camp. The following night the same thing took place again. By this time some of Sitting Bull's men began to sing along with the songs to amuse themselves.

It was not until several nights later that Sitting Bull and his men raided the Assiniboine camp. Sitting Bull went straight to the tripod and took down the drum, which he brought back home with him. The party captured a number of horses and returned to the Blood camps safely. With the songs they had learned on the hillside, and Sitting Bull's captured drum, they introduced the first aspects of the Grass Dance among the Bloods.

Our People learned more about the Grass Dance after the days of raiding enemy tribes were over. Robert Wilson photographed a group of visiting Assiniboines in 1891, while they were exchanging the songs and regalia of the Grass Dance with our People for horses. Such exchanges

Sitting Bull—the Blood—with his two wives and his children. The boy at the left later became one of the last four men to fulfill self-torture vows, during the 1892 Medicine Lodge ceremony. This scene was taken around 1880, and must have been of a hunting camp, due to the unusual crudeness of the tipi poles and cover. Among his sons were Calling High and Jim Wells.

A group of visiting Assiniboine men wearing Grass Dance regalia, which they traded for Blood horses in 1893. Blood spectators are watching the dance in the background. Assiniboine singers are seated around the drum in the foreground. (R. N. Wilson)

220

also probably took place with others, like the Crows and Piegans. The most important Grass Dance items were two feather belts, or "Crow bustles," which were transferred just like other Medicines. They are still among our People at this time.

Two aspects of the Grass Dance Society did not endure very long among our People. One concerned the eating of dogs, which was a custom among those who originated the dance, but was despised by most of the Bloods. The other concerned the method of joining the society. Old members would elect new members, rather than bringing them in by transfer. As an exception, memberships were transferred among those owning important pieces of dance regalia. But eventually it all became a social affair, without memberships of any kind.

Grass Dances were held either outdoors or in dance houses, which were special log buildings. Atsitsina tells this story of one place, down along the Bullhorn River, called Black Place to Dance.

I have been to dances on a lot of different reservations. . . . We have different songs for different kinds of people who come to the Parted-Hairs Dance [Grass Dance]. We will have a song and dance for a very brave man, also for a person who got wounded; for a person whose horse got killed in battle; for a person that got beaten; for a scared person; for a person who has had many wives; for persons that gave many presents; and one for a person who has cut a horse from in front of an enemy's door. The last song was usually for those who were wounded in battle; they are the ones who lead the others out of the dance house after reenacting their war experiences.

Those long knives—some of the members carried long knives [swords] originally taken from the enemy. A person that doesn't want to dance will get slapped on the leg with the long knife. But if they get slapped too hard then they are given a present. . . . And there is a whip. Once it was used to whip Crow horses. We got it in a raid and we used it for getting people up to dance.

A person will make a vow—it is very hard. A person will say, to get better or whatever, that he will eat a dog. We don't usually eat dogs. . . . On the day of the dance a pup will be boiled. The dog is taken out with a special forked stick and an eagle feather is used for licking the dog. The one that made the vow, he will provide all the food, just like at our Nighttime ceremonies. The dance hall will be filled with people. Eight people who will eat the dog will be sitting at the front. They will pray and count coups. Then the ceremony will begin.

First, two handsome men will pick up the boiling kettle. . . . We will sing and the two men will dance around the circle four times. On the last time they will pick up the kettle and bring it to the front and set it down before the eight men. Everyone will watch very quietly. The dog will be really soft-boiled.

When the kettle is set down, the eight men will pray and make oaths that they are telling the truth. The first one who eats will eat the dog's head. It is the most Powerful. In the Old Days when we were really mad and we killed an enemy, we used to eat some part of him—that is what the Old People used to say. That is why we are called Blood Indians—we only quit when we are all bloody. . . .

If some of the younger men can't stand to eat any of the dog, they will ask an older man, "Will you eat this for me? I will give you a horse." They paid a good horse or other goods to have someone eat the dog meat for them. We will sing four times. Everyone will get up after each song and shout [a war yell]. They will raise one hand. After the second song they will raise both hands. Then they will take the dog out of the kettle.

The last time I saw a Grass Dance, Mark Old Shoes was the dancer who picked the dog from the kettle. He stabbed the dog and danced four times around the pot before he picked it up. Some people will say they are Powerful and go and lick the dog. . . .

221

In the Old Days, men danced to express their spiritual and physical powers and to stimulate their enthusiasm for bravery and for thoughts about life in harmony with nature. The dancers wore their fanciest war clothes and most spiritual dream symbols. Often they imitated their spiritual helpers, dressing and dancing in imitation of some bird or animal. The steps were usually slow and all the movements emphasized symbolic meanings. The men danced to inspire each other when they gathered with their society comrades. They danced to arouse the courage of a departing war party and they danced to celebrate the victory when the party returned successfully. In victory dances, the victors often took no part. Instead, their relatives, often wives or mothers, put on their war dress and bonnets and carried the trophies of the victorious battle around the dance circle. Guns and scalps were commonly held aloft, while the bearer called out the relative's name and praised his bravery and success.

As life in harmony with nature changed, so did the dancing. Dancing became more and more of a social affair, where the People gathered to sing and visit. As modern clothing replaced traditional dress, the social dances also became one of the few opportunities for the People to wear the old-time clothing. Those who could afford fancy clothes found this an opportunity to express their wealth and material success. The young men, of course, found these social dances fine for showing off and courting young women. Here is how Atsitsina remembers it:

The ladies will sit to one side, at a dance, and the men will sit on the other side. Before a lady

Mounties of Fort MacLeod, in 1898, look on as Bloods prepare to have a dance. (Steele & Co.)

222

Bloods dancing at Fort MacLeod during the visit of Sir Wilfred Laurier in 1910. The courthouse at the rear is still standing. The dancers wear many sacred articles: headdresses; shirts; feathers; and shields. (Glenbow Foundation)

Men and women doing the Circle Dance, also called the Long-Tail Dance. It was a forerunner of today's Round Dance, the native version of a "slow dance," during which the dancers join hands and arms. Two of the women carry babies in their shawls.

goes to a dance she will think of her boyfriend. She will think, "I will wear my best so that he will see me." A single man will think the same way. The women will sit and the drummers will sing a good song. The men—they will dance the best way they can, to impress their girlfriends. They are just like them new dancers—they move their hips just like them white dancers that look like they are dancing by themselves. The men will dance as best as they can—all the while looking at their girlfriends. They do it very good—some will know how to take good sneaking glances at the girls.

Men who like to show off will paint their faces, and the women will just watch. Those who show off will dance very slowly so everyone will get a good look at them. They will put on their best face. By the end of the dance their eyes will be in the side of their head, because that is the way they will have been looking at their girlfriends all night. The women will do the same way when they get up and they do their circle dance.

Social dances are held throughout the year on the Blood Reserve, and visitors come from all over to attend them. A social dance is also a regular part of each year's Sun Dance Encampment; at our 1972 camp, it was held on the last Sunday of the gathering, a day when many visitors were present. The appearance of the dancers and their dancing styles had little resemblance to what was seen in the Old Days or in the Grass Dance days. Most dance costumes today are bright and flashy and seldom show the quality or craftsmanship of the long-ago. Colored T-shirts, brightly-dyed feathers, and dime-store sequins are very common, and more than one costume sports Japanese-made commercial beadwork. Like the outfits, many dancing styles are flashy and captivating, but based on physical ability rather than on spiritual motivation. The Old People sometimes refer to the new style as gymnastics, though it is more commonly called war dancing or fancy dancing.

A give-away dance during the annual "Indian Days" in Stand Off. The head chief, Jim Shot-on-Both-Sides, leads fellow Bloods around the dance circle before giving out presents to the visitors.

The Close of the Encampment; Returning to Our Homes

A few days after our encampment's social dance, the Horns Society finished its annual public ceremonies, and the gathering was officially over. Most of us had been there for two weeks or more, and for some of us there were cattle and horses at home to care for. Others had hay and grain crops to cut; it was close to the end of August, and time to harvest the fields.

Cattle raising is the most common source of income for ambitious members of our reserve today. Many families have fine cattle herds that are increased by bulls loaned from the tribe-owned herd. However, few of our People still harvest their own fields. Instead, they lease them out to white ranchers who pay a share of the profits. The government encouraged this system, believing that white ranchers could make more "profit" from the land than our People could. Indian farmers may have made fewer dollars per acre, but their efforts were for a sort of family business that gave all involved a sense of pride and a tendency to respect money. Now that our People no longer operate their own all-around farms and ranches, there is little incentive for children to remain at home to help their parents, or for fathers and mothers to stay at home to work their land. There is, however, plenty of easily earned money at harvest time for those who have leased their land, and plenty of spare time to spend it in. Some families have used this cash bonus to increase their herds of livestock, to build new homes, or to provide their children with a future by paying for their schooling or giving them a start with a small herd of cattle. Unfortunately, others have spent the easy money on drinking sprees.

Visits with Some People from the Past

In the Old Days, our People stirred each other's imagination by telling stories of adventure, which they passed on from generation to generation. Most of these stories, originally actual experiences, were never written down and were lost with the Old Ways. In addition, there gradually came a time when the People no longer needed adventure stories, when there was less and less danger from enemies, less and less anxiety about gathering food.

The stories that follow come from the minds and memories of our Old People and their progeny, from an occasional written account, or, as is the case with the one you are about to read, from an unusual, personal venture into the world of the past.

A WARRIOR'S WALK

There is still a "warrior" Spirit within me that makes my heart beat faster when I close my eyes and imagine myself sneaking up to a far-away lodge, ready to get away with the fine horse tied in front of it. Most of our men born around 1900 or before had at least one horse-raiding experience during their youth, even though the war days were over and horse raiding was a thing of the past. Cree horse herds continued to be popular

targets for Blood raiders into the early years of this century. Horses in the corrals and ranges of white ranchers were also well liked.

At the end of a Nighttime ceremony, during the winter following our Sun Dance Encampment, I decided to take a walk of the sort that an old-time raider would have had as part of his warpath. It was around four in the morning, long before Morning Star came up. At this time of the winter, daylight does not come to our country until sometime close to eight in the morning.

I tied a scarf over my head to keep out the cold nighttime breeze and I put on my hooded Hudson's Bay blanket coat, both typically worn by men on the warpath. They also wore wool or buckskin leggings and shirts, and fur-lined moccasins and mittens. In the Old Days, a half dozen or more pairs of extra moccasins would have been tied to my belt to complete my basic warpath outfit.

It is perhaps eight or ten miles from the house in which the ceremony was held down to our home farther south. The ceremony had been held up on the prairie, overlooking the same wide Bullhorn River bottom in which our house is located. My first plan was to travel home along the river bottom. The sky was clear and the stars were shining brightly, but the absence of Night Light, or Moon, made the night quite dark, especially down among the many bushes and willow groves that line the Bullhorn River. Even in the open spaces, between the many growths, it was difficult to see the well-worn paths along the dark ground. My progress was challenged whenever I neared shrubs or bushes. Branches were continually sneaking out of the dark and stabbing me here and there. My scarf covered my earrings, but I'm sure many a war-going man in the Old Days left an earring hanging on an unseen branch, and continued on his trail with a painfully slit ear. Think of the eyeballs that must have suffered similar fates, now and then.

Finally I decided to walk out in the wind of the open prairie. If you have ever felt melancholy while walking alone at night, then you can imagine how it was on that open prairie at that time of night, the nearest house a mile away, its occupants quietly sleeping. I could barely imagine being several hundred miles from home and camps of familiar people, barely imagine how it would be to know that a hidden enemy might suddenly appear out of the darkness or that a war party was behind me on my trail. Can you imagine the bravery needed by a man actually looking for a camp of unfriendly people to steal their horses? Can you see why men were considered very Powerful if they survived many such experiences? Can you imagine how safe the family of such a man felt when he was at home in their tipi? Can you imagine how strong a group of people felt if they were being led by a man who had a successful record of many such experiences?

Walking alone across the prairie quickly impresses one with the vastness of the universe and the insignificance of the self. It becomes easy to see why our Old People relied on spiritual help from the Powers of nature in situations where their physical bodies might be instantly destroyed. The stronger one felt the Powers of nature with one, the more Powerful one felt under physically dangerous circumstances.

Although I feel that everything has a Spirit, and that Spirits are everlasting, I have never particularly believed in "ghosts." I mention them because during my walk home I had an experience that seemed to involve them. This story explains why some of our People don't like to travel at night, especially alone.

For some time, as I walked along, I had the strange feeling I was being followed by something I could not see. I was walking near the edge of the prairie where it drops off to the Bullhorn River below. Suddenly I came to a deep gully that began out on the prairie and opened up into the river bottom. Rather than hike way around it I decided to go straight across, by going down it and then climbing back up. I started to trot downhill when I heard the sound of heavy breathing behind me. My heart grew large in my chest as I came to a quick halt and turned my head to look behind me. I heard one more heavy breath, which sounded as though it had come from something also trying to stop quickly. At that instant there was a thumping sound from behind me, and then a piece of cow dung rolled by and came to rest not far from where I had stopped. I strained my eyes until I was convinced that no person or animal was behind me, and then began singing some of my sacred songs to keep myself company while I continued homeward. The next day I learned from one of the Old People that near this place were several old open graves, and that few people walk past them at night because encounters with ghosts usually result.

There are numerous open graves around the reserve. Most of them are pretty well scattered from the effects of nature. Open graves were usually made by placing a filled coffin or homemade box under a cutbank or next to some large rocks and boulders. Less often, the coffin was covered with a pile of rocks, or placed inside a specially built little cabin. Bodies were usually placed in open graves during epidemics, or by family members who did not believe in burial underground

A long-ago burial in a tree along the Belly River. (National Museum)

but were prevented by the government from placing the bodies on scaffolds or in trees.

According to tradition, the Spirits of our People go to a place called the Sandhills after the person's body dies. Good, bad, or indifferent as the person was when physically alive, so will the Spirit go on forever in the Sandhills. A deceased person's most cherished possessions were usually placed with the body, so that their Spirits could continue to be together. The same was true of a man's favorite horse. It was often shot by his grave. Favorite horses that were not killed often died of starvation while mourning the loss of their master.

It is thought to take some time for a person's Spirit to leave the body completely and go on to the Sandhills. For that reason, a person would

sometimes be brought back from death if he had unusual spiritual powers and had instructed a close friend or relative how to recall them. For the same reason, few people would touch a dead person or go near his burial ground, especially at night. It is said that a dead person's Spirit, or ghost, often tries to persuade others to accompany it. Widows who commit suicide by their husbands' graves are said to have been persuaded to join them on their way to the Sandhills. At the Sandhills it is said that life goes on much like here, only in Spirit. The Old Way of life is the one that goes on, of course.

Some of our People have slept by old graves in search of Power from the Spirits who may be there. I was once inspired to seek such Power. In my dream I was visited by a skeleton-man in a buckskin suit who suggested that I find my Power among living Spirits, not among those of the dead. The dream lasted for some time and convinced me that graves should be left in peace. Unfortunately, some people do not feel this way. They don't even have respect for the dead person's cherished belongings.

The place where I slept was the resting place of a large family that had passed away during an epidemic more than fifty years ago. Their coffins were inside two small cabins. Several ancient trunks and bedsteads were among the many belongings that rested between and under the stacks of coffins. Parts of skeletons, old clothing, and beads were scattered everywhere. Years ago, one of our mercenary people guided white collectors to the place, and they made off with guns, pipes, and large pieces of beadwork. In recent years, others have come and searched carefully for smaller, more valuable items. Some of these have ended up in various museums. The bone hunters came next, first carrying off all the skulls, then picking out other bones. Since my visit, someone made a final, insulting search, during which all the remaining contents of the cabins were tossed out the door. The responsible individuals could probably tell us some interesting stories about their encounters with the Spirits of those buried people.

I learned a few more things during my walk that night. For instance, rocks that lie unseen on the dark prairie are quite a hazard to moccasin-covered feet. Nor is it much fun to step into one of the many holes that lead down to the homes of foxes and badgers. In the Old Days, such holes brought tragedies to men, horses, and buffalo. A concentration of such holes is sometimes a warning for another danger on the nighttime prairie— silent cutbanks with drop-offs of a hundred feet or more into dark river bottoms. I also met a modern, silent danger our Old People didn't have to worry about—barbed-wire fences.

As I neared home, I wondered how it would be to steal up to an enemy camp and raid a horse herd. My neighbor's horses just happened to be grazing along my way, so I walked toward them to try my luck. I learned right away that grazing horses aren't eager to make friends with strangers who appear silently out of the dark. The whole bunch stampeded before I got within roping distance, except for a white horse, which I approached slowly. I thought if I could get a rope on that one I could use it to catch up with the others and herd them away. I was able to walk right up to that white horse. Then I saw that the poor thing was hopelessly lame. I realized why raiders in the Old Days preferred the horses tied to lodges—they were not only the best ones, but maybe the only ones they could get near.

GEORGE FIRST RIDER: EARLY DAYS ON THE BLOOD RESERVE

Among those still living who remember the old stories and their importance back in the Old Days is George First Rider. Earlier, we read some of his doctoring accounts. Here is what he has to say about the early days on the Blood Reserve, as well as his own life.

Oki, I am going to tell the story about the Given to Us [The treaties]. I wasn't at the first Given to Us. [Treaty No. 7, signed in 1877 by the chiefs of the Bloods, North Piegans, Blackfoot, Sarsi, and Stonies. The reserve given to our People by that treaty was farther north than our present one. The Bloods moved to the present reserve in 1883, after Red Crow advised the government that this was a traditionally favorite area for the People and that they would be happier there.] My father was there at the ridge into the river [Blackfoot Crossing, East of Calgary, Alberta— site of the signing of Treaty No. 7]. A lot of the People were given double—after the children were counted with one family the parents sent them over to be counted with another family so they were given again—they got some more money.

We were given seven completes [dollars] and we put the fives [five dollars] into funds, and that's where the promises were made. . . . Shorty [nickname of Colonel MacLeod] said, "You will put these fives into funds," and Tall White Man [Lieutenant-Governor David Laird] gave us rations. When Shorty Gave to Us he announced it hard [he repeated his statements in English after the People were told in Blackfoot by the interpreter]. Shorty said, "The Chief Woman [Queen Victoria] made truce with you with these payments. Now you are all the children of the Chief Woman." He told us she said, "Nobody will bother my children now—they are my children." She told us to put away our weapons, our bows and arrows, our daggers, and the sacred things we used for war. The Chief Woman told us, "Do not steal and do not go on the warpath anymore. I will give you all the birds and animals to eat." That is why trapping is not forbidden on an Indian's land. A person will do what he can to get food. [Hunting and trapping are allowed year-round on the reserve.]

Shorty told us: "These are the promises we make to you. You are promised that the seven dollars will never cease to exist. You will be given rations." Oki, we were also promised education, and medical care. That day, when they were giving the promises, there was no one of us that was educated and spoke white-man talk. The interpreter was not a full Indian, and he left out a lot of words. There were a lot of words that he didn't translate.

The Old People offer holy smokes to each other. They will say, "We will talk straight as the straight hole in the pipestem." The reason why the stem is long on the pipe that we smoke is that a promise will last long. Oki, they looked for a way how they are going to make an oath. The Old People couldn't make the white people swear on the pipe because they didn't believe in it. So, the Old People were shown to swear on the longest term of life. They were made to swear on the

Holy Writings [the Bible]. . . . But they swore in their own way: "When the Sun ceases to shine, and the rivers have flown away dry, and the grass no longer grows, that will be the end of the Treaty —the education, rations, medical care—all these biggest promises in our life."

When I was young, my father and many others trapped coyote cubs. [The newly-arrived cattle ranchers hated coyotes and wolves, so the rancher-controlled government offered large bounties for the pelts of these animals. Many of our People eagerly hunted for the pelts in order to supplement the government's subsistence rations allowed.]

The Many-White-Horns-Owners [ranchers], we gave them our food vouchers and they gave us rations—flour, baking powder, sugar and tea and meat. [The ranchers exchanged the food vouchers for money at the agency.] Then they opened their lands to us to go and hunt coyote cubs. . . .

Those People of that time all had horses. Very few didn't have horses. Some few didn't farm. All they had was a mower. They get a voucher for a mower at Where We Have a Father [the agency] and then they own a mower. The Bloods all move camp out on the prairie. They get money only twice. [The People could camp wherever they wished, within the boundaries of the reserve. Permits from the agent were needed to leave the reserve.] Because of the Big Lease we get twenty-five dollars when it's about to be a Big Holy Day. [Christmas Day; each year at Christmastime every Blood receives twenty dollars as a share paid by several white ranchers who lease huge areas in the northeast part of the reserve. The ranchers pay for leasing the land and give the tribe a percentage of the profits made from the grains they raise and sell. This provides the tribe with its main source of earnings.]

We get our treaty payments at the home of Owns Many Horses [another name for Crop-Eared Wolf, who succeeded Red Crow as our head chief upon the latter's death in 1900], and

Blood meeting at the ration house in 1917. The People were gathered to hear the district superintendent for the Indian Affairs Department give a sales pitch to persuade them to sell parts of the reserve for fifty dollars per acre, instead of leasing it. Next to him stands the Interpreter, Ben Strangling Wolf. The vote was in favor of a sale, but then it was learned that the agent had bribed a large number of the People to cheat by sending underage children and by voting several times under different names. The sale was cancelled and the land was leased. This became known as the "Big Lease," because it involved a large part of the reserve, which is still leased. (Glenbow Archives)

also at Already Singer Woman's home [Mrs. Red Crow; she and the chief adopted several children, including Crop-Eared Wolf]. That was when the sidewalks were still boards in Men with Many Wives [Cardston]. . . .

Owns Many Horses and his wife, Last Rifle Woman, closed the liquor store here in Men with Many Wives. There is a house located here [in Cardston]; the owner's name is Buckskin. The hill where his house is located is called Whiskey Hill. The People that drank were all drinking on that hill. Nowadays the drunks fight. At that time the drunks just danced, they didn't fight. That's what they were doing, they were dancing, when the seizers [policemen] got there. All the

drunks got into the wagon by themselves. But the horses were unhooked from the wagon while the People were getting in. The horses run away and the drunks dispersed and took the wagon with them. A few were arrested the following morning [in those days our People could be arrested and jailed for thirty days for having been seen drunk, or for having alcohol on their breaths], but Red Crow had them released.

Red Crow and Owns Many Horses sat with this Big Grey Mouth [one of the Mormon elders with a big gray beard]. Red Crow told him, "My friend, it was very good the way we took each other for a relative, but there is something that is going to separate us. It is that liquor store."

231

The Mormon elder asked Red Crow, "What do you mean by that?" Red Crow told him, "We are the children of the Chief Woman. She told us not to drink. Now you, why did you give drinks to my children? The way we sat together is going to be ruined." Big Grey Mouth told Red Crow and Owns Many Horses, "My friend, the way you treated us is very good. Where we are settled now, this land connects with the Piegan, you gave me that, and why should we be bad relatives? Now, my friend, I will promise you this: in our country, where we are settled, all the doors of liquor stores will be closed. This way to Glenwood, and all those like Humpback [Magrath], Where Sugar Is Made [Raymond], and at Thorny Place [Spring Coulee] there will be no liquor stores in these towns, and there will be no liquor store here in the Men with Many Wives."

It wasn't long after that when the liquor store burned down, and it was never erected again. Now, I heard that when He Captured Many Guns [Senator James Gladstone, famous as the "first Indian senator in Canada"; he took the Bloods as his People and spent his life on the reserve] went to England, he asked for the liquor rights and now drinking is open for the Bloods. Now it is very lonely the way the Many Chiefs are living. They kill each other every day and they die in accidents. They fight and they separate. Many children are deserted. The new life is very lonely and now, today, the Old People are dying from broken hearts. It's on account of the new law. The first treaty—how happy are the laws that were given to those People. Today, we extinguished the Sun. . . . Life was happy . . . that life will never come back. . . ."

HISTORY OF MY OWN LIFE
Oki, now I am going to tell a story, the story of my life.

The white men herded their cattle on the Blood Reserve and they paid four dollars to each person on the reserve to let the cattle graze there. This practice began when Eagle Bear accepted the first four-dollar payment. That was in the year number 1904 when I was born. Small Priest [the People's name for Father Dusette] baptized me, but he didn't give me a name. I don't know why I wasn't called after my father, Dog Child. When I was not many days old, I was called First Rider and I grew up with that name.

When I was a little bit old-personlike [when first active as a child], my father taught me to ride. This was during the number four winter of my life. There was still a lot of horseback riding then and a lot of travois for transportation. Very few had slim-wheelers [buggies]. I was tied on a horse, and the horse was tied to a picket. Sometimes I used to go to sleep on the horse. My mother made a pad saddle out of blue jeans and stuffed with big-head fur [sheep's wool]. There were stirrups at that time; I used to see them, they were made of wood. But my stirrups were rawhide thongs, which fit my young feet better.

I grew up in the land of the Men with Many Wives [Cardston, Alberta, is a Mormon town]. My father was a hunter and he had many rifles; a slim-gum-arrow [.30/30 caliber]; a double-barrelled hunting gun; also a Number 22, called a gopher rifle. And he was one of the first to own a Number 303 rifle [.303 caliber]. He set traps for coyote, beaver, and muskrat.

My father made me eat all kinds of deer. The People of the long-ago liked to eat the part of the mother animal that the baby animal sucked on. The only thing they didn't eat is the milk of the big white heads [mountain sheep]. I heard that this milk is very bitter.

When I killed an elk, my father showed me they have seven nest lumps [nipples], not four or six or eight. He showed me that badgers have blood clots on their ribs. We sprinkled gun powder on the badger's blood and from looking at our reflection in the blood we knew how long we were going to live. My father saw from his reflection that he was going to be an old man. That is why he was very aggressive. He knew he would not die before reaching old age. Myself, I did not look into the badger blood.

Out on the plains there is a ridge, a place that we call Writing-On. That is where my father went camping and trapping and shooting. He never trapped less than 200 muskrats; usually he got around 500, 600, or 700. I know my father once trapped 1,500 muskrats. In the beginning he could sell the pelts for 15 cents each. Later he was able to get 20 cents, then 25 cents, 30 cents—always more as time went on. When old age forced him to quit trapping, he got 75 cents for each muskrat pelt.

My father was in the Black Seizers Society. Once, when I went to a Black Seizers dance, they painted my face. [Painting someone's face during the ceremony of a society or Bundle makes that person a spiritual associate of the society or Bundle.] My friends, Wore White Pants [Harry Spear Chief] and Tony, the son of Crane Chief, were also painted. Their fathers, like mine, were members of the Black Seizers, as well as elder comrades in our own young man's society, the All Brave Dog Society. ["Elder comrades" were once members of the young society; they taught the songs and ceremonies to the young members.]

My father taught me the life of the Black Seizers, the ones who tear our clothes. [The Seizers had the traditional right to demand food or other donations from the People in camp during the society's gatherings. If refused, the Seizers could tear up their clothing. They were not particularly popular for this.]

My father made me join the Braves Society and he taught me how they dance. I grew up and carried on both the Indian Way of life and the white Way. . . .

One person alone didn't educate me. Ki-soum taught me how to work the sweat lodges for the Horns Society. Natosina taught me how the Horns Society operates. So also did Three Guns

George First Rider, dressed as a minipoka, in 1919.

and Sun Old Man, the wise one of the North Blackfoot Indians. On the North Blackfoot Reserve, me and Berry Eater [Amos Leather] taught each other songs about Medicine Pipes and the Holy Lodge.

Among the Blood Indians, I learned transfer ceremonies from Black Eagle and Dog Ribs. I

233

Dog Child and his wife, the mother of George First Rider, in 1939. (Esther Goldfrank)

Lighter's Staff, and the Blackfoot Rider's Staff. [George only painted for some of these Bundles.]

In one day I took four Medicine hats. My face was painted and wiped and then repainted again, four times, as I went through four ceremonies in one day. [He means that when he was young, four different Medicine headdresses were transferred to him in one day. Thus, his parents spoiled their only child in a socially acceptable way.]

My father's name was Dog Child. My mother's name was The Only Handsome Woman; her other name was Catching Another Horse, but she was never called by that name. She was one of three sisters, and her mother said she was the only handsome woman. So that became her name. My father's name used to be Singing Amongst, but he changed that. My name was given to me from the war deeds of my uncle, Striped Wolf. He was the first one to ride a horse taken from the enemy. So I got the name First Rider. I didn't have the same name with my father. [Most of our People today carry the names of former relatives as their inherited family names. But they also have one or more personal, Indian names by which they are referred to in the Blackfoot language.]

I was born with long hair. My mother used Indian perfume—boiled cedar needles—to wet my hair. That is why I got long hair.

I must have been about five years old when I was able to go riding on my own.

When I was a little boy I was taken to the Holy Lodge. I had two grandmothers [older female relatives, not necessarily biological grandmothers]. They each one gave me a Sun Dance necklace, my childhood property. I must have been eight years old when a horned Medicine headdress was given to me.

When I was thirteen years old I started riding racehorses. I was sixteen years old when I started to learn bronc riding. But soon my father made me quit. He said, "There is no future in it. It is the white man's life. An Indian will compete in a

took them both for my grandfathers. I know all the Horns Society Bundles. At one time or another they were all transferred to me: the Bundle with a Rattle, the Associate Staff, the Leader's Headdress, the Yellow-Ochred Staff, the Swan Staff, the Staff with an Armband, the

rodeo but he will never be given the prize money."

One day a priest came to our place. He told my father, "Your son is a big boy now. He should go to school." My father told the priest, "I love my son. He is not going to school. If I put my son in school, the white men will teach him bad habits. They will teach him to drink whiskey and to steal and to cheat a person and how to gossip about people." The priest told my father, "In the future, people will all talk English and your son will be the only one that will not speak English." My father told the priest, "Our Indian life is not going to be extinct just yet. I am still standing on my Indian life, so my son will not be educated in the school." So that is why I didn't go to school.

I was a farmer. I had all the farm implements —a seeder, a plow, a binder, a cultivator, and a harrow. I didn't borrow these things because I knew the People didn't like me and wouldn't lend me anything. I bought what I needed. I had seven big wagons, two democrats [light wagons with seats], and a lot of workhorses.

Then a bad habit came to me. I started drinking. My life was lonely. I stole a lot of things. I broke into a store and I stole tobacco and forty bottles of lemon extract [a popular and cheap substitute for liquor]. I stole and sold more than five hundred horses. I stole horses from the Blackfoot Reserve, from the North Piegan Reserve, and from the Blood Indians. The horses I didn't sell I slaughtered, and sold their skins. I would slip a rope around the horse's neck, then put a half-hitch around the nose over the nostrils and finally wrap the end of the same rope around the horse's hind legs. As the horse kicked, the rope tightened around its nose, and it suffocated itself. A suffocated horse stiffens up quickly. I skinned the horse and sold the hide for money to spend on liquor.

I sold stolen cattle and wheat. Stealing wheat, that was easy. I simply backed my wagon up to a granary, drilled a hole in the wall, and the grain poured out into my wagon. I spent the money on liquor.

Eventually the day came when I went broke. I went to jail and my wife shacked up with other men. I had eleven children and they went away while I was in jail. The things I stole, which made me act like a rich man, they all vanished. When I got out of jail I had no place to stay. No one cared for me. They knew I was a drunkard and that I had lived a bad life.

But now I pray to God. I quit smoking, I quit drinking, and I quit stealing. I became a Christian. I have a new wife. I pray with her and I don't find life so hard.

MY DAD, HIS NAME IS DOG CHILD

Oki, I am First Rider. Now I am going to tell about my father and mother. My father's childhood name was Singing Amongst. When he grew older, he got a different name. A girl who lived with my father's father, she was a relative, she strung duck beaks and duck legs and tied them around my father's neck. Thus, he became known by the name Duck Necklace.

My father's father was Holy Descent; my father's mother was Under Making Noise. There were four sons: Striped Wolf, the eldest; then my father, Duck Necklace; after him, Mistaken Chief; and the youngest was Shoot at Close Range. Holy Descent was ninety-seven years old when he died; he didn't winter the three [didn't live the final three years to become a hundred].

That old man, my grandfather, as the time came, he told his relatives exactly when he would die. "When Morning Star comes up, then I will depart from you." He prepared himself for his death. He put on his good shirt, a thick, spleen-colored material. He put on his coat, a Hudson's Bay blanket, and his leggings, made from a Hudson's Bay blanket. He put his fine-cut tobacco and his pipe beside him. Then he began to tell stories of the Old Way of life, as though leaving messages for us. At one point he asked, "Look out and see if Morning Star is up." An old woman, Strikes with an Axe, looked outside and said, "No, there is no sign of it yet." Then, with her face and her hands, she made a sign to the others indicating that it was up. Holy Descent said, "Oki, I am tired of sitting up, let me lie down a while, and I will tell you another story." He leaned back on his pillow and held his robe in front of his face with his right hand. The relatives waited, but he did not begin to tell another story. One of them, He Took a Gun by Mistake, said to the old man, "Please tell us your story." But there was no reaction. So he uncovered the old man's face and cried. Holy Descent was dead.

When my father sat with my mother [when they got married in the traditional way], he worked as a seizer [policeman] at Black Rocks [Lethbridge, Alberta]. The policemen who worked with him at The Place with Many People [Blackfoot name for a town] were Slit Ear, Weasel Tail, Don't Lace His Shoes, Calf Child, Black White Man [Blackfoot name for a Negro], White Man, and Flying Chief [Joe Healy]. Their job was to patrol the borders of the Blood Reserve, checking for trespassers and illegal liquor traffic. Through this job, my father learned to speak English, working in the white way. It's the same with some white men. There are whites like That We Buy From [Blackfoot name for storekeepers] that speak good Indian.

My mother's father was Crow Bull. He was short and husky and a powerful shot with an arrow. He chased the buffalo and shot beneath the shoulder like a real hunter. An inexperienced hunter will shoot a buffalo in the belly where there are no bones. [It required great skill to ride a speeding horse alongside a running buffalo and then draw a bow back far enough to send an arrow into the tough part under the shoulder. A shot into this area penetrated the vital organs and brought quick death.] Crow Bull could shoot an arrow right through a buffalo, beneath the shoul-

der. Often, when the buffalo ran close together, he shot two with one arrow. . . .

HEAD CHIEF RED CROW

The most famous chief in our recorded history is Red Crow, who was head chief at the end of the Old Days and the beginning of reserve life. Among our People today his name symbolizes the glory of the past. Red Crow was a brave leader when enemy war parties still threatened our People, but was also a peace advocate when his People were asked to join in the native uprising known as the Riel Rebellion, and when his People were angered by the white settlers and their government. Red Crow certainly helped make it a fact that the Blood (and Blackfoot) People never fought the intruding government with arms.

Like many leaders faced with trials of such dramatic changes as loss of the buffalo and restriction to a reserve of land, Red Crow did not perform his duties in a manner that pleased everyone. Some of our Old People today still talk with bitterness about some of his doings, such as his sale of choice ranchland on the west side of the reserve for fifty cents an acre. He also gave a group of Mormons a ninety-nine-year land lease that includes the present site of Cardston, Alberta. Red Crow later said that he understood the agreement only to be a rental arrangement. The interpreter, a Cree half-breed, admitted years later that the Mormons had paid him well to misinterpret the documents to which Red Crow put his mark. Red Crow trusted his Mormon friends because they treated him well and often filled his buggy with groceries when he went to visit them.

As head chief, Red Crow had the final say in most matters pertaining to the Bloods. Yet he was not known as an orator and preferred to let his subchiefs speak for him. When he went east in 1885 to meet with government officials in Ottawa, he was accompanied by One Spot, then assistant head chief. These two Bloods were part of a

Red Crow, wearing a Cree-made jacket supplied by the photographer, in 1897. (Steele & Co.)

Important men on the Blood Reserve around 1886. From left to right: the chief, One Spot; the head chief, Red Crow; interpreter Dave Mills; missionary Cowan; and, in the chair, agent Pocklington. (Glenbow Archives)

Head Men of the Canadian Blackfoot divisions in Ottawa in 1886. From left to right: North Axe, head chief of the North Piegans; Three Bulls; his brother-in-law Crowfoot, famous head chief of the North Blackfeet, holding an eagle-wing fan; Red Crow; and his assistant, One Spot. Behind the men are their guides and interpreters, Father Lascombe and Jean L'Heureux. (Glenbow Archives)

Canadian Blackfoot delegation that included Northern Axe, head chief of the North Piegans, and Crowfoot, head chief of the North Blackfeet, and his assistant, Three Bulls. Father Lacombe guided the delegation and served as interpreter.

The Blackfoot chiefs received attention wherever their train stopped. In Winnipeg, Manitoba, they were taken out to dine at that city's finest restaurant. After completing their meals, the chiefs sat down on the floor and relaxed while smoking a pipe. Newspaper writers and hordes of onlookers watching the group through the restaurant's windows thought the pipe-smoking quite a spectacle, while the restaurant's head waiter cringed at this show of "primitive behavior." Red Crow returned from this trip with the realization that there was no hope of returning to the Old Ways. His People listened with awe as he told them of the many wonders he had seen—tall buildings, big ships, and endless varieties of strange material goods. But they found it hard to imagine that the white people in the east were as countless as the buffalo used to be.

Another of Red Crow's trusted spokesmen was old White Calf, who was a minor chief and a renowned warrior. He has sometimes been referred to as the war chief of the Bloods, although war for our People in the Old Days was too much of a personal affair to have much use for an official war chief. Whoever assembled and led one or more men on a raid was considered a war chief.

Our Old Man told this story about White Calf as a spokesman:

The agent went around to have all the People put their kids in school. Long-Nosed Crow [Robert Wilson] was the interpreter and another government man was along. They went to see the head chief, Red Crow, who told them, "White Calf will speak for me." When White Calf showed up, the agent said, "Well, we came to ask that every family give up one child to go to school." White Calf and Red Crow discussed what should be done. Finally, White Calf said, "Yes, we will do what you ask. But now that we have satisfied you, you must do something for me." Wilson relayed this to the agent and the government man, and they agreed to return the favor. "All right," White Calf told them, "Since I am a bachelor, and our Chief Woman [Queen Victoria] is also a bachelor, I want you to make the arrangements so that she will be my mate." Wilson had begun to translate White Calf's request, but when he figured out its ending he simply shook his head and said that he couldn't translate such a disloyal request.

The first group of students was sent to St. Paul's Anglican School. For a while, the Old Man was among them. As time went on, schooling became more strictly enforced until virtually every child was placed in a boarding school to be "properly raised and educated." The training began with a haircut and a ban on speaking Blackfoot. The fragile Spirit of the Old Ways was pretty well broken in the minds of most of the reserve's

children after they spent a few years at the school, away from their parents. Red Crow might have known that this would happen, but he couldn't prevent it. After his visit to the East, perhaps he thought that the best thing for the Blood children would be to learn the new Ways so they could deal with them.

We are fortunate to have a written record of Red Crow's adventures; it gives us a sense of the kind of man considered Powerful enough to be a leader of his People. Red Crow related these adventures to Robert Wilson during the winter of 1891. Because Wilson kept these stories in his own files, most of our own People have never read them and do not know them.

LIFE AND ADVENTURES OF CHIEF RED CROW (1830–1900)
Related by Red Crow to Robert N. Wilson December, 1891

I was born at [Fort] Whoop-Up about the year 1830. My father's name was Black Bear and my mother's was Handsome Woman. My father was a great chief. I only knew two of his wives, my Mother and another. I had three half-brothers who were not my Mother's children. They all died young in the days of the smallpox. I also had two Sisters but they too are long since dead and none of their children are alive now. The Blood Chief, Far Seer, was my Uncle [Pinukwiim, or "Seen From Afar," as his name is commonly translated].

My baby name was Captured-the-Gun Inside. This name was given to me in memory of an event in the life of my grandfather. When I first took the war trail my name was changed to Lately Tom, which I greatly disliked and did my best to repudiate. Nevertheless, I bore the name for many years until I became known as Red Crow, the former name of an old relative. [Lately Tom was probably a misinterpretation of a Blackfoot expression suggesting tomcatting. Before he went

239

on the war trail in 1850, Red Crow was an active bachelor, subject to teasing from his friends and relatives.] When I returned from my visit to eastern Canada in 1885 I acquired my present and fourth name, Sitting White Buffalo.

My first war path was with a large party against the Cree. I did not capture anything, but many of the elder men did and returned home on their new horses. Those of us who captured nothing returned home, on foot, this being the custom. [Young men began to accompany war parties in their early teens. They often followed behind such parties for a day or two before letting their presence be known, lest they be sent back home. Once they joined the main group they were treated like servants, carrying the older men's belongings and pack water, and cooking the meals. They were seldom allowed to accompany the main party into enemy camps. Instead, they were made to wait at some distance, guarding the horses. It was not unusual for these beginners to be abandoned by the successful main party, who thought that the young men were in need of such experiences in order to learn the ways of adventure.]

Next Summer I made another attempt and was a little more fortunate, for although I captured nothing, I was presented with a horse by a relative who did.

As soon as we returned home I went off with a small party under Red Old Man of our band. Upon this, my third war path, which was against the Crows, I captured two animals, a buckskin mare and a pinto gelding.

Next summer after that I joined an immense party of Bloods, Sarcees, and Blackfeet under the Chief of the latter tribe, Sun Old Man [better known as Old Sun]. This party was mounted and our direction was North to the Cree Country. Near the Saskatchewan River we sighted three Cree hunters. Knowing they would run at sight of our large party, we hid ourselves in low ground

and some of our men turned the hair side of their Buffalo robes outwards and then went out on foot on a hill nearby and imitated the actions of buffalo. This trick succeeded, for the Cree hunters came for them and ran into the ambush. We all rushed and killed them easily, but not before one of our men got a bullet in his shoulder and another, Big Plume, a stab in the back with a broad dagger. Two of the Crees were armed with guns, which were captured by Bloods.

A Blackfoot took the bow and arrows of the other Cree. I contented myself with capturing a white Hudson's Bay Point Blanket, which [was] then very much prized, and relieved one of the dead Crees of his scalp.

Later that Summer I joined a small unmounted party going to raid the Crows under Morning Paper [or Morning Writing]. This party was so small that we only required one brush lodge at nights. [Men on the war path usually built simple lodges of brush for their sleeping quarters. Eight or ten men could sleep in one lodge. These lodges were usually well hidden, but located close to some lookout point where the members could take turns sitting and watching the enemy's movements. Some of these old brush shelters became landmarks and were used for many years.]

Upon our arrival in the country of the Crows our raid was bungled by a Blackfoot of our party. It happened in this way: One of the Crow Indians had a valuable horse, probably a racer, standing in a lodge, the front of which had been unlaced and spread out. The Blackfoot in our party saw this animal, and, knowing that none but a good horse would be cared for in that way, he desired it very much. The fearless fellow jumped on the horse's back thinking to cut him loose and boldly ride him out of camp. But the Crows were not to be deprived so easily of their favorite steed. Before the horse, up sprung Crow with gun in hand. Our Blackfoot, being as nimble as he was reckless, slipped off the horse and escaped to the friendly bushes, with only a bullet hole in his robe. That shot alarmed the Crow village and they all arose in an instant. I was at that time in another part of the camp quietly looking for some horse to lead out, but upon hearing the shot, I left as fast as I could run. Away out on the hills I came across three others of our party who had taken many horses. We then started for home; our other companions had scattered from the Crow camp and gone home by other routes.

Upon our Northward way we four met a war party of Crows, chased and fought them to no purpose in a running contest in which no one was hurt. We arrived home without other adventures and found our missing friends there before us.

My next trip was in the fall of my second year of raids. I led a party of four myself. Our object was as usual to take horses from the Crows. We went to the Bears River and followed it down to the Missouri. There I had a dream that at a place I knew well, the "big hill," there was a large herd of horses. When I awoke and told my friends we set out to find them. In going towards the "Big Butte" we discovered a large camp of the Crows. I went in alone and took a gray mare. After that, we all went up into some pine timber on a hill and made our little brush camp. Three nights we laid low, then I visited the Crows again and brought back a black stallion and a pinto. Four more nights we remained in our camp, then all of us went into the Crows camp, but we captured only two horses. Now having horses for all of our party, we left for the Big Butte and we ascended to look about. From there I saw the big herd of horses exactly as I had dreamed. We descended and went in the direction of the horses, but to reach them it was necessary to cross the frozen river. While carrying dirt, making a path for our horses to walk on the ice, a large party of Blackfeet came along and joined our party. A few of them on foot crossed the river without any trouble and went ahead and stole a great number of horses from the big herd we were after. When

we finally crossed and approached the remaining horses, one of their owners came forward. I was just about to shoot him when he announced that he was a Blood. He informed me that he was one of a party of Bloods and Piegans who had taken the big herd of horses from the Crows and that he was now looking for more than half of them, which had lately disappeared. I explained that some of the Blackfeet of my party had relieved him of his horses and were now on their road north with them.

Our party now split up, five went back to the Crow camp we had just left. Some went home with the Bloods and Piegans who had taken the horses. I sent back my four horses with a young man to whom I gave one for his trouble of delivering them; one horse I sent to my uncle, one to a female relative, and the other I sent to the woman who had supplied me with moccasins when I left home on this trip. I also sent to my relatives a message that when I had captured many horses I would return home, and not before, even should it take me until the next summer to do so.

Five of us started out on a new expedition and were soon joined by 12 more. For many days and nights I slept and fasted by myself, seeking an indication as to what to do. Finally, one night I dreamed that at a certain mountain were a great number of horses. At once we went there and found the dream to be true, for in the neighborhood was a large village of Snake Indians [Shoshones], their horses grazing in every direction around the camp. The first night I captured 6 and sent them home by two young fellows. The next night with some others, I returned with a large herd, as many as I could drive. Upon my reaching our camp I said to Eagle Ribs, my friend and a chief afterwards [the uncle of Mokakin], "Take your choice of all these horses, my friend, for you are a married man and I am single." After he had done so I picked out two and told the others to help themselves, to divide them amongst them.

241

On our way home we saw some horses hobbled, indicating a camp was nearby. I took 4 of them, making in all 6, which I brought home safely, except that a black one played out. We made quick time out of that country, for we kept up a fast pace for three days and four nights without any sleep or food. On our way we found a late campground of the Snakes; it was so fresh that the fireplaces were still warm. But we had had enough and were anxious to see our people, so pressed on.

At the Red Deer [River] we saw a large village, which we avoided and circled, but our trail was discovered and we were followed by a numerous party who would have overtaken us had not a blizzard struck. In that friendly storm we made our escape without even losing our horses. At the South Piegan camp I found my uncle who, with my other relatives, had moved there during my absence. We were all very much played out and ragged when we arrived. It was springtime, the ducks had arrived ahead of us.

One night only did I remain at home. A large war-party was about to start to the Crow country, again under the guidance of Red Old Man, and I could not resist the desire for more adventure. At once I prepared and went with them.

Early one morning I was out scouting after we had reached the hostile country. Large parties like ours travelled in the daytime and rested at night. And because of the size of the party, many scouts would be thrown out in front and at each side so that there was not much risk of the whole group being seen. Good experienced men were generally chosen as scouts.

From a hill, I saw some buffalo running in the distance and heard a faint sound of gunshots from the same direction. I rejoined our group and told them that we were very near our enemies. We at once painted up and prepared for battle. We found the hunters busy skinning the animals I had earlier heard them shooting. We approached them without showing ourselves. On one of their horses was a Gros Ventre saddle from which we judged that the people were Gros Ventres and friends. We left our cover and went towards them, at which they fled in haste towards a hill. Their five horses scampered off also, the owners not having time to mount them. Over the hill disappeared the fleeing Indians, we in hot pursuit.

Before we reached the hill, however, a great crowd of people appeared upon it coming towards us. To our surprise and discomfort, they were Snakes, not Gros Ventres. Seeing that we were vastly outnumbered, we turned and ran away at our best speed. Looking back we saw that the prairie behind us was black with people, many of them mounted and coming for us, yelling like fiends. They soon overtook the hindmost of our men and killed two Bloods and a Piegan. Another of our party was about to suffer the same fate, but when we heard him appealing to us for help, we ran back and made a stand. In the fight that followed, Red Old Man was shot through the thigh. But the Snakes, it seems, were satisfied with having killed three of us without losing any of their own number, for they now withdrew and went home.

We made a bier with willows and robes upon which we laid our leader and carried him away homeward. Six men at a time would carry the wounded chief; with frequent shifts we were able to do fairly good travelling. At Snow Mountain we left Red Old Man with one attendant and pushed on so that we could more quickly send assistance and horses to bring him home. We had not gone far when we met a very large party of Piegans. It was a war party with women and lodges. They immediately sent to their main camp for help to go to Red Old Man.

With the large party of Piegans we returned toward the Snake village. We were anxious to have satisfaction for our late defeat. When we discovered our enemies again they were on the move. With my field glasses, I watched them all day and saw when they camped at night. I guided our men to the spot, but when we approached the campfires, we discovered that the people had fled. They had made a night move, thinking to evade any pursuers, and had left fires burning. Our men scattered all over the surrounding country, searching for them, and located the Snake village, neatly hidden on a creek, the branch of the stream where they had pitched camp once before. We captured an immense band of their horse and did it in such a bold style that we were seen. The owners turned out in force to retake them but when they saw how many we were they gave up. One of our Piegans killed one of their foremost braves. We were thus able to go home with blackened faces.

With the Blackfoot chief Big Snake leading our party, we started out once again for Crow horses. We soon came upon a village where there were horses, but their owners were too much on the alert. From the position and appearance of the camp we knew they were apparently expecting an attempt upon their stock. So we drew off and went in search of other villages. After not being at all successful, we decided to return to the alert Crow camp. Early one morning when we were setting up nearby, we were attacked by a large number of our enemies. We lost four of our men, whose bodies fell into the hands of the Crows as we were retreating in search of a suitable position to make a stand and defend ourselves.

We reached a hollow in the hills and there fought for some hours. During this fight we killed a Crow and caught his horse, a black, which I mounted, and left my companions to search for a better location. Our enemies were constantly being reinforced and we knew that unless we gained a very strong position we would have little chance of surviving. I dashed out on the black horse and galloped here and there looking for a suitable nook. At last I found a natural fort and rode into it to inspect it; some Crows saw me and made a rush at me, but I returned to my friends unhurt.

I had some difficulty in persuading them to leave their hollow because of the risk in exposing themselves directly to the fire of the Crows. Finally they all agreed and we made a break, as I led on the Crow stud.

Our movement was made so quickly and [was] so unexpected by our enemies that all but one of us safely reached the more advantageous place. The exception became separated from us and hid himself in a crevice of the rocks some little distance away. We were no sooner in our new hole, which proved to be a perfect stronghold, than the Crows closed in upon us. They were so close that our separated companion could not reach us without making himself a target for a hundred weapons. Fortunately, the Crows did not notice where he was and he remained out of sight all day, unharmed and amusing himself by singing. All that long summer's day the battle lasted. The Crows made four great charges upon our position but each time we drove them back with heavy losses. They came so close to us that we seldom missed a shot. Had they been careful with their shots and charges, we would not have seen the Sun rise very high that day. At one time, they came within ten feet of us, and I sprang up on our rocky breastwork, drew my bow in a threatening manner, and they retreated. It was always with great risk that we showed ourselves to them. Some of their men had moved a lot of stones to the top of a little hill nearby, and from behind them they would fire a volley every time they saw one of our heads. A Crow called out in the Blackfoot language, enquiring who we were. I replied that I was a Blood. He assured me that no one of us would live to tell the story of this fight. Said he: "We have you securely and you cannot escape." We laughed and taunted them to do their best, telling them that they could not hurt us, though they were as numerous as trees.

Our position was surrounded by big stones and rocks and fir trees, making it impossible for a number of horsemen to ride in upon us. Their charges were very exciting; gun shots and yells; the Crows calling to each other to have courage and not retreat; and we shouting yells of defiance. At sundown they all drew off and we could see them having a talk, after which there was singing, dancing, and more preparations made for war. We thought this meant another charge but they had a different scheme. They made a circle of fires around us. The crafty fellows were not going to let us steal away in the darkness. The one who spoke our language again called out that they were going to starve us out, because among the men we killed was a great chief, a young man, who must be avenged. Our reply was as before, "Do your best." In truth, thirst was the only thing that was bothering us.

As soon as it was dark, our man in the crevice made his escape and we saw no more of him.

Several times we attempted to get away. One of our men would remain in the fort and keep up

Red Crow and his head wife in a Blood camp in the late 1800's. Some people today question the showing of sacred bundles in photographs, but the people of the past did not have such concerns. Red Crow's Medicine Pipe Bundle hangs over the doorway of his lodge. The ends of the Shawl are pulled back to expose parts of the Bundle on each end. At that time he was owner of this painted tipi design, known as the Single Circle Lodge. It now belongs to the South Piegans. To the right is a frame made of travois poles, which could be used as a rack to hang things from or as a frame for a sun shelter. (R. N. Wilson)

A sacred Pipe, possibly from Red Crow's Medicine Pipe Bundle, which he owned in 1892. The Bowl is of the type made by eastern tribes; the sacred Stem may have come with the Bowl from one of those tribes. (R. N. Wilson)

a mock conversation with himself to make our foes think that we were all there. Then we would all crawl out and try to pass between the fires when the Crows were not in sight. We were driven back each time. They had us so completely hemmed in that a hundred of them seemed to spring up in whatever direction we started for. After half of the night had passed, I thought of an old trick and decided to give it a try. I set fire to a big pine tree, which made a very dense black smoke. The prevailing breeze kept the smoke in a large black cloud down close to the ground. Keeping well within the smoke, I led them out, crawling past our enemies, and we reached the bushes unseen. I expect they watched our burning tree a long time before they guessed its purpose.

We arrived safely at our main camp, which was at Bear Paw Mountain, and learned that the man in the crevice had arrived some time before

us and told the chiefs of our plight. The chiefs had decided to wait 4 days for us. They said that no besieged party could hold out for more than 3 days without water and little ammunition. But during those three days we escaped, travelled home and arrived on the 4th. The people were very angry with Big Snake for making such a bungle of the expedition. All the chiefs accused him of cowardness and bad judgment; his life was even threatened. I was given much praise for having saved the lives of the party. My coat was full of bullet and arrow holes, as were also the garments of many of the others. After the escape, the first time I unbraided my hair a big lock of it came loose in my hand; it had been cut off by a Crow bullet. You can judge how busy we were defending ourselves when I did not notice that bullet.

On the Red Deer were pitched the lodges of the Bloods, Blackfoot, Piegans, and Sarcees. [The Sarsis were always allied with our People. A small tribe who would probably have been wiped out without this alliance, the Sarsis are from a different family of the People than the Blackfeet, and their language is not the same. Yet they adopted most of our culture, such as dress and ceremonies.] The Sarcees had lately suffered rather severely in war with the Crees; a favorite chief and many others had fallen. On an errand of revenge a very large party was organized under the Blood Bull Shakes His Tent. We set out, all mounted, and travelling Northwards at a place called Round Bushes or Round Timbers we saw a Cree camp in the distance. Some of our wild young men wanted to ride boldly and attack it, but we wiser ones told them that they would certainly be killed, for the distance was so great that if pursued, they would be overtaken before they could return to us. These young fellows attempted several times to go in spite of our advice, but I headed them off and made them wait and listen to reason. One of the chiefs called our attention to a road by which we could all ride almost unseen to within a short distance of our enemies' camp. We covered the fronts of our light-coloured horses with buffalo robes and made the party look like buffalo and walked our horses towards a hill between us and the camp. Several times we had to move through open prairie, but we walked slow like buffalo, lowering our heads and horses' necks. When we reached the hill, we all painted and made ready for action. Leading my horse, I crawled to the top of the hill where I saw the Cree men were away running buffalo. In the short distance between us and the camp were ten people who were returning with water to the village. There were two women on ahead, then six women and one mounted man, and a single woman bringing up the rear; 9 squaws and one man, all loaded with water kegs. As soon as I saw our party behind the hill mounting, I sprang on my horse, and started down the opposite slope after the squaws. I had a good start of any of our party and was soon close behind the water carriers, who had heard nothing and were slowly plodding along. Soon, however, our big party came running around the hill, all yelling. The squaws, throwing water kegs in every direction, ran for their lives. I rode up alongside of the hindmost squaw and shot her dead with my flint-lock and called to Eagle Head to take her clothes and scalp. The man who was mounted escaped to camp, but the nine squaws were all killed.

That was not all. We were hardly through when we discovered over a bank quite close to us a great crowd of squaws, also getting water, hidden from us by the high bank. Although there must have been a hundred there, not a woman escaped. I did not kill any more, but contented myself with riding around and heading off and driving back any who were getting away. When the last squaw was dead and scalped we started for home.

The Crees were soon in hot pursuit. We went slow, allowed them to catch up to us, then we turned and charged, killing their leader. We retreated, the Crees followed, and we turned to charge a second time but they gave up the fight and went home to their dead wives.

We reached home in two days. There was great jubilation in our camps, especially among the Sarcees.

Once, when I was a mere lad, I was permitted to go with a large war-party under the chief One Spotted Horse [also known as One Spot]. The Crows had been stealing our horses and the purpose of this expedition was to retaliate. At the Elk River was a trading post frequented by the Crows. We arrived there and hid ourselves at sufficient distance to watch the large numbers of Crows camped about the Post. Other lodges were continually coming in and camping there to trade. One Spot called us together to discuss the situation. A large party like ours always has men who are either too old or too young and are liable to tire and get in the way of the good men. The ground around the fort was very muddy and travelling was most tiresome work, so our leader ordered most of the men to return home; some were old, some were young, including myself. But I and two others made up our minds not to leave and said so. The Chief at first explained that none could remain but the strongest and most experienced. Finding persuasion useless, he abused us and called us all sorts of nasty names for our disobedience. We did not mind the abuse, so we stuck with them and followed wherever they went. The culling out had cut us down to only three brush lodges.

We three boys were punished in many ways for not doing as we were told. A buffalo was killed and we were forced to pack nearly the whole carcass. We were continually carrying water to the men and whenever they could catch one of us sitting down, they would find some errand to keep us busy. But we took all in silence and remained.

A rocky place on a hill was fixed up as a fort in case we should be pressed to retreat. Early next morning some of the men on watch on the hill saw a great crowd of Crow Indians coming straight towards our camp. Of course they thought that we were discovered, but it soon turned out that it was only a buffalo hunt, for one of them chased an animal and killed it. Their reason for hunting so early was that the muddy ground in the morning was stiffened with frost when the buffalo could be more easily chased than later in the day when the heat of the Sun thawed the ground. All during their hunt, we three boys were kept in a hole and were told all sorts of lies about what was going on. When the Crows had gone out of sight, our men descended to our brush camp and prepared for action by painting themselves. We boys were told to paint our faces and to take horses and go off by our-

selves. No men would accompany us. No one had a pleasant word for us, nothing but insults. We simply sat in perfect silence and acted as if we heard nothing.

We all approached the Crow village and found that it was a large one stretching far up the river and down, so we went into cover waiting for night to come. We watched the playful crowds of young People outside their lodges. As the Sun began to sink they transferred their merriment inside.

At last the welcome darkness enveloped the scene and our time for action had arrived. One Spot told a tall man of our party to go with a scout and very cautiously enter the camp before the others. One Spot pitied him because he was poor and wanted him to be successful. The tall person went as he was told and came back in a short time with three horses. The chief sent him to the fort with his animals. The rest of the party were now told to scatter and each to act according to his judgment. Our leader said, "There are the horses before you and their owners asleep." Away we all went, some up the river, others down, and in a little while the village of the slumbering Crows was being approached from all directions.

Another boy and I went up-stream toward a group of lodges. We were crawling along through the grass and bushes, close to the lodges, when we heard something behind us. It was my companion's older brother, called High Sun. He offered to stay with us and lead us. He led us closer to the lodges where we could see the horses in their corral. We waited a long while, then he returned and gave us a spear which he had captured. We could not see it plainly but by feeling it we could tell that it was richly ornamented and a valuable trophy. He went back and returned with a big grey horse.

Satisfied with his take, he told us to leave and return with him to our retreat. But my friend and I told him that he had got all he wished for and we had nothing. We said we were going to get at least some small article for each of us before we went home. High Sun exchanged his rifle for his young brother's bow and arrows and parted. We returned and took the same path between the lodges that High Sun had. The corral was full of horses, and my companion wanted to go in and take some. But I had noticed shields and other articles hanging on the usual tripods near some of the lodges and I preferred them to horses. Like fools, we stood there and argued in whispers about it. Finally we parted, I to the tripods and he to the horses. At the first lodge I took from a high tripod a shield and some bags of Indian goods. In front of this lodge was a horse which I untied and led away. Leaning against another lodge was a tripod also supporting a shield and some bags. It was not an easy task to remove these articles as the others. Leaning, as they were, right against the lodge, the least sound or clumsy movement would awaken the inmates. But I was cautious and not in a hurry, so made no noise.

I spread my robe upon the horse's back and tied each pair of bags together and slung them over the horse; the two shields I put on my back with their straps around my neck. I discovered another horse tied near a lodge, untied it and led both horses away from the camp. I was obliged to go very slow, for all the stuff I had was covered with bells and would make an uproar at the least quick movement of the horse. I went near to the corral and found that my friend had gone. After slowly walking the horses out of the earshot of their late owners, I mounted the one with the bags and directed his steps toward our fort, leading the other.

All was well until I had reached quite a distance from the Crow lodges. The horse I was riding became impatient to return home, and when he found that I would not allow it, he began to pound and dance up and down. The bells all made a row and the two shields on my back rattled together so loud that the horse became more unmanageable each moment until finally, down went his head and I was bucked off. I did not let go of the bridle but the animal I was leading got away when I fell, galloping back home at his top speed. I led my horse far out on the prairie, until I grew tired of walking and again ventured on his back. Fortunately, he had recovered from his uneasiness and gave me no more trouble. As day broke, I saw for the first time that my horse was a fine buckskin. When I neared the fort, my stud again began to dance, and in that style I went in, the horse prancing sideways, showing first one side then the other, my goods with many bells jingling in time to the horse's movements. When I saw the black looks of envy upon the faces of the warriors observing my return, I felt amply revenged for all their insults.

I tied up my horse and unloaded my captures. The men all came around as I turned out the contents of the bags. Everyone admired the number and quality of my trophies. In one pair of the bags was a man's suit complete, shirt, leggings, all of the very finest of an Indian chief's ornamented clothing. Those bags contained much more than we Bloods put in our bags. The Crows seemed to keep all of their finery in their bags, even beads and women's trinkets. I was soon plied with many requests for this article and that. Most of the things I gave them, reserving for myself the shields and some of the best things from the bags. One of the shields was a beauty. It was fringed with eagle tail feathers and red cloth. On the front a mountain lion was painted and there was a bullet hole through it, blood all over the inside. The strap was a band made by doubling the whole deerskin over and over.

When I asked about the fortune of my companions, I learned that only a few of them had been successful. The Crow horses were too securely corralled and only a few of our oldest men were able to take some. The spear taken by High Sun was one of the best I have ever seen. The handle was covered with buckskin and decorated with crows' feathers. A stuffed crow's head was tied to it; the owner tied it in his hair before going to war.

Next night under cover of darkness we left our hiding place and started upon our home journey. After many days we arrived at Fort Benton, and then came up home to the Blood camp on Belly River.

Wolf Chief [Makwi Ena, better known as Big Wolf; he was once an owner of the Long-Time Pipe] was the leader of a war-party. It was my third trip to the Red Mountain country. Just before we reached the country of the Crow, we met a single Blood Indian coming home with two horses he had taken from these people. He had lost the rest of his party at night, and now he returned with us. He rode ahead with three of our party and the rest followed not too close behind. It was night, and suddenly we saw the flash of many guns ahead of us. We thought the four ahead were discovered. Realizing that nothing could be done for them, we climbed the Red Mountain in the dark and there passed the night.

After daylight one of our men noticed an object down upon a distant hill. While we watched it, a long line of horsemen came in sight on top of that same hill, and then we discovered that two of our men were not with us. They had fallen behind in the darkness and had slept by themselves away down the mountain. It was towards them the Crows were going; they had not discovered us. We all ran down to help our men, and from rocks and trees held back the Crows. They evidently thought us too strong for them, for two riders were dispatched to camp, as we guessed, for more help.

There was a young Blood with the Crows. He had been captured as a child, when his parents were out hunting. This youth called to us in our own language, enquiring who we were. We told him some of our names. He named many of his relatives and asked if they were alive. Some of them were in our party and we told him so and asked him to come over to us, that we would not hurt him. He seemed agreeable and came closer for a moment, then retreated. We decided that if he came, we would force him to stay, but would do him no harm. Soon he returned with two others who stayed a distance back as he rode toward us. Before he had quite reached us he halted. One of our party was a relative of his and we went out and met him. Our man enquired if he was armed, and he replied not. They stood a few yards apart, each afraid of the other. All the time the two Crows kept calling the young Blood to come back. He told us that if we had lots of ammunition we would require it, as reinforcements were on the way from the camp, which was a triple one composed of Crow, Snake and Nez Perce Indians. The Crow camp alone, he said, was very large and from such a number of lodges there would be a great crowd of men. "Do your best!" said he. "The people from the three camps are going to make it hot for you."

After giving us this news, he turned and rejoined the others. We could see the Crows sitting on a hill waving their hands to us to go home. In reply we waved to them to do likewise. We busied ourselves making our position stronger, rolling plenty of big stones in place. Near sundown the Crows on the hill began to move about. Through my glass I saw them all saddle up and leave. They came near us, shouting that they were going home and telling us to do so too. They had not seen anything of the expected reinforcements and were not inclined to attack us alone. Just about when they passed out of sight, we saw from the same direction approaching horsemen, whom we at first thought to be the four men we lost the night before. In ones and twos mounted men came in sight until the hill was black with people. Then we understood how matters were. The retreating Crows had met the reinforcements and now we were going to catch it.

One man rode far ahead of the others. He wore a hat, a buckskin shirt and had an American flag wrapped about his body. Riding a buckskin pacer, he came up within speaking distance and called out, "My friend! I am a Nez Perce." He then rode up to within twenty paces of us, dismounted and deliberately let go his horse and drove it away with his whip. This seemed to be a signal, for at once a great charge was made upon our stronghold. Mounted and yelling men were upon us in every direction. Some of our party were stationed out a little distance around us, hidden in holes and behind rocks.

The enemy rode right in between these out-pickets and the rest of us. I fired a shot, missed my man and while loading my flintlock I turned and saw behind me a man on a blue roan horse. On his head was a horned war-bonnet streaming away out behind him. He carried a shield, and an American flag was tied about his person. My chum and I had earlier agreed not to empty our guns at the same time, but in turns. Since his gun was loaded he fired and brought down the wearer of the fancy clothes. I ran forward to capture the trophies, but the man was only wounded. He got up before I reached him and escaped.

All the Crows near us seemed to have fired at me as I snatched the shield and spear lying beside a dead Crow. There was a lull in the battle after that; they all retreated to a distance, probably to have a talk. One of them then showed himself upon a neighboring hill and signalled to us to go home. As before we made the same signal to him. They wanted us to leave our position so that they could charge us in the open. I gave our chief Wolf Chief all the things I had taken. At sun-down the Crows all went out of sight. At dark our leader proposed to start for home, but I would not agree. I thought that we ought to do some-thing more before we left, and said so.

Our party split into two; half with Wolf Chief went home. Most of the younger men were in that band. The older and better men all remained with me to seek fresh adventures. I led my men away around to the country on the oppo-site side of the Crow village, where we arrived at daylight. We heard shots in the direction of our late retreat, and with the aid of my glass I saw the Indians running buffalo. There were many buffalo about and the Indians were busy all day killing and taking in meat. I was suffering much with rheumatism and said: "Tonight I will accomplish something or get killed; in the latter case my limbs will pain me no more." So at night we filed down the hill and noiselessly approached the camp. It was moonlight, and some of the Crows were parading their village, which was immense, signalling and calling out at intervals. Several times they shouted out in the Blackfoot tongue: "My friends, beware; my friend, go away. Do not come closer."

These remarks had a bad effect upon some of my comrades, who wanted to turn about at once and go home. I lost patience with them and said: "All right, you all go home leave me alone to do the work." I took off my leggings, prepared to act and asked who was going to follow me. No an-swer. I enquired again and a Piegan named Lazy Boy volunteered to come. I told the others to go to a certain place and wait for us. The Piegan and I waited a long time. A cloud darkened the moon and caused a little rain to fall. The singers went into their lodges and long afterwards the horses began to stray out of the circle, grazing. My com-panion thought that he could distinguish riders amongst them, but it was only his imagination. I roped a black and the Piegan a gray. We drove away a big herd to where the rest were waiting and then all were soon engaged at the pleasant task of catching horses to ride home. We drove away our new property, and a snow storm came up. We went around the mountain and ascended the other side, and we camped at our late battle-ground, keeping the horses well out of sight in the timber.

All the next day we watched the excited Crows, a large party of whom went north in pur-suit of us. They never guessed that we were look-ing down upon them from their mountain. Next night we set out for home, but we took the pre-caution to make a great half-circle towards the North; the straight line we left to our pursuers. We saw no Crow or other hostiles on the way home.

Winter had set in when we reached our Blood camp which was pitched on Stand-off bottom.

Although we were at peace with the Cree, they stole a number of our horses at that time. I led a war-party of seven men to see what we could do in retaliation. The Cree were bad Indians, who deserved to be punished. They were not honest, they stole horses. [It would have been difficult to form any sort of stable peace with the Crees in the Old Days, since the People of that tribe lived in many scattered bands over the plains. Each band was governed by its own chiefs, who could not make peace for any of the other bands. The stealing of horses, of course, was an accepted means of testing bravery and personal skill among most all of the People who used horses in North America.]

We being mounted made fast time, and going in a North easterly direction, saw in the distance a big blue hill looming up, and near it a large Indian camp. Between us and the camp the country was very level so that it was not safe to travel any closer in daylight. During our waiting hours that day I went up on top of a hill with my glass to see what might be in sight. I saw a large war party enter the camp. Later in the day I saw a single tall man following up the trail of the war party. He appeared to be unarmed. I ran to my horse, mounted, and followed by some young companions, galloped after the lonely man. We reached him just as he was down, drinking from a little rivulet or spring. I searched him for arms, but found nothing. The man was poor, he had not even a knife. I was so disgusted that I left him to the boys, to do as they liked. One said to kill him. I did not like Cree Indians well enough to say no, so I said nothing. And, as there were no arms to take, I did not say, "kill him." The end of the matter was this: I blackened his face, praying to the Sun as I did so, and gave him to the Sun, unhurt, as a present. When I told him that he was free and might go he looked very much

surprised. But he did not wait for us to change our minds; he walked rapidly a few yards then broke and ran like a deer, until out of sight. I guess he had never heard of one of his people falling into the hands of the Bloods and living to tell about it. He simply was not worth killing!

We rode during the entire night and at daylight we were close to the village. The people saw us and came out in a big crowd. One mounted, man enquired who we were; we told him and he returned to the village. We rode right into the camp and the Indians had a big talk. They were Assiniboines, but the lately arrived war-party were Cree.

We saw our tall friend again, who was relating to his people his adventure of yesterday. It appeared that they all called him a liar and then some came to me and asked if what the tall fellow said was true. I, of course, told them it was. A chief told me that I had a very strong heart, to turn loose a man like that, unhurt.

We remained there two days. The war party had a dance on the second day and two of us went to see it, although we were warned by a friendly Assiniboine not to go near the dancers or they would kill us. They had a very fine dance. Their war bonnets, shields and things were good, but the dancers acted in a queer manner. They would come near us and point their guns at us in a nasty way. Between dances they counted coups, which all seemed to be about Bloods, Blackfeet, and Piegans. One of them spoke in our language. He named a Blood that he had killed, he described the horse the dead man rode, and which he had captured. This was too much for my good temper. I peeled out my knife and walked into the circle shouting, "You are no good! You are no good!" I then began to sing and yell and count coups against them. I told them that I had killed three Cree in one day. It was a lie, but I was an eyewitness to the event I referred to, so I was able to discuss it to their satisfaction. They thought I spoke truly. I only wanted to make them angry because they had succeeded in making me so. I told them lots of lies about Cree that I had scalped, killed, and taken guns from, and the women all began leaving the camp, taking their children away to the bush. On a pole in the dancing circle was a Hudson's Bay Company flag, and on the ground beside it was a bow and thirty arrows. With a yell, I cut loose the flag and took the bow and arrows. Then, turning my back upon the Cree dancers, I told them once more that they were no good and stalked away with their things.

When we entered the lodge of our Assiniboine host, he informed us that some of the Cree war-party had been trying to bribe him to give up our horses to them. This news made me even more hostile. I called aloud to the Cree to bring out all their warriors and fight us seven Bloods, but my challenge was unheeded.

Shortly after that we started for home. I presented the flag to my chum, Big Plume.

Not a Favorite Child was the leader. From our camp on Sun River we went to the lodges of the Crows that were pitched on Stinking River, where the Crows often made their winter camps. It was a hard place to take horses from, because it was in the middle of a perfectly level prairie which was too wide to cross twice in one night. A war-party starting out at nightfall to walk across the prairie could not reach the camp, capture horses, and get out of sight again before daylight. Furthermore, the Crows had constructed permanent corrals which they used year after year. These enclosures were very well made, and constructed so that horses on the inside could not be seen from the outside. Moreover, all sorts of thorny bushes were used in the construction, making it nasty work for anyone who tried to tear them down. In times of very deep snow I have known the Crows to cut down young cotton trees and feed them to their horses, [who] would eat the bark and thrive as well as on oats.

We saw that there was a camp on the river and late in the afternoon we struck boldly across the plain, unseen, and at dark we were not far from the village. When we went close to examine the lay of the land, we discovered a fresh difficulty. The wily Crows had picked out a most strong position. The village was nearly surrounded by the river, which then made a bend of almost a circle. In the circle was built the horse corrals, and beside them were pitched the lodges. At the narrow neck of land leading to the circle some boys were building a fire, so that it was impossible to pass out that way with horses. The river was covered from bank to bank with a sheet of glare ice.

We had our choice: Go home on foot. Or get those horses. It was decided that none but the older and most experienced men should go near the village. When they had departed upon their dangerous errand, one called Spotted Wolf enquired who would follow him. No one answered until he had asked the question a third time, then I said, "Go on, I will follow you." I was both young and foolish then and had no right to go, but he wanted a companion. Spotted Wolf was a great walker. He started off at such a pace that I had to trot to keep him in sight. He stalked straight towards the place where the boys were building the fire, and although it was getting dangerously light there, we managed to crawl past on the dim side, unseen.

We reached the corral, got inside, and after a lot of trouble succeeded in making a hole big enough for a horse to pass through. Suddenly, we heard a great row at one of the other corrals. One of our men, a blundering fool, had entered that corral and caught a mare with a bell on her neck. He attempted to lead her out of a place where she would have to jump high to get through. The mare tried but fell back, her bell making a row that roused the whole village in an instant. Then the women began throwing burning sticks on the ice so that their husbands could see to shoot. At the first yell, I and my friend sprang upon our horses and jumped them onto the ice nearest to us. My animal was surefooted and after many slips and much struggling carried me safely to the other side. Looking back I saw that my comrade was not so fortunate, for his horse was down. My first impulse was to let him shift for himself, but I changed my mind, dismounted, tied my horse to a tree, and ran back on the ice. I pulled the horse by the tail, Spotted Wolf pulled him by the rope on his neck, and thus we slid the animal over the slippery ice to the edge, where he quickly gained his feet. We mounted, and not an instant too soon, for the Crow had seen our actions and were almost upon us. Away we galloped with a shower of arrows and bullets after us.

Our chief had taken out a horse from one of the corrals before the row occurred, but no others than we three did so. One called Many Strikes obtained the trimming of a war shield, but not the shield. The fellow who caused all the row carried away the mare's bell, which he had taken off and put over his shoulder when he saw the mistake he had made. My capture was a bald-faced bay.

While at camp on the Red Deer, a party of Blackfeet went down the south branch of the Saskatchewan and captured some Cree horses. Upon their return, they informed us that the Cree were only a few lodges that could easily be wiped out. A large party was organized and went down to perform that always pleasant task, under the leadership of Weasel Horse [Blackfoot Old Woman]. Instead of the expedition returning in triumph with many trophies of war, such as scalps, guns, and horses, only a few returned. These survivors had found many more Crees than they were in search of and had been nearly wiped out themselves. A great council was held to decide how to retaliate. The result was that the Bloods, Blackfeet, Piegans, and Sarcees moved in a single immense camp down the river. A war camp of the whole nation upon an errand of vengeance.

When we had moved a long way down the

Sacred headdress belonging to Red Crow in 1892. (R. N. Wilson)

river, White Calf and Eagle Head with a few men went out upon a scouting trip. After they had been gone two or three days, they returned flourishing a scalp. They had discovered a Cree village and at some little distance away were a man and a woman. The man escaped, but the woman, who was heavy with child, fell into the hands of the scouts, who killed her.

The news spread rapidly through the camp, and soon men were catching and saddling their war horses. A great war-dance was indulged in by the mounted men until all were ready, then off they started, hundreds and hundreds of them. A fine sight. As the Cree camp was not far from ours, our scouts were able to note the size, shape, and position of it before sundown. It was a large, circular camp, situated on the open prairie. After dark we went in close and took up a position in a large coulee quite near the camp. It began to rain and did not clear up until daylight. We made ready to strike as soon as there was enough light. In the camp amongst the lodges were a lot of hobbled horses. Our men untied and drove them away to a safe distance. The noise aroused the slumbering Cree and in a few seconds they all were alarmed. The women and children quit camp and flew to the timber. The men at once opened up a fierce fire upon us. Our leaders ordered us to retreat slowly away out to the open plain, so that the Crees would follow, which would enable us to charge them. We fell back from the village, the Crees pressing in pursuit. When a sufficiently long distance was between them and their camp, we turned and went at them. They did not attempt to make a stand but fled in the wildest disorder, and were slaughtered like buffalo. I rode after three Crees, who turned to meet me. One had a gun, two were armed with bows and arrows. The latter shot many arrows at me as I went towards them, then they turned and ran away. Their companion with the gun waited for me to get quite close; he evidently intended to make sure of me. On I rode, straight for him, and at last, when almost upon him, he fired at me and missed. It was his last shot on earth, for although he bravely clubbed his empty gun to strike me, he fell in an instant with my bullet in his breast.

The gun was taken by a young relative of mine. I picked up a fine robe with a chief's coups painted upon it. We again started away as if to retreat and a number of Cree fools mounted and came yelling after us. Again we turned and drove them back. Our people would ride alongside of them, and catching them by the feet, would throw them from their horses. A Blackfoot chased one Cree, who was so thoroughly frightened that he soiled his horse's back. The man was killed, and the horse taken by the Blackfeet. Only one young Blood on our side was killed.

We now returned to our lodges. Calf Shirt, father of the killed boy, waived the mourning custom. He said, "Be joyful, do not mourn for my son, you have killed many enemies and captured much." So in great glee our camps were moved back to our own country.

These are the principal adventures of my life. I am not in the habit of talking about them, for I am not a boaster. Only upon a few occasions when I lost my temper have I said that I was strong. All the People know me and my doings. I have had enough war and trouble in my time and know what it is. That is why I try of late years to keep the young men quiet. They do not know what they say when they talk of war.

I was never struck by an enemy in my life, with bullet, arrow, axe, spear, or knife!

Red Crow's adventures on the warpath are typical of those experienced by most of our men back in the Old Days. His are honest and realistic accounts. In all, he took part in thirty-three war adventures, which was not unusual in the Old Days; that he was never injured was quite exceptional.

It was certainly not necessary for a man to be raiding continually in order to live the Old Ways. Many men were satisfied to test their courage once or twice and then obtain their needed horses in trade. Such men were either holy men, skilled doctors, exceptional hunters, or noted craftsmen. Any of these "occupations" brought a man respect and stolen horses in exchange for his services.

It is strange that Red Crow did not mention the last major battle in which the Bloods took part. Perhaps he was gone from the camps at the time it occurred. This battle was fought during the early winter of 1870. An epidemic of smallpox had killed many of our People the previous winter, and the Crees decided that we were so weakened we could be attacked and wiped out. Over five hundred Crees and Assiniboines headed south under the chiefs Piapot, Big Bear, Little Pine, and Little Mountain. (These chiefs later led their People in the ill-fated Riel Rebellion of 1885.)

As the massive enemy force came south they sent ahead scouts to locate the Blood camps. The scouts found our tipis along the Belly River, near the present city of Lethbridge. Our People were trading buffalo robes at nearby Fort Whoop-Up. The scouts stole several horses from the camps and then returned to the main force to relay the news. The enemy forces eagerly headed for the Blood camp and attacked as soon as they got there, in the middle of the night. A few Bloods were killed before resistance was properly organized. While the enemy forces assembled themselves in a front line and prepared for the massacre, word of the initial attack went up and down the river bottom along which the Bloods were camped. The Cree scouts had failed to check out the nearby area and thus had no idea that there was more to the Blood camp than they had seen. Not only were the rest of the Bloods camped nearby, but almost the entire South Piegan division was camped just a short distance south.

The Piegans had arrived in the Blood country after one of their large bands had been wiped out in an unprovoked attack by the U.S. Army in Montana. Only the strength of the Piegan chiefs kept the rest of their People from wiping out the Army forces in revenge. Instead, the Piegans moved over to Canada in a fine mood to be attacked. Many of them were armed with new U.S. repeating rifles, while the enemy had only flint-locks and bows and arrows.

The dawn showed the Crees their mistake.

As day broke, they saw an endless body of warriors all around them. They tried to retreat but it was no use. As they scattered, some were trapped in cottonwood groves, some were slaughtered while trying to swim across the river, and some were killed hiding in coulees, where our men threw large stones down at them. The Piegan and Blood chiefs finally called their men off to avoid further bloodshed, and the remaining Crees were able to make their escape. Exact figures are not known, of course, but it is believed that fatalities on our side were around 40, while the Crees lost 300 or more.

STORIES OF NATOSINA, OR EAGLE PLUME

One of my favorite Old People from the past was our uncle's father, Natosina. During most of his life he was known by the name Pita-Sapohp, or "Eagle Plume." Although he has been gone for close to forty years now, his name is still frequently mentioned at ceremonies and other gatherings of our Old People. He knew about all our Old Ways, and was a skilled Teacher of them. One Old Person described him to me as "Professor Eagle Plume."

Old Natosina was born around 1850. His father was named Not-Scared-of-Gros Ventres. Among his father's wives was his mother, whose name, *Otsani*, can no longer be translated. Because it was misunderstood, she was called Old Charlie, which stuck with her. Among her children were Natosina's brothers Running Wolf, Big Snake, Many Chiefs, Last Star, Crow Tail Feathers, and Dog. She also had a daughter, Three Owl Woman.

Natosina married his main wife, his sits-beside-him wife, as we say, while she was very young. Her name was Prairie Dog Woman, and she is best remembered as a holy woman who put up several Medicine Lodges. Around the year 1900, he took the widow of Low Horn for a second wife. Her name was SikskiAki, and she

255

Atsitsina with his parents, Natosina and SikskiAki. He is wearing a blanket coat and holding a pipe bag. Natosina holds a buffalo tail whisk, which he uses for fanning himself and for sweat bathing.

brought with her an infant son, Jack Low Horn. With Natosina she soon had another son, who is our uncle, Atsitsina. For a short time Natosina had three wives, all related, but the youngest one died without having children.

Old SikskiAki was given her name, "Black-Faced Woman," because of her dark skin. In spite of that, she had blue eyes. Her mother, Blonde Big Nose, also blue-eyed, had been part French and part Mexican. *Her* father (Atsitsina's great-grandfather) had been a French trader also known as Bill, who was noted for having very long red hair. Old SikskiAki's father was a Blood named White Crane.

Natosina was the leader of every kind of Sacred Ceremony—Medicine Pipe, Beaver Bundle, Horns Society, Nighttime, and Medicine Lodge. He was a noted doctor and spiritual advisor. His war records include twenty-two different raids, on which he killed seven enemy men and captured well over one hundred horses. Like many Old People he was baptized into the Catholic Church in a mass ceremony that was explained

to them as a blessing from the holy white man, as priests are called in Blackfoot. Not long before his death, when a relative volunteered to go for a priest, he picked up a cup and said to those with him, "In this cup is my Catholic religion." He slowly turned the cup upside down and sat it down on the table, without saying another word.

Natosina's brother, Big Snake, died around 1915. He was well known among all the Blackfoot People for being both fearless and reckless. Because his parties always returned successfully, he had a large following whenever he announced plans to leave on a raid. Experienced older men, however, seldom went with him because he was so wild. They preferred the company of more serious and conscientious men.

One man who knew old Natosina was the writer James Willard Schultz. He lived with the Piegans for many years, beginning in the 1870s. He learned the Blackfoot language, went on buffalo hunts and war raids, and was known as Apikunni, or "Far-off-Scabby-Robe." He left the Piegans in 1903, after the death of his wife, but came back to visit often and wrote many fine stories about the Old Days. In the 1920s he recorded a few adventures of his Blood friends, who included Natosina and old Weasel Tail. I read Apikunni's story to Atsitsina, who had not heard it for many years. He said that most of the details in it are correct and that it is a good version of the way his dad used to relate this adventure. I will give you the story in Apikunni's words—he writes it as though old Natosina were speaking.

EAGLE PLUME

One beginning-of-summer-time, when we Ka'ina were encamped on Belly River, close up to the Backbone [the Rocky Mountains, the "Backbone of the Earth"], I called upon nine men, good warriors all of them, to go with me on a raid south; a raid upon the Crows. Before leaving, we built a sweat lodge of good size, and asked Three

256

James Willard Shultz, the writer, with some of his Blood friends at Waterton Lake in 1928. From left to right: Bobtail Chief; his wife; Schultz, or Apikunni; Many Mules; and Weasel Tail. In the foreground is the wife of Weasel Tail. Though it may look odd for a woman to wear a war bonnet—and this one belonged to Bobtail Chief—her adventures and coups on warpaths with her husband gave her that right.

Bears, owner of the Beaver Medicine Roll, to join us in it, and pray for our success and safe return. He was very glad to do that, and, after we left for the south, he mounted a horse, near going down of Sun of every day, and rode all through the camp, shouting the name of each member of our party, and calling upon the People to pray for us. That in itself is a powerful aid to a war party. It sustains them, gives them courage. Each evening, the warriors think and say to one another: "Right now, our Sun priest is riding about in camp, praying for us, asking the People to pray for us. It is good, it is powerful. We must deserve their prayers."

Many youths wanted to go with us, to wait upon us, and so learn the ways of the warrior. I selected one of them, a good hunter, a good shot, a youth named Wolf Plume. He carried my Thunder Medicine Pipe, my shield and my ropes. [Atsitsina thinks that instead of a Thunder Medicine Pipe, specific to our Sacred Bundles, his father was carrying a small war-pipe.] When we made camp, and I went off by myself to rest, to sleep, and try to obtain a vision of that which was ahead of us, he brought me food, water, coals for my pipe, made me comfortable.

We started out on foot, travelled only in the night-time. We crossed Bear River [Marias River] straight down from Sacred Red Rock, before which we stopped to give it a few presents, and ask it to pity us, to aid us in that which we had set out to do. We crossed Milk River [Teton River] just below the butte for which our far-back fathers named it the Breasts [because of their appearance] and, just below the mouth of Point-of-Rocks River [Sun River], crossed Big River [Missouri River]. Yes, right where now stands that town of many houses [Great Falls], there we stopped that early morning, to rest and sleep until night should come again. Our shelter was a small grove of cottonwoods and willows along the river-bank. We had no meat, and were very hungry that morning. On the plain, well out

in front of us, were several herds of buffalo and antelope. Said one of our party: "If we only had the meat of one of them, how safely we could broil it with this smokeless bark." He pointed to the dead, dry bark of a fallen cottonwood.

Said another: "The animals are all quiet; there seems to be no enemy war party hereabout; let us go out there and make a killing."

"No. We will take no chances; no risks whatever. Quiet though it seems to be out there, somewhere, hidden from us, a large enemy party may also be hungrily looking at the herds," I said.

"We cannot travel without food. As you will not allow us to go out there and make a killing, just you make some of the animals come right in here," said another, Bear Bones [Bear Shin Bone], who was always cross, always complaining, but a brave, successful man of many war trails.

"I will try to bring some of them in," I answered, and had Wolf Plume hand me my medicine-pipe roll. I did not expose the pipe. Simply held the roll up to the Sky and prayed to Sun, Thunder Bird, and Ancient Raven, to make food come to us.

We watched the herds; particularly the one nearest us, a small herd of buffalo, all of them save one old cow, lying down and chewing again the grass with which they had filled themselves. The cow was standing with lowered head, motionless, asleep on her feet. But now she raised her head, stretched out her legs, shook herself, and started slowly walking toward us. Up rose the herd then, two or three at first, then all the others, and in single file came on behind her. And I said to the cross one: "There, Bear Bones, as you asked so have I done with the help of my medicine. And now you do the killing. Not with your gun, but with your silent bow and arrows."

"Yes," he answered.

"A fat one. A cow without calf, or a one-winter or two-winters one," said I.

All of my party were looking at me, thinking that I had great favor with the Above Ones; that my medicine was powerful. I said nothing. I was not proud-feeling. Bear Bones asked us to move back, to leave him alone to make his killing. We went down to the shore of the river. Presently we heard a great pounding and rattling of hoofs, smashing of brush and dead sticks, and some of the herd came running out to the shore below, and turned and ran up past us and then back through the timber to the plain, all but one, a cow of two winters, with an arrow deep in her side, just back of her shoulder. Right in front of us she fell, blood streaming from her nose and mouth, and she died. And out from the timber came Bear Bones, who said: "Ha! There she lies. I knew that she could not go far with my arrow in her lungs."

So was it that, by the favor of the Above Ones, we ate fat, broiled meat that morning, and had meat for several days to come. And my companions were happy, eager to go on. That which I had done, my bringing the herd of buffalo to us from the plain, was, they said, a sign that our raid was to be successful. After we finished eating, I went apart from my companions, and, before I slept, smoked and prayed to the Above Ones, and sacrificed to Sun a piece of tobacco from my Thunder Pipe Roll.

Going on south, night after night, we crossed the Yellow Mountains [Judith Mountains] through the low gap in them, and one morning, just before Sun appeared, arrived at Dried Meat River [Musselshell River]. We crossed it, and stopped in a small grove of timber. We still had meat of the buffalo that Bear Bones had killed; thin cuttings of it, now partly dried. Wolf Plume broiled some of it for me, and, after eating, I had him prepare a resting-place for me, in some thick willows a little farther down the grove, and, after naming two of my companions to go on watch until the middle of the day, I lay down, my sacred pipe roll at my side, and soon slept.

I had a vision. I saw a camp of many lodges. It was night, yet I saw the lodges plainly, and horses tied close to them. And then I saw riders going away from the camp, driving before them a herd of horses. I awoke. Sun was nearing the middle of the blue. I lay there until my helper came and called me, and then joined my companions, all of them up and broiling meat at a little smokeless fire. My helper gave me some meat, and, as I ate, I told my vision. All agreed with me that it was a good one; that its meaning was that we were to have good success and get many horses from an enemy camp somewhere ahead.

We heard a raven making its hoarse cry. It came from the north and rested upon a branch of a dead tree under which we were sitting. Again and again it gave its loud hoarse cries, looking down at us, and off to the south. My companions looked up at it, looked at me. As I was a sacred-pipe man, I sang the raven's song: "Wind, it is my element, powerful is the wind."

And then: "Buffalo I am looking for. I have found them. I have found them upon the ground. The ground is my element. It is powerful." [The last words are from an Iniskim song; Iniskims were part of most war-pipe Bundles, but not sacred-Pipe Bundles.]

The raven listened to my singing, looked down at me, turning its head sideways, looking at me first with one eye, then the other, and when I had finished, it gave four cries, spread its wings, and went flying on to the south. That was another sign that we were to have good luck. We were impatient for the coming of night, so that we could go on southward.

When the new day came, we arrived at the north end of the Bad Mountains [Crazy Mountains], and stopped at the head of a small river, Bad River [Shields River], that flows down the west side of them, southward into Elk River [Yellowstone River]. Some time before the coming of the next day, we neared the junction of the two rivers, and saw fresh horse-tracks in a dusty buffalo trail that we were following. That meant that we were probably near an enemy camp. The far

259

side of Elk River was Crow country. We went up onto a near hill that was well grown over with juniper and other brush, and there awaited the coming of day. It came, and to the south of us, where Elk River comes from the mountains out into the plain, we saw rising the smoke of many lodge fires, of a big Crow camp, of course.

Leaving me alone on watch on the hill, my companions went down into the timber bordering the river and built a war lodge of poles and brush, and, when it was completed and a small fire of dry bark burning in it, I went down into it, Wolf Plume taking my place on the hill. I called upon Black Elk to assist me, and together we burned some sweetgrass, purified ourselves in the smoke of it, and, with the prayers and songs belonging to it, went through the complete ceremony of my Thunder Medicine; praying each of us, as the pipe went the round of our circle, for success against the enemy, and safe return to our People. [This is the common procedure with a war pipe. A regular Medicine Pipe would not be smoked at such a time.] That done, we rested there for the remainder of the day, keeping good watch upon the country from the hilltop, but failing to see enemies anywhere about. There were plenty of buffalo between us and Elk River; more herds were on the other side of the river. The Crows, we thought, must be making their killings of meat very near their camp.

Came night, and we went on down to Elk River, built a raft of driftwood, placed upon it our weapons, clothing and various belongings, sacrificed to the underwater people some small presents, praying to them that we might safely cross their element, and so took to the water, holding onto our raft while swimming. We easily made the other shore, some distance downstream, dressed, and went on, following up the valley of the river. Morning had not come when we heard, far ahead of us, the dogs of the camp answering the howling of the wolves about it. We did not want to go on and raid the camp; we wanted first

to see it, see how the people cared for their horses, and how we could best get some of them. We therefore went up onto the slope of the valley, where was plenty of cover, small pines and juniper brush, there to remain until night should come again.

Day came and revealed to us that which made our hearts glad: A little way farther up the valley, in a wide, grassed flat and near heavy timber bordering the river, was a circle of more than two hundred lodges. Lodges of new, white leather, whitely gleaming in the light of rising Sun. And tethered close to the lodges of their owners were many horses, the war horses, the fast, trained buffalo horses of which their owners were so proud. Other horses there were, many, many bands of them, grazing in the great bottom above, below, and out around the camp. Smoke was rising from the lodges. Women were hurrying to the river for water, to the timber for fuel. Men were going to bathe, others were caring for their horses. They were rich, powerful people, our enemies, the Crows.

Said Bear Bones: "It will be easy to take all of those far-out grazing horses that we can drive, but I don't want them. I want, I am going to have, some of those big, powerful, swift ones that are tied here and there in the camp."

So said all the others of our party.

In all the great camp, there was but one painted lodge. The Crows seemed to have few sacred-pipe men. Anyhow, there was but this one lodge that had sacred paintings upon it. A very large lodge it was, and well apart from the others, in the lower side of the circle. Two black-and-white spotted horses were tied in front of its doorway. Pointing to them, I said to my companions: "Those two there in front of the painted lodge, they are mine."

"Yes, yours, the two spotted ones," they answered.

Just then a man came out of the painted lodge, untied the two horses, smoothed their manes and tails with a handful of brush, then led them to the river to drink. Presently he brought them back into the open; [he] hobbled one and let it go, led the other back to his lodge, and saddled it. Many other men were saddling their swift animals. They were going out to run buffalo. I prayed to my medicine, to the Above Ones. "Pity me; help me. Let this be the last time that painted lodge man will ride that spotted fast one. Help me to take it and its spotted mate."

Sun was but a little way up in the blue when a hundred or more riders gathered at the lower side of the camp circle. They came down the valley, past us, talking, laughing, singing, happy all of them. And following them were their women, with travois, horses, and packhorses, for bringing in the meat and hides of the killing that was to be made.

I named two to remain on watch, and we others lay down and slept. Came the middle of the day, and we sat up, and the two lay down. I wanted no more sleep that day. I was uneasy. We had dangerous work to do, and my companions looked to me as well as to their own sacred helpers for protection in it. True, my visions had been favorable but I could not be sure that we should not, some of us, get into trouble. I prayed again and again to the Above Ones. I promised Sun that, provided we survived our raid that night, my woman would build for him a sacred lodge.

The day was hot, and we became very thirsty. In going up onto the valley slope to watch the camp, we thought we were to suffer from want of water. We had food, dried meat, but dared not eat of it, for that would make us still more thirsty. Idly we watched the big camp; men visiting one another, sitting out in the shade of the lodges, talking, smoking; women busy tanning robes, and leather; children playing everywhere about. We knew that there were a few women of our own kind down there, women whom the Crows had captured many winters back when a large war party of them had ambushed a number of our hunters out after buffalo, on Yellow River. We wondered if they were happy; contented. Black Elk said that they probably had become Crows in all but their blood. Had we not in our tribe Crow women, Snake women, Kutenai women, Cree women, and women of the West-Side tribes, whom our warriors had captured, and with their children, plenty of food, good clothes, were they not happy? Yes. They even said, many of them, that they would rather die than return to their own kind. And there was Painted Wing's woman, Pine Tree Woman; she went with him to war against her own People, the West-Side, River People.

Said my younger helper, Wolf Plume: "I am so poor that none of the girls of our tribe will so much as look at me, so I will try to capture one of the girls down there. It is said that the Crow girls are very beautiful."

"You will make no attempt of that kind this night. You are to stand in that point of timber there below the camp, and take care of the horses that we bring to you," I told him.

"You know that I was but making nothing-talk," he answered.

Sun was not far above the mountains when the Crow hunters came riding back up the valley, their women trailing after them with their travois horses and packhorses drawing and carrying big loads of meat and hides. Again the men were singing happily; their women, too. I watched my spotted horse and its rider. The man was short and slender. The horse seemed not to be tired, for now and then he pranced, trotted sideways.

I said to my companions: "See my beautiful spotted horse. See him prance. He is not tired, he, my spotted horse."

"But after being used all day, and tied again for the night, he will have little strength to make the long, fast run we will have to make," said one.

"Ah! But the rider is going to let him graze until night," I answered.

261

Ha! Arrived at his lodge, the rider unsaddled the spotted horse, hobbled him and turned him out to grass. Yes, as I willed the rider should do, so did he.

I said to my companions: "My friends, very powerful is my sacred medicine."

"Ah! Powerful! Powerful!" they repeated.

Sun went to his island home. Night came, and we sneaked down into the valley and through the timber to the river, and drank plenty of water and ate of our dried meat. I then led my companions to the point of timber, a little way below the camp, that I had selected for our gathering-place, and there we remained in the camp, until visiting, feasting, smoking, dancing, and singing ceased and the lodge fires all died out and the people slept. I then told Wolf Plume to watch for our return to the point with horses, and again advised my companions to be very cautious in approaching and entering the camp, and to go into it separately in its north, south and east sides. We then left the point and soon lost sight of one another in the darkness.

The night could not have been better for our raid. Clouds hid Night-Light, above us, yet it was not too dark. We could see objects, make out what they were, at a distance of twenty or twenty-five steps. So was it that I surely but slowly approached the big painted lodge. To go to it, I had to pass between two lodges at the outer edge of the circle. When quite near them, I stopped, listened, heard in one of them the heavy breathing of a sleeper. I went on, and made out that a dark object that I was approaching was a horse; and then I saw that it was one of my black-and-white spotted buffalo runners. It did not flinch from me when I went right to it and stroked its shoulder. Its rope, I made out, was fastened to a peg of the lodge skin. I stood beside the horse, looking, listening. All was quiet. I believed that I knew where my other spotted one was tied. I went on past the doorway of the lodge and right to it, its rope end also fastened to a lodge peg. I noiselessly

untied it, coiled it as I moved on to the horse, and then started leading him to the other one. But slowly; only a step or two at a time. When I had got right in front of the lodge, a sleeper within began dream-talking, not loud, a few words at a time. I didn't like that. People who talk in their sleep wake up. This one might awake, hear the horses moving off, and come out. I was very uneasy. I led the horse still more slowly, and at last came to the other one. I cut his rope at the right length for leading him, and then I went on with the two, backing away from the painted lodge until I could no longer see it, watching the two other lodges as I passed between them. I went out from the camp and at a faster pace to the point of timber. Several of my companions had already arrived there with their takings of horses, and had gone again for more of them. Wolf Plume took charge of mine, and said: "Ha! The two spotted ones. You said, there on the valley slope, that they were yours, and you spoke the truth; they are yours."

"Yes, and now I go to the camp for more of them," I answered.

"Wait. Hear me. Pity me, Sun-Power man," said he. "I have worked for you, carried your medicine things; do pity me. Let me go at least once into this enemy camp and take horses, even one horse. I want to be a warrior. I want to be able to count at least one coup, when, this summer, we build Sun's great lodge."

"Yes, I do pity you," I answered. "When I come again, I will make someone take your place here, and you shall go into the camp with me."

Again I led two horses to the meeting-place, and close following me came Bear Bones with three, making five that he had taken. I asked him to remain there until Wolf Plume could make one entrance into the camp with me. He objected; said that he had not come with me as a servant.

"You were once as is this youth, anxious to

count your first coup. Someone did for you as I now ask you to do for him," I answered.

"True. Go, you two. I will watch our takings here," he said.

I believed that my companions had none of them been in the upper part of the big camp, so I decided that we would try our luck up there. With Wolf Plume close at my side, and moving slowly, noiselessly, I passed between the two lodges just below the painted lodge, went by it and two others, and was then in the grass and sagebrush bottom land that the circle of the lodges enclosed. It was maybe two hundred steps across. We were nearing the lodges at its upper side, were rounding an almost shoulder-high patch of sagebrush, when a man rose up close in front of us and spoke three or four words, no doubt asking who we were or where we were going. He never spoke again nor even groaned. I struck the top of his head with the end of my rifle barrel with all my strength, and he dropped. Wolf Plume, who carried no gun, only bow and arrows in the case upon his back, gave a downward spring and stabbed him in his breast. Then whispered to me: "Here. Take my knife and scalp him."

"I will take one side, you the other," I answered. And when we had done that, we felt about for any weapons that the dead one might have had, but could find none, not even a knife in his belt. He was not a night watcher for the camp, else he would have had a gun or bow and arrows. He had recently come from his lodge for one purpose or another, had probably awakened his woman when leaving his couch, and she would become alarmed if he did not soon return to her, and would arouse the camp. I whispered to Wolf Plume that we must go on.

We soon came to the lodges in the upper part of the circle and found that there were horses tied before all of them. We each took two, from lodges at the outer edge of the circle, and led them well out toward the edge of the bottom,

and then down to the meeting-place. Besides Bear Bones, four others were there with second and third takings, and close after us came in the rest, with one, and two, and even three more horses each.

Said Bear Bones: "I thought that you two would never return. Now I go again for more."

"No. With the takings that we have, we start for home right now," I answered.

"No, I want more of these Crow horses."

"So do I," said several others.

"We cannot go into the camp again. We have killed a man. He will be missed. The whole camp will soon be called upon to look for him," I explained. But even then Bear Bones was strong for us to raid the camp again. All the others sided with me, however, and he had to give in.

"True, we have not taken many horses, but those that we have are every one of the fast buffalo runners, fast and powerful war horses; better these few than a big herd of those slower ones, grazing out there in the bottom."

Mounting, each one of us, one of our takings, I led off, the others driving the loose horses after me. We were not out of the bottom when we heard great shouting and crying back in that enemy camp.

At that, we went on with all the speed that we could make with our little band of loose animals. But that, we felt, was fast enough, for we could frequently change on to fresh horses, and so outride any who might pursue us. Three times we so changed before we came to Elk River, twice more after crossing it. If any of the Crows did take our trail, we never saw them. We made the long way back to our People without trouble, and got great praise for our success. Yes, and one of the Sun-Lodge builders of that summer was my woman.

Kyi! I end my tale.

OLD CHARLIE

Natosina's mother, Old Charlie, lived to a very old age. She stayed at the home of her son, along the Bullhorn Coulee, where she could see her grandchildren growing up. She was a very successful doctor. She used cactus spines and porcupine quills to perform a kind of acupuncture that was used by some of our doctors. Here is a story about her told by Atsitsina.

I will tell you a story of my grandmother, Otsah. She was my father's mother. She used to carry me on her back in a blanket. She was a very Powerful person. She used acupuncture to take the evil out of an affected person's body.

At my father's house they had no food. Doesn't Own Nice Horses [Jack Low Horn] and a cousin of ours said, "We are going to go out and raid a cow so we can have some food." Somebody told them, "You better not do it. The Old Man will hear about it and he will get pretty mad. He doesn't like us to do anything against the law. Anyone that is caught killing will get lots of years in jail." They didn't listen. They went out and killed a cow along the Bullhorn. They really needed food badly. They butchered the cow in a real hurry because they were scared they might get caught with it.

So they packed the meat home. When they got home with it my cousin found out that he had lost his knife. He said, "If the police find it I will be caught. I have my brand carved in the handle." My father's brother-in-law, Sits-with-His-Chest-Out, told his son, "That old lady, she has Power to find things that are lost. Give her this real tobacco and ask her to find your knife."

My cousin took the real tobacco over and gave it to the old lady and asked her to find his knife. She tasted the tobacco, she couldn't see too well, and she said, "Oh, some real tobacco." She got out some dishes and she put some raw kidney and

liver on the table, and a glass of water. Then she sang some songs. She told us to turn the lights off. She sat there quietly and we all waited. Pretty soon the dogs started barking outside and there was a noise like someone running up to the house and breathing hard. It was a ghost!

The old lady told the ghost, "Oki, there is some water for you. Drink it." There was a sound like glass tinkling against something solid. Then she said, "Oki, there is some food for you." There were more funny noises. Then she offered the ghost a smoke and we could see the tobacco being smoked. Then she told the ghost what the problem was, and asked him to go and look for the boy's knife. The old lady told us to turn the lights back on. Nobody was there and all the food and water were gone.

A while later the dogs started barking again. The old lady said to hurry up and turn the lights off. Then we heard a loud thumping noise. After that she offered the ghost another smoke and then he left. We turned the lights back on and found the knife lying on the floor. I know that old lady was very Powerful because everybody saw this happen. She didn't know where the knife was and she never left us to go and get it.

Natosina was kept so busy with his sacred duties that he never cared much for the modern ways that were coming to our People. Most of his visitors followed the Old Ways. His Powers were so strong and had so many obligations associated with them that others were afraid to come near him. Whenever he had a bad dream he would call his children and grandchildren to him, as well as any other nearby relatives, and pray for them while painting their faces with sacred red earth.

One of his dream obligations required that he never be interrupted while smoking. He communicated with Spirits then, and an interruption might break his contact and leave his Spirit outside his body.

One time SikskiAki's father and uncle, when

Natosina (Son Chief) or Eagle Plume, as he was in 1920's. The shirt was his prize one, decorated with locks of hair from friends and relatives. (Glacier Studios)

When they got there the door was closed and blocked from inside. Bernard told his brother, Edward, "Darn it, that old man is smoking again and I'm cold and want to go inside." They stood around for a few minutes and then Bernard suddenly pushed hard on the door and opened it up. Natosina was sitting in a chair near the door, his pipe in hand. As they came through, the pipe fell and his head fell forward; blood trickled from the side of his mouth. His old wife told the boys to hurry and close the door and then to stand still. She began to sing the song of his sacred Power and pretty soon he lifted his head, looking somewhat dazed. While the boys looked on in amazement, Natosina coughed loudly, his hand held in front of his mouth. He took the hand and rubbed it on his forehead, which became covered with sacred yellow paint. He coughed again into his hand and wiped it on one of his cheeks; it became covered with sacred red paint. One more time he did this, covering his other cheek with red paint. Then he told the boys, "Don't walk in like that again when you know I'm smoking. I might not be able to come back next time."

STORIES OF WEASEL TAIL

A contemporary of Natosina was Apachsoysis, or "Weasel Tail." Although he knew a great deal about our sacred ceremonies, he was not a leader. His fame rested on his fearless bravery. He was also noted for being something of a historian, as well as a great comedian who specialized in tall tales.

Weasel Tail was born in 1859. When he became orphaned, he wandered and ended up living for a time among the Crow People. He was still young when he married his only wife, Hate Woman, who went with him on several of his war parties. Like his partner, Bird Rattler, Weasel Tail went back to Crow camps during some of his later horse raids. During one horse raid, he was caught with Bird Rattler and imprisoned at Fort

they were little boys, found out what might happen if Natosina were interrupted while smoking. The two boys had been out for some time chopping firewood. It was a cold day and they were tired, so they eagerly headed for the warm house.

265

Weasel Tail, around 1910, wearing his sacred shirt and his Weasel Medicine, which helped protect him on his war trails. (Pollard Photo)

MacLeod. He was one of the group that escaped from that stockade and sought sanctuary in the States among their Piegan relatives. Unlike Bird Rattler, however, Weasel Tail returned to his Blood People after the escape was officially forgotten. He stayed on the Blood Reserve until his final years, when he again moved south to the Piegan Reservation. He died in 1950, at the age of ninety-one.

Weasel Tail attributed his Power to several visions and Medicines. Among them were his own personal sacred helpers, the otter and the kingbird. He carried parts of both with him wherever he went. When he went on raids and battles he usually wore a small bunch of sage hen tailfeathers that had once belonged to his father. His grandmother had saved the sacred feathers upon the death of his father, and given them to him when he was old enough to go to war. Another Medicine he wore to war consisted of a wolf cap and robe, given to him in a dream.

Eagle Child taught Weasel Tail how to paint his horse for battle. He told him, "This you will do to prevent the bullets and the arrows of the enemy hitting you or your horse. You will paint the horse's right shoulder and right hindquarters with red dots. Why? Because when you shoot a bullet through the flame of a fire, the flame is not injured, not even touched by the bullet; and red paint represents the color of the fire flame. You will paint the horse's left shoulder and left hindquarters with white clay spots. Why? When you shoot a bullet or arrow through the smoke of a fire, the smoke is not injured or touched; therefore, the white dots upon your horse represent smoke, and that gives you the power of smoke, you and your horse, even as the red dots give you the power of fire flame, to be unhurt by the bullets and arrows of the enemy."

Before leaving on their journey, the members of a war party usually met in front of their leader's lodge and sang songs. One of Weasel Tail's favorite songs for such occasions had these words in it: "Girl I love, don't worry about me. I'll be eating berries coming home." Some of the time, however, the girl he loved had no reason to worry about him, for she went with him on his war adventures. He explained it this way: "My wife said she loved me, and if I was to be killed on a war party she wanted to be killed too. I took her with me on five raids. Some of them I led, and my wife was not required to perform the cooking or other chores. She carried a six-shooter. On one occasion she stole a horse with a saddle, ammunition bag, and war club."

In 1929 Weasel Tail was camped by Water-

Eagle Child. He was apprehended at the end of his last horse raid by an Indian policeman named High Tree. He aimed his gun and the policeman fled. He then claimed the name High Tree and gave it to his grandson. (Glacier Studio)

267

Weasel Tail ready for battle. His face is painted and he carries his Medicine shield, rifle, and coup stick. He often wore an eagle feather in his hair. He is also wearing his sacred shirt, designed with paint and perforations and said to be impenetrable by bullets or arrows. And in fact, he lived through many battles to tell about them. His horse's tail is tied up in the war party style, and is symbolically painted: the hands represent enemies killed by Weasel Tail in hand-to-hand encounters, while the white spot on the hip shows where one of Weasel Tail's horses was once hit during battle. At the left is his Yellow-Star Tipi, with his wife standing outside. (Glenbow Archives)

Weasel Tail dressed for adventure. He was famous for wearing the front of his hair roached in the style of the Crow People, with whom he lived for some time. His Medicine skin hangs at the bottom. Around his neck he wears the claws of a grizzly bear that he had killed with a large dagger. (Glacier Studio)

ton Lake with a number of our Old People. They told their stories to the writer Apikunni, who published some of them in his book, *Sun God's Children*. Weasel Tail told a long story about one war raid on which his wife accompanied him. The party went first to the Crows and successfully stole a number of horses. On their way home they were surprised and attacked by a large party of Crees who took the recently captured horses and rode off with them, leaving Weasel Tail and his party again on foot.

According to the story, Weasel Tail and his group then headed north in search of a camp of friendly Gros Ventres, but they mistakenly walked into a camp of unfriendly Assiniboines. The first person they met was a Blood named Sliding Down, who offered to speak for them in the lodge of the Assiniboine chief. The People of the enemy camp surrounded the chief's lodge and threatened Weasel Tail's party. The chief was not much friendlier than the rest, and it soon became evident that they were in for trouble. They were finally provoked into an argument that resulted in the whole group standing up and aiming their rifles at the chief. Weasel Tail said that his wife carried her six-shooter and aimed it along with the rest. He said that he gave a terrible roar to show them his Power.

Sliding Down, who had married into the Assiniboines and spoke their language, told them that Weasel Tail was a ferocious warrior who had killed many but had never been injured himself. The Assiniboines fled and Weasel Tail and his party promptly withdrew. They were not followed and made a safe escape.

Weasel Tail said that the party then split up. He and his wife and one other man went south to try again for Crow horses. On the way they encountered a lone Crow man who had lost his wife and was wandering around, mourning. Weasel Tail caught the man by surprise, but pitied him and gave him his life, with a prayer to Sun to help him if he should ever be in a similar situation.

Weasel Tail concluded this fantastic adventure by locating a Crow camp and, while his wife waited in the nearby timber, he and the other man managed to steal fourteen good horses and they all returned home safely.

Weasel Tail also told Apikunni that he had been on very many raids, and that he had counted one or more coups on ten of them. He said that not all of his raids were successful, but that he always came back home safely. His favorite time to go on a raid was during the winter, when there was a chance of snowfall to cover his retreating tracks. He counted his final coup around the end of the war years, along the Belly River not far from Stand Off. He met a Kutenai man on a butte by the river. The man had three horses with him. Some say he had just stolen them, others say he was coming to trade them to the Bloods. At any rate, Weasel Tail prayed before the fight and said that this would be his last killing. He was the winner of the fight, and the place is today still known as Kutenai Butte.

In later years, Weasel Tail was a frequent participant at Sun Dance Encampments, powwows, and other gatherings of Old People. He was often called on to relate his exploits so that the ceremonies could proceed.

CALF SHIRT AND HIS RATTLESNAKES

Calf Shirt was one of the last of our Old People who could prove to skeptics, including white people, the Power of his own Medicine. His sacred helper was a rattlesnake, and he always carried a live one with him until his death, not long after 1900.

Most of the Blood Reserve is not troubled with rattlesnakes, but at the north end, near the city of Lethbridge, they are very common. At the narrow head of a long and steep box canyon there

Calf Shirt shows the People how much harmony there is between himself and his Medicine Power. The rattlesnake was alive and not defanged, of course. Calf Shirt was only bitten once, at which time he was forced to go to an old lady who had the Power to doctor rattlesnake bites. (Thomas Magee)

is a place known as the Snake Pit, which few people have gone into to investigate. Even today, early on a cool morning, one can see the steam rising from the entrance to a large den. It was in that area that Calf Shirt once went to seek a vision, through which he was given the Power of Rattlesnakes. I have never heard the exact story of his vision but the following story is an indication of the Powers it gave to him.

Calf Shirt's sister was married to a Blood named Cree Man, who did not treat her properly. According to custom, a girl's brother could go and take back his mistreated sister, which Calf Shirt did. When Cree Man came to see about his wife, Calf Shirt told him, "If you want your wife back you will have to prove to me that you will devote yourself to her better. To do this you must obtain for me one of my Medicine animals." He then told Cree Man how to get to a particular snake den and how to identify a certain large rattlesnake there. He told Cree Man that the large snake would be curled up outside the entrance to the den. He told him to look for a certain plant in the vicinity. He said, "Put some of this plant in your mouth and chew it. When you see the snake, rub some of it on your hands and pick the snake up by the neck, not too tight, and hold it next to your bare skin until it gets to know you."

Cree Man went to the other side of a place called Turnip Hill, near Lethbridge. When he got there the snakes were just coming out for the morning. He watched until a very large snake emerged and curled up by the doorway. Cree Man spit some of the chewed-up plant on his hands and some on the snake's head. The snake lay very still. Cree Man prayed fervently as he reached forward to pick up the snake. He told it, "I came to get Calf Shirt's Medicine. I am going to take you home with me." He held the snake up against the bare skin of his stomach and the snake coiled itself around his waist. He got on his horse carefully, so that he would not injure the snake or arouse it, and rode back home as fast as he could. When Cree Man arrived at the camp, Calf Shirt asked for the snake. Cree Man began to shake and cry. He was afraid to touch the snake again lest it bite his stomach. Calf Shirt told him to spit some more of the plant on his hands and on the snake's head, after which Cree Man was able to pick up the snake. Calf Shirt put it into a white sugar bag.

Cree Man returned to his home with his wife, but he was unable to sleep for several nights. He continued to have nightmares about rattlesnakes. Calf Shirt sent some sacred paint to him and told him to keep using rattlesnakes for his Power, now that he knew how to handle them. Cree Man just wanted to forget the whole experience.

Calf Shirt used his Rattlesnake Power to doctor various ailments. One of his specialties was sterilizing women. Among his doctoring articles was a buckskin snake that was painted black and had a green glass bead attached to the head and a small bell to the tail. He would lay this snake next to a woman's body, sing his song and give her some kind of Medicine, and the woman would never have children again.

Oddly enough, however, he did not have the Power to doctor rattlesnake bites. One time he was careless with the one that he carried with him and it bit him. His relative, old Weasel Head, paid a good horse to a deaf old woman who was able to doctor Calf Shirt until he was well.

The Old Man said that Calf Shirt was famous everywhere, but that few people came very near him, because they feared his snakes. He always kept one in a cloth or buckskin bag inside his shirt, by his stomach. The Old Man said, "If he came and sat down at a dance or gathering, everyone around him would get up in a hurry and sit somewhere else. We always wondered what he fed his snakes."

Calf Shirt's Powers taught him to design a sacred tipi. It was painted blue and had rattle-snakes drawn around its sides. John Red Crane was one of the later owners of this tipi.

Calf Shirt was the son of Spotted Bear, and he was noted for his bravery during the war days. I have not heard of any stories in which he took his rattlesnakes along to war. In 1870 it is recorded that he led a war party that killed seven Crees, and during which he captured a pipe-tomahawk. Seven Persons Creek, in southeast Alberta, is said to have been named for this incident.

There was another Blood named Calf Shirt who is sometimes confused with "Rattlesnake Calf Shirt." This other one, sometimes referred to as "Mad Calf Shirt," is thought to have been the strongest and meanest Blood that ever lived. He was a minor chief who kept his People in line by beating them up and occasionally killing them. His terrible temper was all the worse because of his fondness for liquor. He had two wives, and the older one was the only person who could control him at all. Sometimes when he was drunk she would grab him by the ear and tell him, "Listen to me, you old man!" His younger wife once tried to keep him from fighting by offering him a kiss, but he almost bit her lip off.

Mad Calf Shirt met his end at the hands of Joe Kipp and some others operating a whiskey trading post by a place called Left Bank, some ways east of Fort MacLeod. Calf Shirt entered the trading post late one night in an awful mood, demanding more liquor. The traders mixed strychnine with the brew and expected to see him drop to the ground. Instead, he became even more violent, threatening to kill those who were near him. Someone hit him over the head with an axe, from behind, but the handle broke and the axe only bloodied his head. The traders then fired several shots from close range into Calf Shirt. That ended his fighting. They dragged his body down to the frozen river, chopped a hole in the ice, and stuffed his body through. The next morning his wives went to look for him and found his body lying down, outside of the hole. They began

271

to sing his Power song which he told them would bring him back to life. Others from the camp persuaded the women to stop, for fear that Mad Calf Shirt would return even madder in the form of a grizzly bear, which was said to have been his Power.

WHITE WOLF

In his old age, White Wolf looked like a fierce old warrior who had never given up his thoughts about war trails. And until his death early in this century he was, indeed, one of the bravest warriors of the Old Days. Nevertheless, White Wolf is best remembered as a very kind and able holy man. He was Teacher to Natosina, who later became Teacher to Heavy Head, who was then Teacher to our Old Man.

White Wolf was also known by the names White Bull and One Week. The latter name was given to him because he so often said, "Rations in one week." It was the only expression he could say in English, having learned it around the agency.

Three of old White Wolf's war adventures are recorded with picture drawings on a buffalo hide in the collection at the Glenbow Museum. The story of one of the adventures goes like this:

White Wolf. One of the greatest holy men. His Teachings were passed on to Natosina, then to Heavy Head, and from him to the Old Man, among others. (Glacier Studio)

My partner was Pinukwiim. We went together on most of our trails. On one of these we were led by Sun Calf. There were eight of us. We went to raid the Crows, approaching their camps by going from coulee to coulee, so as not to be seen on the open prairie. Some early-morning hunters from the enemy camp spotted us just as we were going into a coulee to camp for the day. We should not have been out in the open after daybreak, so close to their camp. They went back to the Crow camp and returned with more than a hundred mounted men. Meanwhile, we got busy digging a pit, because there was no place for us to escape to on foot. We used our big knives for *shovels and dug a pit deep enough to hide in. The battle lasted all day. We were safe inside our pit. The Crows couldn't come close without us shooting a couple of their horses each time. By afternoon there were dead enemies and horses lying all around us. We fought this way for four days, going on without food and water. On the fourth night we had a chance to sneak away from the place in the darkness and escape. All eight of us got back home safely. Many Feathers and Little Dog were also along on this trip.*

Wolf Child, Guy Wolf Child's father. He was also known as John Epps, for his fondness for turnips, which he acquired while working for nearby settlers and farmers.

WOLF CHILD

The following anecdote is remembered by old Wolf Child's son, Guy Wolf Child:

My father went on many raids, just like other men in his time. Because of a dream he always painted himself yellow all over, from head to toe. That is the color of Sun. When he went to war he always tied a bunch of feathers to the topknot in his hair. He got the feathers from different people. They would pray for him and paint his face for success on his warpaths. They would give

him a feather from their own Medicine or from a Medicine Pipe Bundle or something that they had. He tied them all together and kept them for good luck.

BIG WOLF

The name *Makwi Ena* means "Wolf Chief," but was translated as "Big Wolf" and written that way on the agency records. After that the People began calling Wolf Chief by the English name Big Wolf. He was an experienced warrior and a leader of holy ceremonies. He once owned our Long-Time Pipe and is thought to have been the last man who knew the proper ceremony for it. According to him, that Pipe had a complete set of its own songs; they resembled sacred tipi songs and could be sung only by former Owners of the Pipe. The Long-Time Pipe was never opened by anyone other than a former Owner until its sale to the Provincial Museum.

Big Wolf was the first father-in-law of our Old Man, who told me this story.

Oki, at this time, my father-in-law, Big Wolf, was called Hind Man. He and some others started traveling at the time of changing weather, just before summer. It was raining and snowing, and they went on horseback. They rode along until they came to this big road. He told two of them to go and check the road to see if anyone had been moving along it, for the tracks might lead them to a camp to raid.

It was raining and snowing so hard that the two men waited in some bushes for a while, until the storm cleared a little. Then they saw a single rider going along the road with a travois attached to his horse. One of the men hurried back to the rest of the party to tell them that it looked like a man coming back from Where We Buy [trading post]. Before they all got back to the road, the man was gone out of sight. They went up on a hill to look down the road and they saw three men

273

away but the third one got back on the horse and rode off. Big Wolf chased him and shot him from his horse. The Cree was badly wounded but he was acting very wild and growling like a bear. One of Big Wolf's friends rode up and shot the Cree in the head. He was very bloody. Big Wolf said it was awful, he still kept growling and trying to get up after them until he finally died. That is what Big Wolf told me.

BLACK PLUME

Old Black Plume was a kind man whose intentions were so good that the People asked him to lead their ceremonies, even though he often

Big Wolf. Powerful warrior and former Owner of the Long-Time Pipe (Glacier Studio)

coming down the road. One of them was riding a horse, the others were walking. So they all rushed out and attacked them. Big Wolf chased the one on the horse. Before anybody got hurt, Ermine Horse found out that the men were friends, they were Northern Real Crees. Ermine Horse told the others to return all the things that they had taken from the Crees, then they all sat down to smoke.

After a while the Bloods started arguing with each other. Some of them said they didn't come to make any treaties. Maybe the Crees figured out what they were arguing about, because one of them lifted his gun and fired at the Bloods. A fight started. Two of the Crees were killed right

Black Plume dressed for raiding in the 1920s. The case around his shoulder holds a looking glass.

274

Black Plume and his wives in 1892. A Medicine Pipe Bundle hangs over the doorway of his lodge and other Medicines hang from the tripod at the rear. He is wearing his hair in a topknot, as befits a Medicine Pipe owner. The old horse was his favorite war horse, which he originally captured during a raid on an enemy camp. (R. N. Wilson)

mixed up some of his songs. For some years he kept a Beaver Bundle, which was later sold to Mrs. Walters by the man he transferred it to. He was Keeper of the Black Seizer's Society Pipe. He also owned a Medicine Pipe Bundle at one time, and from his friend, Robert Wilson, obtained the famous Weasel Medicine Robe that once belonged to Red Crow.

Black Plume had two wives while he was a young man. They were Long-Time Gun Woman and Black Horn. The latter was the mother of Dick Soup and Bob Black Plume. In his later years, he was married to an older woman for a short time, and then became the husband of Pretty Wolverine Woman, former sweetheart of Medicine Pipe Stem, whose romance led to the death of that young man along with her former husband, Charcoal. She lived with Black Plume until his death, around 1940.

Black Plume is said to have gone on about ten war raids. On one raid, he joined three of his friends to form one of several Blood parties that retaliated against the Crees for breaking a recent peace treaty. The Crees had raided the Blood camps in the summer of 1883 and made off with some eighty horses belonging to Head Chief Red Crow. Black Plume and his group located a Cree camp out on the prairie just before daybreak. They decided to take cover in a grove of trees and wait for nightfall. During the day some of the horses from the Cree camp wandered out to where they were, and the men immediately noticed that many of them were from Red Crow's herd. Each man captured one of the horses and headed back home.

When they arrived at the Blood camps, the Mounties were already waiting to arrest the raiders for horse stealing, which was by then "against the law." But when it was learned that all four horses had been stolen from Red Crow, the Mounties were forced to give up the arrests. Red Crow was so happy the Crees had lost some of his horses, he let each man keep the one he had brought home.

MANY MULES

Many Mules was another member of the group that went on some of the final war parties and lived well into this century to tell about it. He belonged to the Fish Eaters band. In 1910 Many Mules was still living with his two wives, Medicine Strikes and Crow Woman. Among the Medicines he owned was the famous Never-Sits-Down Shield, which he got from the South Piegan chief, Curly Bear. The writer Apikunni recorded the following stories that Many Mules told him in the 1920s.

I went on many war trails and counted coups on two Crees, two Kalispells, one Assiniboine, and one Crow, all of whom I killed. I also captured a woman from the River People on the west side of the Rocky Mountains.

I once had a very narrow escape from the Crows. We were a very small party, only five of us. From the big camp of our People, then on Bow River, we went south to raid the Crows. After traveling many nights, we at last found a Crow camp. It was on Bighorn River, a little way up it from its junction with Elk River [the Yellowstone]. Night Light was showing all of herself; we could see almost as well as though it were daytime. We went into camp to take the good buffalo horses and war horses that were tied close to the lodges of their owners. I got four of them out without arousing the sleeping people. A little way from the camp circle, I mounted one of them, leading the others down the valley to meet my companions.

Ha! I had gone but a little way when I came

Many Mules. His Medicine Power is tied to his head. (Glacier Studio)

almost face to face with six riders. One of them spoke to me. He was a Crow. No doubt he said, "Who are you?" For answer, I aimed my rifle at him and pulled the trigger, but there was only the click of the hammer. The cap was a bad one. At that, I let go of the ropes of the three horses I was leading and rode as fast as possible for the timber bordering the river, the six Crows following, shooting at me. At the edge of a big patch of willows, I sprang from the horse and ran into the willows. My enemies surrounded it, firing into it, yelling loudly, and so awakened the People in the big camp. Many of them came running, eager to fight. I thought that they would soon have my scalp. I prayed to the Above Ones, to my sacred helper, to help me in some way to survive.

Ha! Before the men from the camp arrived, one of the six set fire to the willow patch. It was in the time of falling leaves; the grass in the willows was brown and dry; many of the willows were dead and dry. The fire burned fiercely. I prayed still harder for help and got it. A very strong wind suddenly sprang up, blowing across the valley toward the river, and causing the fire to make a very thick, black smoke. I went with the smoke, as noiselessly as possible, but choking, eyes smarting so that I was almost blinded. But I kept on, and, without being seen by any of the enemy, stumbled down a steep bank and into the river, which was not deep. Still concealed in the black smoke, I crossed to the other side, and went down the valley, keeping in the timber and brush as much as possible, until at last I was safe. I kept going, crossed Elk River before daylight, and remained in a grove until night, when I went on again. I saw nothing of my companions as I traveled night after night until I arrived at Fort Benton. The Piegans were encamped there, and one, a close friend, gave me a horse, and I rode back to Bow River and my People.

A PRAIRIE ENCOUNTER ON THE WARPATH

Many Mules, Heavy Shield, Running Sun, Running Calf, and Gambler left together on a warpath to raid the Crees. They headed east and encountered a small war party of three men. The Bloods were not sure if the others were Crees or North Blackfeet, since they were all dressed in the common striped blanket coats. Many Mules told the others to dismount and aim their rifles, while he would ride over to find out who they were.

He approached the trio with his hand in the air and spoke to them in Blackfoot. They said nothing. He spoke the Cree words for a greeting, and was given a reply. Dropping his hand, he thus signaled to his partners that the three were enemies. They fired off a volley, killing one enemy and wounding another. Many Mules caught the wounded one and killed him, while the third man tried to escape. Heavy Shield had a fast horse and chased him. The others were shouting to him, "He hasn't shot his gun yet! Watch out for him!" Heavy Shield had already fired his gun and did not have a chance to reload it. He was armed only with his knife and his favorite elk-horn whip.

Heavy Shield caught up with the Cree and rode alongside of him. The Cree leveled his rifle across his saddle and fired. The bullet tore the feathers off Heavy Shield's Medicine Bird, which was hanging from a thong at his side. Many Mules caught up to the two and jerked the gun from the Cree's hand. The Cree then took a hatchet attached to the horn of his saddle, which was a real saddle, and tried to hit Heavy Shield with it. By this time Running Sun had also caught up to them and knocked the hatchet from the enemy's hand and captured it. Heavy Shield and the Cree were still riding along, trying to knock each other off their horses. Heavy Shield stuffed the end of his whip into his enemy's mouth while the latter grabbed one of Heavy Shield's braids. At this point their horses separated and both men fell to the ground. Before the Cree could get up to resume the fight, Gambler came along and ran over him with his horse and someone else counted coup on him.

TOUGH BREAD, A DOCTOR WHO USED ACUPUNCTURE

A well-remembered doctor who lived well into this century was a man named Pastahmp—"Flint." Somehow his name was misinterpreted and recorded as Tough Bread, by which he became commonly known. His daughter is Porcupine Woman, who is the wife of Bob Black Plume, or Skunk.

He used thorns from rose bushes to draw the sickness out of bodies. He put those thorns all

Heavy Shield. The scarf on his head was his trademark; it was a Medicine Power he got from his father, whose name was also Heavy Shield. (Glacier Studio)

Tough Bread, wearing an iron necklace. (Glacier Studio)

Running Sun, with the type of pipe carried along on war parties. (Glacier Studio)

Striped Wolf, with the feathers of his Medicine bird, a sage hen, tied to his hair. (Glacier Studio)

over the place where the sickness was in a person. Sometimes he left them there for a long time; other times he burned them with the end of a glowing stick, right down to the skin. He once cured a half-dead (paralyzed) Chinese man in this fashion. After Tough Bread's death, nobody knew how to carry on his unique curing methods. He had offered to teach Mokakin and to give him all his doctoring things, but Mokakin was scared because he hadn't yet had any dreams that gave him the Power to doctor. Tough Bread was also a leader of Medicine ceremonies.

STRIPED WOLF MEETS
A FORMER ENEMY

As a young man, Striped Wolf took part in a few of the last horse raids against enemy tribes. It is said that his name came from a wolf that was seen on a hillside "striped" with many buffalo trails. His brother was Dog Child.

Striped Wolf went on a raid toward Looks-like-a-Belly. On the way, he met a Gros Ventre coming toward the Blood camps for the same purpose. Both were at the head of their parties, and when they saw each other, they fired simultaneously. Both men went down, each thinking he had shot the other. Actually, they both took off and hid.

Later, Striped Wolf told the others about the man he shot and they all went to find the body. They looked all over but couldn't find it. The Gros Ventre did the same thing, but his party could find no trace either.

Many years later, there was a dance they both attended. Both Striped Wolf and the Gros Ventre still remembered the time and place they shot at each other. Somehow they found out about each other at that dance. They took each other for brothers and talked about what happened. It turned out that one of them had been shot through the legging flap and the other

through the edge of his shirt; neither had gotten hurt.

Now this is strange: one's name was Striped Wolf and the other's Striped Bird—just about the same name. They exchanged names. They shook hands and kissed, and became like brothers. All the Gros Ventre's relatives gave Striped Wolf a lot of presents—money, blankets, and other things. They remained good friends until they died.

THE HANGING OF CHARCOAL

Charcoal's days ended in 1897 at the age of thirty-nine, on the gallows at Fort MacLeod. Before his death, Tsako, as our People nicknamed him, became the most wanted man on Canada's western frontier.

Wilson wrote of Charcoal as a participant in a Nighttime Ceremony and recorded that he had owned a number of Medicines for which he sang songs: painted lodge and flag; painted lodge; Sioux sword for the Grass Dance; Horns Society; Mountain-Trim Tipi; Soldier's Society Pipe; Weasel-tail buckskin suits; Dogs Society; and bear knife. This last sacred article was a huge dagger with a handle made from a bear's jawbone. It was sought after and owned only by Powerful warriors. During the transfer ceremony for this knife, the new Owner was forced to strip and roll on a bed of thorns. At the end of the transfer the former Owner would hurl the sacred knife at the new Owner, who could have it if he survived and caught it.

Charcoal had two wives. One was faithful to him, but the other, Pretty Wolverine Woman, was fickle and wild. Although she had been married to Charcoal for about five years, everyone in camp knew that she and a young man named Medicine Pipe Stem were lovers. They had been seen together while she went out after water. Charcoal's relative, Eagle Bear, had talked to her several times and warned her that her husband could punish her for her actions. Charcoal was known

Charcoal, shortly before he was hanged in 1897, for the death of a Mounted Police sergeant. His fancy shirt was supplied by the photographer, who didn't have a spare pair of moccasins to lend. It is assumed that the hat is hiding Charcoal's handcuffs. (Steele & Co.)

for his collection of weapons—guns, shells, and knives—and for his ability to use them. Nevertheless, he was a well-liked and respectable man. He was noted for having some Powers to doctor.

It was haying season in the land of the Bloods, and Charcoal cut hay with a group led by Eagle Bear. Sometimes one or both of Charcoal's wives came along to help. One night the haying party returned home and saw Medicine Pipe Stem leaving Charcoal's tipi in a hurry. When Charcoal went inside he said nothing to his younger wife, but he noticed that her lover had left his hat behind.

The next day Charcoal asked his young wife to help him with the day's work. She complained of a headache and remained at home. The haying party spent the day hauling hay to Fish Creek, where the Mounted Police had their horses. At lunchtime Charcoal also complained of a headache and went back home.

Charcoal timed his arrival in the camp quite well—his wife was gone, and so was her horse. He took along one of his rifles and went out to search for her. He saw his wife's horse tied to a tree. He dismounted and quietly went up to surprise the pair as they were making love in the bushes. He shot Medicine Pipe Stem once. The bullet was said to have gone through the eye, leaving no trace when the eyelid closed over it. Charcoal took his wife back to camp with him, and she said nothing about the incident to anyone.

Charcoal feared punishment by the white man's law so he prepared to leave the reserve. (According to our old customs, he was justified in his shooting. The payment of some horses and goods to the dead man's family would have settled the issue.) One evening he rode past the home of the store-owner and farm instructor, McNeill, and shot at him through a window. McNeill was not liked by all our People, and it is said that he and Charcoal had feuded some time before. His shot injured McNeill.

Charcoal went back to his family and told his wives to pack up their camp. He took along his mother-in-law, his daughter, and his two sons. They headed west toward the Rocky Mountains.

In the meantime, Medicine Pipe Stem's body had been found, and the Mounted Police soon connected the murder with McNeill's shooting and Charcoal's hasty departure. They quickly got on his trail.

The Mounted Police found Charcoal's camp in a hidden meadow at the foot of the Rocky Mountains. They were greeted with a round of rifle fire. By the time the police managed to crawl up to Charcoal's lodge, they found only his old mother-in-law and his daughter inside. Charcoal, meanwhile, had gone around the other way to make his escape, along with his wives and sons. In the process they captured some of the police horses and stampeded the rest.

With the Mounties left behind on foot, Charcoal and his group headed north on fresh horses and found sanctuary in the south end of the Porcupine Hills, the country of the North Piegans. They built a sturdy brush lodge for shelter, since they had lost their tipi along with the mother-in-law. For some time the group remained hidden and was not discovered. However, after Charcoal had killed several cows on nearby ranches and stolen horses from the Piegans, his presence in the area was suspected. The Mounties closed in after a shoot-out he had with one Piegan who had caught him stealing horses. No one was injured. At this point Charcoal's wives took the boys and returned home to the Blood Reserve.

The Mounties, led by Sergeant Wilde, trailed Charcoal in the area west of present-day Pincher Creek. On a cold winter day in November, they found his fresh camp along Beaver Creek. The sergeant instructed his men, "Shoot if he doesn't stop." They plowed through the deep snow and finally spotted him in the distance. Everyone's horses were too tired to catch up to him except for the sergeant's. As he rode alongside of Charcoal and demanded his surrender, Charcoal pulled back the hammer of his rifle and shot the Mountie off his horse. Another bullet in the forehead ended the career of Sergeant Wilde, and brought much local sentiment against Charcoal.

Charcoal took the sergeant's horse and rifle and went on. One of the dead sergeant's Piegan scouts followed on Charcoal's horse. In a while he met up with a white rancher, a former Mountie, who joined the Piegan in his chase. Just before dark they came close, but Charcoal's close rifle shots made them reconsider the importance of their effort. Charcoal got away in the night.

Charcoal then apparently made several visits to the camps of his People, who supplied him with food and moccasins. They pitied him, even

Pretty Wolverine Woman, about twenty years after Charcoal was hanged and her lover was killed. (Joe Young Pine Collection)

in to the police by his own People. The following March, 1897, Charcoal was hanged for the murder of Sergeant Wilde. He was not convicted of the murder of Medicine Pipe Stem, because there was not enough evidence to prove his guilt.

HOW SPIDER GOT HIS NAME

The finest dancer in the memory of most of our People was a man named Spider, who died a few years back. He was not known for having much interest in our sacred ceremonies, or for having fancy clothes like eagle headdresses and buckskin suits. Yet he was always perfectly groomed, kept his face and hair painted, wore pleasing clothing, and carried an oblong mirror in one hand while he danced (a custom among many Grass Dancers).

Spider's favorite dance shirt was made from green wool cloth. It had strips of beadwork on the arms and over the shoulders, like a buckskin shirt but more subtle. This shirt was originally given to our uncle, Atsitsina, by a Sioux man. Atsitsina gave the shirt to his brother, Jack Low Horn, who later gave it to his relative, Spider. Spider was buried in that shirt. He usually used yellow paint to cover his face and bangs, which he wore straight-up, over his forehead, in the style of the Crows. Mrs. Walters wrote that she saw Spider dance during the social dance at a Sun Dance Encampment, and that he wore a "buckskin outfit colored green, with wide bands of lavender and green beadwork and matching moccasins. . . . In one hand he held an oblong mirror about fifteen inches long, with a hand loop that also had green and lavender colors on it. With his mirror held stiffly downward and his other hand on his hip, he drifted around that circle like a bit of down. His feet seemed scarcely to touch the ground. Even the Indians burst into applause." At that time, in the early 1930s, he was sixty-five years old. His other name was Long Hair; he never cut his hair.

though they knew the Mounties would jail them for giving him help. In fact, Charcoal's two brothers had already been jailed, along with their families, in a police effort to force Charcoal to surrender. One of the brothers was very ill, so the other brother asked the police to release him. Instead of releasing the ill brother, they kept him and both families. They let the healthy one go and told him that the rest would be freed when Charcoal was brought in.

Thus Charcoal was overpowered and turned

Spider was given his name by an old man named Yellow-Painted Lodge, who had the Medicine Power of the Spider. Here is the way he used that Power.

Yellow-Painted Lodge and others in his camp went on a hunt for buffalo. While they were gone, their camp was raided by a Cree war party, which captured most of the women. When the men returned they were quite upset about their loss, but knew that the Crees outnumbered them greatly so did not try to follow. Yellow-Painted Lodge heard that his wife had been captured alive, so he made plans to go and get her back.

Yellow-Painted Lodge took with him a number of horses and other goods to give to the Cree in exchange for his wife. Before long he was at the Cree camp and he learned which lodge his wife was in. Yellow-Painted Lodge kissed his wife when he saw her. She told him that she feared for their lives, because her captor had a Medicine that was very Powerful.

The Cree were gone hunting. When they returned, her captor asked, "Who is our visitor?" The woman said, "It is your brother." The Cree had seen the horses outside, so he knew the purpose of Yellow-Painted Lodge's visit. He was not willing to give the woman up so easily, however. He said, "I will show you the Power of my Medicine. If you are stronger, then I will take the horses from you and you may have your wife back."

The Cree took from a small pouch the red-painted wooden figure of a man. The Cree began to sing and drum and soon the figure got up and started toward Yellow-Painted Lodge. His wife called to him, "Don't let that thing touch you or you will be dead!" Yellow-Painted Lodge untied a small buckskin bag from his back braid. He took out of the bag a piece of rawhide cut into the shape of a spider. He picked up a patch of grass and placed the spider on it, while he sang his own Power song. He covered up the spider with his hand for a moment and blew down between his

Spider, or Long Hair, the handsome man of the Bloods. He is well remembered for his careful grooming, fancy dress, and perfect dancing. He has on a bead-decorated green wool shirt that was given to Atsitsina during a visit among the tribes in the east. (Arnold Lupson)

fingers. When he lifted his hand, the spider had become real and was walking around on the bunch of grass.

Yellow-Painted Lodge sat the spider down on the ground, right in the path of the Cree's little man. The spider jumped forward and grabbed the little figure. In a moment he had the figure all bound up with his thread, dragging it along behind him as he climbed up one of the lodge poles.

The Cree knew that he was defeated. He begged Yellow-Painted Lodge to spare his life. He told him to take back his wife and keep his horses. He offered to give him any other goods that he wished to have. Yellow Painted Lodge sang another song and the spider dropped his burden and hurried back to the bunch of grass. He covered up the spider and blew on it, and again it looked like a spider-shaped piece of rawhide. He put it back in its buckskin cover and tied it on to his braid. The little figure of the man lay crumpled up where the spider had dropped it.

Yellow-Painted Lodge then told the Cree, "I didn't come here for anything else but my wife. If you will just give me a meal, we will be on our way home. I want you to have the horses I brought and you will be my brother. You can come to our camp and be my guest anytime." The Cree was happy to hear that, and he knew that no further trouble would come once Yellow-Painted Lodge had accepted food in his tipi.

At this time old Little Bear (SikskiAki's great-grandfather) had a very sickly baby. While Yellow-Painted Lodge was visiting, he was given the baby to hold, and Little Bear asked the old man to pray for the strength of the child. Yellow-Painted Lodge asked, "Do you want this baby to become a man?" Little Bear told him he did. Then he told Little Bear to make incense. He said, "I will sing my Power song. If my Power comes alive then I will give its name to this baby and it will grow up to be a strong man. He brought out his rawhide spider and placed it on a bunch of grass and began to sing. After he breathed on his hand, the spider began to move around, then ran across the floor to Little Bear and his wife. They saw it. Then it went back to Yellow-Painted Lodge, who put it away. He said, "Since my Power has come alive for your child, I will give him the name Spider."

CROW-SPREADS-HIS-WINGS

At the time of his death, during the winter of 1953, Crow-Spreads-His-Wings was about ninety years old and the last man among the Bloods to

Crow-Spreads-His-Wings at Fort MacLeod in 1947.

have two wives, both of whom outlived him.

Crow-Spreads-His-Wings was the son of Wolf Old Man and the half-brother of our Old Man, the two having different mothers. His head wife was a holy woman and a very successful doctor. He, too, was a good doctor, in addition to leading Medicine Lodge ceremonies and all kinds of other holy gatherings. The family were Keepers of our Medicine Pipe Bundle many years ago.

The head wife adopted her grandson, Harry Shade, after his own mother passed away. The Old Man later adopted Harry and raised him. Harry Shade said that Crow-Spreads-His-Wings was the only doctor among our People who was ever heard of being threatened with imprisonment if he continued his practice. This happened around 1921. A woman had an infected breast and Crow-Spreads-His-Wings doctored her and gave her some strict instructions, which she did not follow. Shortly after his visit the woman died. Authorities made an autopsy and ran laboratory tests on the infected part to check for poisoning from improperly used medicines. They found nothing, but the agent and a Mounted Policeman came out to his house and told him he would go to jail if he was heard doctoring again. Apparently the threat had no effect to speak of, and the agent never came back to carry it out.

SHOT-ON-BOTH-SIDES

It is difficult for a head chief to satisfy all the People in his tribe, but old Shot-on-Both-Sides must have done so. The Old People of today have only good memories of him. He was born in 1874 and succeeded his father, Crop-Eared Wolf, as head chief in 1913, a position he held until his death in 1958. His son, Jim, succeeded him.

Some of our Old People refer to Shot-on-Both-Sides by his father's name, Crop-Eared Wolf, which he once used, and by his old-age

Shot-on-Both Sides about 1940. (Arnold Lupson)

Long-Time-Pipe-Woman, wife of Head Chief Shot-on-Both-Sides.

285

Head Chief Shot-on-Both-Sides and his council around 1930. From left to right: Cross Child; Fred Tailfeathers; John Cotton, Owns Different Horses; the chief; Percy Creighton; and Running Antelope, who was a full brother of John Cotton. The uniforms are government-provided, that of the head chief having embroidered bands on the collar, sleeves, and trousers.

name, NatosApi, or "Sun Old Man." For most of his life he was married to Long-Time-Pipe-Woman, who died in 1955 at the age of eighty-seven. For many years she was Pole-Owner and leader of the Motokiks.

Shot-on-Both-Sides was very faithful to the Old Ways. He always wore his hair in braids and wore shells as earrings. For more than thirty years he and his wife took care of the Long-Time Pipe. A member of the Horns Society nine times, he also belonged to lesser societies, including the Pigeons, Mosquitoes, Braves, Crazy Dogs, Crow Carriers, and Black Seizers. He owned a number of painted lodges at different times, as well as the famous One-Horn Headdress. He cut the hide for the Medicine Lodge and owned both the big drum and a sword from the early Grass Dancers, or Parted-Hair Society.

In their old age, Shot-on-Both-Sides and Long-Time-Pipe-Woman lived in a one-room frame house on the west side of the reserve. Their house was furnished very simply—a wood stove, a table, and a few chairs. They spent most of their time on the floor, in the Old Way, where they kept beds for sleeping and for entertaining most of their visitors.

Old Shot-on-Both-sides will be best remembered for his encouragement in keeping alive the Old Ways and for his defence of his People's rights, including his refusal of many offers to give up parts of the reserve.

CALF ROBE AND YOUNG PINE STEAL A PINTO

Calf Robe and Young Pine were partners. One time they went down to the Crows to steal horses. They each took a fast horse from in front of its Crow-owner's lodge, and then headed back home. After they had gone quite a way, one of the horses went lame and had to be abandoned. The remaining horse was a really fine-looking pinto. They took turns riding him.

Some time went by and a single Crow raider came to the Blood camps to steal horses. He went into the camp on a moonlit night and saw the pinto tied in front of a lodge. "Hai-Jah," he thought to himself, "there is that fast pinto stolen from us a while back." So he cut the pinto loose and took it home.

Again some time went by. In 1908, the Bloods held a big July dance in their new dance hall on the reserve. Many visitors came from all over, including a number of Crows. Calf Robe had, long before, made a wooden replica of the prize pinto that he had stolen and then lost, and he carried the replica whenever he danced. On this occasion he hung the replica from a stick at one corner of the dance hall. Sometime during the celebration, the old men took turns getting up and telling about their war experiences, using sign language for the benefit of the guests. When Calf Robe rose, he told about the capture of his pinto, and that someone else had stolen it from him later. At that point, one of the Crow visitors got up, took the replica down, and announced that since he was the one who had recaptured the original horse, he might as well take the replica of it, too.

THE LAST REAL WAR PARTY

In the spring of 1889, the last war party left the Blood camps for enemy country. The party was gone for one whole moon and traveled a long way through most of what is now the state of Montana. This story was told by its last surviving participant, old Running Wolf's nephew, Last Gun, while I visited with him before his death at the age of 116.

My father was old White Calf, head chief of the Piegans. My home was with the Piegans in Montana, but I spent a lot of time with my Blood relatives in Canada.

Among my brothers in Montana was one named Cross Guns. Somebody had stolen his best horse, and he was able to trail it as far as the line [border], but then he lost the tracks. He came to visit with me in Canada and told me about the loss of his favorite horse. Somebody from over here must have gotten away with it. Before he left we agreed to go on a horse raid during his next visit to make up for his missing horse. We thought we might raid some Crees or the white ranchers down east.

One day, before my brother returned from Montana, Morning Writing came to see me. He told me that I should go downriver to the camp of the Lone Fighters band, where Young Pine wanted to see about something important. When I got to Young Pine's tipi, there were a lot of

Calf Robe in 1910. (Pollard Photo)

Jim White Calf, or Last Gun, in front of his famous Yellow-Buffalo-Lodge, a few years before his death at the age of 116.

visitors, mostly young fellows. It looked like they were either planning a society take-over or a war party. He gave me a seat next to him and told me that he and Calf Robe and Prairie Chicken Old Man were planning to lead a war party and that they wanted to invite me along. I told them that I was waiting for Cross Guns to come back from Montana with more bullets and that the two of us had already planned to go on a raid. They agreed to wait until Cross Guns came back up.

In a couple of days Morning Writing came to see me again. He said that Young Pine was anxious to leave, even if there was no sign of my brother. Young Pine's tipi was even more crowded than before. I guess all the young guys in camp wanted to come along on this raid. Young Pine told them to go and steal horses from the nearby white ranchers that night and to hide them in the river bottom. He said that we would be leaving the next night. Most of the young guys took off right away to find horses to steal. Young Pine told me to sit still and wait, so I did.

After all the young guys were gone, Calf Robe told me that it would be impossible to get very far with a large group like that without being seen by the Mounties. So he had sent them off to find horses just in order to get rid of them for the night. Young Pine told me that he and Prairie Chicken Old Man and Calf Robe and Crazy Crow wanted me to join them that same night. I told them that I was not ready to go that soon, and that I needed the bullets that Cross Guns was going to bring. They told me that they had extra bullets for the .30–40 that I was carrying; it had a lever action and used shells. They told me to meet them that night at a place we called the Pine Tree, a place along the St. Mary River between Stand Off and Magrath where a large, lone pine used to stand.

That night we all met at the Pine Tree. We had to be careful not to be seen leaving camp. There were many Indian policemen watching for horse raiders. That had been against the law since

Young Pine in his minor chief's outfit, around 1915. (Joe Young Pine Collection)

the treaty. By morning we had walked some ways past where Magrath now stands. We only had two horses along with us. Young Pine and Prairie Chicken Old Man rode double on a roan while Calf Robe and Crazy Crow rode on a bay. I walked alongside the riders. East of Magrath we made camp in a grove of willows and Calf Robe rustled up a two-year-old heifer for us to eat. We spent the day making dried meat over a small fire in the bush.

Calf Robe and I were sent up on a hill as scouts during that day, and we soon spotted a lone rider coming our way. He looked to us like a scout, so we went down to distract him from finding our camp. We told him that we were hunting antelope and had just seen a couple in a direction away from our camp. Since nobody in his right mind would walk so far out on the prairie—on foot!—to hunt antelope, the scout knew what we were up to. He said, "I hope you have a good warpath. Myself, I will go and see about those antelope." We hurried back down to our party and all packed up and headed east, in case the scout came back with Mounted Policemen. The next morning we did not stop until daylight.

Our second camp was made in the brushy part of a small coulee. Crazy Crow was the youngest member of our group. He was little more than a boy, so he was asked to go and rustle up some water. But he was afraid to go off by himself, so I volunteered to go. Crazy Crow had acted foolishly on the whole warpath, and we were all sorry that he had come with us. I found some water in a little slough and carried it back in a water bag that we had made by peeling the tripe from inside the stomach of the two-year-old heifer, leaving the outside part as the water bag. None of us overdid our drinking of that slough water from the stomach bag!

The next night we traveled all night through rain and dampness. We went by the place where Bad Head was killed and we got as far as Writing-on-Stone by the next morning. We sent Prairie Chicken Old Man to scout around for police. They watched that place because they knew that any war parties in the area would go by that sacred stone to pray and leave offerings. Since no police were in the area we made our camp by the stone, for good luck. But we were not yet asleep when we heard sounds in the distance that made us reconsider our camping spot. In a heavy fog we moved on across the line, into the States. At a place called Greasewood we rustled up another beef and butchered it to dry the meat. We couldn't eat any part of it because it tasted like dried onions, so we packed up our things and moved on. The mounted men decided to go ahead at a faster pace to scout for enemy camps, while the two of us on foot would keep heading in the same direction.

We walked along until we accidentally came upon a sheepherder's camp along a small creek. No one was around and there was a fresh quarter of beef hanging from a tree. We cut some good pieces off the beef and raided the tent for a raincoat. Then we moved down the creek to a place where there was an old war lodge that I had stayed in during an earlier raid. To dry the meat, we made a great big smokey fire with green brush piled on top. We figured that any other raiding parties would think it was a white man's fire and not dare to come near for fear of being shot at. The rest of our party saw the smoke and showed up before long with no news of enemy camps. We stayed at that camp for the rest of the day.

Near dark we went on our way, following the same creek. We came to a place owned by a white rancher and decided to look around for horses. We left our stuff on one side of a nearby hill and quietly approached the place. There was a house and a large barn and a bunch of horses in a big corral. The other guys scouted around while I went into the barn to see if there was a saddle lying around. I had some matches with me—those old kind that sputter and burn with a blue flame. My second match lit up the barn so clearly I could see two men sound asleep in a stall. I beat it out of there in a hurry.

I went outside to the corral and was just getting my rope ready for a horse when a man came out of the house in his nightgown and shouted at me. I pulled the gate open and let all the horses out before I ran off in the darkness. I hurried back to our things and met the rest of the group. We got our stuff and went on our way to look for Crow camps. We crossed the Missouri River. At that point the mounted men decided to ride ahead. We agreed to meet by a certain coulee the next day.

When my partner and I reached the coulee we made camp. We saw a couple of head of beef nearby, so we went over to butcher one. By the time we got back to our camp with the meat, the rest of our party showed up, still with no news.

We needed water again. This time Crazy Crow volunteered to carry it if I would come along. It was raining lightly, so we stayed in the brush along the coulee to scout around. We followed up one branch of the coulee and found a running creek and a log cabin nearby. Crazy Crow wanted to raid the cabin, but I hold him it was too dangerous for two of us without our guns. Finally he talked me into it and we sneaked up quietly. When we got close, we hid behind a bush and threw a rock on the roof. Nobody seemed to be at home. We threw another rock at the wall. When nobody moved again, we ran up to the house and went in through the unlocked door.

The inside of the house was very neat and well supplied with food and other stuff. By the time we got our bundles on our backs we could hardly walk, much less run. The house was out in the open for a ways, so we were pretty worried about running into the owner on our way. Somehow we made it, and even managed to stop and fill our water bag and haul it back to camp. When the others saw us with our loads they knew that we had made a raid, so they sang a victory song with our names in it.

The others helped us carry our loads, as we decided to move camp right away; we didn't want to stay so close to our recent raiding site. We found a more secluded spot and made a good shelter with the canvas. Then we opened the different cans of grub and really had a banquet. All we had been eating was dried meat. After we ate, we decided that it would be a good time to sing some songs and pray for success on the rest of the trip. This was a customary thing to do when nearing enemy camps on a war raid.

Each of us prayed and sang our special good-luck song. Young Pine started out by singing: "If we are married or single, a woman always waits for us when we go on a war party, and she makes us think about her while we are gone. She gives us a good-luck charm to carry and a song to sing."

My own song had these words in it: "Last Gun, if I never see you again, I will do nothing but cry all day long."

Because we were far from our home, we all decided to add to our good luck by taking on new names that belonged to some relative of ours. I took my uncle's second name, Everyone Talks About. Young Pine took the name Fine Young Man. Calf Robe took his brother's name, One Spot. Crazy Crow took the name Looks-like-a-Coyote. Prairie Chicken Old Man took the name Many Mules.

We stayed in our victory camp all that night and decided to travel in the daytime. We saw a lone antelope some way ahead of us. I took a long shot at the animal and knocked it down. It tried to run but was wounded in one leg. Calf Robe chased it and killed it with a knife. We took the antelope up on a hill to eat and dry some of the meat. We had lots of tobacco from our recent raid, but we had no pipe to smoke it in. Young Pine was the only one who brought a pipe along, but he had left it at an earlier camp. We cut up one of the leg bones from the antelope and made a good stem out of it; then we made a bowl by shaping some clay and baking it in our fire.

The first horse we stole on this trip was a sorrel that belonged to some traders at a place called Wide-Leafed Bush, in the Missouri River Valley. Years before, these same traders killed one of my stepfather's earlier wives. She would have

Calf Robe. The rawhide rope is for horse raiding. (Glacier Studio)

been my mother in the Old Way. Her name was Sharp Ears, and she was shot with a bullet intended for my stepfather, who was trying to run the traders out for selling whiskey to his People. I stole the horse from them in revenge for that murder. The other fellows got angry at me for stealing a horse from white people. They said that the U.S. Army might come after us now. [Horses stolen from such people could usually be identified by their brands.]

When we got to a place called Snake Nose Butte, our party split up because of an argument. We never did decide who was our leader, al-

though Young Pine was the one who had organized the raid. Calf Robe and Prairie Chicken Old Man didn't accept him as a leader when the two disagreed over a chipped knife blade. The knife belonged to Calf Robe, who was so bitter about its chipping that Prairie Chicken Old Man finally jumped on it and broke it in half. Calf Robe and Crazy Crow took one horse and parted from us, but joined us later when we reached the Elk River [Yellowstone]. At the junction of that river and one called Pryor Creek there is a butte that we call the Beaver Head, because that is what it looks like. Fom on top of that butte we got our first view of a Crow camp—two of them, in fact. One camp was small and the other was average, but there were many horses all over, especially pintos.

We stayed up on the butte all day, and made camp in some dense brush. It rained and the clouds made the night black so we could see hardly a thing, but we headed for the Crow camps anyway. Crazy Crow and Prairie Chicken Old Man were the ones who had spotted the enemy camps, so we let them go in first to take their pick from the horse herds.

Calf Robe and I decided to go over to the smaller camp and see what we could find. We went past a lodge that was away from the other ones, and we looked inside. I saw a woman combing a kid's hair, and I got excited at the thought of getting a scalp. I told Calf Robe that I would go in and kill them both and scalp them. But he told me that I was crazy, that we came for horses, not to kill people. What he said was right. I was still young and crazy then. Besides, it turned out that those people were distant relatives of mine— some years later some Crows were at our camps and I told about this warpath, and they knew right away who it was.

We couldn't find any horses because of the rain and darkness, so we went back to the rest of our party. They had already captured a large herd and then lost them in the darkness. They were angry with us for not being there to help them. We decided to move on, and look for another Crow camp and hope that the weather would clear enough so that we could see what we were doing. We went on toward the east until daybreak, then made our camp in some woods.

The next night we kept going east, toward Sheep River [Bighorn River], until daylight came and we made our camp on top of a hill, where we could keep a lookout on the surrounding country. During the day a wagon train heading east stopped to make camp near us. We had no field glasses, but it looked like they had a lot of horses. We waited until dark to go and steal some. The horses turned out to be mules, which were not of much use to us. We decided not to steal anything from the white men because of possible trouble with their army. We went on to the Sheep River, where we knew there would be Crow camps.

We paired up and split into three groups. Crazy Crow came along with me. We found a camp before long and located a herd of plain horses, but none of them were worth coming this far for. Two of the others took horses and moved on to search for another Crow camp with better horses. We didn't see them again for a few days.

We left the herd and went to look at some other horses nearby—they were everywhere. It seemed the Crows probably didn't expect any more horse raiding from enemies. Crazy Crow decided to stay by our first bunch of horses, in case I ran into trouble anywhere else. I herded the second bunch away from where they were grazing and met up with Calf Robe and Prairie Chicken Old Man, who kept the herd going away from the camps, while Calf Robe turned back and went with me to another Crow camp.

It was daylight by the time we reached the Crow camp. It was so large we decided to walk right through the center of the camp and look things over. We pulled the hoods of our blanket coats over our heads and walked at a steady pace. We looked just like any two Crow men, and Calf Robe, who had lived among them as a young man, knew how to speak Crow pretty well, in case anybody talked to us.

We walked all the way through the camp without being stopped. By one lodge I saw a large Medicine Bundle that I wanted to steal, but Calf Robe told me I was crazy, since there were people nearby. I had to settle for getting seven of the best horses from a herd of good ones that we found at the bottom end of the camp. We herded the horses away from the camp until we caught up to Prairie Chicken Old Man. I took one of them and went back to get Crazy Crow, whose horses we no longer needed. He wasn't where I left him, and I had a hard time to find him. When I did find him he was walking around with one moccasin on, looking around the ground for the other one. He had gotten on an unbroken horse while I was gone, and it threw him off so he lost his moccasin. I hold Crazy Crow to get on the back of my horse. But he insisted on trying to catch a certain pinto that he recognized as having been stolen from his father some time before.

By the time I caught the pinto, Crazy Crow had his other moccasin on. I brought him the horse and started to ride off, but I soon noticed that he couldn't get on it. I rode back in the slough and caught him a roan, but he couldn't mount it either. Finally I caught him a buckskin, but when he asked me to get down and help him up on it I just rode off and left him there. When I caught up with the two older men they told me that I better go back for Crazy Crow, so I brought him a real gentle roan that he was able to get up on without trouble.

The four of us headed north with our large herd of horses. One of us rode at each corner to keep them in control. At one point we rode a long way up a canyon before we found it was a dead end. We had to ride all the way back down, which worried us, in case we were being followed. At another time we came to some railroad tracks just as a train was passing. The people on board waved to us and we waved back. Along the railroad tracks was a fence we managed to break down so we could cross. By the time we reached the Yellowstone River some of our horses had already given out, but we still had as many as we cared to handle. We kept looking around for army scouts, since we were a pretty conspicuous group headed away from Crow country.

As we rode along we kept losing more horses. A lot of them were still weak from the hard winter that had just finished. When we crossed the Musselshell River we had a hard time, because the river was flooded, and three colts drowned. A while later we passed by a sheepherder's camp and we told him, in sign language, that there were a bunch of played-out horses back along our trail if he wanted them.

We kept riding until we came to Wide-Leafed Bush, where I had stolen the sorrel from the ones that killed my stepmother. I turned the horse loose and it headed back home. We made our camp and were so tired that we all fell asleep, even though one of us was supposed to stay on guard.

The next day as we rode along we saw a cloud of dust in the distance. We thought the Crows were after us. Before we had a chance to run for cover we discovered that it was just a herd of cattle. We traveled until nighttime again, and after hobbling some of the horses, we made camp. While we were camped, a white man came by who Calf Robe wanted to kill. I reminded him of what he had told me the other night in the Crow camp, that we came to steal, not to kill. We told the man in sign language to keep going.

When we went on our way again, I rode ahead to see if the white man had come from an army fort or a town, but I couldn't see anything except wild prairie. We got to the Missouri River and crossed it all right. Prairie Chicken Old Man found a small boat and started to go across in it,

but he didn't know how to handle it and soon went under with the boat. We had to rescue him. Some ways beyond there we found some tall sage where we could make our camp safely, and we all went to sleep again.

The next morning we found all our horses gone except one. I thought they had been stolen, but Prairie Chicken Old Man found signs of a picket-rope dragging on the ground, which convinced him that the horses had strayed off. I kept waiting for an ambush while we followed the horses' tracks, but we finally found them grazing by themselves.

We rode on until we came to the hill where Young Pine had left his pipe. We asked Crazy Crow to look for it, but he was afraid. I was wearing plain blue woolen leggings, a blue shirt, and a blue cap that I had stolen from the house earlier. I put my braids inside the cap and went on up the hill. If any enemies were around I figured they would think that I was a white man and they wouldn't bother me. Nevertheless, before I went very far, I decided to take my rifle. When I got to the top of the hill I could find only the tobacco pouch, which had been torn open. The pipe was gone. About that time I saw a man in the distance, then another one. I thought that I was going to be approached, so I hid my rifle behind my back and slowly moved toward the edge of the bluff, where I could take cover. Then I recognized the men as Young Pine and his partner, who left our group a few days ago. We went down to the rest of our group. They had each three white men's branded horses and hadn't eaten all day. I suggested that they let the horses go and take three each from our herd, in case we got caught somewhere—ours were not branded. I told them that Crazy Crow was carrying a large sack of fresh meat.

When we reached the rest of our party, Crazy Crow told us that he had lost the meat some ways back, and he refused to go back and look for it. I went back and found it in a short time. We all sat down to cook and eat, although we didn't know that it would be our last meal for some time. It started to rain while we were eating, and it didn't stop for the next ten days.

South of the Bear Paw Mountains we found an empty shack, where we camped for a while. By this time the rain was turning into snow and it was getting colder. The next day when we got to the foot of the Bear Paws, it became so cold and miserable that we decided to make camp and wait for the storm to pass. We made a brush shelter and stayed in it for four days, but the storm just kept up. We had nothing to eat the whole time, even though we all took turns going out to hunt. One of my best horses died while we were camped there. It was a mare; she had a colt that died, too. They must have frozen to death. Both of them were wearing bells, and I had grown very attached to them.

Our last day in that camp was the sixth in which we had gone without food. We were getting sickly from not eating. That night I went down to the creek and took out a calf hide that I had been soaking all day. It was my riding pad. I brought it to the camp and scraped the soaked hair off, then singed the rest. After that I cut the hide into strips and covered them up with coals. Young Pine was awake and he saw what I was doing. When I took out one of the fried rawhide strips, he asked me for one, too. Before we got finished chewing on them all the others were awake and chewing on rawhide strips. We ate up the whole calfskin.

The next night I had a dream. When I awoke I told the others about it: "In my dream we came up to an abandoned cabin. Part of it was collapsed. There was a hill by the place, and we killed two antelope there. We split up and were butchering the antelope when we got attacked."

Calf Robe interrupted me and said, "Hold it, I don't want to hear the rest of your dream." I told him that the dream ended all right for us, so he told me to go on. I said, "After the fight we

were sitting on top of the hill cleaning a scalp. Young Pine asked me if he could have first choice on part of the scalp."

Young Pine started to fill up his pipe while he told me that he accepted my dream. He handed me the filled pipe. "When your dream comes true I will ask you for first choice on part of the scalp." I took the pipe and told him that he could have it.

The next day we continued on our way home. The weather was a little better. As we rode along the bottom of a hill we came to an abandoned log cabin that was partly collapsed. It was the cabin in my dream, I was sure. While approaching the cabin we saw fresh cow tracks, so we followed them until we got near the top of the hill, where we killed two cows. Young Pine and

Calf Robe with his last wife, in 1930. (Glenbow Archives)

295

his partner and I started skinning one of the cows while the others skinned the second cow. While we were skinning and butchering I happened to look down the hill and I saw a man in a white blanket coat looking over one of our horses. I told Young Pine to look down there, and suddenly a bunch of other men showed up at the same place. They spotted us and began to shoot. We figured it was the Crows after their horses, so we prepared to defend ourselves. Young Pine and his partner covered me while I ran to the rest of our party and got them to help me in driving the horses to a safer place in some brush and timber. The other two joined us and we took cover to see what would happen next. When the enemy appeared, Calf Robe asked them in the Crow language who they were. For an answer, they all fired at us.

Young Pine knew the place where we were pretty well. He had camped there on other war raids. He told me to take the lead and ride up the creek bottom to a place where the canyon walls were high and steep. He said we could make a better stand there. He told Calf Robe and Crazy Crow to drive the horses behind me while the other three covered us. We slipped away while the shooting was going good and strong. We headed up the creek very slowly. It was slippery and the snow was deep. As we rounded a bend we found that some of the enemy had already headed us off. One man was on a horse just in front of me. I had a hard time to turn my horse around while the other man was trying to get off his in order to get a good shot at me. Before he got off his horse, I aimed my rifle with one hand and fired at him. I hit his horse and they both went down. I finally got my horse to turn by slapping it on the nose with my gun, and I rode for cover. At that point a lot of shooting began behind me and we soon discovered that the rest of our party had headed off the enemy. I dismounted and went to help them when Calf Robe called for me to come back. I went to where he and Crazy Crow were guarding the horses, but all he wanted was for me to stay by them, so I left.

When I found the rest of our party they were up in good cover and had the enemy pinned in some willow bushes below them. Young Pine had figured out how to head the enemy off and that was how they had gotten such a good spot. When the enemy heard my rifle shots they must have decided there were more of us than they first thought, so they made their way out of the bushes, all but the last one. I aimed carefully and fired just as he came into the clear. I saw his body jerk and he went back into the willows and shot at us some more. Each of us took another shot at the man and Young Pine was the one who hit him a second time. We saw him spin around and fall over. The enemy had abandoned their horses near us, so Young Pine's partner went over and hit each horse with a stick to count coup on them. Young Pine, Prairie Chicken Old Man, and I ran down to the fallen enemy. I reached him first and counted coup, but Prairie Chicken Old Man captured his good rifle. We rolled the man over on his back to scalp him but were shocked by his appearance. He had blood running out of his nose and mouth and he looked like he had glass eyes. Young Pine fulfilled his wish and scalped one braid first, then I scalped the other one.

By this time the enemy had found better cover and they started to shoot at us again. We went up to our cover and found Calf Robe and Crazy Crow waiting for us on their horses. They had abandoned all the others. We didn't have time to say much about it, so we ran over and took the abandoned enemy horses. Young Pine got a nice roan with a white mane and tail, while his partner took the best one of all, a buckskin with one white eye and a beaded bridle and saddle. Each of us got a horse and we all took off. Calf Robe and Crazy Crow were the only ones who didn't take much part in the action and didn't count any coups. While the others rode on I decided to

Young Pine wearing his war Medicines. On his head is the stuffed body of a raven, which was given to him in a dream. Another dream Medicine, the skin of a blackbird, is tied to his hair lower down. Around his neck he wears an iron necklace, obtained in trade, and an Iniskim necklace with a piece of cottonwood punk attached for incense. Around his wrist is a bear claw bracelet.

go back and get a couple of the best horses from our abandoned herd. On the way I found a good blanket that one of the enemy had dropped.

When I caught up to the others, they were headed for the top of a hill. We felt pretty safe by this time, since I had stampeded the rest of our horses and thus left the enemy on foot. We stopped to rest and eat. When the battle first started I had packed along some tripe, a kidney, and a tongue in my pockets, and all those things were still there, along with my half of the scalp. We were so hungry that we didn't even have a chance to clean the food, much less cook it. We all ate the fresh stuff with some of the dead enemy's blood on it. That was the only time I ever ate human blood.

After eating we made camp in some of the brush on top of the hill. Calf Robe and I stayed up to keep watch while the others went to sleep. Calf Robe started feeling sorry for himself because he did not take part in the fighting as we had, and he swore to fight in any further battle until all the enemies had dropped their blankets and run. While he was talking like this, he suddenly got a strange look in his face. When I looked in the direction he was watching, I saw a bunch of riders heading our way, following our tracks. We woke the others up, but couldn't see the riders anymore. They were behind a hill. The snow was pretty deep, so they could not follow us very quickly, but they could see our tracks clearly. When they came closer we noticed that they were U.S. soldiers in cavalry uniforms. They might have been nearby and heard all the shooting earlier. Luckily for us, when the soldiers came to the steep part of the hill where we were hiding they turned and followed our tracks back down to where we had fought our battle. We packed up and went on our way as fast as we could. The soldiers outnumbered us and probably had lots of ammunition.

We made our next camp at Grassy Lake. One of my legs was really in pain. My horse had slipped on the way and I had fallen off and cut my knee on sharp rocks. We didn't stay in this camp long before we went on again, with me in great agony. We went as far as Big Rocky Coulee, where we camped again. I kept watch, since my leg would not let me have any rest, while the others slept.

After a while I spotted a lone antelope heading our way. I sat still and just moved my head slightly, now and then. Antelope are pretty curious animals. This one kept coming closer to see who I was. When he got close enough I slowly raised my rifle and knocked him over with one shot. The rest of the party jumped up from their sleep, thinking the battle was on again. They were quite angry with me for scaring them that way, but we all felt much better after roasting a bunch of fresh meat and having our first real meal in many days. We ate some raw liver first, then made some blood soup to get our stomachs ready for the meat we were roasting.

To make the soup we used the paunch of the antelope for a kettle. We tied it at both ends. Then we dug a pit and lined it with the antelope's skin, so that it would hold water. Into the pit full of water we dropped hot stones from the

Young Pine, who was a minor chief, with his head wife and his oldest son, Black Sleeps, in front of their tipi in 1901.

fire, and pretty soon the water was boiling. Then we put the blood-filled paunch into the boiling water for a little while, until we figured the blood soup was ready to drink.

By the time we made our next camp we were out of spare moccasins, and a couple of us, including myself, were actually barefooted. We stopped at a place near present-day Shelby, Montana. There we found a stray cow that we shot and butchered. I still had some sinew with me for sewing, so we each made ourselves a pair of crude moccasins from the raw cowhide. We didn't stay in this camp very long, because we wanted to get back across the line into Canada, in case the soldiers were still on our trail. We moved north until we got near the present town of Sunburst. There we made a good camp and had a victory celebration. One of us would sing while the others would dance. We painted ourselves for victory with black charcoal from our fire. We didn't know at the time that the soldiers were still on our trail and that the Mounties were looking for us, as well. We were traveling at night again, so that we wouldn't be seen by scouts or ranchers.

The next day we made camp back at the Pine Tree. We slept there and had another small victory celebration. From there we had an easy ride back to the Blood camps. It was daylight when we reached the Lone Fighters band. When the People there heard our story they all painted their faces black and we had a big victory celebration. They gave me a good pair of blue pants—mine were very dirty and torn—and a white blanket coat and even some bullets for my rifle. I felt much better after I got cleaned up and put on the fresh clothes.

In the afternoon I left and rode down to my uncle's camp. When I got close to it, I began to sing the victory song, and Running Wolf came out to meet me. I told him the story and gave him the scalp, and the People in his camp had a scalp dance and celebration, too. My uncle later did a ceremony with his Beaver Bundle and put the scalp inside. I don't know what became of that scalp, because when I got his Beaver Bundle, many years later, it was not there anymore. I still have that Beaver Bundle.

Unfortunately, the war party did not end as well as it seems at this point. Red Crow soon showed up in the camp and talked to my uncle and then both of them talked with me. Red Crow said that the Mounties were looking for us and that it would be best if I turned myself in. I went with Red Crow, and he took me to the agent, whose name was Pocklington. The Mounties had a two-wheeled Red River cart, like the Crees used, and they chained me into it for my trip to the stockade at Fort MacLeod. As we crossed the Kootenai River [Waterton River], the high water almost knocked the cart over and I thought that I was going to be drowned. Somehow we made it across safely. Young Pine and his partner also turned themselves in, and soon joined me at the stockade. The interpreter there was Bear Child [Jerry Potts], and he tried to scare me by telling me that I was going to be sent to the prison in Sasketchewan. He told me that I was crazy for going on a war party, since everyone knew that we were gone and the police and soldiers were all looking for us.

We were in the MacLeod stockade for about four weeks, during which time they gave me the job of waiting on the tables in the dining room. Finally they took the three of us to the courtroom. The Indian commissioner was there, and some Mounted Police officers, and Red Crow with some other chiefs. The agent stood up and spoke for us and the judge decided that there was no evidence to keep us in jail. They weren't sure about the killing, or who did it, and none of the horse owners had complained to the authorities about their losses. They gave us some rations and sent us back home.

The next day we had a really big victory dance at the Blood camps. There was so much *excitement and shooting that some of our horses stampeded out of the camp. I became a member of the Crazy Dogs Society at that time. I stayed with my relatives at my uncle's lodge until the Medicine Lodge ceremony, when we had a lot of trouble with the Mounties. The Mounties wanted to arrest Calf Robe again, because he had threatened them with a gun the first time they arrested him. Calf Robe decided to make up for not fighting in the battle with us, so he fought the Mounties in the Medicine Lodge, and the Mounties got beat up pretty bad. And that is the end of my story.*

THE FIGHT IN THE MEDICINE LODGE IN 1889

The incident in which the Mounties tried to arrest Calf Robe inside the Medicine Lodge is talked about by our Old People as "the time we had a war with the Red Coats." Some of our People thought that the Mounties came to stop our men from performing the self-torture ceremony.

Two men underwent that ceremony in 1889, Heavy Head and Tough Bread. However, the Mounties did not arrive until the day after this took place.

Here is how Grandma AnadaAki remembers her stepfather Heavy Head's story of his self-torture and what followed:

My father said that he went through the torture barefooted and without any clothes except a breechcloth. They cut him in the tipi where the holy woman stays. He said that other men were usually cut in the Medicine Lodge. He said that somebody told him to ask for deep cuts, so that they would not cut very deep. They painted him all over with sacred white clay, and designs were painted on his face with red paint and black paint. They tied sage around his wrists and his

ankles. When they cut him, he said that he felt like his heart was being cut out of his body. His body was all bloody by the time they got him fixed up. They even cut his back and tied a shield to it.

From the holy woman's tipi he was made to dance to the Medicine Lodge. The wind blew on his wounds and caused him so much pain that he cried all the way there. When he got inside he hugged the Center Pole and prayed, then he leaned back on the ropes that somebody tied from the top of the Pole to his chest. He leaned back real hard and jumped up and down and sideways while the drummers sang a song. He said that he jumped real hard because the pain was so bad that he wanted to tear the ropes off fast, but they didn't tear out. Black Eagle took a stick and hit the rope hard and the skin broke on that side. But my dad stopped him from hitting the other side because of the pain. Big Wolf grabbed him by his hair and pulled him back so hard that the other side broke. Black Eagle was counting some coups so that he could cut the loose skin off my dad's body. He cut the skin off and he put gunpowder on the wounds. After that my dad was sent away to sleep and look for a vision. That was when they had the riot inside the Medicine Lodge.

My father said that he walked westward from the camp until he came to the Belly River where he slept on top of a cutbank. He could hardly sleep that night from all the pain of his wounds. The next day he was walking around by the river when his relatives found him. They warned him not to walk back into the middle of the trouble at the Medicine Lodge. By the time they all got back home together the trouble was over and the People were packing up their camps to go home. The men were angry and had their guns all ready in case the Mounties came back to fight again. Some of the Mounties had gone into the Medicine Lodge to arrest old Calf Robe while the men were just in there telling war stories. Those police had no right to walk into the Holy Lodge that way. They were crazy. By the time they left they didn't have their guns anymore and some of their clothes were torn from them. They didn't take Calf Robe with them either. That is what I remember about my stepfather's story—Heavy Head.

Mounted Police Superintendent Steele wrote a lengthy report to his superior about the last real war party and about the fight in the Medicine Lodge in 1889. Although Steele was known for being a gentleman, his views about our People and our Old Ways was typical of the white settlers. Listen to some of his comments:

The Blood and Piegan Indians, whose reserves are located in this district [Fort MacLeod], have given considerable trouble and annoyance during the past year, and unless some great change takes place, it will not be lessened. The members of both tribes take every opportunity of procuring liquor of any description on every possible occasion. In fact, they even indulge in smuggling it across the line for their own use. This and horse stealing are the main causes of all our trouble with them; it seems impossible for them to resist indulging their apparent natural inclinations in this direction.

On the 2nd of July the "Sun Dance" commenced on the Blood Reserve. On the 4th, a constable from the Stand Off detachment then on duty at the Sun Dance reported to me at MacLeod, that Sergeant Hilliard and two constables had tried to arrest an Indian, "Calf Robe," for pointing a gun at constable Zinkham, when trying to arrest him for horse stealing some time previous, and as the Sun Dance was then in progress, some 200 or 300 of the Bucks assisted in rescuing "Calf Robe" from the police. On the following morning I ordered Inspector Wood, in command of a small party, to proceed to Stand Off and investigate the matter; he returned the following

day, bringing with him several of the Indians who participated in obstructing the police in doing their duty. They were placed in the guard room.

On the 8th of July, the five Indians that were placed in custody were brought before me and Inspector Wood, for their preliminary trial, Indian Agent Pocklington appearing for the defence. They were committed for trial at the next sitting of the Supreme Court, which was held on the 5th August, Indian Agent Pocklington and their chief, "Red Crow," going their bail pending the sitting of the court. The Crown prosecutor thought before the trial came off that there had been a good case made out, that the Indians had no cause or right to assault the police, even had there been no arrest warrants issued; but the judge . . . threw out the case. . . . In making this arrest, the non-commissioned officer was not in possession of a warrant, but I consider he acted perfectly right, there being so many bad Indians wanted at times that unless a man takes every chance offered he will likely lose his man altogether, as they give very few opportunities for arresting.

The impression has gone abroad that the Sun Dance is a religious festival; it may have been regarded as such at one time, but the experience of nearly all those whose dealings and occupations have brought them in close contact with the Indians, and who are well acquainted with their manners and customs, do not now consider it as such. It has degenerated into a gathering merely for the purpose of using up presents of tea, tobacco, &c., given them by their agents or begged from their white neighbors. It is a festival that should be discouraged; it has the effect of reviving too vividly old associations. Old warriors take this occasion of relating their experiences of former days, counting their scalps and giving the numbers of horses they were successful in stealing. This has a pernicious effect on the young men; it makes them unsettled and anxious to emulate the deeds of their forefathers.

It was reported to me on the 30th of April that a party of fifteen Blood Indians had left for the Crow Reserve in the United States for the purpose of stealing horses. Sergeant Hilliard . . . got the names of the Indians absent from the reserve. . . . On the 22nd I received a telegram from R. S. Tingley, of Big Sandy, Montana, to the effect that some of our Indians were stealing horses in that vicinity, and requesting me to take action. . . . On the 4th of May I received another message from R. S. Tingley that they had stolen seventeen saddle horses from him. I immediately dispatched Inspector Macpherson and all available non-commissioned officers and men to intercept, if possible, this band of Indians, and also notified all outposts.

On the 7th of May I received a further dispatch from . . . Helena, Montana, stating that nine Bloods had run off forty horses belonging to the Crows. . . . I also received a telegram from . . . Fort Assiniboine, U.S., that nine Bloods had passed through the Bear Paw Mountains, having stolen stock belonging to the Crow Indians in their possession.

Several rumours came in from the reserve, brought in by Indians who claimed to have seen "Prairie Chicken Old Man's" party, and who reported that they were all killed by Gros Ventres in the Bear Paw Mountains.

On the 16th Inspector Macpherson's detachment captured the "Bee," who was one of the party, and sent him in here.

On the 18th he sent in "Hind Gun" together with "Young Pine" and the "Scout," who by the advice of the chiefs gave themselves up to the Indian Agent. . . .

"Young Pine" made a confession regarding the trip, and stated that the party comprised five Bloods and one South Piegan, and that on the Big Horn at the Crow Agency they drove off about 100 head of horses, the most of which were very poor and dropped along the trail. When returning on the second day they were surprised by a large party of Gros Ventres, who commenced shooting at them . . . they firing in return, saw some of the enemy drop; they continued to retreat, and noticing two Indians in the trail in front of them, they pursued them and killed one of them. . . . They however, arrived on the Blood Reserve with five of the stolen horses and one stray horse. . . . Owners for these horses have not yet been found. . . . They are at present running with our herd here.

CRAZY CROW'S STORY

In conclusion to the story of the last real war party, let's hear Crazy Crow's version as told in a letter to Mrs. Walters by his daughter, Mrs. Ethel Tailfeathers. The letter accompanied Crazy Crow's yellow feather mascot, which was sold to Mrs. Walters upon Crazy Crow's death in the 1930s.

I was only 16 when I went on my first warpath. My father was not very keen on my going so young. He would say, "Son, there is plenty of time for you." But my spirit of adventure was too strong. I would not listen. So my father invited one of the very old timers of the camp to come and pray, paint, advise and impart his blessing on me. He sang the war song as he was tying the eagle feathers and dipped them in his yellow war paint and tied them on my head; all the while praying that the mascot on my hair would keep me from all harm of the enemy and bring me success in raids among other tribes.

When we go out to raid we do not set out to kill, but to raid and only kill in self defense. We put on our best regalia so that if we get killed, the enemy will have something worthwhile. I went with an older friend [Calf Robe]; he would look after me as he had experience. I rode on a gray horse and the enemy was on a pinto. I especially wanted a pinto as a pinto is dear to the heart of an Indian. It was worth risking a life to secure one. We pursued the enemy and shot him in fair fight at close quarters. He fell off when he was wounded. I jumped off my horse and ran to him, killing him and scalping him. We halved the scalp and that is why it is rather thin. I took the pinto and we started for home. We got home safely without the enemy taking after us. When we got home my father told me, "Son, give that pinto to the old man who gave you his blessing. It is due to the mascot that you have been able to get that pinto." I gave him the pinto but was very sad for I wanted the pinto for myself. But my father comforted me and said, "Son, never mind. The pinto is just going to be one of many horses you will bring home," and he was right.

These were his own words.—ETHEL TAIL-FEATHERS.

THE DUNCAN SHADE GANG

Our Old People continued to prove their bravery and skill by going on horse raids well into the present century. Some went for adventure, others went for personal or material gain. But most mature men around the turn of the century did it simply for sport at least once.

For some years there was a loosely organized group of horse raiders who went mostly to the east to raid the white ranchers in the prairie country near the Cypress Hills. Sometimes they raided nearby Crees and sometimes they went across the line and raided ranchers in the States. They often gave away their captured horses to relatives, or sold them on the black market; they seldom kept the horses for themselves. The recognized leader of this "gang" was a man named Duncan Shade, better known as Dog-in-the-Shade. Among his regular followers were Stephen Fox and his brother, Crazy Crow, Hungry Crow, Percy Creighton, Shot-on-Both-Sides, Black Rabbit, and Charley Goodrider.

Because of their generosity, their practice of an old tradition, and the fact that they never be-

Charlie Goodrider dressed in his finest, as he often was.

came involved in any shooting, the Duncan Shade Gang was respected by the People of the reserve. But it happened that they were eventually traced back to the Blood Reserve when one of the gang was discovered selling a stolen horse with a recognized brand. The Mounted Police brought several of the white ranchers to the reserve to look over the horse herds; they found many horses they'd been missing. A few of the gang were actually captured by the Mounties.

Hungry Crow was sent to the penitentiary in Rocky Mountain House for a five-year term. Black Rabbit was captured across the line and sent to the Deer Lodge Penitentiary. Later, when he was released, he was given enough money to take a train to Browning, Montana. From there he started to walk home, until he saw a camp of covered wagons on his way. He waited until dark, then went to the camp and got himself some four-legged transportation. Shot-on-Both-Sides was captured and then released on the recognition of his father, who was head chief. Crazy Crow was captured later and sent to the penitentiary for six months. While he was gone it is said that his brother, Plain Woman, ended up with his wife. When Crazy Crow came back and heard about it, he said, "That is all right. She is not the only woman on the reserve." He found himself a new wife and stayed on good terms with his first one.

Hungry Crow in 1958. (Glenbow Archives)

Some Scenes from the Past

EARLY DAYS

Northwest Mounted Police headquarters at Stand Off in 1894. Police Scouts from left to right: Calf Tail; Black Eagle; Big Rib; Many White Horses (later a holy man known as Bachksine); Tail Feathers; Many Mules; and Bear's Teat or Meat Mouth. Next to Meat Mouth stands an interpreter, then Sergeant Chris Hilliard, who kept a diary of his experiences as a Mountie. The older man with the buffalo coat is Mounted Police Superintendent Steele. (Steele & Co.)

Bloods and Piegan visitors at the Blood Ration House in 1881. In the foreground is the Negro interpreter, Dave Mills. Next to him is Running Rabbit. Center row, from left to right: Bull Backfat; Old Eagle Ribs; the agent; Four Horns, a South Piegan; and Jack Miller, or Three Bulls, a half-breed from the South Piegans. Back row: Two agency employees; Eagle Head; an unknown man; another employee; Last Gun—nephew of Running Wolf and stepson of the South Piegan head chief, White Calf; then Hind Bull; and finally, Blackfoot Old Woman, or Ermine Horse, who was then a minor chief. (Glenbow Archives)

Old agency at the north end of the reserve, along the Belly River. This is where the People used to come to get their rations, their treaty money, and their bad news about the latest in government plans and restrictions to their life. Tipi camps, dances, and horse races were a regular part of treaty payment days. Few of the men came to the old agency during ration days—the women brought their family's ration cards and loaded the supplies on travois or in wagons. (Glenbow Archives)

Dressed and ready for a horse race along the Highwood River in 1893. (Glenbow Archives)

A prairie camp along the Rocky Mountains in 1899. On the far side is the Big-Striped Lodge of Red Crow, the head chief. (Edward Curtis)

Omachksi-gohkstotaksin, or "Big Corner Post," in the Medicine Lodge of 1928. Big Corner Post was a dummy made up by a band of the same name. For four years it traveled all over the reserve on missions of humor. At Medicine Lodges it often served as the enemy in battle reenactments. The dummy met its end in a fire at the hands of an irate horse-owner. Someone had stolen the man's finest pinto and tied the dummy on top of it. On the following ration day, a crier went around and announced that Big Corner Post had been arrested for horse stealing and punished by being burnt up. In this photo, with the dummy, from left to right, are: Dog Child; old Bill Heavy Runner; and Rough Hair. (Glenbow Archives)

Members of a warrior's society inside a Medicine Lodge around 1880. They all have their guns and coup sticks and are ready to reenact their war adventures. At the right is the Weather Dancer's Booth—one of the dancers can be seen looking through an opening. To its left sit the drummers and singers for the ceremony. (Ernest Brown)

Setting up the circle camp at Lethbridge in 1912. The Blood Buffalo Painted Lodge is at the center.

Yellow-Painted Lodge of the head chief, in the center of the camp. An Otter Flag tops the tipi, although this was not an Otter Tipi; flags could be transferred without the tipis. Seated in the carriage are the two head chiefs of that time: Ermine Horse, or Blackfoot Old Woman; and Crop-Eared Wolf.

Young Bob Steel, son of Steel the holy man, and his pony, dressed for the dance at Lethbridge in 1912.

Visitors at Fort MacLeod in 1907, supposedly members of the Horns Society. From left to right: Heavy Shield; a North Piegan; Eagle Ribs; Goose Chief; Black Horse Rider; two unidentified; Hind Bull; Eagle Child; and Mike Oka.

Warriors from the Old Days, in 1907. In back, left to right: Unidentified; Good Striker; Packs His Tail; Calf Robe; Weasel Tail; and two North Piegans.

Spectators at a dance in Fort MacLeod, in 1907. In the foreground is Black Looking, with a Black-Covered War Pipe slung across his back. He was arrested by the Mounties for horse raiding, but he escaped from the Fort MacLeod stockade and hid in Montana for several years, until his "crime" was forgiven. Behind him is Calf Robe, who also has a Black-Covered Pipe across his back. It might have been a war pipe or a society pipe. In the foreground is a member of the Dog Society. (Glenbow Archives)

Three old women at Fort MacLeod in 1924. On the left is Double Victory Woman, mother of John Cotton. She holds a staff with hooves and bells attached. In her other hand is a horsetail switch. The woman in the center is Heavy Face, mother of Jim White Bull. She holds a stone hammer for pounding berries and dried meat. On the right is Takes-a-Man, who was then the widow of White Calf. On her dog's travois is a hide scraper made of bone and a small kettle of the kind that was obtained from traders. Black Looking is the man on the horse. (Glenbow Archives)

PORTRAITS OF PEOPLE FROM THE PAST

Mean Bandolier, or "Minnie," as Wilson called his adopted brother. (R. N. Wilson)

312

An unidentified but typical Blood warrior around 1885, at the end of the war days. His fine flintlock rifle is decorated with brass tacks, as is his horse whip, which doubled as a war club, his wide belt, and the large knife case in front. His war Medicine consists of a bandolier made of large seeds to which is attached a bunch of hawk and owl feathers. (Ernest Brown)

313

BLOOD WARRIORS AT THE FIRST CALGARY STAMPEDE IN THE YEAR 1912 From left to right: Duck Chief, a North Blackfoot; Heavy Head, with some kind of war Medicine tied beneath his horse's chin; Bob Riding Black Horses, with a long coup stick (although I have not heard of any coups he got); Cross Child; unknown; Gets Wood at Night, who was a doctor; Joe Healy, or Flying Chief; Antelope Whistler with a bone necklace around his horse; Black

Opposite page: Three Guns, again; then Weasel Tail with a gun case and coup stick; then Calf Robe, with his famous pinto horse replica, which was reclaimed by the Crows. Riding double on the next horse is Black Plume, with a Medicine Shield, and Mike Oka. Next to them is a North Piegan minor chief, Tom Scott; an interpreter; and the Rev. John McDougall. Calf Robe is the only one riding without a saddle or bridle and bit.

314

Looking with a shield; and Weasel Fat; Ghost Chief with a blanket coat. Red Beads is next, with a coup stick. Running Antelope, a minor chief, holds a spear. Natosina has on his favorite buckskin shirt, which is now in some museum in the States. He has an eagle plume on top of his black hat, perhaps to symbolize his other name. Next to him is Three Guns in a horned Medicine headdress.

Bear Shield, around 1900. Also known as Pig Shirt, he was a brother of the chief, One Spot, and was best known for being a lady fancier and user of Love Medicine. He married a number of times, once even to a white woman. He is wearing one of the holy war-shirts, said to have been bullet proof. Around his neck is a large brass bell, perhaps to call attention to himself, and a beaded case for a pocket mirror. His rings are made of brass wire. From his gun hangs an iron, which was struck with flint to make sparks for fires. (Pollard Photo)

316

Mountain Horse. (Glacier Studio)

Three Suns. (Glacier Studio)

Mike Oka. (Glacier Studio)

Good Striker. (Glacier Studio)

Eagle Speaker. His mother was captured by the Assiniboine and he was born with them. When he came back here, with her, he learned to be a leader of our sacred ceremonies. (Glacier Studio)

Rough Hair in 1910.

White Man Running Around. He was a Beaver Man and leader of Medicine Lodge ceremonies. (Glacier Studio)

Ermine Horse, or Blackfoot Old Woman, the other head chief during the time of Crop-Eared Wolf, in 1905. (Glenbow Archives)

Part of the Blood delegation in Banff during the summer of 1922. Their camp was set up next to the elegant Banff Springs Hotel. Because of its hot mineral springs, the Old People called Banff "Holy Springs." In the foreground is Atsitsina's father, Natosina, or Eagle Plume, wearing his favorite war shirt, which is now in some U.S. Museum. The last scalp he took is hanging from the stick in his hand. The next man cannot be identified. The first man with a headdress is Rough Hair, wearing a trade sash around his waist. Next is Flying About, stepfather of John Many Chiefs; then Gets Wood at Night; Heavy Head (with the beaded strip on his blanket); Black Horse; Calling First; Owns Different Horses; Shot-on-Both-Sides; Hairy Bull; Morning Bird; two unidentified; Jack Low Horn; Coal; unidentified; Bruised Head (brother of Shot-on-Both-Sides); Plume; Many Braided Hair; and Guy Wolf Child. (Pollard Photo)

319

Day Chief in 1903. He was a head chief for a short time, after the death of Red Crow. He wears the coat of a head chief, and has his tweezers for plucking whiskers tied to his braid.

Nick King and the famous One-Horn Headdress. This photo was taken just before he left for overseas duty with the Canadian forces during World War I. The headdress was considered a very powerful war medicine, so Nick King took it apart, packed it inside of its rawhide container, and took it with him to the war in Europe. It is not known that he actually wore it in battle, but it is said that someone in Europe took a great liking to it, for he did not bring it back to the Blood Reserve. (Glenbow Archives)

320

Weasel Fat, around 1910.

Old-timers gathered by St. Paul's School, on the reserve, to welcome a royal visitor. From left to right: Joe Healy, or Flying Chief; Mountain Horse; Spear Chief; Crazy Crow; Natosina, or Eagle Plume; Bobtail Chief, or Line Medicine Pipe Owner. (Glenbow Archives)

321

Percy Creighton, or Chief Little Dog, as he often signed his name. He is wearing the famous Half-Red Medicine Headdress, burnt in the fire at the old dance hall, in which he was killed. Creighton was caretaker of the hall. (Arnold Lupson)

Rides-at-the-Door in 1951. His widow is today the only holy woman left on our reserve. He is wearing his Sun Power necklace. (Phillip Godsell)

Give-away in honor of the late Big Wolf, in 1939. The poster shows Big Wolf and illustrates his coups. The upside-down U's represent horses he stole, while the semi-circles with wiggly tails tell the number of times he acted as scout for war parties—a duty of honor. Two fine horses were given to friends and visitors, during the social dance at the Sun Dance Camp, in addition to the blankets seen in the photo and other goods and food items. Jack and Jim Low Horn are in the foreground. Big Wolf was Jim's father-in-law.

SUN DANCE ENCAMPMENTS OF THE 1940s
A series of photographs taken by Arnold Lupson
Courtesy of the Glenbow Archives

Bobtail Chief leads the capturing party back to the ceremonial tipi during the transfer of the Long-Time Pipe to Henry Standing Alone, who is being carried in a blanket. Behind Bobtail Chief are Iron, Morning Bird, and Crow-Spreads-His-Wings. The last man is John Many Chiefs.

Bobtail Chief leading the new Medicine Pipe Owner and his party back to their own tipi. The Owner is carrying the sacred Pipe under his blanket, while his wife carries the rest of the Bundle on her back. (Arnold Lupson)

323

Early part of the public dance by the Horns in the 1940's. Jim White Bull leads the dancing Horns, wearing the Head-dress-with-an-Arrow. Former members are seated within the dance circle. These scenes look much the same today.

At the end of the public dance by the Horns. Jim White Bull wears the ancient Headdress-with-an-Arrow-in-Front. The children on the right represent enemies, who are trying to keep back the advancing Horns. On the next round they will scream with excitement as the dance leader charges towards them with a loaded rifle. As the shot is fired and they fall in symbolic defeat, the Sun Dance Encampment comes to an end for another year.

Dog Child sings an honoring song for his son, George First Rider, while he leads a saddle horse and a team around the camp circle to show what is to be paid for his son's membership in the Horns Society. (Arnold Lupson)

Construction of the sacred sweat lodge for the Medicine Lodge ceremony. One hundred willows are used for its frame. Dog Child is inside the circle, on the right.

Members of the Horns Society heading out of camp for the Center Pole. Driving the lead wagon is Head Chief Shot-on-Both-Sides. On the back of the wagon sits Tom Morning Owl.

Bringing back the Center Pole with a modern rubber-tired wagon in the late 1940s. Four members of the Horns Society are sitting on the Pole, drumming and singing.

A holy party passing the Center Pole of the Motokiks on their way to the unfinished Medicine Lodge. The man in front is Day Rider, whose wife was the new holy woman of that year. She is the second lady, bending over, with the sacred White Elk Robe. The second man is Crow-Spreads-His-Wings, whose wife is at the rear. The third man is Rides-at-the-Door, who is carrying a scalp from the Natoas Bundle—it is symbolic of the People's victories in life. His wife is behind him. At this time she is the only holy woman among our People.

Center Pole raisers waiting with their paired tipi poles to converge on the Medicine Lodge.

Raising the Center Pole.

327

A sacred Pipe about to be offered to the members of the Horns Society for smoking. The Pipe is being held by Day Rider. The Owner of the Pipe stands next to him, wearing the sacred headband. Last Gun, a South Piegan, is calling out his war exploits, while Weasel Tail stands nearby.

Charlie Reevis, the priest, leading the procession from the holy woman's tipi. The construction in the foreground is an ordinary sweat lodge and not the 100-willow one for the Medicine Lodge people.

Completed Medicine Lodge. The Striped Tipi is at the right.

Inside the Medicine Lodge during a give-away. John Cotton gives a present to one of the visitors seated in the foreground. Behind him, wearing large headdresses, are Jack and Jim Low Horn. Standing in the back, with dark sunglasses, is Guy Wolf Child, dressed in part of his dance outfit.

Social dancing.

The painted new Horns members listen while old members pray and recite coups in order to paint the staffs and cover them with their sacred wrappings. On the left is Dog Child.

Circle Dance during social dancing at the Sun Dance of 1939. The designed robe worn by the man on the left used to be a chief's emblem.

Meet the Old People of Today

SikskiAki and I asked a few of the Old People living on the Blood Reserve to comment on the past, present, and future of our Old Ways. Most people on the Blood Reserve have at least some respect for their traditions and for those who are still trying to follow them. Nevertheless, few know how the Old Ways really were. Most of our People today were taken from their parents and placed in boarding schools at an age when their minds were forming permanent patterns. In the schools, their contacts with the Old Ways, both spiritual and physical, were always discouraged and sometimes forcibly severed. By the time they left the schools, the children had been taught to judge life according to the standards set by white society, standards that were meaningless to their parents who lived simple, natural, spiritual lives. This forced-separation of children from their families and culture continued until just a few years ago, but it had already broken the Spirit of our Old Ways in the daily lives of our People.

OUR HEAD CHIEF, JIM SHOT-ON-BOTH-SIDES

My father had the Long-Time Medicine Pipe for many years. He taught me to treat our home like a church. Every morning and every night he made incense. He asked for life in his prayers. He prayed for all of us. . . . At the beginning of summer he would be really happy when he first heard thunder. That is when he opened his Bundle. He would butcher a cow and use it to feed those who came to the ceremony. We had a good life because our home was very holy.

Jim Shot-on-Both-Sides is the present head chief of the Blood People. The Bloods have had five chiefs from his family over the past hundred years. His father, old Shot-on-Both-Sides, was the son of Crop-Eared Wolf, who was the adopted son of old Red Crow, who was the nephew of Pinukwiim. All of them were head chiefs.

Except for one two-year term, Jim Shot-on-Both-Sides has been head chief since the death of his father in 1958.

The Old People still respect me the same way they respected my father. I don't know about the young people. For instance, when we went down to Ottawa, they put me first in everything. Before every meeting began I was asked to pray. We had meetings at different places and I prayed at each of them. I prayed so that we would get what we went for.

The last wife of old Shot-on-Both-Sides, Long-Time-Pipe-Woman, was our chief's step-mother.

My real mother died when I was about ten or eleven. Her name was Drums-in-the-Water, and she belonged to the Knife Owners band. The only member of that band who is still living is that old lady whose father was the Negro interpreter, Dave Mills. My mother's brothers were Willie Wadsworth and old Weasel Moccasin. Nowadays I've got all kinds of relatives on the reserve, full bloods, half-breeds, and Negroes.

His father had many sacred Medicines, including the Long-Time Pipe and Backside-to-the-Fire Pipe. He belonged to the Horns nine times.

I was very young when things were first transferred to me, before I went to school. When I went to school I gave away my weasel-tail buckskin suit. Bob Big Sorrel Horse transferred it to me. I think he transferred a horned Medicine headdress to me also. When I went to school I just gave them away. I was crazy. I should have kept them. I just gave them to my friend, Leo Crazy Bull. I didn't transfer them. He never did go to school.

The last thing that was transferred to the chief was the rights to the famous One-Horned Headdress. The original, lost in Europe during the First World War, was given to him by Big-Faced Chief, a North Piegan. Bear Shin Bone painted him for it. He also had the Children's Medicine Pipe once, and he belonged to the Pigeons Society twice. He said that he would like to attend our Nighttime ceremonies if he ever gets enough sacred songs to do so. At this time he is only allowed to sing twelve songs.

I think the Old Indian Way is good for young people. That is why I am helping the Horns to try and get their sacred Bundles back. A Medicine Pipe Owner we used to think was very holy. He dressed holy and acted holy. Nowadays they don't behave like the ones from the past. The People don't find them very holy any more. . . . But maybe things will get better again. If we start to live a holy life again, maybe there won't be so many deaths. In the past there were not many sudden deaths; the People lived in a holy way then. . . . In the Old Days the Old People often followed both religions. They liked to go wherever there was praying. Now not only the Indian religion is being forgotten, the white religion is falling the same way.

ALBERT CHIEF CALF

Two of our Old People who still attend every ceremony are Mr. and Mrs. Albert Chief Calf. The old man was born in a tipi in 1895. He is known by his father's name, NinnaOnesta, or "Chief Calf"; his other name is Wrapped Up. His wife's name is Little Nice Face. The two make a distinctive couple on their daily walk through town—he is over six feet tall and sturdy-looking; his wife is quite short and plump. He usually wears an old black cowboy hat with an eagle plume attached; she always covers herself with a woolen shawl.

Although NinnaOnesta has attended ceremonies of our Old Ways all his life, he has been leading them for only the past few years. Last winter he alone led more Nighttime ceremonies than all the other leaders. He is always available for praying and is very easy to please and willing to please. He wears sunglasses because of his poor eyesight, which allows him to overlook details and distractions that would bother other leaders.

NinnaOnesta went on a number of raids during his young days, but like most of our Old People, he has said, "I can just talk about my raids when I am confessing them during holy ceremonies. I can't talk about them just anytime." He went on his most notorious raid with the late Henry Standing Alone. They were discovered trying to steal horses and a gunfight followed, but no one was seriously hurt.

NinnaOnesta transferred his last Horns Bundle during the Sun Dance last year. He said he had had it for thirty-two years. He has also been a member of the Horns Society five times. "Being a Medicine Pipe Owner and belonging to the Horns both brought me a lot of happiness. They are both the same to me. You can see how many children and grandchildren I have around me. They were all raised safely because we took good care of our holy things. We raised our kids by them."

All winter long he looks forward to the return of Thunder. "I really enjoy Medicine Pipe ceremonies. I wait with happiness for Thunder to come so that I can get ready for the Pipe dances again. I really feel good going to them." He owned one Medicine Pipe Bundle for "many years." He said it was "the one that crazy Black Plume kid sold to that white man that's trying to get all our holy things away from us."

NinnaOnesta and his wife would like to see the Old Ways kept up properly by the young. "These young people that are trying to follow the Indian Way. It is very good. There is nothing at all wrong with it. It is very good for them." Asked if he had any advice to offer to young people, he replied; "If one of them will come to me for advice, I will tell them how to live. But no one has come to me, so far."

BOB BLACK PLUME

Apikayi, or "Skunk," is a short, little man in his mid-seventies who has a smile and handshake for anyone who passes him. Some of our People refer to him as "the preacher," because he is involved in all sorts of religious affairs, from Horns Society to Full Gospel and the Catholic Church. Perhaps to suit that title, he is usually well dressed in a dark suit and white shirt, with a clean cowboy hat or a slouch cap over his pure white hair.

Apikayi was the son of old Black Plume and one of his wives, Black Horn, who had a number of white relatives. His full brothers include Dick Soup. His father's grandmother was a noted doctor. She used to apply a special skunk skin to the afflicted area of a patient's body. If the skin came alive, the person would survive and she would begin to doctor. If it did not come alive, she would know there was no hope. When Apikayi was young he was a very sickly child, so his great-grandmother used her sacred skin to check him. It came alive, so she told his parents that he would grow to become an adult. Later she gave him the skin, as well as the name. He used to tie it to his braids, when he still had them.

Apikayi was once a leader of our sacred ceremonies, but not this past winter, due to conflicts with some of our Old People. He has often been criticized for mixing up the songs of various ceremonies, and for leading ceremonies that were not actually transferred to him. He and several relatives sold their sacred Bundles, which made him unpopular. His active participation in various other religions added to his unpopularity. Here is what he says about all that:

I haven't quit going to our ceremonies for good, even though the People are saying that I have given up the Old Ways. That isn't true. I once had a dream that told me I would grow old by them. I was praying very hard and I left my body. I went far into the Above. There was a yellow-painted tipi there and I was invited in. The people in the tipi told me that I would live to be a hundred by keeping up my Old Ways and by leading all the ceremonies that I am asked to lead. I am looking forward to seeing if my dream will come true. I am still very healthy at my old age.

The reason why I have quit going to ceremonies lately is because some of the People don't treat me good. Some from Gleichen [North Blackfoot] asked me to lead the Medicine Lodge ceremony that they were going to give down here last summer. I told them that I would, because my relatives on both sides took part in Medicine Lodge ceremonies in the Old Days. One time I was in a restaurant in town and Wolf Old Man [our Old Man] came in and saw me. He came over and asked if it was true that I was going to lead the Okan. I told him it was. Then, right in front of everybody, he told me that I had no right to lead that ceremony and that I didn't know enough about it and might hurt others who were taking part in it. But that isn't true. I know most of the songs from it and I know what to do to lead it. He's just mad because his brother [Crow-Spreads-His-Wings] used to lead them and he studied for a long time before he could do it. I can open a Beaver Bundle, too, even though I never had one. My father had one and my wife's father [Tough Bread] had one and I learned the songs from them.

The reason my songs are different from everybody else's is that I had a different Teacher. Most of the ones who lead the Medicine Pipe ceremonies learned their songs from Heavy Head, but I learned them from Tough Bread. I'm the only one still living who learned them from him, so I'm the only one who sings them that way.

The reason why I sell my things is because I believe in the Old Ways. In the Old Days, when the Old People were asked for something holy they always gave it, they never held back, and I am the same way. The white men sometimes want the holy things much more than an Indian will want it, so I let them have it to make them happy. The Crow Beaver Bundle that I sold was not being used any longer by the People. My sons sold the Medicine Pipe and the Horns Society Bundle. They didn't ask me about it before they did it, so I am not to blame for that. I always pray for my family and for anyone that needs my prayers. I am not stingy with them. The Creator
hears my prayers whether I say them at a Night-time ceremony or at the Catholic Church or during a Full Gospel meeting. I am not shy to pray any place. That is how I live.

MARK OLD SHOES

Mark Old Shoes, or Rusty Boy, is probably the youngest and healthiest of our Old People. He is learning to lead some of the ceremonies, mainly our Nighttime ceremonies and Medicine Pipe Bundle openings. He is also head Weather Dancer on the Blood Reserve, in case there is ever another Medicine Lodge ceremony.

Mark's father was the famous warrior Morning Writing, who was registered on the agency rolls by his earlier name, Old Shoes. Morning Writing raised his children in the Old Way and did not allow them to go to school. When Mark was twelve years old, his father died and he was sent off to school, where they forced him to cut his braids. Since then he has always worn short hair.

Mark has been a member of the Horns Society three times, once as a bachelor and twice with his wife. The first time he joined as partner to the Owner of one of the leaders' staffs. At later times he owned the Staff-with-a-Rattle and the Headdress-with-an-Arrow-in-Front. As he looked through the photographs of past scenes he had some comments: "I find it strange how much everything has changed. For instance, in those days the Old People all allowed their pictures to be taken at the Sun Dance. Now, if anyone is seen with a camera, the Horns will sure get after him."

Like many of our Old People, Mark has much faith in the new Horns to help keep our Old Ways alive. He has said, "I think that as long as the new Horns really believe in what they are doing, our Old Ways will keep going. Young people didn't care much about the Old Ways, lately, when it was just us Old People. But now a

335

lot of young people are thinking about trying to join in."

Mark was greatly disappointed when the Long-Time Pipe was sold to the Provincial Museum. His brother-in-law, George Long-Time Squirrel, wished to become Keeper of the ancient Pipe, so he sent Mark to see John Red Crane, because the two were related. Mark said, "It sure

Mark Old Shoes, in the center, as the head Weather Dancer during the Medicine Lodge ceremonies. In the foreground is the Old Man, who was then his Teacher for the sacred duty. On the other side of him is old Heavy Head, dressed and painted just as he was some sixty years earlier when he underwent the self-torture. Each Medicine Lodge dancer must dress the same way as first instructed by his Teacher. Thus, the Old Man and Mark are both wearing shirts, with blankets wrapped around their waists. (Mark Old Shoes Collection)

was hard for me to go back to my brother-in-law and tell him that he couldn't take the ancient Pipe because that white man was going to take it to Edmonton." He added, "It was just as hard for me when John Red Crane asked me to drum for him at the transfer. I didn't believe in it at all, but by the rules of our Old Ways, I couldn't refuse. He was my relative and I knew the songs. I lost my son not long after that. Just about everyone who was at that transfer suffered some misfortune soon afterwards, especially John."

Mark's father-in-law was old Long-Time Squirrel. He died while he was still Owner of the Different-People Pipe. At that time his son was not prepared to take the Pipe, so Mark's mother-in-law asked him if he would take it, since it could not stay in the home where a member of the family had died. So Mark and his wife took it to their home, and had it transferred to them during the following Sun Dance.

Mark is the Weather Dancer as the result of a relative's dream. A woman named Prairie Chicken Calling was visited by a holy man while she was sleeping. The holy man pointed into the distance and asked, "Do you recognize that man over there?" The man was Mark, dressed as a Weather Dancer. The holy man said, "I am telling you that if that man becomes the Weather Dancer and devotes himself to his duties, he will have a long life."

The woman told Mark about her dream. She said, "Please pity me, relative, and do as my dream instructed." Mark spoke to the Old Man, who was then the Weather Dancer. The Old Man agreed to transfer his rights during the next Sun Dance. Mark has been Weather Dancer at three Sun Dance ceremonies so far. He said, "That's the most Powerful thing that I have, now. It's my life, and I will live by it so that I can reach old age."

GUY WOLF CHILD

Guy Wolf Child, at ninety-two years, is usually the oldest dancer at our ceremonies. Until a couple of years ago, he came to the dance circle dressed in only a breechcloth and moccasins, his face and body painted, and carrying two or three large willow hoops so that he could do one more encore of the old hoop dance. He used to keep up to six hoops moving on each of his arms and legs, as well as one on his head, each hand, and waist.

Today, Guy Wolf Child is white-haired and blind. He usually sits quietly in the corner of a room and tries not to trouble anyone. If there is any sign of drunkenness, he asks to be escorted outside and away from the house. When we came to see him, he was thrilled to have company. He made sure he knew who everyone was, and said, "When we meet we shake hands. That is the way we have relatives. That is the only way that I will know them now." We told him about the nice photo of his father, old Wolf Child, and he asked if we had it with us. He told us, "Lay it in my lap so that I can at least touch the picture of my father, since I can no longer see it."

We asked him what thoughts about the past made him happy, and he replied as follows:

I always enjoy thinking about the past, back when I was young and could dance good. I don't remember the times before I went to school too well. I don't know how long I was in school, but I remember that when I came out, the modern life had started. Things already seemed very modern to me. I used to do all kinds of work for different white men, they used to treat us pretty good back then.

All things are different today. In the Old Days we all wore leggings, only lately they started to wear pants. Even the Sun Dances are different today. Everyone used to get together for them when I was younger. We used to play a game with

bows and arrows; we put mud balls on the points. We had mock wars. People from the opposite ends of the reserve would shoot at each other with the mud-tipped arrows and the winners would keep all the arrows. We played a hoop game and in the spring when the geese came back, all the women and the men played ball games. Kids used to go out on the prairie and play. We would snare gophers, then take them home and cook them and eat them. They were not too bad.

I was a very good dancer. Everyone used to watch me. I was always the first one out on the dance floor when I was young. . . . I always danced at the stampede and exhibitions they had in Fort MacLeod and in Lethbridge and several times I danced at the Calgary Stampede, once on the back of a flat trailer.

The most important place I ever danced at was in Banff, when Long-Faced Crow [Wilson] took us up there to entertain some officials. Fifty-five of us went up there by train. We took along several painted lodges to sleep in. They drove us out to the buffalo paddock in cars and I remember some of the Old Men, like Natosina, talking about how they would like to have a bow and arrow and go in there for just one more buffalo. They really liked seeing buffalo again. We had ten tipis set up; most of the men brought their wives along.

When we got ready to dance for all the white people in Banff, Wilson told me not to wear any clothes, just to wear my breechcloth and to dance with my hoops. My moccasins were fully beaded with white background and I had paint all over my body. There were several people taking pictures of me, some of them with those big cameras that they put their heads inside of. I never saw any of the pictures. The other Bloods that were along illustrated all kinds of things from the Old Days. They had mock battles and horse raids and they put up tipis. Natosina even led a Nighttime ceremony for them inside the big

337

house; the white people were standing all around them watching.

I always look forward to going to any kind of dance, even though I can only hear the drums and bells. I remember just what it looked like in the Old Days, and I always get up and pretend that I am dancing like when I was young again. My grandchildren sing Indian songs and drum and I get up and dance every night.

DAN WEASEL MOCCASIN

Dan Weasel Moccasin has worn his hair in two braids all his life and is often called "Braids," although his actual name is Yellow Horse Rider. He parts his hair down the middle, instead of to one side as was our usual custom. It is not proper to ask someone questions about personal habits, but it is known that Yellow Horse Rider keeps his hair long for holy reasons.

His father, old Weasel Moccasin, was a member of the Knife Owners band and the Horns Society. His mother was a member of the All Short People band. Yellow Horse Rider was their minipoka, and the usual favorite children's sacred articles were transferred to him.

When he was seven, old Heavy Shield gave him a Medicine Lodge necklace. A Piegan holy woman named Handsome Gun Woman gave him another necklace during a Sun Dance ceremony. While he was young he also had the topknots from both the Backside-to-the-Fire Pipe and the Cree Medicine Pipe. Later he was given the rights to the sacred Lynx Tail Headpiece from Calling Last's Beaver Bundle. He never transferred it to anyone else, although Calling Last left it in his Bundle when he sold it to the museum.

Around 1943, Yellow Horse Rider took the Children's Medicine Pipe with his daughter, Eleanor. His father gave up his fine buckskin outfit and seven good horses for it. They kept the Pipe for five years before giving it up to John Red Crane.

Today, Yellow Horse Rider lives with his family in a modern home on the same land his father owned, at the south end of the Belly Buttes near the Belly River. Except for singing at summertime powwows and at an occasional Medicine Pipe ceremony, he is very shy and quiet. So many sacred things have been transferred to him that he can sing the required sixteen songs at our Nighttime ceremonies. But he says he does not like to attend unless the sponsor of the ceremony specifically asks him to. This is a traditional custom.

Yellow Horse Rider has said, "I live the Indian Way. That is the Way in which I was raised and it is the only Way I know how to live. I only do those things that I am meant to do, and I try very hard to do them right. I have a lot of children. If I don't treat my Indian Ways right, it might hurt them."

JOE YOUNG PINE

About ten years after the last real war party, one of old Young Pine's two wives gave birth to a son, whose name became Joe Young Pine. He is known today as Dog-With-a-White-Spot, one of his father's names. He is most often seen around the reserve while traveling in the ditches next to the roads. That is because he is one of the last to use a team and wagon. Here is what he says about that simple method of travel:

Very few people on this reserve had an automobile when I first got one. I was still young, then. Now that most everybody has at least one auto or truck, I'm back to using my team and wagon. I like it real well. I'm never in a hurry and I always have time to stop and visit with whoever I want to. I don't just go by in a cloud of dust. Of course, I like it because it's cheap, too. I never have to worry about gas money or oil changes or stuff like that. When there's any drinking going on around the house I don't have to

Joe Young Pine, around 1915. He cut his braids shortly before going to Australia. To his right stands Ernest Brave Rock, brother of Mrs. Wadsworth. Seated before them is the wife of Joe's older brother, Black Sleeps. (Joe Young Pine Collection)

worry about somebody taking off in my car and wrecking it. That used to happen a lot.

I used to race chuckwagons at all the rodeos and stampedes. In 1939 I was one of the fellows that was sent to Australia from this reserve. We

were gone for three months. It's pretty tough when you are so far away from home and you get homesick. I used to just get into my wagon and drive around and try to pretend that I was back at home, here. But that was kind of hard. We never saw any kangaroos when I went for a ride in my wagon here, but we sure did there. We raced chuckwagons and horses while we were down there; we showed their cowboys how we do it here.

A lot of Old People prayed for me before I left. They were pretty worried about us going so far and across so much water. We went from Vancouver by boat, it took us twenty-six days.

Joe's wife joined the Horns Society once, with her first husband, and recently she joined again with Joe. He is the oldest member of the society. His wife said, "Don't ask him if he's ever had a vision. He was too scared to go out by himself to do that; he just chased the girls, instead."

MRS. ANNIE WADSWORTH

Eighty-two-year-old Annie Wadsworth was a cousin of Charcoal. She can still remember when he came to her mother one night, when he was wanted for murder, and asked for food and sewing materials, which her mother gave him at great risk.

The most outstanding fact of Mrs. Wadsworth's life, however, is that her parents gave her away as a bride in the Old Way when she was only seven years old. Her father was Moon Calf; her mother, Forward Stealing Woman. They gave her to eighteen-year-old Willie Wadsworth, then better known as Wearing-a-Tailfeather-Headpiece. She says that she does not regret being married so early because her husband treated her very well throughout their life together. They had twelve children.

She speaks of her early marriage:

Yes, I was still running amongst the girls. I was still small and naughty. My father told me one day, "You will get married. There is a boy that just came out of school. He is a gentle boy, so he will be kind to you."

I was very proud that I was getting married. I should have been educated first, but I obeyed my father to get married so that someone would look after me. He was getting ill then.

My mother sewed moccasins for me to get married in. When winter came, it was on Christmas, they got me my horse and they tied a travois to him. I had my bedding and I had two parfleches; one was full of moccasins and one was full of dried meat. Those that are called pillows [backrests] were loaded, too, and some blankets were put on top. I rode on one horse and there were two more horses with many blankets tied on them; they were all presents from my folks. I don't remember everything about it, because I was small. I don't know how many more horses were sent later; my husband traded off some of them for cows.

I wore a buckskin dress. My leggings were beaded, and I wore a fancy blanket with a safety pin in front. My shawl was a fancy woolen blanket. We arrived at the old place where we used to get our rations. An interpreter lived there. His name is Young Scabby Bull, a black white-man [the Negro, Dave Mills]. My mother told me to stay in there for a while so that she could go and get rations. This was ration day.

So I sat there. Then a woman came in and kissed me and said we were going. I was hoping to see my mother, but I never saw her again that day. She took me out and put me on the horse with the travois. So we started off again. The woman led the two other horses. She was on horseback, too.

We came to a house. It was the house of my deceased brother, Bull Shields. A man lived there

Mr. and Mrs. Willie Wadsworth and family during a Sunday outing with some of their children.

by the name of Bull Head. He had two wives. One of them was named Shaggy. They both jumped out and took me down. I must have looked funny. A woman by the name of Annie started to laugh at me. She was John Cotton's wife. I must have looked really funny. It was in the winter and I had on my buckskin dress, and my shawl was a small fancy blanket.

They fed us and then we started off again, on and on. Finally I couldn't see my homeland, which was beyond the ration house. We came to a place that is called Willows-in-the-Water. As we came into the open, there was a house with a sod roof. We went in and they took my belongings. At one side there was a wooden bed, an old bed of the past, carved fancy. It was the bed of the one that I was going to marry!

My blankets were all brought in. The boy had a sister. I asked her, "Have you got any toys?" She brought out a small rawhide container full with her toys. She sorted them out and she gave me some. Then she gave me the rawhide container to put my toys in.

I got very lonesome after I was there for three days. There was a lump in my throat. I wasn't thinking of my mother. I was thinking of my father, because I loved him the most. A person asked me, "What is the matter with you?" I told her, "My necklaces are too tight, that is why I am crying." So she tied them looser. She knew that I was lonesome and longing for my parents. She said, "Both of you will go down, you will go to see your mother." I was anxious to go, so we went.

When we came to the top of the ridge I saw my home down in the valley. I was really happy. I didn't even greet my mother. I jumped on my father and was hugging him. I was so glad to see him. We slept there, and in the morning we started coming westward.

After two years, the mother of the one that I married went up west. . . . I proved myself, and now what kind of fingers I have for all the work I did? I started cooking right then. I was nine years old when she went up west, and the other mother of my husband, his real mother's sister, she was very mean to me. That is why I am not mean to my daughters-in-law, because this woman was very mean to me. I used to carry two big buckets of water, and she never fed me any bread. Before I went to sleep I used to steal some bread and I went to bed with it and ate it. My husband used to get mad at me because the crumbs were all over the bed. There, I told you the story plainly, just the way I know about my marriage.

Mrs. Wadsworth and her husband took an active part in the Old Ways of our People. For several years they had the Backside-to-the-Fire Pipe. The Pipe was transferred to them while they were living on the land east of Stand Off. The ceremony was held inside of the Upside-Down-Buffalo-Head Tipi, which was given to them by old Shot-on-Both-Sides. Natosina helped with the

Pipe transfer. He sang the songs for them to wake up by.

MRS. FRANK RED CROW

Mrs. Red Crow, who is known as Singing-in-the-Water, is the sister of Ponah and the widow of Frank Red Crow; her father was old Iron. She was born in 1902 and spent much of her life married to Frank's uncle, Francis Red Crow. She became a widow, then married Frank some time after his wife died.

Mrs. Red Crow says she always had respect for the Old Ways, but she never cared to have sacred things transferred to her. One time, when she and Ponah were still quite young, their grandmother put up a Medicine Lodge:

Nobody made a vow to cut up the hide, so our dad, Iron, told everybody, "My daughters, they can do it." He came and he told us to come up to the front with him. I didn't want to but he made me. While they were getting the things ready I saw that no one was watching and I just ran away as fast as I could and found a place to hide until they were finished.

Before she married Frank Red Crow she had lived a fairly modern life, without following most of the Old Ways. She didn't know Frank very well but thought that he was very faithful to the Old Ways. She didn't know anything about him selling sacred Bundles to Mrs. Walters during the 1930s.

She learned about his selling holy things quite by accident—literally. Not long after their marriage they loaded their truck with camping gear and headed for Great Falls, Montana. Frank brought along an ancient-looking rawhide container, which he wrapped in cloth and laid on the front seat beside him. She did not ask what was inside. Not long before Great Falls, while driving in the dark, they ran into some livestock on the highway. Their truck was quite damaged, although they escaped injury. The driver of a passing auto offered them a ride. They took most of their equipment and crammed it into the cab, to lock it up.

The next day when they returned to their truck, they discovered that someone had stolen everything. This made Frank quite upset. So she asked him what was inside the old rawhide container. He told her that it had contained the flag and other sacred articles for the ancient Mountain Sheep Painted Tipi, and that he was going to be paid well for it in Great Falls. That made her quite upset and she told him so and got Frank to agree not to sell any more sacred things.

Apparently, Frank and his previous wife had made quite a business of selling Indian things. When she first married him, one wall of his house was covered with shelves containing all sorts of craft materials—beads, shells, hides, dyed porcupine quills, and even sacred paints. His first wife was an excellent craftsman who could reproduce most any item and make it look quite old.

Mrs. Red Crow gave us the woman's collection of odd-shaped stones from which Iniskims could be made. She also showed us a bag of shells, some of them already strung up and painted as Medicine Pipe Owners' necklaces. She said that Frank told her he used to help Robert Wilson with his picture-taking during the Sun Dance Encampments. Later he admitted that he sold two Bundles that had been transferred to him—a Soldier's Pipe that he got from a man called Small Buttocks, and a Crow Water Bundle (which was somewhat similar to our own Beaver Bundles) that he got from Gros Ventre Boy.

In his old age, Frank Red Crow joined the sacred ceremonies in a sincere way and had the respect of his People. He adopted his little granddaughter Agnes as his minipoka, and taught her about some of the Old Ways.

Ponah once asked us if we ever wondered why the shawl covering our sacred Pipe Bundle looks so clean and new. When we said yes, she told us this story: One time Ponah was visiting the Red Crows. She knew her sister was always a good housekeeper and never liked to see dirty things around. When the Red Crows had gotten their Pipe, the old shawl covering it clearly showed its many years of protecting the Bundle. So during this visit, when Ponah noticed her sister washing what looked like the Bundle's shawl, she went to look at the Bundle and saw that an ordinary blanket was covering it. "You must be crazy," she told her sister. "Do you want us all to drown in a big thunderstorm? You're not supposed to wash holy things like that!" Poor Mrs. Red Crow felt very badly. She had never been told such a thing.

Now she holds sacred duties as the Scabby Bull for the Motokiks, a position transferred to her a few years ago by Doreen Day Rider, the previous Scabby Bull.

MRS. ROSIE DAVIS

Mrs. Rosie Davis is the oldest person on the Blood Reserve.

I don't know how old I am. Nobody ever told me the exact year of my birth. People usually say that I am one hundred years old, and they are probably right. I was still a little girl when the 1877 Treaty was signed.

I was born in Fort Benton. My mother married a white man named Smith, who worked on a Missouri River steamboat out of Fort Benton. We lived there when I was young; my father would come to see us between trips. My mother's father, Iron Pipe, took my mother and me up to the Blood Reserve so that we would be registered on the band rolls for the signing of the 1877 Treaty. He told my father he would try to send us back down to Fort Benton somehow.

When the treaty was finally settled, my grandfather could not find anyone to accompany us back down to Fort Benton. It was very dangerous to be alone out in that country, because of the enemy war parties. So my mother never saw my real father again. She then married Flying Chief, who was better known as Joe Healy. He was my stepfather.

Joe Healy had become an orphan when he was very young. His parents were camped in a tipi outside of Fort Whoop-Up, near Lethbridge. During the night, some enemy People from the west side of the mountains came and shot rifles into the tipi. They killed Joe's parents and his two sisters. He was wounded in the thigh. Two traders named Healy and Hamilton found Joe, who was still a little kid, so they buried his family and adopted him. He was doctored by some nuns, and later he was sent to school at Fort Shaw, in Montana. He was about the first boy on this reserve to go to school. He learned English and became a scout and interpreter for the Northwest Mounted Police.

I was at the Riot Sun Dance, the one during which Heavy Head tortured himself. I was sitting inside of the Medicine Lodge, near my grandfather, Iron Pipe, who was one of the Medicine Men. People would come up to him and bring him a filled pipe and sometimes an offering and he would pray for them.

As Rosie Davis grew older, she became a student of Miss Wells, an English lady who taught a number of Blood girls the ways of being housewives, British style. Her students became noted housekeepers and influential wives of men on the Blood Reserve. Even at her old age, Rosie Davis speaks very clearly, in a British accent, and uses very good grammar.

Rosie married Charlie Davis, also the child of a white father and a Blood mother. His father was the first government-appointed official for the Northwest Territories. His uncle was the mayor of nearby Fort MacLeod for many years. Charlie was still very young when his mother passed away.

His father took the three oldest children back East and put them in school in Winnipeg. Charlie and his older sister were given to relatives on the reserve. His mother's brother, White Buckskin, took him and raised him in the Old Way, although he looked very much like his real father. Charlie's father came after him several times, to take him away to school, but old White Buckskin would always see him in time and sneak out a back window with Charlie to hide him in the brush.

Charlie and Rosie took on the care of the Long-Time Pipe in their old age. They had it "for four or five years," according to Rosie, and she still regrets giving the Pipe up to John Red Crane, who sold it to the museum. She said, "I would have never given it to that man, but he said he made a vow, so there was not much that I could do about it."

Charlie Davis never joined the Horns Society because old White Buckskin told him, "Your wife lives like a white lady, so you had better not join the Horns with her. She might do something wrong."

Rosie Davis wears glasses for reading but she gave up doing beadwork just a couple of years ago. She said she likes to read all kinds of books, but that some writers are "too far-fetched." She just got through reading *Bury My Heart at Wounded Knee,* and her conclusion was that she "liked it real well, but it was sad and pathetic."

343

White Buckskin, stepfather of Charlie Davis, in 1910. (Pollard Photo)

Back to Wintertime

OUR NIGHTTIME CEREMONIES

It is late winter now, not long before Thunder returns and the season of outdoor life and holy ceremonies begins again. But even during winter we have come together to pray and sing our holy songs in Nighttime ceremonies two or three times each month.

Ach-kanotsisi—"All-Smoking-Together"—is how our People announce a Nighttime ceremony. People devoted to our Old Ways are invited to someone's house to sing the songs of the sacred articles transferred to them during their lifetime. The sponsor of the ceremony provides a leader, as well as plenty of tobacco and food. In exchange, he and his family will receive strength by hearing each participant sing sacred songs and say prayers for their benefit.

The Nighttime ceremony is commonly referred to as a Big Smoke, or Sacred Smoke. During the night-long ceremony, each participant counts coups—he calls out the Medicines he has owned and sings the Medicines' songs. Usually each person sings sixteen songs recalling experiences with Medicine Pipe Bundles, Beaver Bundles, Horns Society, Medicine Lodges, sacred tipis, sacred necklaces and headdresses, and other society memberships and Bundle transferrals. The singing of all these songs is a summary of the holy life of our Old Ways.

According to the Old Man, who was a leader of these ceremonies, the All-Smoking-Together began very long ago. His Teachers, men like Natosina and Big Wolf, told him that the first participants in these ceremonies were holy leaders of the formal summer ceremonies. They used to gather regularly during the wintertime to rehearse all the songs of their Bundles and to discuss the plans for the next Medicine Lodge ceremony. The Nighttime ceremonies developed from these gatherings and from dreams of some of those participants.

Joe Gambler told a story about a Nighttime ceremony to the Provincial Museum:

Big Smoke: People will make a vow to it. They think it is holy. A person that is going to die will say, "I will put up a Big Smoke so that I may survive," and he will not be sick very long and he will get better.

A person who had many Sacred Bundles will participate. A person who never had many Bundles will not participate, except the two orderlies, who give out the pipes for smoking, burn the incense, make the fire and serve the food, and the orderly who cuts the tobacco and gives out the smokes. These three don't sing, the rest will all sing.

There are lots of People who will officiate, such as Wrapped Up [Albert Chief Calf], Brown [Brown Chief Calf], Wolf Old Man [our Old

Man], and Skunk [Bob Black Plume]. Those four people are the shamans of the Big Smoke. When people make vows they will say to the one who will officiate, "Pray for my child so that he or she may get better. I will treat you very good."

To make the incense altar, a part of the ground will be scraped clean and Earth will be added on top, and at one end a pillow-shaped thing will be placed and a piece of manure will be laid on it. The little pipe is laid on this piece of manure, and there is another large piece of manure on which some pipes are laid. The pipes are given to the singers who will pray with them and then they will sing.

The ceremonialist [leader] will select who will sing and how many songs they will sing.

Big Smokes are held at my house. Big Smokes can be held in any place where people can sit conveniently, as long as there is a stove in the house, as we use the hot charcoals for burning the incense.

The one that made the vow and prepared the Berry Soup will sit with the ceremonialist. The one that made the vow will take his shirt off and he will be painted on the face and body with the paint. He will take the pipe that is to be handed out first and he will offer it to the ceremonialist. The one that made the vow will give a smoke to the ceremonialist and the ceremonialist will pray for him in return for the pipe.

The one that prepared the Berry Soup will not sing. He will just sit at the back. He will be called the Holy Sitter.

After the ceremonialist finishes his facial paintings he will take the rattles and rattle them four times and then give one to each of the four singers. The first man will then start. He will pray, he will not sing. When he gets through praying, he will sing. He will say, "I made an offering at such a place," and he will give four accounts.

The four men will sing about their most important sacred Bundle. They will sing of a sacred Bundle that they depend on [for spiritual strength]. That is how the participants will complete their singing in the first round.

After this they will sing a second round—that will make eight songs. They will sing of the miscellaneous Bundles, like tipis, that were transferred to them. First they sing of the Medicine Pipes, the Horns Society, and if a person owned a Beaver Bundle, he will sing of his Water Pipe Bundle [another name for a Beaver Bundle]. They also sing of their tipi designs, and Sun Dance necklaces, and Medicine Pipe necklaces, Weasel Tail suits, Medicine headdresses, All Brave Dog Society. They'll sing of all their miscellaneous Bundles that were transferred to them. That is why the singing takes so long.

Robert Wilson attended several Nighttime ceremonies during the 1890s. Those differed in some details from the similar ceremonies of today, as well as others of the same period. Most of our Medicines were then still with us and numerous people had owned enough Medicines to sing at least sixteen songs. Today, only a few have owned enough Medicines to sing four rounds of songs, and most of these have never learned to sing all of their own songs, so they ask the leader of the ceremony for help.

Here are Wilson's observations.

NOTES ON SACRIFICIAL CEREMONY
Feb. 26

One Spots Lodge, 15 people in the lodge, nearly all men. At the usual spot in the lodge was the altar, made in shape of a mound of clay about 4 inches high, an elongated cone. Opposite the door and in front of the altar was a space afterwards occupied by Old Moon [Ki-soum, or Sun, who was the leader of this ceremony]. Between his seat and the altar was a pile of cow chips and spread on top of them was a lot of wild sage, two eagle feathers, and some little paint bags. Incense was made on a large coal of fire, not on the altar but between it and the fire. A feast of tongue soup was handed around and Moon prayed alone. He was followed by all the others, except some late comers who were handed their food and then prayed, as usual holding up a little piece [of tongue] and at the end of the prayer shoving it into the ground [as an offering]. Old Moon began the songs at 2:15, all the men and women joining in the gestures, comprising holding all the fingers up, tips touching, and the sign to take something and put it on the breast. While singing was in progress, a filled pipe was handed to the oldest man, who, holding stem to the sun, prayed in a loud voice, the others singing throughout. Squaws were in the meantime putting red paint on faces of children who were to be painted afterwards by Moon. Singing ceased and another pipe was handed to Moon, who turned the stem quite around. Then, pointing the stem up over the fire, he prayed and afterwards pointed it to the earth. . . . One Spot sat at right of Moon and Three Bulls at the left. One Spot now took off his shirt, moccasins, leggings, and presented them all to Moon, also a piece of tobacco. He retained only his blanket, which he now wrapped around himself. Moon renewed the songs, One Spot let the blanket fall and sat upon it naked [with his breechcloth on, I'm sure]. Moon took a piece of fat meat and with many waves and signs from altar to One Spot and all over the latter's body, he handed to him, who rubbed it all over the head, arms and legs and body then handed it to Moon, who, after passing it all over his own body, passed it to the left and it went around. Moon now took red paint and, with some signs, rubbed it on his body, arms, legs and all, the others remarking with laughter how fat he was. One Spot turned his back and Moon rubbed paint all over it. One Spot's hair was tied up over his head and Moon painted his face all red. One Spot's son, a child of six or seven years, was brought forward and stripped to the waist . . . painted by Moon. . . .

Another child was painted, then One Spot's grandson, Jerry Pott's child was brought in, his face already painted red. The Mother's face and arms were painted red, then the child's face; in the child's hand was a quarter which was given to Moon, who again renewed the singing at 2:55 with gestures. One Spot, Moon and Three Bulls did the gestures. Moon took One Spot's right hand in his, straightened out the forefinger and made it point to the ground, and then up to the sky. Then, still holding the hand, it took up one of the feathers from off the sage bunch and, One Spot holding it, crossed his arms on his breast, the feather against his shoulder. Moon took the feather from the other and passed it, quill end down, once around One Spot's head, then gave it to him again. Again he took the hand and made the feather sweep around the little mound of clay back to his shoulder as before, then took the left hand and did the same, sweeping the little mound half done. [The feather represented the Power of the wind as it was scattering the mound, which represented a cloud. None of these symbols are placed on our altars of today.] Then he took one of the moccasins, turned the heel inside out, levelled the mound of sand and handed the moccasin to another man to finish the job. Singing, Moon took hand of One Spot and with feather marked out a pattern on the sand. [The pattern had a round circle in the center, to represent Sun. A circle on each side was for the Sun Dogs, while one above was for Morning Star. A crescent at the bottom stood for Night Light, or Moon.]

Moon took One Spot's hand and made it take some black paint from the sack and sprinkle a little in all of the marks on the sand, still singing. The man who had helped before now took bag and put more black in the marks. While he was doing this, Moon was busy picking off pieces from a root, which, when he had enough, he mixed with grease. Singing, he guided One Spot's hand to and took from bag yellow paint and scattered a little outside of the marks in the sand.

347

. . . No yellow was put around the top spot. [The yellow represented daylight; Morning Star was left black because he is not visible in the daytime.]

Moon put an eagle feather in his own head at back and gave directions to the assistant who went out and, going around to back of lodge by east, took down the pole bearing the offering. While he was out, Moon put a coal of fire in the top spot and guided One Spot's hand to put the stuff he had been mixing, and which he gave him, upon the coal of fire [as incense], singing and waving the hands to the coal fire [to take the incense smoke]. They sang to the man outside to come in, and brought in the offering and gave it to Moon, who took it, praying, and laid it on the sage brush. Moon now, with black paint mixed with grease in the palm of his hands, put a black spot on the bridge of One Spot's nose, on each cheek and on his chin and then made a broad streak, or ring, around each wrist and ankle. Then the offering was waved by Moon on each side of One Spot's head, back, and body; and a child was brought up, face painted same way and wrists and ankles, offering waved . . . also Potts' wife and child, and Calf Robe. . . . Moon now guided One Spot's hand with black paint to mark little short stripes at the top and bottom of the blanket of the offering. Moon always touched the bowl of the pipe to ground before smoking it. Moon and One Spot held up the offering there and singing, an old man called off two coups and then another old man called two. Towards the middle of the songs they lowered top of offering to the altar waving the points of feathers to the figures in sand, and, at intervals, the squaws would let up a yell. Finally, they with the feathers at top of offering, sweep out the figures entirely, and Moon then placed the sage in little bunches leading to the door . . . assistant stood up and, carrying the offering, Moon guiding his first step, walked out, stepping upon the bunches of sage, of which there were four. [The offering symbolically con-

tained all the prayers, at this time, and was taken out and tied to a tree or left amid rocks. The bunches of sage were used to keep the bad Spirits, which was the purpose of this ceremony, from remaining behind to trouble the occupants of the lodge any further.] Tea and berries were now handed around. Ended at 5 p.m.

That ceremony was similar to our Nighttime ceremonies of today, except that it ended after the details of the introduction were completed; there was no singing of transferred songs.

Here is an interesting excerpt from Wilson's notes on a ceremony that took place on July 28, 1891. It illustrates the earnestness and the faith of the participants.

A woman . . . entered the lodge . . . stating that a relative of the devotee's, a brother who was ill in an adjoining lodge, wished to partake of the sacred facial decoration. As the man was in an advanced stage of consumption the priest made no answer at first but grumbled in an undertone to the effect that people must think him possessed of superhuman power. After a moment's thought, he gave a reluctant consent and the sick man entered and was painted as the rest. . . . The priest afterwards explained to me that that sick a man should not have requested the painting of himself, because the immediate object of the sacred face-painting was to ensure good health and long life to the participant; and that the painting of the face of a person who was visibly dying was in his eyes almost an act of sacrilege, hence his reluctance to make a mockery of a ceremony the efficacy of which he, the priest, firmly believed in.

Wilson himself once used offerings in our Old Way to overcome a problem. This story comes from Atsitsina.

The offering in place over the tipi while the ceremony is held inside. A Horns Society Bundle hangs from the tripod at the rear. (R.N. Wilson)

I will tell you a story about Long-Faced Crow. My brother, Looks-like-Black-Hide [Paulus Low Horn] told me this story. He used to work for Wilson at his store. He said to me, "For a while one of Wilson's pigs would get killed every night. He would ask me if I had any idea what was killing them, but I didn't."

Wilson rode up to him one day right after another of one of his pigs was killed. He told my brother, "I can't figure out what is killing those pigs. I make good money on them when I take them to Fort MacLeod. I am going to fix this. I am going to make an offering, because I know the Indian Way is Powerful. I act like an Indian, so I will take care of this problem like an Indian. I was told by the People who go to Sacred Smokes that I could do it." My brother said Wilson took

his shirt off right there, while he was sitting on his horse, and he told my brother to get some sage and he showed him how to fix it up as an offering. He took his scarf off and he told him to use part of it for tying the offering together. My brother was going to smile, but Wilson told him, "Don't laugh. I am going to try to get over this in the right way." He said that Wilson knew the Indian Ways very good. He rode over to his house and he called in to his wife, in Blackfoot, to give him some twist tobacco. [His wife was the daughter of the agent on the North Piegan Reserve, and she had learned to speak Blackfoot fluently.] She gave him the tobacco and he rode back over and told my brother to tie it on to the offering with the rest of his scarf.

When my brother finished the offering Wil-

349

son took it—he never got off his horse—and he faced toward Sun and he started to pray. He prayed just like an old holy man: "HiYo Sun—HiYo Moon! Help me, save my pigs. The one that is killing them has no pity, so I give you this offering. Please make them stop killing my pigs. . . ." My brother said he prayed really hard, and for a long time. When he finished he told my brother, "I give this to the Sun. Climb that tree and put it up there. They're not going to kill my pigs anymore!" When my brother finished he went home and told his wife and they were both really amazed at how Long-Faced Crow believed in the Indian Way.

The next day Wilson went out and counted his pigs; then he went over to my brother and he said, "The Sun heard me. I gave him something good and he helped me." After that, my brother said that nothing killed his pigs anymore.

NIGHTTIME CEREMONY ON THE PRAIRIE

"Oki, Napi, we will make a holy soup for you. We have come to ask that you pray for our grand-mother, AnadaAki, while she is ill."

"Ah," answered the Old Man. "Yes, I will pray for her, and when she gets well, you will make the soup for me."

Thus we announced our vow to the Old Man, early one winter, after Grandma AnadaAki had suffered a heart attack. We asked him to use his influence with the spiritual powers by praying and by agreeing to lead a Nighttime ceremony, to give strength to Grandma in her effort to recover.

Some time passed after we made the vow. It was late in the winter season. Grandma had been well for some time, but we waited for favorable conditions before holding the ceremony. By then, because of his old age, the Old Man attended few of the Nighttime ceremonies and he hardly ever led them. Although he assured us that he was able and willing to lead this ceremony for us, we prayed that the weather would be mild, which it was, on the day of the ceremony. There was snow on the ground from a few days before, but the air was barely cool enough for freezing.

The ceremony was to have been held seven nights before, but a sudden death among the Old Man's relatives meant that he could not attend any public gathering for four days. He told us that everyone's good Spirits would be back if we set the ceremony for seven days later, which we did.

I wore my blanket coat for the ride over to our relative's house, where the ceremony was held. We had driven over there earlier that morning to drop off mattresses for seating, dishes for cooking, the foodstuffs, and our blankets and other things needed for the ceremony. We fastened the offering to the house wall outside the place where the Old Man was to sit and pray later that night.

It was still daylight when we arrived at the house where people were going to gather. No one had arrived yet. The offering swayed in the breeze that often blows from the mountains. The prairie between the house and the mountains, perhaps half a day's ride away, was a patch-work of farms and ranches. The light covering of snow reflected differently, depending on whether the fenced sections of land were for pasture or crops, and whether they were plowed at the end of the last summer or left with their stubble standing.

The house was an older one, made of milled lumber. A few relatives were inside, to do the cooking and to lend their help, should it be needed. The room was crowded with many bags and boxes of food. Another room was crammed with furniture, leaving the room where the ceremony was to be held cleared of all furniture—only mattresses covering the floor along the walls. Two of the canvas linings from our tipi hung on the wall to lend the room some atmosphere. None of the relatives took a direct part in the ceremony, so none had gone inside this room for fear of disturbing its sanctity.

Down along the Bullhorn Coulee.

I began my preparations by pouring some fine earth from a paper bag onto a small board. This was to be the incense altar. The layer of dirt was the thickness of two hands and "mirror-shaped," as the Old People call a rectangle. At the end closest to the Old Man was a higher ridge of earth, which caused the complete altar to look like a made-up bed with pillows.

The Old Man arrived with his brother, Mike Yellow Bull, who cut the tobacco and filled the pipes. After a brief glance in the ceremonial room, he asked, "Everything is not yet ready?" I answered, "Almost." He asked me to get him a chair so he could sit and have a smoke while I finished the preparations.

I leaned some bunches of man-sage against the head of the altar and placed two pieces of dung next to them. On the brass-studded tobacco cutting board, I placed some prepared bearberry leaves and commercial tobacco. Then I brought in the Old Man's bag of ceremonial articles and arranged them in place. I laid the wooden incense tongs to the right of the altar and some braids of sweetgrass to the left. I also put down two sharpened willow sticks for lighting the pipes, and a long piece of wire for cleaning the stems.

I guided the Old Man to his seat in the ceremonial room. It is not proper for anyone to sit until the leader has assigned each person a place. The place to the right of the leader is for the

Our Old Man and me.

sponsor of the ceremony, who sits very quietly and humbly listens to everyone's prayers which are for the benefit of himself, his family, and the one for whom he vowed the ceremony. We call this "sitting holy." If the sponsor of the ceremony is a participant who sings his songs, then he asks some relative to take his place next to the leader, for it is not proper to sing while sitting holy.

Atsitsina arrived and the Old Man directed him to a place on his right. Atsitsina helped start the second part of the ceremony by reciting four spiritual offerings made in the past. The participant with the bravest war coup would sit at the far left and recount four brave deeds, when that part of the ceremony was reached. My seat was next to the Old Man on his left. As a Medicine Pipe Owner, this was my seat of honor.

The Old Man inspected the altar and approved it. He arranged before him the sacred bags from his paint outfit: one contained the black paint, another contained the sacred red earth, and a third contained pieces of kidney fat.

352

Then, while we sat waiting for the others to arrive, Atsitsina asked the Old Man, "Omach-Kinna [Old Man], why don't you tell our grandson the secret for reaching old age? Maybe he will tell me, and then I will become as old as you are."

The Old Man kept looking at the altar for a time, then he began to speak:

My parents took me to an old holy woman who had a lot of Power. She was the one who foresaw that I would reach old age. Her name was Otter Woman. She told my parents, "This boy will reach old age. I have foreseen it. But he will have to face a test right now to prove that he is the right one. Do you wish to risk his life to have him meet this test?" My parents had a lot of faith in that old woman's Power, so they told her, "Yes, go ahead."

I was only about five months old when all this took place. The old woman began by piercing my ears with porcupine quills. Next, she buried me under the earth; I was not told how deep, but she must have left my face free so that I could keep breathing. Then she built a fire of dry cottonwood sticks over my body. She told my parents that the Earth Powers would protect me from harm if I was the one in her dreams. No harm came to me. Then she bundled me up in blankets and tied me into the branches of a tree. She and my parents stood below and mourned for me as though I were dead. She told them that from then on, the Spirits of death would be satisfied and would not come to bother me with misfortune. When they brought me down from the tree she told my parents, "This boy has proved that he is the one who will have the Powers I saw in my dream. He will belong to Sun from now on. Sun will care for him and he will have the Power to help his People."

Then the old woman prayed: "Sun, I give you this boy so that you will guide him like I saw in my dream. Here is a part of him to prove that we are sincere and that he will always remember you." That old woman took out her knife and cut off the end of my little finger from my left hand, you can see where it is missing, and she left the end of my finger out there on the prairie as an offering. That is when I was first told that I would have old age.

After the Old Man's story, we sat quietly for a while. Then Atsitsina remarked that he had not yet been purified for the recent death in his family. He could not attend a holy ceremony until he symbolically cast the Spirit of death away from himself. He asked me to step outside with him and to bring along a few leaves of sage from the bunches by the altar. He had already taught me what to do to purify someone in our Old Way. I rolled the sage leaves into a small ball between my palms and prayed, asking for help that Atsitsina may forget what has happened and go on with the Good Spirits again. Four times I prayed and asked the various Powers to give him strength and encouragement, and then I handed him the ball of sage. He prayed and brushed his body four times with it, then told the sage to take the evil from his body as he cast it away toward the east, the direction of the new day.

A truck arrived bringing SikskiAki's parents and our two boys. Wolf Child quietly walked into the room and sat by me. The Old Man squinted to see who it was, then greeted Wolf Child: "Ahhh, Makwi Poka, shake hands!" The Old Man was very fond of Wolf Child. The boy prayed enthusiastically and made hand signs while trying to sing along with our holy songs.

NinnaOnesta and his wife arrived with a box full of bowls, utensils, pipe and blankets, and two cushions—in case our seating proved uncomfortable. The Old Man gave NinnaOnesta a seat on the far left, where he usually sits to call out his raiding exploits.

By the time it was dark, all had arrived for the ceremony, having been dropped off by young relatives. In the Old Days, ten to twenty participants could be expected for a Nighttime ceremony, but today only half as many showed up.

When all were seated, the relatives in the kitchen started passing out the food. Each bowl was filled with chunks of boiled meat, eggs, oranges, apples, rolls, and fresh-baked cookies. Most of the food was to be taken home in paper bags for the Old People's grandchildren.

Each of us took a small piece of meat between our first two fingers. The Old Man handed the incense tongs to the orderly, SikskiAki's young nephew, who took a coal from the wood stove and deposited it in the middle of the earth altar. The Old Man sprinkled sweetgrass on the coal, guided by my hand. As the sweet-smelling smoke rose he held his piece of meat into the air and began a prayer:

HiYo holy Spirits, help us as we are gathered with you again. Hear our prayers tonight. Hear the songs that we will sing for you. Give us your Power and help our children and our grandchildren. . . .

To conclude his prayer he placed the meat as an offering at the edge of the altar and said, "Oki, Earth Spirits, take this food and bless my life so that I will always have enough to eat." All of us joined him in praying out loud and we passed him our pieces of meat which he deposited as offerings to our Earth Mother.

Then we ate a little of the food before we took a break and went outside.

After we returned, we got settled to begin the first part of the ceremony. Incense was made first. Then the Old Man took some of the sage from in front of the altar and peeled the leaves from the stems. He coated his hands with kidney fat and mixed it with sacred red earth. Then he rolled the leaves into a ball, all the while praying

353

to remind us of the Powers of Earth and all that grows upon it. When the ball was ready, he turned toward me and dropped it into my cupped hands. I rolled the ball between my palms and then brushed it, slowly, twice down each side of my body, while praying to ask that the cleansing Spirits of the sage purify my body and replace any evil in it with the natural goodness of the Earth. When I finished, I passed the sage sacrament to the person at my left, and so it went around the room. More incense was made, and then the young helper was instructed to go out and bring in the offering. He covered himself with his blanket for this sacred duty, and went out to bring in the holy object from its quiet, sacred resting place.

The object represents the Spirits who are with us, in our life here on Earth. Fastened to it are symbols that recall to everyone the Powers of the Universe. For instance, the frame of the offering is made of two willow sticks tied together in the shape of a cross; the willows represent trees and bushes, as well as the material from which we build our sweat lodges; and the cross the sticks are tied in stands for the junction of the four sacred directions, which is the place where we stand, each of us, no matter where on this Earth we are. Fastened on top of the cross, the willow stick tied to form a circle speaks for the roundness of our Sun, our Moon, and our Universe, the sacred circle in whose honor we arrange our lodges and our camps. Fastened to the circle are seven black-and-white eagle feathers. Seven is our sacred number, as there are seven moons in each season, and seven stars help us tell time at night and remind us of all the other stars in the nighttime sky; the feathers are black-and-white to remind us of day and night, good and bad, life and death. Bunches of sage are tied to the ends of the arms on the cross because sage is pure and holy in the prairie-life of our Old Ways, and represents the sacredness of all the plants on Earth. Black and red pieces of cloth are tied to the arms of the offering with buckskin thongs; the thongs remind

us of the animals that supply us with meat and hides, just as the feathers remind us of the birds that fly, and the cloth represents the life of the People on Earth, red being for holiness and black for victory. It is the People's gift to the Spirits of nature.

Outside, the helper said, "Hoi"; he took down the offering and stood toward the east, holding it in his hand. The Old Man began a song whose words tell that the sacred offering will be brought in, in a holy way. After the song, everyone was quiet. Then we heard the signal from outside again. The Old Man began the same song again, everyone joining in this time. Four times we sang, each time the helper standing at one of the four directions to let all the Universal Powers have a symbolic look at the offering before it was brought inside. In Sun-wise direction he went around the house, and before the fourth song ended came inside and handed the offering to the Old Man.

The Old Man prayed with it, giving it a spiritual welcome into the midst of our gathering, then put it down. He rubbed kidney fat between the palms of his hands, and took some sacred red earth. The young man sitting holy took off his shirt and kneeled before the Old Man. The Old Man sang the song for the red paint, while covering the boy's face, shoulders, chest, arms, and wrists with it, smearing the last over the boy's hair in ceremonial blessing.

He wiped the red paint from his hands and took the black paint pouch and a fresh piece of kidney fat. Singing the song for the sacred black paint, he dipped two fingers into the pouch and mixed the powdered charcoal with the grease in his palms, as though he were washing his hands with a bar of soap. With his blackened thumb he put a mark on the boy's temples, and his nose, then traced a black circle all the way around the boy's face, over the red paint. He also put black circles around the boy's wrists. The Old Man then told him to turn around in a Sun-wise direction to bless him with the offering, rubbing it

354

twice over each side of the boy's body. The boy then put on his shirt and continued to sit holy.

Next, some of us came forward who wished to have the Old Man's blessings by being painted. First went Grandma, the helper, and Mike Yellow Bull. Then Wolf Child and I went around the altar as the last ones to be painted.

After that, Mark Old Shoes told about four sacred offerings he made in the past, as the Old Man sang the fourth song of the ceremony. During the song the Old Man held the offering toward the east, calling out for Sun to see it, then tracing Sun's path to the west. He did that four times. Then he handed the offering to the boy next to him, who prayed with it and handed it to the pipe attendant, Mike Yellow Bull. He untied the offering and removed the cross-arm to which the cloth was attached. The cloth was spread out beneath the brass-studded tobacco cutting board. The rest of the offering was tied to the wall, above the Old Man's head.

One of the raw tongues was placed on a cloth in front of the Old Man. He took the right hand of the one sitting holy, dipped one finger into the black paint, and prayed while marking a line down the center of the tongue, doing this four times. Next, the boy was given a knife and file to hold, while the Old Man guided him to symbolically sharpen one with the other. That constituted the asking and receiving of ceremonial permission for cutting the tongues and tobacco. When this was done, we took another break.

After this second break, we made incense again, then filled the pipes from the large mound of smoking mixture on the cutting board. The largest pipe was filled first and handed to Atsitsina, who held it four times toward the incense, twice with the bowl-end and twice with the mouthpiece. One by one, the incensed pipes were then leaned against the large piece of dung, which had been secured to the right of the altar by three nails driven around it. Everyone was careful not to move the pipes resting this way because they were considered to be sitting holy.

Using the small pipe, the Old Man was the first to smoke. He asked me to take his blanket and cover his body from the top of his head down. The tobacco was lit with the glowing end

Wilson's photo of his recorded "sacrificial ceremony," taken in the 1890s. The sponsor of the ceremony is holding up the sacred offering. The leader sits next to him. The altar in the foreground is different from the altars we make for this type of ceremony today. In the center is an earth-painted symbol of Sun, a crescent Moon, Sun Dogs on each side, and Morning Star above Sun. Bunches of sage lie on the ground. The incense tongs and paint bags lie next to the leader.

of a willow stick. He then blew offerings of smoke to the Spirits who dwell in the Above, in the Below, and on Earth. Everyone was very quiet, for the Old Man was symbolically smoking with the Powers of the Universe. He blew smoke in various directions until all the tobacco in the bowl had been smoked.

The main part of the ceremony was now ready to be started. Incense was made, and the Old Man held four rattles over the sweet smoke. He shook the rattles, to prepare the Spirits for singing, then passed them to the man who was farthest to the right. The others sang a song while he prayed and told about one offering. In the same way, each of the four men sang four rounds of the song and called out four offerings.

The four men prayed for the other participants, calling each one by name, and their families. As each one heard his name, he placed his hands on his chest, signifying that he was taking the prayers to his heart.

When each man finished praying, he sang his first four songs, representing the most Powerful Medicines transferred to him during his lifetime. Atsitsina and I were the only participants who had not belonged to the Horns; our first songs were for our Medicine Pipe Bundles. Medicine Pipe Owners were allowed to sing four songs for the Bundle they were keeping. Beaver Bundle Owners could sing as many songs as they wished for their Bundle. All others were allowed to sing only one song for each sacred thing that had been transferred to them, even if that object had a great many songs.

As a current Medicine Pipe Owner, a special ceremony was held at my turn to sing for the first round. A blanket was spread to the left of the altar. The Old Man sat to my left on the blanket. A coal was deposited at the rear of the altar and I held a pinch of sweet pine needles over the hot coal, the Old Man's hand on top of mine. He began with a prayer, then sang four Medicine Pipe songs, slowly lowering my hand with the in-

Singing the Medicine Pipe Songs: Makwi Api and me.

cense during the beginning of the first one. We took the sacred smoke and symbolically purified ourselves with it, while we sang of the holy Bundle that had given its Spirit to both of our lives.

After everyone had sung his first four songs, we took another break. The first of four rounds was over.

The second round of songs began with the rattles over the incense like the first round. Most sang songs during this round for Medicine Pipe Bundles. One song was sung for the Bundle itself, another for the necklace or some such sacred article. After each man had sung his four songs, he told which sacred article they were for, who gave him that article, and whom it was finally given to. Some singers ended their round by saying that their holy object had been given to the white man by so-and-so, and it was now on display at such-and-such a place.

Those who have sold our major Bundles, and

356

Having a smoke after singing Medicine Pipe Songs: Atsitsina and me.

are still alive to tell about it, seldom come to our Nighttime ceremonies. When they do, they usually sing the songs for what they sold, though others feel that this is sacrilegeous, that no one can benefit from the Spirit of a holy thing that was given away for money.

The pipes were smoked continuously during the rounds of singing. At the start of each round, the first pipe was handed to the one sitting holy, who presented it to the Old Man. The Old Man held the mouthpiece to the Above and prayed for the boy and for those for whom the ceremony was held.

During the next break we ate some raw kidney and a bit of kidney fat, a delicacy among our Old People. There was talking and joking while we ate.

The next two rounds of singing were just like the first two, but the songs representing sacred articles not so Powerful as those sung about at first. The songs were for Iniskims and Iniskim necklaces, painted tipis, Sun Dance necklaces, for the duties of Weather Dancers, for parts of Beaver Bundles, and for lesser societies such as the Crazy Dogs and Pigeons.

The Old Man started the third round with a song about the Power of birds. During the song, he waved his right hand in the air to resemble the sailing of a bird. Most of our songs used to have symbolic hand and body motions to accompany them, but few of our People still know these or bother to use them when they are singing. But the ceremony was not yet over.

After the last song of the fourth round, someone brought in a bowl with tongue taken from the sacred blood soup. The eight pieces were used to ask for blessings. The one who was sitting holy took one piece from the bowl; taking and holding up that hand, the Old Man called out, "Oki, Natosi, Sun, this is for you. SikskiAki and Natosina promised to feed you this when they asked you to help AnadaAki, and now they are fulfilling their promise."

He lowered the boy's hand and let the piece drop at the edge of the altar. They took up another piece, which was offered to Moon in the same way. They did the same with a piece offered to Morning Star and a piece offered to Earth Spirits.

The remaining four pieces were held up, one at a time, in the same way, as the Old Man called out, "Oki, Sun, this young man is going to eat with you so that this meal will be holy. Give him your strength and guidance." He then pushed the piece into the boy's mouth, and it was eaten.

After the Old Man did this with the four pieces of tongue, the boiling kettle filled with the sacred soup was brought into the room. It had been boiling all night long, from the time the tongues had been cut up. The sacred soup is a mixture of tongue, serviceberries, and blood. The pieces of tongue are first boiled in water. Then the blood is mixed with flour to form a smooth

357

paste, which is stirred into the boiling water along with the berries. A dark, creamy soup results. Each person's wooden bowl that night was filled.

Incense was made for the last time, and each person held up a piece of tongue and prayed for strength and long life for ourselves and our families. Then we ate.

Three more "soups" were brought out—stewed apricots, rice and raisins, and stewed tomatoes. Four soups, one for each round of singing.

The Nighttime ceremony was over. Through the window came the first sign of the new day, a thin, light line separating the dark, starlit sky from the horizon. The songs were over, the pipes smoked out, the prayers all spoken; the People left for home, all as One and all happy.

□

On my way home, I paused on top of a hill to watch Sun rise, breathing the universal air that all of us must breathe, that makes us all a part of the Universe. To the never-ending Spirits of this Universe I gave my prayer of Good Thoughts:

Okohe Natuyetuppi! HiYo! HiYo Natosi— HiYo KokomiKisoum—HiYo Ksachkomituppi! Now then, holy people! Hear me! Hear me Sun! Hear me Night Light! Hear me Stars! Hear me Earth Spirits!

HiYo all of you Holy Powers in the Universe. I am thankful to be able to see those holy mountains where I will soon be in body and Spirit. Help me to grow closer to you in this Way that I have been learning to live with all of you Powers who make up this Universe. Let me learn to be humble and to feel small so that I may see the greatness of your Powers, so that I may treat them with respect, and look to them for strength while living on Earth.

HiYo Natosi! Let me continue to see you as you make your daily path across the sky. Continue to let me see your light so that my path

will continue to be bright, so that I may see it well and not lose my Way along it. Let me continue to feel your warmth in my body so that I may have good health. Let me continue to feel your warmth in my heart so that my heart may be good to others, so that I may give that warmth to all whom I meet along my life's path.

HiYo Night Light! HiYo Stars! Let me have many more holy nights beneath you in the coming years of my life. Let me feel safe in your light. Let me look up at your vast home and feel the smallness of myself, so that my troubles and hardships may seem even smaller.

Okohe—HiYo all of you good Old People from the past, all of you who lived in a holy Way and have brought me to your Spirits. Continue to let me find your Spirits wherever I go. Let them continue to guide me along this path and inspire me to learn these good Old Ways. Let me continue to devote myself to your Spirits, continue to show me how to live, how to pray, how to sing your songs and dance your dances. Let me learn your sacred ceremonies. Let me learn all those holy Old Ways that will help me and my family to live a holy New Way on this Earth. Let me continue to share your Powers of Good Medicine with all those who wish to hear my words. Let those words continue to be inspired by your Spirits, you holy Old People. Come to my brothers and sisters and inspire them to live a holy life in harmony with nature. Inspire them to follow some of these holy Old Ways. Use your holy Powers to bring together those People who wish to live a holy life with your Spirits. Let those People join together as a spiritual family. Let me bring my family to join them, no matter where each of us may be in body. Keep us together in Spirit. Let us be as holy families. Let us be as holy tribes. Let us be a holy nation, all together. Kimatokit—Kimatokit! Hear me and help! Hear me and help!

Okohe—HiYo all of you Good Spirits in nature. Help us to live a holy life in harmony with all of you. HiYo Earth Spirits! HiYo Earth Mother! Let us find that part of you where we can live this dream and follow these holy Ways. Let us live in our lodges on you in peace and happiness. Let us grow our food and our sacred tobacco in a holy Way. HiYo birds and animals! Let us learn to live as one with you. Let us learn your songs and your Ways so that we may use them in our own Way. Let us treat you with respect, and let us learn to give to you whenever we must take from you. HiYo trees and flowers. Let us learn to know each one of you and give us your help as we learn to live in harmony with you. HiYo mountains! Let us climb your heights and let us find our sacred visions there, visions that will keep our Spirits as high as you are.

Okohe—HiYo holy Pipes, HiYo Good Medicines! Let us learn to know your Spirits and Powers so that we may use them to give strength to the holy life we wish to live with you. Help us to share those Spirits and Powers with all those who wish to share them with us. Let our good Old People continue to teach us what they know about you, and about all of you Good Spirits, and let us continue to treat you in a holy Way so that our Old People will continue to be with us in happiness. Let the holy Spirits of your sacred past live again in sacred ceremonies, sacred songs, sacred dances, sacred lodges, and in the sacred minds of many young people who are looking for

a sacred Way of life. Forgive us if we make mistakes as we try to learn this holy new life with you Holy Ones from the past. Let us know that we are doing the right thing by giving us success and happiness, by letting us raise our children with success and happiness, by letting us treat our Old People with goodness so that they can share our success and happiness. Let us learn to use your holy Old Ways with respect and goodness, not for personal glory or power, but for the good of all our brothers and sisters who walk this Earth in search of that sacred path that will lead them to a holy life in peace and harmony. Let this be one of the Ways to peace and harmony on this Earth, and let those of us who follow it learn to make it a good and holy Way. Let each of us know how many steps we should take as we go along this Way, and let us know when we should pause in order to feel the fullness of what we are learning. Let us learn not to criticize each other for the method which we use to travel along this Way, as long as it is holy, nor for how far each of us travels, as long as we stay holy and cause no harm to one another. Let us reach old age with happiness.

That is what I say in my prayer. Hear me! Let me meet with all of you again, and in happiness.

I am Natosina

Epilogue

Time has passed since the Sun Dance Encampment of 1972, when I sat and wrote down the stories that make up this book. The Sun Dance Encampment for 1976 will soon be set up on the Belly Buttes.

The Old Man is gone now. Last spring, when he opened our Medicine Pipe Bundle, he said: "This will be the last time that I open a Medicine Pipe. . . . Next year someone else will have to do it for you." During last summer's encampment he came only for a brief visit. He sat with us, among the crowd of spectators, as the Horns Society gave their public dance. The leader of the society brought his swan-skin-covered staff and asked the Old Man to call out the four required coups and to give his blessings. For the last time the Old Man held the Powerful staff that once was his. It was his last ceremonial appearance.

The summer before that, the Old Man had given a special name to our new son. "Heard Again," the Old Man called him. During the naming he said: "When the Spirit came to give me Power I didn't hear him right the first time, but I heard him very well when he came again." To celebrate his being born during the Sun Dance Encampment, we gave our boy the official first name of Okan.

Last fall, while the Old Man was making his final efforts to remain on this Earth, another son was born to us. To honor the Old Man's spiritual ties with sacred stones, Iniskims, we gave this boy the official first name of Iniskim. Sometime later our old uncle said: "This boy has a legal name, but he has not yet been given a name in the Old Way. Myself, I am no longer using my young-man-name. Since you two are carrying the names of my father and mother, I give this little boy my own name. He will grow old like me, known as Atsitsina."

Each of our children will be able to call on the Old Man's Spirits with Iniskims—his were passed on to us, still sitting up in his old altar, where he put them. The rest of his holy things were placed in the grave with him. An old metal suitcase held his doctoring articles. A cloth bag contained his old, rawhide-covered drum. On top of the suitcase lay his two painted and carved canes. Thus his body went on its final journey.

The Old Man's passing caused someone to look up his official birthdate on the records. It turned out that he was older than he had thought —his birth was recorded for the year 1877. He was the oldest man among all the Blackfoot People when he died. The next oldest was Guy Wolf Child, who passed away not long after.

A few months before the Old Man's passing, we had lost another one of our ceremonial leaders —old John Many Chiefs, or White Horns. His death came about the same time as that of Mrs. Mountain Horse, the lady who prepared medicinal herbs. Shortly after that came the death of White Horns' eldest son—Ray Many Chiefs, who

A sacred gathering during the 1975 Sun Dance Encampment. At the right sits Laurie Plume, better known as Emonissi, or Otter. As a child he owned a sacred buckskin shirt decorated with weasel tails. Here he transferred the songs and rights accompanying this shirt to young Wolf Child. Next to him sits Many Grey Horses, the Owner of the Long-Time Pipe, and next to me is 85-year-old Tom Morning Owl. His mother was old SikskiAki, so he was Atsitsina's half brother. He also held sacred rights for a weasel shirt, which he transferred to me at this ceremony. The shirt is hanging between us. Atsitsina and Apikayi (Bob Black Plume) were the singers for the occasion. They used two drums from the Long-Time Pipe. With their passing the following winter, Laurie Plume became the last of the Blood elders able to lead the Medicine Pipe ceremonies.

was the dance leader for the Horns Society and possessed the society's Headdress with an Arrow in Front. He had also been a minor chief in the tribe.

The Horns Society lost an important spokesman with the passing of Ray Many Chiefs. A tragic accident recently claimed the lives of two more important members of the Horns—Charlie Weaselhead, the eldest son of Mokakin and Ponah, and Hugh Calf Robe. Both men were ac-

companied by their wives, and each of them left behind ten children.

But before all these losses, the Horns were able to recover some of their important sacred Bundles from the Alberta Provincial Museum. The exact settlement has yet to be worked out, but the Bundles are with their real owners on the reserve. Another Alberta museum—the Glenbow—has refused to consider returning the important Horns Bundle which they bought in a

362

The Long-Time Pipe after its return to the Blood People. Its new Owner, Many Grey Horses, wanted this picture to be included in the book so that history would see the ancient Bundle as more than just a museum relic. The Owners are seated on the left. Barely visible is the wife of Apikayi (Bob Black Plume). He led the opening ceremony before his final switch to the Full Gospel faith and his death right after that. The ancient Bundle rests in the center.

secret transaction from the widow of John Red Crane, who had sold our Long-Time Medicine Pipe. The Old Man's grandson, Harry Shade, made a vow to become Keeper of that Horns Bundle. He and his partner, Jim Red Crow, have recently decided to follow Mokakin's advice and will ask older Horns members to remake the Bundle for them.

A most exciting event occurred last year, in time for the Old Man to help celebrate. Our ancient Long-Time Medicine Pipe came back to stay with our People. It happened this way:

Several summers ago the Bundle was brought to the Sun Dance Encampment and ceremonially opened. By tradition, the leader of the ceremony should have been a former Owner, who would have known the special songs for it. But none are left among the People. Thus, White Horns led the ceremony in the best way he could. Many Grey Horses came and brought his drums, which had originally belonged to the Bundle. He himself was one of the drummers for the ceremony. At the end of it he surprised everyone by announcing that he was taking the Bundle back to his own home and that he would shortly have it transferred to himself and his wife. The white man from the museum, who occupied the Owner's place during the ceremony, had already offered to transfer his rights if anyone wanted to take them. He seemed pleased by the announcement of Many Grey Horses. The transfer ceremony took place not long after. The payments included several fine horses and many dry goods. However, the white man had said nothing about all this to his former employer—the Provincial Museum. When they learned of the affair they rushed down to see Many Grey Horses and used threats of law and order to frighten him into returning it. They told him that he would be allowed to have it for the annual ceremony, provided he sign many complicated legal papers first.

The following winter I had a vivid dream in which I saw the Long-Time Pipe being brought back home for good. I went to see Many Grey Horses and his wife, and told them about the dream. They offered to accept the dream and to follow its directions. Accordingly, SikskiAki and I joined the elderly couple for a trip to the Provincial Museum in Edmonton the following spring.

At the museum we were treated courteously. Permission was granted for Many Grey Horses and his wife to pray with the Bundle and to give thanks for the return of Thunder. First, parts of the Bundle had to be brought together—some were on display and some were in storage. Many Grey Horses then placed the Bundle on his wife's back, while he carried the bags and other accessories. Dressed in moccasins and blankets, we made a colorful procession outdoors, where we could pray directly to the Spirits of Nature. We went around the museum building, stopping at each of the Four Sacred Directions to pray. Some distance behind us followed two of the museum officials, while plain-clothes guards remained farther away. After the fourth stop Many Grey Horses and his wife took their Bundle directly to our car. We explained our purpose to the amazed museum officials, who made no effort to stop us. Shortly we were headed south, joyfully bringing the ancient Bundle back home.

Four times we stopped on the way home with the Long-Time Pipe to make offerings of sacred berries and tobacco. Many Grey Horses prayed fervently that the sacred Bundle should never again leave our People. He asked it to stay and help the People through these trying times, and to remind them of the ancient Powers that gave strength to our ancestors of the long-ago.

There was much joy among the People when the news was heard—everyone was thankful for the Bundle's return. Old Bob Black Plume came out of semi-retirement to lead the ceremony for its opening, as he has done each time since. People from far and wide came to see the sacred Pipe and to receive its blessings. Several hours were required just to paint those who had come for that reason. Surely here was physical proof of the spiritual Powers that dwell in the Land of the Bloods—from the days of dogs, through the days of horses, and into the age of modern cars and airplanes, the Medicine Pipe has held the People together.

Index of Proper Names

Page numbers in italics indicate illustrations.

Adolf Hungry Wolf lives with his wife, Sik-skiAki, and their children in a small cabin at the foot of the Rockies near Invermere, British Columbia. Their nearest neighbors are ten miles away. Contact with the outside world is usually limited to occasional trips to town for supplies or to the Blood Reserve to visit relatives and join in religious ceremonies.

In addition to this book, Hungry Wolf has written and published himself a series of paperback books on the Blood way of life, called *Good Medicine Books*. Of his writing, he has said, "I felt that the spirit of the old people and their ways could be presented to readers as more than just history or anthropology. I wanted to share some of the spirit of the old people with the many new people who might otherwise never experience it."

THE BLOOD PEOPLE IS THE EIGHTH BOOK IN HARPER & ROW'S NATIVE AMERICAN PUBLISHING PROGRAM. ALL PROFITS FROM THIS PROGRAM ARE SET ASIDE IN A SPECIAL FUND AND USED TO SUPPORT PROJECTS DESIGNED TO AID THE NATIVE AMERICAN PEOPLE.